'Sex and gender have become highly politici[zed, with much] ill-informed debates. This book, with schol[arship across] disciplines, throws a clear and immensely we[lcome light on] [how s]ex and gender matter, and how the relationship betwe[en them is] a matter of evidence, not of personal opinion. Societies invent gender, but sex is an immutable biological fact. A public policy that ignores this difference risks unravelling many gains in women's rights. This is not just a matter of obscure academic argument, but one that concerns us all.'

Ann Oakley, *Professor of Sociology and Social Policy, Social Research Institute, University College London, UK*

'An important and extremely timely collection of essays that presents a valuable overview of current research investigating the relationship between sex, gender and gender identity in the UK today. The contributors to this volume are all senior researchers in their fields who conduct evidence-based research and believe, in issues as diverse as criminology, sports science, children's literature, education and many others, that sex matters. This book pays tribute to their tenacity in researching the erasure of sex categories in their fields in the face of the many obstacles that have been placed in the way of "gender-critical" scholars.'

Sarah Pedersen, *Professor in Communication and Media at Robert Gordon University, UK*

SEX AND GENDER

Sex and Gender: A Contemporary Reader is a much-needed exploration of the relationship between sex, gender and gender identity. Its multidisciplinary approach provides fascinating perspectives from the sciences, social sciences and humanities, as well as biology, neuroscience, medicine, law, sociology and English literature. The 15 chapters are original contributions, authored by scholars who are leaders in their respective fields.

This thought-provoking collection offers significant methodological, theoretical and empirical insights into one of the most fraught debates in contemporary politics and academia. It provides a broad-ranging introduction to the issues central to questions about how and why sex matters from a range of disciplinary perspectives, drawing out the social, political and legal implications.

Questions addressed include:

- Is sex binary?
- What is a woman?
- Why do we need data on sex?

Also discussed are topics widely debated today such as sports, feminism, sex and inequality, sex-based rights, puberty suppression, criminal justice and gender dysphoria.

Sex and Gender: A Contemporary Reader is a timely introduction to contemporary debates on sex and gender. It is an accessible text for both general readers and for students of gender issues across a wide range of disciplines including sociology, education, history, philosophy and gender studies.

Alice Sullivan is Professor of Sociology at University College London, UK. She was director of the 1970 British Cohort Study (BSC70) for ten years from 2010 to 2020. She has published extensively on social, educational and health inequalities using longitudinal data analysis.

Selina Todd is Professor of Modern History at Oxford University and a Fellow of St Hilda's College, Oxford, UK. Her books include *The People: The Rise and Fall of the Working Class 1910–2010* (2014) and *Tastes of Honey: The Making of Shelagh Delaney and a Cultural Revolution* (2019).

SEX AND GENDER

A Contemporary Reader

Edited by Alice Sullivan and Selina Todd

Routledge
Taylor & Francis Group
LONDON AND NEW YORK

Designed cover image: © Shutterstock

First published 2024
by Routledge
4 Park Square, Milton Park, Abingdon, Oxon OX14 4RN

and by Routledge
605 Third Avenue, New York, NY 10158

Routledge is an imprint of the Taylor & Francis Group, an informa business

© 2024 selection and editorial matter, Alice Sullivan and Selina Todd; individual chapters, the contributors

The right of Alice Sullivan and Selina Todd to be identified as the authors of the editorial material, and of the authors for their individual chapters, has been asserted in accordance with sections 77 and 78 of the Copyright, Designs and Patents Act 1988.

All rights reserved. No part of this book may be reprinted or reproduced or utilised in any form or by any electronic, mechanical, or other means, now known or hereafter invented, including photocopying and recording, or in any information storage or retrieval system, without permission in writing from the publishers.

The views and opinions expressed in this book are those of contributors and do not necessarily reflect the views and opinions of Routledge.

Trademark notice: Product or corporate names may be trademarks or registered trademarks, and are used only for identification and explanation without intent to infringe.

British Library Cataloguing-in-Publication Data
A catalogue record for this book is available from the British Library

Library of Congress Cataloging-in-Publication Data
Names: Sullivan, Alice (Professor of sociology), editor. | Todd, Selina, editor.
Title: Sex and gender : a contemporary reader / edited by Alice Sullivan and Selina Todd.
Description: Abingdon, Oxon ; New York, NY : Routledge, 2023. | Includes bibliographical references and index.
Identifiers: LCCN 2022061470 (print) | LCCN 2022061471 (ebook) | ISBN 9781032261201 (hardback) | ISBN 9781032261195 (paperback) | ISBN 9781003286608 (ebook)
Subjects: LCSH: Gender identity. | Sex role. | Sex differences (Psychology) | Sex discrimination.
Classification: LCC HQ1075 .S4628 2023 (print) | LCC HQ1075 (ebook) | DDC 305.3—dc23/eng/20230130
LC record available at https://lccn.loc.gov/2022061470
LC ebook record available at https://lccn.loc.gov/2022061471

ISBN: 978-1-032-26120-1 (hbk)
ISBN: 978-1-032-26119-5 (pbk)
ISBN: 978-1-003-28660-8 (ebk)

DOI: 10.4324/9781003286608

CONTENTS

Notes on Contributors   ix

1   Introduction   1
    Alice Sullivan and Selina Todd

2   Two Sexes   16
    Emma Hilton and Colin Wright

3   Sex and the Brain: I Still Haven't Found What
    I Wasn't Looking For   35
    Sophie Scott

4   Is Womanhood a Social Fact?   51
    Kathleen Stock

5   The History of Sex: Sex Denial and Gender Identity Ideology   69
    Jane Clare Jones

6   Sex and Gender in Second-Wave Feminism   86
    Selina Todd

7   Why Do We Need Data on Sex?   104
    Alice Sullivan, Kath Murray and Lisa Mackenzie

8	Sex and Gender in Law *Rosemary Auchmuty and Rosa Freedman*	125
9	Sex, Gender, and Equality in the United States: Confusion, Conflict, and Consequences *Callie H. Burt*	139
10	Psychosocial Factors and Gender Dysphoria: Emerging Theories *Lisa Littman*	156
11	The Technology of Puberty Suppression *Michael Biggs*	175
12	Schools, Feminism and Gender-Identity Theory *Shereen Benjamin*	194
13	The Children Who Wouldn't Grow Up: Gender in Children's Literature Over Fifty Years *Susan Matthews*	214
14	Sex, Gender Identity and Sport *Cathy Devine*	232
15	Sex, Gender, Identity and Criminology *Jo Phoenix*	259
Index		*278*

NOTES ON CONTRIBUTORS

Rosemary Auchmuty is a pioneer of women's studies and feminist legal studies in higher education in Britain. She has been a professor of law at the University of Reading since 2007. She is a member of the Law, Justice and Society grouping at Reading, with a particular interest in the Legal History and Gender and Law sub-groups.

Shereen Benjamin is a senior lecturer in primary education at the University of Edinburgh and is a former teacher in primary, secondary and special schools. She now works in teacher education and researches the intersection of disability, gender and social class in schooling. Her publications include 'Sexuality, Sex and Gender: Respect and Recognition' (2019) in the edited collection *Social Justice Re-Examined: Dilemmas and Solutions for the Classroom Teacher* (Stoke-on-Trent, Trentham).

Michael Biggs is an associate professor of sociology and a fellow of St Cross College at the University of Oxford. His research has focused on social movements and collective protest but was diverted when students exhorted him to educate himself on the subject of transgender children. Searching for evidence he discovered a British experiment on 'puberty blockers' whose results had disappeared. His investigation led to publications in medical journals (*Journal of Sexual Medicine* and *Archives of Sexual Behavior*) and was central to the landmark judicial review (*Bell and Mrs A v Tavistock*, 2020) which curtailed the use of puberty blockers in England and Wales.

Callie H. Burt is a sociologist and criminologist in the Department of Criminology and Criminal Justice and the Center for Research on Interpersonal Violence in the Andrew Young School of Policy Studies at Georgia State University. Her areas of expertise include developmental and life-course criminology; crime and inequality;

sex, gender and the law; genetics and society; and research methodologies. Much of her research focuses on the developmental effects of social inequalities, especially the effects of social risk and protective factors in adolescence, from a biopsychosocial perspective. She has a long-standing research interest in sex differences and how these differences are shaped by gender as a social force and the ways in which law and social policies reflect, reinscribe or challenge these differences. In recent years, she has published in a variety of outlets, including the *Annual Review of Criminology, Behavioural and Brain Sciences, Criminology, Feminist Criminology,* and *PLoS Biology,* among others.

Cathy Devine is an independent researcher and is a former senior lecturer at the University of Cumbria. She previously worked at the National Coaching Foundation and the National Federation of Women's Institutes as Head of Sport. She was a member of the organising committee for the inaugural International Women and Sport Conference in Brighton in 1994, organised by the British Sports Council and supported by the British Olympic Association and the International Olympic Committee. Her research is on the human rights of girls and women in sport. Her publications include 'Female Olympians' Voices: Female Sport Categories and IOC Transgender Guidelines', *International Review for the Sociology of Sport* (2021) and 'Female Sports Participation, Gender Identity and the British 2010 Equality Act', *Sport, Ethics and Philosophy* (2021).

Rosa Freedman is the inaugural Professor of Law, Conflict and Global Development at the University of Reading. She received her LLB, LLM and PhD from the University of London and is a non-practising barrister and member of the Honourable Society of Gray's Inn. Freedman is a member of the UN Secretary-General's Civil Society Advisory Board on prevention of sexual exploitation and abuse, is a specialist adviser on safeguarding to the UK government International Development Committee and sits on the UK FCO Women, Peace and Security Steering Group.

Emma Hilton is a developmental biologist at the University of Manchester. Her academic research has focused on the study of genetic disorders, including sex-specific disorders, in humans. Regarding social issues arising from sex and gender, her academic publications include 'The Reality of Sex', *Irish Journal of Medical Science* (2021) and 'Transgender Women in the Female Category of Sport: Perspectives on Testosterone Suppression and Performance Advantage', *Sports Medicine* (2021). She has written opinion pieces and letters in the mainstream press including the *Wall Street Journal* ('The Dangerous Denial of Sex' with Colin Wright, February 2020). She is a director of Sex Matters, an academic policy group advocating for reality-based discussions of sex in law.

Jane Clare Jones is a feminist writer, philosopher and activist. She is the founder of the Institute of Feminist Thought, an online feminist school, and the founder and editor of *The Radical Notion*, a feminist quarterly examining and extending materialist and sex-based class analysis.

Lisa Littman is a physician researcher who conducts research about gender dysphoria, desistance and detransition. The findings of her 2018 publication, 'Parent Reports of Adolescents and Young Adults Perceived to Show Signs of a Rapid Onset of Gender Dysphoria', generated hypotheses about the potential role of psychosocial factors in the development of gender dysphoria. Dr Littman is currently the president of the Institute for Comprehensive Gender Dysphoria Research and has previously held academic positions at the Brown University School of Public Health and the Icahn School of Medicine at Mount Sinai.

Lisa Mackenzie is an independent policy analyst and a member of the policy analysis collective MurrayBlackburnMackenzie. She is a former civil servant in the UK government, where she worked as a communications specialist in a number of Whitehall departments, including the Department for Social Security and Home Office, as well as the Commission for Racial Equality. More recently, she has worked on policy for a penal reform campaign group and a trade union.

Susan Matthews was a reader in English literature at the University of Roehampton. She has published widely on the history of sex, sexuality and gender (including *Blake, Sexuality and Bourgeois Politeness*, Cambridge 2011) and on children's literature. Her work on gender ideology includes 'Gender Guides and Workbooks: Understanding the Work of a new Disciplinary Genre' (in Brunskell Evans and Moore, eds., *Inventing Transgender Children and Young People,* 2019).

Kath Murray is a research fellow in criminology at the University of Edinburgh and has a background in criminal justice and policing. Her doctoral research on stop-and-search led to major legal and policy reform in Scotland, for which she received an ESRC Outstanding Early Career Impact prize. She also undertakes research and analysis as part of the MurrayBlackburnMackenzie Policy Collective, whose outputs on sex and gender identity include peer-reviewed publications, parliamentary evidence, briefings and media commentary.

Jo Phoenix is a professor of criminology at the University of Reading in the School of Law. Her current research interests include gender, sexualities and justice, academic freedom, youth justice and punishment, the production of criminological knowledge and research ethics. She is the author of *Making Sense of Prostitution* (2001); a co-author of *Sex, Regulation and Social Control* (with Sarah Oerton, 2005); and the editor of *Regulating Sex For Sale: Prostitution Policy Reform in the UK* (2010), as well as numerous articles and book chapters on child sexual exploitation and sex, sexualities and justice. In 2011, she launched Durham University's Centre for Sex, Gender and Sexualities. Exactly 10 years later, and in the face of a public harassment campaign that led to her taking her former employer (The Open University) to an employment tribunal for harassment, bullying, direct discrimination and constructive dismissal on the basis of her gender-critical beliefs, she and Jon Pike launched and co-convened The Open University's Gender Critical Research Network.

Sophie Scott, CBE FMedSci FBA, is a neuroscientist and Wellcome Trust Senior Fellow at University College London. She is known for her public engagement work, including stand-up comedy, and gave the Royal Institution Christmas Lectures in 2017. She was appointed Commander of the Order of the British Empire in the 2020 Birthday Honours for services to neuroscience.

Kathleen Stock is a former professor of philosophy at the University of Sussex. She is the author of *Material Girls: Why Reality Matters for Feminism* (Little, Brown 2021) and has also published extensively on imagination, fiction, sexual objectification and sexual orientation. She regularly discusses gender identity ideology and its effects on women and girls in public writing and speaking and was awarded an Order of the British Empire for services to higher education in 2020.

Alice Sullivan is a professor of sociology at University College London. She is a quantitative social scientist and was the director of the 1970 British Cohort Study (BCS70) from 2010 to 2020. Her academic contributions to the sex and gender question include 'Sex and the Census: Why Surveys Should Not Conflate Sex and Gender Identity' (2020, *International Journal of Social Research Methodology*) and (with Judith Suissa) 'The Gender Wars, Academic Freedom and Education' (2021, *Journal of Philosophy of Education*).

Selina Todd is a professor of modern history at Oxford University and a fellow of St Hilda's College, Oxford. Her research focuses on the history of women, feminism and the working class in modern Britain. Her books include *The People: The Rise and Fall of the Working Class 1910–2010* (John Murray 2014) and *Tastes of Honey: The Making of Shelagh Delaney and a Cultural Revolution* (Chatto and Windus 2019).

Colin Wright, PhD, is an evolutionary biologist, formerly of the Pennsylvania State University, US. He now writes as an independent scholar.

1
INTRODUCTION

Alice Sullivan and Selina Todd

This book is about the meaning and significance of sex (a biological category) and gender (a social category). The introduction explains our definition of sex and gender and the relationship between them. We also explain why studying sex and gender matters, and our aims for this book. The chapters that follow span, collectively, the sciences, social sciences and the humanities. The contributors – all senior scholars in their respective fields – examine the biological basis of sex, the construction of gender and how sex and gender inform academic, social, legal and political debate. Each chapter presents original scholarship of relevance to students and scholars of the subject, but this book is also written for the general reader interested in sex and gender.

The erasure of sex categories from language, public policy, discourse and data collection is a recent phenomenon. The idea that sex should not be referred to, analysed or taken into account has achieved dominance with extraordinary speed.

The Lancet medical journal's statement that "'Historically, the anatomy and physiology of bodies with vaginas have been neglected'" (Gribble et al. 2022) provides a vivid example of the expunging of sex categories, and women in particular, from language. Health services increasingly refer to women according to body parts or functions, such as 'people with a cervix' or 'menstruators'.

The denial of sex has had concrete effects on everyday life, including the removal of single-sex spaces and female-only sports categories. Rapid changes in the medical and social treatment of children who express confusion about their gender have occurred despite a lack of supporting evidence (NHS England 2022). Parents and schools have had to contend with a rapid increase in the number of children and young people presenting with gender-related distress, in an emotive climate, in which even asking for better data to support decision-making is presented as suspect (Barnes, 2023).

DOI: 10.4324/9781003286608-1

Many people may be bemused by these developments and wonder where they have come from. Those implementing policy change on the ground may be largely ignorant of the academic origins of the campaign to abolish sex categories. Change has often been pushed through quickly and quietly, without due scrutiny or discussion. This type of 'policy capture' has occurred in areas of policymaking where sex is a consideration, from data collection to prisons to sports (Murray and Hunter Blackburn 2019; Devine 2022; Sullivan 2021; Biggs 2022).

In this climate, the current book provides a much-needed resource for anyone interested in how we got here and who wishes to understand current debates on sex and gender from a multi-disciplinary and evidence-based perspective.

We were motivated to write this book for three reasons. The first is that we cannot understand the world without reference to the fact that humans are sexed. Removing sex as a conceptual and empirical variable leaves the human and the social sciences and the humanities hopelessly hamstrung. This matters for science and scholarship, regardless of whether one takes a feminist perspective or not. But it matters particularly for women, because women remain unequal to men. Only by understanding sex and gender can we identify where such inequality exists, analyse its causes and consequences, and seek to eradicate it. Women across the world are subject to sex discrimination in the workplace and beyond and are subjected to male violence, sexual assault and harassment (Abdel-Raouf and Buhler 2020; Vail et al. 2018; Francis Devine and Booth 2022; Allen et al. 2022; Bryson et al. 2020). Many academic feminists have moved away from the analysis of these material problems, influenced by aspects of postmodernist thought and by gender-identity ideology (influences that we outline below). We agree with Martha Nussbaum (1999) that '[f]eminism demands more and women deserve better' (45).

The contributors to this book believe that researchers and policymakers should examine the extent of inequality between the sexes, the reasons for such inequality, and who perpetuates and benefits from it. Acknowledging the biological differences between women and men is important if we are to understand their distinct needs and vulnerabilities (for example, women are on average physically weaker than men). But these biological differences do not explain or justify women's inequality. The social and political construction of gender creates and justifies this inequality by suggesting that women should play 'feminine' roles and men 'masculine' ones and by valuing the latter more than the former. Studying gender, and its relationship with sex, is therefore crucial.

Our second motivation is a recent challenge to this understanding of sex and gender and the view that sex affects people's lives. Since the late twentieth century, gender-identity theorists have argued that gender is a personal identity that has nothing to do with an individual's biological sex (we explain and evaluate gender-identity theory later in this introduction). During the early twenty-first century, this idea has gained traction in academic debate and policymaking, especially in the world's richest Western countries. Those who believe that men and women should be defined by how they feel, rather than by their biology, focus on the need to accommodate individuals who do not believe they belong to the biological sex they were born into. Those people who believe they have an innate gender identity at odds with their biological sex are defined as 'trans'. This debate has focused particularly on how the desire of some men to be treated as women can be addressed. How the sexes, and particularly women, are defined and whether women as a sex should possess distinct rights to protect them from sex discrimination and harassment have become burning questions for academics and politicians alike. This volume will help readers to navigate this debate.

The third motivation for writing this book is to communicate evidence-based views which have been suppressed. The advocates of gender-identity politics have silenced dissent and suppressed women's voices, for example by targeting feminist meetings with violent threats (Kirkup 2018). Their actions have highlighted and exacerbated the conflict between gender-identity activists and feminists advocating for women's rights. The slogan 'no debate', adopted in political campaigning for gender self-identification and the erasure of sex as a category, has also had a chilling effect within universities (Suissa and Sullivan 2021). This book is underpinned by the need to reassert scientific and scholarly values in the face of attempts by postmodern sex denialists to curtail scholarship through campaigns of slander and abuse, often targeting employers and publishers, something many of the contributors to this volume have experienced. Calls for 'no debate' on sex and gender seek to prevent both democratic and scholarly discussion. Yet the open exchange of ideas is essential if we are to develop mutual understanding and work towards solutions to social problems and conflicts of rights.

The wide-ranging multi-disciplinarity of this volume reflects the fact that sex, and the gendered norms associated with sex, matters across the disciplines represented here, including biology, history, law, sociology and English literature. The contributors to this volume argue that the attempt to erase sex, both as a conceptual category and as an empirical variable, has consequences for all the disciplines which take human beings as their subject.

Defining sex and gender

The scholars in this volume share a broad understanding of sex and gender. Sex is biological, immutable and binary (there are only two sexes, as Hilton and Wright explain in this volume). Scholars and policymakers need to understand the biological differences between women and men because these create distinct, sexed experiences and needs. For example, only women have the potential to bear children, so even the experience of *not* childbearing is different for women than for men. Only men can get prostate cancer, and only women can menstruate and breastfeed. Everyone needs to be able to recognise these differences so they can understand their own bodies and requirements. Scholars need to be able to analyse men and women as groups to identify their needs, and policymakers need to be able to address those needs (or be held to account if they do not). The category of sex enables us to do this.

Differences do not inevitably turn into inequalities, so biological differences between the sexes alone cannot explain sex discrimination. To understand how inequality is created and maintained, we must study the relationship between sex and gender. Gender is often used as a synonym for sex. In fact, as linguist Deborah Cameron (2016) has pointed out, people have been using gender as a fancy term for sex for over 500 years. But in the 1970s, second-wave feminists began to use gender to define a socially and politically constructed set of roles and behaviours that constrain individuals according to their sex. The *Oxford English Dictionary* attributes the definition of gender as 'sex as expressed by societal or cultural distinctions' to Ann Oakley (1972): 'Sex differences may be 'natural', but gender differences have their source in culture' (189). Many social scientists use this social definition of gender and so do we.

Sex and gender are connected, because gendered constraints are imposed on individuals according to their sex. For example, girls may be expected to play with 'feminine' toys like dolls, while boys may be encouraged to play with 'masculine' toys like guns, although both sexes are capable of playing with both or neither. Women may face discrimination if they seek to work in a 'masculine' job such as a senior leadership position (which partly explains the significant pay gap between men and women), although there is no biological reason why men make better leaders. We are therefore interested in why women are expected to perform certain roles and not others, how certain roles and behaviours are designated 'feminine' or 'masculine', and who benefits from this.

Gender does not just create distinct roles but is also hierarchical. Feminine tasks and roles are generally granted less value (in terms of money and/or status) than masculine ones. But even if women undertake roles that are considered to be masculine, they are likely to be paid and valued less than men in the same roles. This shows how sex and gender interact: women, as a sex, are valued less than men. Women, as a sex, are subject to gendered exploitation: for example, their unpaid care work is relied upon by the state as a desirable alternative to providing a comprehensive social care system (Bedford et al., 2022), a state of affairs justified by treating such work as women's natural role. Gender restricts both men and women, but *women* are oppressed because they are treated as inferior to men and subjected to gendered forms of exploitation.

The importance of sex and gender in differentiating women's lives from men's means they need to be taken into account in law and politics. In Britain, the Equality Act 2010 recognises sex as a protected characteristic, which means it is illegal to discriminate against someone on the basis of their sex. Some organisations and services are granted an exemption from this when there is a demonstrable need. For example, a rape crisis centre may decide to employ only women (because it caters to women victims), political parties are allowed to create women-only shortlists (because women are under-represented in politics), and competitive sport can exclude the members of one sex from sporting competitions (because women are physically weaker than men). In addition, some services are single sex (such as toilets and changing rooms) because of the need to uphold the dignity and privacy of both sexes but particularly of women. Although men can also be victims of male sexual violence, and, of course, not all men are perpetrators, it remains the case that the overwhelming majority of perpetrators of sexual harassment and sexual assault are men and the majority of victims are women. While other countries differ in the provision they make, most nations do recognise sex in law.

Competing understandings of sex and gender

The scholars in this book can be described as 'gender critical'. Gender-critical beliefs are defined in UK law as the belief 'that biological sex is real, important, immutable and not to be conflated with gender identity' (Brione, 2022). The case of Maya Forstater, who lost her job at a think tank following tweets expressing gender-critical views, has established that gender-critical beliefs are 'worthy of respect in a democratic society' and therefore protected under the characteristic of religion or belief within the Equality Act 2010 (*Forstater vs CGD Europe and Others*, 2021). It is illegal to discriminate against someone because of their gender-critical beliefs.

As academics, we are ambivalent about describing ourselves as 'gender critical', although we certainly share the gender-critical view that sex is real and sex matters. Sex certainly matters to our academic work. Our ambivalence stems partly from the fact that our beliefs are not new – in fact, they were widely taken for granted until very recently. Many academics who believe that sex is real and that it matters may be unfamiliar with the label gender critical or not realise that it applies to them. There is a danger that the term could mislead some readers into thinking that the belief that sex matters is a new theory, formed in response to 'gender-uncritical' scholars.

In fact, gender-critical views do not constitute a theory about sex and gender and are compatible with every political philosophy, with the sole exception of gender-identity theory. That gender-critical beliefs are compatible with both socialism and conservatism, Islam and atheism, feminism and opposition to feminism should come as no surprise, since all these belief systems existed long before gender-identity theory. The view that sex matters does not reflect a belief in a particular theory or creed. It is an unassailable empirical fact. As such, 'gender-critical' people should be no more likely to agree on other matters than people who agree that the Earth orbits the sun.

However, beyond this minimal definition of gender-critical beliefs, some scholars use the term 'gender-critical feminism' to signal that they are critical of gender, including both gender-identity theory and traditional conservative views about gender roles (Stock 2021; Lawford Smith, 2022). This position still accommodates a wide range of views but puts gender-critical feminists in opposition to people who acknowledge the reality of sex but repudiate feminism.

The view that sex matters certainly does not imply that there is no role for social factors in determining the behaviour and social position of the sexes. This caricatured view is sometimes labelled 'biological essentialism', while the opposite view, that biology has no role, is labelled 'blank slatism'. In practice, while scholars (including contributors to this book) disagree on the relative importance of nature and nurture, biology and society, it is generally acknowledged that human behaviour is determined by a complex interplay between these factors.

Gender-identity theorists sometimes disavow any role for biology, arguing that both sex and gender are culturally or linguistically constructed. They disagree with our understanding of sex as biological and gender as social. The most prominent advocate of gender-identity theory is American philosopher Judith Butler, whose seminal work *Gender Trouble* (1990) has informed subsequent studies on both sides of the Atlantic.

Although Butler and her followers argue that both sex and gender are constructs, in recent years many gender-identity theorists have also claimed that gender is an innate, 'natural' identity. They believe that biological sex is 'assigned' to a person at birth, not determined at conception as gender-critical scholars believe. Many gender-identity theorists view trans people as those whose gender identity differs from their biological sex. Others argue that people can freely choose their gender identity and change it at will over their lifetimes. It is not clear how gender can be both a linguistic construction and an innate identity. Because of its contradictions, some of our authors prefer to refer to this school of thought as 'gender-identity ideology' rather than as a theory.

Regardless of whether gender-identity theorists treat gender as an innate, fixed identity or one that is freely chosen and fluid, they believe that society should give greater weight to gender identity than to biological sex. The supporters of gender-identity theory argue that sex is oppressive because it is binary: everyone is obliged to identify as female or male. According to this view, this binary system oppresses both women and men, especially those whose gender identity differs from their sex. This conflicts with the gender-critical argument that *gender* is oppressive because it restricts both men and women to certain roles and ascribes low value to the roles that women are meant to perform. Far from being an innate or freely chosen identity, gender is a tool of oppression.

Gender-identity theory was developed in North American universities, and until the 2000s, it was confined to university humanities departments. It is rooted in postmodernist queer theory (we discuss what "queer" means later in this introduction), which overtly opposes scientific values and the notion of truth. Despite this, since the early twenty-first century gender-identity theory has had a great influence on public discourse and policymaking internationally. Its adherents now include many activists, politicians and lobby groups. The supporters of gender-identity theory oppose feminists' claim that women should be entitled to certain single-sex services (such as women's refuges), spaces (such as changing rooms) and other provisions (such as women-only sports). For theorists like Butler, feminists' insistence on women's rights and resources reinforces the binary system and privileges those whose gender-identity aligns with their biological sex.

Gender-identity theory rejects the evidence that biological sex exists and downplays the social and political construction of gender. Gender-identity theorists appear to believe that acknowledging biological differences between the sexes causes inequality. But acknowledging sex difference is not the same as arguing that such difference justifies social and political inequalities. Treating gender as a personal identity fails to interrogate how certain roles and behaviours become understood as 'feminine' or 'masculine' and in whose interests. Promoting gendered identities risks reinforcing the power relations that underpin gender and perpetuating stereotyped roles for men and women.

Gender-critical scholars differ in our understanding of how gender is constructed and who gender benefits. Many gender-critical scholars are feminists who believe that men construct and use gender to justify and perpetuate their power over women. Feminists call societies in which this occurs 'patriarchal'. Feminists believe that in a patriarchy, men use gender to oppress women by ascribing little value to 'feminine' roles like caring (which are portrayed as 'natural' and thus requiring neither praise nor much pay) and by suggesting that women's value is defined by men's desire for them. Feminists do not believe that patriarchy is the only form of oppressive power that exists or that all women are oppressed to the same extent or that all men benefit equally from patriarchy. But men, as a sex, have a vested interest in sustaining patriarchal practices whereas women, as a sex, do not.

But there is no single gender-critical view on gender. Some think that sex differences, and the need to recognise these socially, mean that some form of gendered behaviour will always exist. Others are sceptical of patriarchy as an explanation of power. And some, regardless of their views on gender, are more concerned with examining biological differences between men and women than the construction of gender.

Given the wide range of views that are compatible with gender-critical beliefs, it is not surprising that this volume reflects heterodox perspectives. This book shows the rich potential that open scholarly discussion generates for our understanding of sex and gender in the past and the present. We hope that the volume will encourage further debate and research, helping promote greater fairness for women and girls in the future.

Trans people

Contemporary debate about sex and gender is at its most polarised when centred on the definition and rights of transgender people. We use 'transgender' to refer to those who believe both that they possess a gender identity and that this identity conflicts with their biological sex. According to the glossary of the UK lobby group Stonewall (2019):

> Trans people may describe themselves using one or more of a wide variety of terms, including (but not limited to) transgender, transsexual, gender-queer (GQ), gender-fluid, non-binary, gender-variant, crossdresser, genderless, agender, nongender, third gender, bi-gender, trans man, trans woman, trans masculine, trans feminine and neutrois.

In this sense, *trans* is an umbrella term, used to refer to a diverse range of identities and experiences. Where possible, we distinguish between transsexuals, transvestites and transgender people to make clear exactly who we are discussing.

Until the twenty-first century, very small numbers of people identified as transvestites (who adopt the appearance of the opposite sex on certain occasions) or transsexuals (who wish to live as members of the opposite sex on a permanent basis and have surgery to help them achieve this goal). It was widely understood that people could not actually change sex, because they could not change the biology with which they were born. But by the end of the twentieth century, many Western countries recognised 'gender dysphoria' – the inability to live as one's natal sex without significant mental distress – as a medical condition. Many governments enabled transsexuals to change their legal sex in what is recognised as a legal fiction: the law recognised a small number of people as the sex they wanted to be rather than the sex they were born. In Britain, this was enacted by the 2004 Gender Recognition Act. In order to get a Gender Recognition Certificate, applicants have to prove they have lived as a member of the opposite sex for two years and be medically diagnosed as gender dysphoric.

Some gender-identity theorists and trans-rights activists have argued that more reform is needed: that people should be allowed to self-identify as male, female or neither and access the services and rights afforded to the group they have identified into. This has implications for how we define males and females: Are people men or women on the basis of biology or on the basis of how they feel? Contributors to this volume argue that men and women should be defined by biology. It is vital that the state can categorise individuals according to sex in order to address biological differences between them (such as different healthcare needs) and identify and ameliorate sex discrimination. Replacing sex with gender identity would change who can use single-sex changing rooms and toilets, compete in single-sex sports, use women's refuges or be housed in the female prison estate, with detrimental effects for women.

It is unclear that such reforms would benefit trans people. We still know very little about trans people's health needs and their life experiences. Being able to identify and count trans men and women as distinct groups in social surveys and healthcare, to take just two examples, would allow us to discover more about their needs and experiences. By arguing that transmen should be identified solely as men, and transwomen as women, gender-identity theorists ignore the fact that these groups have distinct needs – based on both their biology and their gender identity – which we don't yet know enough about.

People who do not conform to the social expectations for their sex often face prejudice, whether or not they identify as trans. All the contributors to this volume believe that trans and gender-non-conforming people should be able to live without discrimination or harm. We emphasise this because some proponents of gender-identity theory argue that discussing the origins of and reasons for gender identity is unnecessary and even prejudicial to trans people. Some claim that any critical evaluation of gender identity or assertion of the reality of sex is a denial of trans people's identity and even their existence. The authors in this volume share the view that sex is biological, determined at conception rather than 'assigned' at birth. We also believe that trans people should be legally protected from harassment and discrimination. Some of the chapters that follow examine how trans people might be accommodated in (for example) competitive sports or the prison estate without encroaching on women's right to single-sex space. Opposition to gender-identity theory does not imply disrespect for trans people. In fact, trans people have a range of views on sex, gender and gender identity.

Lesbians, gay men, bisexuals and 'queer' people

The debate over the meaning of sex and gender also affects the definition and rights of lesbians, bisexuals and gay men. Scholarly studies of their lives and histories began to appear in the 1980s and often treated each group as distinct from the others, albeit often united in their fight for rights. But by the 1990s, the pioneers of queer theory argued that lesbians, gay men and bisexuals should all be categorised as queer, because they were rebelling against heteronormativity.

It is certainly true that lesbians and gay men faced similar prejudice in the 1980s and 1990s. In Britain, the Conservative government's introduction of Clause 28 in 1988 banned local authorities from 'promoting' homosexuality in schools. And between the mid-1980s and the early 1990s, the British government's response to the HIV/AIDS epidemic treated homosexuality as the root cause of the virus – as was true in many other countries, including the United States. Lesbians and gay men recognised their shared political interests by establishing campaign groups, such as Stonewall, which was formed in Britain in 1989.

In the 2010s, queer theorists, and some campaign groups established to represent lesbian and gay rights, became increasingly concerned with gender identities. Whereas campaigners had previously been concerned with sexual orientation and *practices*, queer came to encompass an increasing variety of sexual *and* gender *identities*. By 2020, some gender-identity theorists, and the lobby group Stonewall, argued that men who identify as female and are attracted to other females are lesbians. This stress on gender identity ignores the reality of same-sex attraction. This has led to a rift between groups such as Stonewall, which now prioritise gender-identity theory, and those lesbian, gay and bisexual people, including founding members of Stonewall, who continue to advocate for the rights of same-sex attracted people (*Sunday Times*, 2019; Rhodes, 2019).

Queer theorists and gender-identity theorists both aspire to a future in which opting out of the binaries male/female or heterosexual/homosexual becomes more common. But why this would be liberatory is never explained. The authors in this volume argue that far from subverting gender norms, this version of queer theory has ignored the basis on which gay men and lesbians have faced discrimination (because they are same-sex-attracted) and has reinforced or revived prejudice towards them. Contributors show that both parents and medical practitioners have treated gender-non-conforming adolescents as potential transgender adults, despite much evidence that, without medical intervention, they are likely to grow out of their gender dysphoria and are disproportionately likely to become gay men or lesbian women.

We use 'queer' to refer to groups or individuals who ascribe to queer theory. We do not define lesbians, gay men and bisexual people as 'queer' per se, partly because queer is a porous category. The fact that some heterosexuals identify as queer, and many gay, lesbian and bisexual people do not, makes it an unclear category to use when discussing sexual orientation. The experiences of gay, lesbian and bisexual people are distinct from those of people who feel they have a gender identity.

What this book covers

This book draws on work from across the sciences, social sciences and humanities. This means that authors use different sources and research methods. Each author briefly explains these at the beginning of their chapter, and we have tried to use language accessible to the general reader.

We do not aim to offer a comprehensive account of why sex and gender matters, or how their meanings have been debated, across academia and society. Rather, we seek to familiarise readers with some of the most salient debates in academic discourse, policy and cultural life. This means tackling the recent influence of gender-identity theory and explaining the benefits of taking a gender-critical approach to sex and gender in key areas of scholarship, culture and policy.

Our focus is primarily on Britain, where gender-critical thought and scholarship have flourished in recent years. Gender-identity theory is a product of elite campuses in the US and has met with significant resistance in Britain, notably from feminist campaigners (Pederson 2020). Britain's 'exceptionality' in this regard has been noted by both gender-critical thinkers and gender-identity theorists. It is therefore a valuable locus in its own right.

A number of factors may have contributed to the greater capacity for resistance in the UK. While free speech is protected as a principle in the US Constitution, in practice, US workers have few protections from unfair dismissal and lack a welfare safety net, including universal healthcare. The lack of a socialist tradition in the US may have contributed to the appeal of identity politics to US 'progressives'. In addition, the feminist movement in the US has been far less effective in gaining material rights for women compared to the UK movement. For example, US women are not entitled to paid maternity leave, free contraception or free and legal abortion. In the UK, both sex and gender reassignment are protected characteristics, meaning that people are protected from discrimination based either on their sex or on their trans status.

Crucially, the 2018 consultation on reform of the 2004 Gender Recognition Act brought the concept of 'gender self-identification' into public consciousness and provided a focus for campaigning in the UK. The proposed change would have allowed anyone to change their legal sex, without the need for a medical diagnosis (Harrison 2018). The consultation undermined the usual tactics of the gender-identity lobby, which has relied on changing policy and practice behind the scenes without public discussion. Whereas in the US, a polarised politics has discouraged liberals from challenging gender-identity theory for fear of being deemed right-wing, in the UK, the resistance to gender-identity theory has been pluralistic, with strong leadership roles for Woman's Place UK (WPUK), a group formed of labour movement activists, as well as non-partisan groups such as Fair Play for Women. These and other dimensions of British opposition to gender-identity theory and activism are worthy of further study. We hope this volume will encourage such research.

This focus on Britain is also valuable given recent international developments. More national and international bodies are adopting, or re-adopting, a gender-critical understanding of sex and gender. In 2021 the Swedish National Board of Health and Welfare recommended that children under the age of eighteen should no longer be prescribed puberty blockers or cross-sex hormones. In the UK, the Cass Review (Cass 2022) has pointed out the lack of a firm evidence base to support the use of puberty blockers and social transition for children with gender-related distress. In 2022, FINA (the world governing body of swimming) voted to exclude transwomen from female competitions. Similarly, World Rugby has banned males from the women's game for reasons of fairness and safety (Pike 2021) and World Athletics announced in 2023 that they would exclude individuals who have been through male puberty from elite female competition.

But Britain also shows that there is no political consensus on sex and gender. The definition of sex in the UK's decennial census has apparently become a devolved matter. While the 2021 census of England and Wales instructed respondents to record their legal sex (and included a new question on gender identity), the 2022 census of Scotland allowed respondents to record their gender identity as their sex – a decision welcomed by the Scottish government. Debates over sex and gender show no signs of abating in Britain or beyond, so academic interrogations of the subject are vital.

We include a small number of comparative contributions. Some of these help identify the reasons for Britain's exceptionality; most focus on countries that have been at the forefront of relevant debates or developments; all provide illuminating analyses of the societies on which they focus. Chapters on lawmaking in Britain and in the United States demonstrate why Britain's treatment of sex and gender is, in some respects, strikingly different from many other western countries. Because gender-identity theory originated in the United States, it is particularly pertinent to include a chapter on lawmaking there.

Other comparisons highlight connections between different societies. Susan Mathews's examination of children's literature on both sides of the Atlantic shows that influential cultural narratives can cross borders even when political differences are stark. Studies of the treatment of children and adolescents labelled 'trans' demonstrate similarities in the medical practices and philosophies of the Netherlands – which pioneered the use of puberty blockers – the US and Britain, despite significant variation in healthcare systems.

Our comparative chapters show that while national differences in political and legal systems are important, they do not determine how sex and gender are defined. These authors suggest that recent challenges to the gender-critical understanding of sex and gender are best understood as trans-national. They also indicate that ignoring biological sex, and treating gender as a personal identity, is detrimental to women and young lesbians and gay men across a wide variety of societies. We hope that further scholarship will shed more light on these transnational developments and what they tell us about the powers and limitations of national political and welfare systems, and the influence of national and international policymaking bodies, lobby groups and campaigns.

These comparative chapters provide a glimpse into the international context, literature on which is limited but growing. The emergent scholarship is highlighting exciting, if disturbing, new areas of interest. These include the 'cultural and linguistic imperialism' enacted by international aid organisations that insist recipients – generally low-income and middle-income countries – 'desex' language regarding maternity and breastfeeding (Gribble et al. 2022).

The structure of this book

This book has three main aims. The first is to define sex. This is realised by Chapters 2, 3 and 4. In Chapter 2, Emma Hilton and Colin Wright outline that there are two biological sexes which are immutable: in other words, it is not possible to change one's sex. In Chapter 3, Sophie Scott examines sex differences in the brain. She demonstrates that there are some important differences between men's and women's brains which are determined by sex, regardless of a person's gender identity. Contrary to biological essentialists, Scott shows that sexed brains, while important, do not explain differences between men's and women's behaviour. In Chapter 4, Kathleen Stock evaluates competing philosophical arguments about definitions of womanhood and shows why a robust definition must centre on biology.

Our second aim is to analyse the evolution of gender-critical and gender-identity understandings of sex and gender. In Chapter 5, Jane Clare Jones traces the history of gender-identity ideology and analyses how it became so influential. In Chapter 6, Selina Todd examines why and how second-wave feminists developed an understanding of gender as a social and political construction, with beneficial consequences for women's legal and political rights. These chapters show that gender-critical and gender-identity understandings of sex and gender are irreconcilable and that scholars and policymakers must choose between them.

Third, we examine how conflicting understandings of sex and gender affect policy and cultural life and show why a gender-critical approach is the fairest and most robust. This is realised by the authors of Chapters 7 through 15. As Alice Sullivan, Lisa Mackenzie and Kath Murray explain in Chapter 7, it is vital that data collection exercises can categorise individuals according to sex and gender identity, rather than conflating the two, in order to allow examination of the experiences of different groups. The reasons why British and some international law safeguards sex-based rights are explained by Rosemary Auchmuty and Rosa Freedman in Chapter 8. In Chapter 9, Callie Burt examines the basis of challenges to sex-based legal rights in the US and the consequences of these. Together, these chapters argue that legal recognition of sex, and sex-based rights, is essential.

The negative consequences of ignoring biological sex in medicine are explored in Chapters 10 and 11. In Chapter 10, Lisa Littman assesses the therapeutic practice of affirming gender as an identity and shows how this fails to interrogate the reasons people feel uncomfortable in their sexed bodies. Littman demonstrates that this practice is detrimental to young gender-non-conforming people, particularly lesbians and gay men. In Chapter 11, Michael Biggs examines how medical professionals have downplayed the importance of biological sex and given precedence to gender identity. Biggs reveals that this has exposed gender-non-conforming children and teenagers to risky medical interventions.

All our authors believe that legal, sex-based rights are a foundation on which to build rather than an end in themselves. This is made particularly clear in Chapters 12 through 15. In Chapters 12 and 13, Shereen Benjamin and Susan Matthews deal respectively with education and children's literature as important sites of gendered socialisation. They demonstrate that culture and social policy are highly influential in creating or challenging sex inequality. Benjamin and Matthews argue that encouraging children to believe that men and women are defined by gender identity perpetuates older sexist stereotypes about what males and females can do; for example, girls are those children who like to play with dolls or wear dresses. By contrast, feminist pedagogy and literature give children the tools to break out of these stereotypes, by teaching children that girls and boys can behave in a variety of ways and play myriad roles, regardless of their sex.

The contributors to this volume are opposed to discrimination on the basis of sex or gender identity. Chapters 14 and 15 address this directly regarding two areas where single-sex provision is crucial. In Chapter 14, Cathy Devine evaluates the impact of sex differences and the need for sex-based rights, in both professional and amateur sport. She shows that achieving fair competition means dividing the sexes because of the biological differences between men and women. However, she also suggests how trans people could be accommodated in distinct competition categories. In Chapter 15, Jo Phoenix examines how the justice system can treat men and women equitably. She highlights important sex differentials in patterns of offending, regardless of offenders' gender identity. She also shows that gender-identity theory and queer theory offer no strategies for protecting women *and* trans people in the prison estate. Phoenix uses a gender-critical approach to suggest how both groups' rights could be upheld.

Conclusion

This *Reader* provides a wide-ranging, multi-disciplinary overview of sex and gender. Discussions about this subject have become fraught with difficulty in recent years, particularly because of the claims of some gender-identity theorists that gender-critical views are inherently prejudicial. Statements of fact which would have been seen as uncontentious until very recently, such as the statement that sex is binary, have been met with denunciation and threats, generating a climate of fear and making nuanced discussion seem all but impossible (Hooven 2022). This volume contributes to breaking this spell. We hope it will provide a starting point for constructive, evidence-based conversations about sex and gender across disciplinary boundaries.

References

Abdel-Raouf, Fatma and Patricia M. Buhler. 2020. *The Gender Pay Gap: Understanding the Numbers*. London: Routledge.

Allen, R. et al. 2022. *The Femicide Census 2020*. https://www.femicidecensus.org/wp-content/uploads/2022/02/010998-2020-Femicide-Report_V2.pdf.

Barnes, H. 2023. *Time to Think: The Inside Story of the Collapse of the Tavistock's Gender Service for Children*. London: Swift.

Bedford, S et al. 2022. *Universal Quality Social Care. Transforming Adult Social Care in England*. London: New Economics Foundation and Women's Budget Group.

Biggs, M. 2022. Queer Theory and the Transition from Sex to Gender in English Prisons. *Journal of Controversial Ideas*, 2(1), Article 2. https://doi.org/10.35995/jci02010002.

Brione, P. 2022. Employment Tribunal Rulings on Gender-Critical Beliefs in the Workplace. House of Commons Library. https://commonslibrary.parliament.uk/employment-tribunal-rulings-on-gender-critical-beliefs-in-the-workplace/

Butler, Judith. 1990. *Gender Trouble*. London: Routledge.

Bryson, A., Joshi, H., Wielgoszewska, B., & Wilkinson, D. (2020). A Short History of the Gender Wage Gap in Britain. *Oxford Review of Economic Policy*, 36(4), pp.836–854.

Cameron, D. 2016. A Brief History of Gender [Blog post]. https://debuk.wordpress.com/2016/12/15/a-brief-history-of-gender/

Cass, H. 2022. *The Cass Review: Independent Review of Gender Identity Services for Children and Young People: Interim Report*. February.

Devine, C., 2022. Female Olympians' Voices: Female Sports Categories and International Olympic Committee Transgender Guidelines. *International Review for the Sociology of Sport*, 57(3), pp.335–361.

Forstater v CGD Europe and Others: UKEAT/0105/20/JOJ. 2021. Employment Appeal Tribunal judgment of Mr Justice Choudhury, Mr C. Edwards and Mrs M.V. Mcarthur on 10 June 2021. https://assets.publishing.service.gov.uk/media/60c1cce1d3bf7f4bd9814e39/Maya_Forstater_v_CGD_Europe_and_others_UKEAT0105_20_JOJ.pdf

Francis-Devine, B. & Booth, L. 2022. *The Gender Pay Gap: Research Briefing*. London: House of Commons Library.

Gribble, K. et al. 2022. 'Effective Communication About Pregnancy, Birth, Lactation, Breastfeeding and Newborn Care: The Importance of Sexed Language'. *Frontiers in Global Women's Health*, 3. https://doi.org/10.3389/fgwh.2022.818856.

Harrison, K. 2018. A System of Gender Self-Identification Would Put Women at Risk. *The Economist*. 3 July.

Hooven, C.K. 2022. Academic Freedom Is Social Justice: Sex, Gender, and Cancel Culture on Campus. *Archives of Sexual Behavior* (52), 35–41.

Kirkup, J. 2018. Why Are Women Who Discuss Gender Getting Bomb Threats? *Spectator*. 21 June.

Lawford-Smith, H. 2022. *Gender-Critical Feminism*. Oxford: Oxford University Press.
Murray, K. & Hunter Blackburn, L. 2019. Losing Sight of Women's Rights: The Unregulated Introduction of Gender Self-Identification as a Case Study of Policy Capture in Scotland. *Scottish Affairs 28*(3), pp.262–289.
NHS England. 2022. *Public Consultation Interim Service Specification for Specialist Gender Dysphoria Services for Children and Young People*. 20 October.
Nussbaum, M.C. 1999. The Professor of Parody. *New Republic, 220*(8), pp.37–45.
Oakley, A. 1972. *Sex, Gender and Society*. London: Temple Smith.
Pedersen, S. 2022. 'They've Got an Absolute Army of Women behind Them': The Formation of a Women's Cooperative Constellation in Contemporary Scotland. *Scottish Affairs, 31*(1), pp.1–20.
Pike, J. 2021. Safety, Fairness, and Inclusion: Transgender Athletes and the Essence of Rugby. *Journal of the Philosophy of Sport, 48*(2), pp.155–168.
Rhodes, M. 2019. Co-Founder of Stonewall Calls for Calm. *Holyrood*. 4 November.
Stock, K. 2021. *Material Girls: Why Reality Matters for Feminism*. London: Fleet.
Stonewall, 2019. What Does Trans Mean? https://www.stonewall.org.uk/what-does-trans-mean.
Suissa, J. & Sullivan, A. 2021. The Gender Wars, Academic Freedom and Education. *Journal of Philosophy of Education 55*(1), pp.55–82.
Sullivan, A. 2021. Sex and the Office for National Statistics: A Case Study in Policy Capture. *The Political Quarterly 92*(4), pp.638–651.
Sunday Times. 2019. Letters to the Editor: Gay People Losing Faith in Stonewall. 22 September.
Vail, S., Corradi, C. & Naudi, M., eds. 2018. *Femicide Across Europe: Theory, Research and Prevention*. Bristol: Policy Press.

2
TWO SEXES

Emma Hilton and Colin Wright

> [W]hy the sexes are, in fact, always two.
>
> —Sir Ronald Fisher, 1930

Sex is an evolved mechanism of reproduction, fundamental to the existence of almost all complex life and forming a biological pattern that is not merely descriptive of form but also predictive of function. So foundational is the functional property of sex, an astrobiologist discovering complex alien life—necessarily replicating as individuals, assumed to be subject to natural selection acting on the variation of physical form and having experienced the major transitions that lead to complex life (Levin et al. 2019)—would likely look for mechanisms of sex in our extra-terrestrial friends (although, of course, the physical form may be rather different). However, the empirical facts and principles of sex, ascertained and synthesised over centuries of scientific study, are often forgotten by postmodernist commentators, intent on framing sex as a human-centred, human-invented—and thus malleable—construction of social understanding (see Jones, this volume).

The aim of this chapter is to review the biological understanding of the phenomenon that is sex. In the first section, we ask the question: Why does sex exist? We explain its evolutionary origins and the binary gamete system on which sex—'female' and 'male'—is founded. We explore some of the diversity of sex in the natural world yet understand how reproductive bodies are organised around two functional reproductive roles. In the second section, we focus on developmental biology and how sex manifests in humans: how we make babies and how female and male humans develop. In the final section, we critique emerging misinformation about sex, arising from an anti-science movement driven by gender identity ideology, and address arguments that assert the existence of a third (or more sex) in humans, that seek to deconstruct understandings of sex as a binary phenomenon and that frame sex as a social construct.

The incursion of ideological misinformation about sex into the academic fields of medicine and biology generates confusion in research and presents potential for harm. 'Sex matters' in basic and applied health research (Wizemann and Pardue 2001) and major health organisations, research funding bodies and academic journals increasingly demand that researchers account for 'sex as a biological variable' in their design, analyses and reporting, whether they include studies of whole animals or simple cell lines. Despite this, the United Kingdom National Health Service maintains a system where biological sex cannot be disaggregated in patient records (Forstater 2021) and the World Health Organization (WHO, 2022) promises to 'achieve greater impact [using] sex disaggregated data' (WHO/Health topics/Gender) while updating guidance asserting that 'sex is not limited to male or female'. From a wider perspective, we have argued that ideologically driven scientists are in danger of sacrificing 'empirical fact in the name of social accommodation' and that this is both 'an egregious betrayal to the scientific community they represent' and 'undermines public trust in science' (Hilton and Wright 2020). By countering deconstructive discourse, this chapter may be considered a reconstruction of sex.

A note on language. Physiologist Ernst Wilhelm von Brucke said, 'Teleology is a lady without whom no biologist can live. Yet he is ashamed to show himself with her in public' (Davis and Uhrin 1991, 549–552). It is possible in discussions of evolutionary biology to avoid teleological language, but sentence constructions are often verbose and clunky. For the ease of readability, we sometimes use language that is teleological in tone, but, in the words of zoologist Simon Maddrell (1998), '[t]his should not be taken to imply that evolution proceeds by anything other than from mutations arising by chance, with those that impart an advantage being retained by natural selection' (2461).

What is sex?

And why does sex exist? Given the deliberately destructive discourse around sex, it is not uncommon to find purportedly scientific articles that neglect to mention its evolved function in reproduction (e.g., Ainsworth 2015; Sun 2019). Indeed, that science communicators writing about sex neglect function means that, despite the authors' claims, such articles are not actually addressing the biological phenomenon of sex: What is it? Why does it exist? Why do humans have sexed bodies? Rather, they are examining how the sex of a given individual may be identified via some sex-linked checklist of physical features that—ironically—only exists from understanding how those physical features are associated with function. We return to this conflation of sex (what it is) with the physical characteristics associated with sex (how we recognise the sex of a given individual) in the final section of this chapter.

Reproduction

The phenomenon of sex is rooted in reproduction, the process by which new individuals are produced from parents. There are two types of reproduction in the natural world: asexual and sexual. In asexual reproduction, a parent replicates its genetic information and generates new, genetically identical offspring by processes such as binary fission—the division of a parent into two similar cells, observed, for example, in bacteria—and budding—the generation of a new individual from a parental outgrowth, observed, for example, in yeast. Expansion, via asexual reproduction, of a genetically identical population is of relatively low biological cost to each parent and rapid to enact: consider how quickly mould, which can reproduce asexually via the production of spores, can colonise a loaf of bread. There are also benefits to a parent, as its genetic information is passed in its entirety to the next generation.

Yet despite the existence of a low-cost and rather straightforward method of reproduction, the natural world is dominated by species that employ a different reproductive strategy: sexual reproduction. Unlike asexual reproduction, sexual reproduction involves two parents, almost always from two different classes of individuals called 'females' and 'males'. Each contributes a halved amount of their genetic material—carried on chromosomes—which is brought together to generate a new and genetically unique individual. This mixing of genetic material from each parent is achieved, in a process called 'fertilisation', by the fusion of two specialised cells called 'gametes'. Gametes, carrying only half of a parent's chromosomes, are a unique cell type, and the function of the gamete is singular—to effect sexual reproduction.

Sexual reproduction is biologically costly. From a gene-centred perspective, genetic relatedness between parent and offspring is half that achieved by asexual reproduction, and the loss of large amounts of genetic information with each round of reproduction—a huge penalty compared with asexual reproduction—means individuals must invest biological resources in multiple offspring to maximise their genetic legacy ('the cost of meiosis', where 'meiosis' is the cellular process that halves genetic material during gamete formation; Williams 1975). At the population level of most sexually reproducing populations, half of the offspring will be males who cannot themselves bear offspring, and these populations will experience lower growth rates than asexual populations where all offspring can themselves bear offspring ('the cost of males'; Maynard Smith 1978). Finally, at the organism level, individuals must invest resources in systems to produce specialised cells, and mating requires energy to move, locate and secure a partner, with associated health risks like disease transmission and exposure to predators. Explaining why, despite the costs, sexual reproduction is maintained in complex species has been called the 'queen of problems in evolutionary biology' (Bell 1982).

The advantages of sexual reproduction need to be large to balance the biological costs, and its prevalence suggests a strong evolutionary advantage for a mechanism of reproduction that mixes genetic material. Such advantage is typically conceptualised as novel combinations of genes and changes in them (mutations) upon which evolutionary selection can act—the foundation of Darwin's (1859) theory of evolution by natural selection. It can be divided into two broad hypotheses: the accumulation of beneficial genetic changes and/or the removal of detrimental genetic mutations. The accumulation of beneficial genetic traits is advantageous in adaptation to changing environments (the 'Fisher-Muller model'; Fisher 1930; Muller 1932) or co-adaptation alongside interacting species who are trying to harm you (delightfully called the 'Red Queen hypothesis' after Lewis Carroll's (1871) character in *Alice Through The Looking Glass*, who observed, 'Now, here, you see, it takes all the running you can do, to keep in the same place'; van Valen 1973). However, the benefits of bringing together useful genetic traits during sexual reproduction must be balanced by the possibility that already-coexisting beneficial traits are separated among offspring (Desai and Fisher 2007). Finally, sexual reproduction permits harmful genetic mutations—those that compromise evolutionary fitness—to be weeded out to prevent them from accumulating in a population (see 'Muller's ratchet' from Muller 1964; also 'Kondrashov's hatchet' after Kondrashov 1988).

The fitness advantage conferred by sexual reproduction helps explain its near ubiquity among complex species, although several biologists argue they remain insufficient to balance the costs. But even if the full evolutionary picture is not yet evident, sexual reproduction is clearly an incredibly successful evolutionary strategy. Most complex species, including humans, have completely lost the ability to reproduce asexually in favour of obligate sexual reproduction. Spontaneous asexual reproduction in some sexually reproducing species can occur (e.g. when a female generates offspring from an unfertilised egg, a process called 'parthenogenesis') but does not usually outcompete sexual reproduction mechanisms, despite the predicted advantages for an asexually reproducing female population. Plants and simple animal species that typically reproduce asexually in stress-free environmental conditions to which they are comfortably adapted can switch to sexual reproduction during times of stress, when genetic mixing may produce a survival advantage among offspring (Becks and Agrawal 2010). No wonder Erasmus Darwin (1800) remarked that '[s]exual reproduction is the chef d'oeuvre, the masterpiece of nature'.

Gametes and sexes

While genetic exchange mechanisms exist where DNA is transferred between different individuals in a non-sexual fashion, for example between bacteria and between virus and host (Callier 2019), the evolutionary root of sexual reproduction via specialised gametes sits with the evolution of multicellularity, at least 1.5 billion years ago (Fu et al. 2019). Modelling of evolutionary scenarios for a variety of gamete characteristics to maximise properties like frequency of fusion and health of offspring shows that the evolution of a binary system of gametes is optimal, comprising large gametes and small gametes and with gamete fusion occurring only between one small and one large gamete (no small–small or large–large fusions). On this extreme divergence of gamete types, evolutionary biologist Brian Charlesworth suggests that 'anything in between [smaller but less robust eggs or larger but sluggish sperm] would be at a selective disadvantage' (reported in Schaffer 2007). We call this binary system of gametes 'anisogamy', and it exists in almost all animals and many plants. For an excellent overview of gamete evolution from isogamy to anisogamy, see Lehtonen and Parker (2014) and the references therein.

In anisogamous species, the large gamete (and associated biology) is termed 'female' and the small gamete (and associated biology) is termed 'male'. In animals, the female and male gametes take the familiar forms of egg and sperm, respectively (in plants, the female and male gametes are contained in the ovules and pollen, respectively). Large and small gametes have evolved different specialisations. The female gamete, with greater physical volume, single-handedly provides to the developing embryo basic cellular components, many molecules and signals required to direct early growth and energy generators (with their own DNA and replicating via binary fission) called 'mitochondria'. Maternal inheritance of cellular components is typical of anisogamy and predicted to promote embryo health by eliminating any negative effects that might arise from competition between incompatible mitochondria inherited from two parents (Greiner et al. 2015); indeed, this process and how it is optimally coordinated may dictate the existence of only two gamete types (e.g. Hurst 1996). As a consequence of maternal inheritance, the male gamete needs only to contribute genetic information during fertilisation and participates competitively to do so, typically becoming specialised for mobility to better access female gametes—consider the tail-like structures of sperm that propel it towards the egg (Lessels et al. 2009) and pollen grains sticking to bee legs (Hu et al. 2008)—and created in large numbers to improve the chances of both an encounter with a female gamete and the outnumbering of small gametes from other males (Parker and Lehtonen 2014).

Anisogamy is the evolutionary origin of sex—the reproductive roles associated with female or male gametes. The evolution of two classes of individuals, one for each reproductive role, is thought to have arisen multiple times in animals and plants, suggesting an evolutionary benefit. The divergence into two separate sexes of individuals has been described as 'an almost inevitable consequence of sexual reproduction in complex multicellular organisms' (Lehtonen and Parker 2014; answering the question, 'Why are there girls and why are there boys?').

We opened this chapter with a partial quote; in full, it reads,

> No practical biologist interested in sexual reproduction would be led to work out the detailed consequences experienced by organisms having three or more sexes; yet what else should he do if he wishes to understand why the sexes are, in fact, always two?
>
> *(Fisher 1930, ix)*

So why only two, and not more, sexes? Considering the nature of sexual reproduction, gamete evolution and anatomy, we answer that question with a question (perhaps a challenge): What function could a third sex have? Science fiction (and we emphasise 'fiction' here) offers possibilities. When considering the Tralfamadorians in Kurt Vonnegut's *Slaughterhouse Five*, Billy Pilgrim puzzled:

> They said their flying saucer crews had identified no fewer than seven sexes on Earth, each essential to reproduction. Again: Billy couldn't possibly imagine what five of those seven sexes had to do with the making of a baby, since they were sexually active only in the fourth dimension. . . . It was gibberish to Billy. (145–146)

Sexual systems and bodies

Across almost all complex life, evolution has favoured just two sexes, but this does not impose restrictions on how sex is allocated in different species at the individual and population level (described as a 'sexual system'; Charnov 1982). Although we are most familiar with the allocation of two sexes split across two classes of individuals ('gonochorism'), evolutionary biologist Lukas Scharer (2017) illuminates: 'The male and female sexes are not two types of individuals; they actually represent two different reproductive strategies, and in many organisms, these two strategies are distributed among individuals in a population in a variety of ways'. That is, across the natural world, there is diversity regarding the allocation of male and female sexes within and between individuals and across populations.

Gonochorism is nearly ubiquitous in animals. Typically, male or female sex is fixed early in embryonic development and immutable to change during the lifespan of any individual, even though, of course, the physical characteristics associated with sex may be subject to expected age-related changes or changes acquired via injury or disease (or, at the hands of humans, surgery). Humans have not evolved as hermaphrodites—individuals who fulfil both male and female reproductive roles in their life span—though hermaphroditism is a natural body plan in many anisogamous species and can represent a stable strategy for sex allocation. Many plants—particularly flowering plants—and a few less-complex animals exist as simultaneous hermaphrodites, with both female and male sexes manifested in the same flowers and/or the same individual plant or animal at the same time of life.

A few aquatic species—most notoriously, clownfish—are sequential hermaphrodites, where changes in reproductive role during the life span ('sex change') are evidenced by the switch in production of one gamete type to the other, underpinned by anatomical changes in gamete-producing tissues (gonads). In the case of clownfish, this switch of sex (male to female) is driven by the loss of the single breeding female from the colony (Casas et al. 2016). Sequential hermaphroditism seems to occur only in species where 'sex change' requires no or minimal remodelling of gross reproductive anatomy. Fertilising externally, male and female clownfish both have a similar ductal system that permits the sperm and eggs, respectively, into the aquatic environment. With highly specialised and qualitatively different reproductive anatomies, neither obviously nor easily remodelled post-development, 'sex change' in humans is impossible.

Even considering species with same-sex allocation, evolution provides a dazzling array of anatomies and appearances. It is often true that gonochorist males whose reproductive role is to contribute sperm have evolved appendages for the direct introduction of that sperm into females, while the females of many species have evolved internal biology that receives sperm and protects the developing offspring from the outside world. But appearances can be deceptive. For example, male seahorses have a brood pouch in which developing seahorses are incubated, a functional role more usually associated in the natural world with female individuals. However, these seahorses are the sex class that contribute sperm to the offspring, and it is that, not their gross anatomy, which defines those individuals as male. Another curious example is that of female spotted hyenas, which have a hyper-enlarged clitoris that resembles a penis, yet they produce eggs that are fertilised by a male hyena and are, by definition, female. Human-centred biological expectations about anatomy, which include, for example, penile appendages in males and pregnancy in females are undoubtedly too narrow to capture the diversity of sexed bodies in the natural world.

Hermaphrodites incorporate both male and female sexes, and gonochorists one or the other. And while gonochorism and simultaneous hermaphroditism represent stable arrangements of the two sexes within a species, there are many that buck these trends. There are species composed of females and hermaphrodites (McCauley and Bailey 2009), of males and hermaphrodites (Weeks et al. 2009), and of males, females and hermaphrodites (Oyarzun et al. 2020). The two sexes can be differentially allocated in individuals and between species. Yet, despite the variety of bodies and sexual systems found in the natural world, reproduction within and between individuals occurs by the meeting of female and male gametes, one of each type, in that precise combination, in a pattern recapitulated across almost all complex life. The binary system of sex is an evolutionary thread stitched through life on earth.

Human sex

From an evolutionary perspective, we have established what sex is (reproductive role by reference to gamete type) and that, despite the fascinating manifestations of the two sexes within individuals and within populations, there are only two sexes. In this section, we turn to developmental biology—the study of how organisms grow—and the development of the reproductive human.

The developmental biology underpinning this section is largely sourced from standard reference textbooks. Interested readers should explore Baresi and Gilbert's (2020) *Developmental Biology* and Wolpert et al.'s (2019) *Principles of Development*.

Making a baby

Humans are gonochoristic mammals and are divided into two classes of individuals according to their reproductive roles. In humans, the act of reproduction itself requires, in the first instance, male sperm to fertilise female eggs, achieved during intercourse between two sexually mature people. Male reproductive anatomy includes testes, contained in the scrotal sac, that make sperm to be delivered to a female via the vas deferens and then the penis. Both testes and penis are external organs, while female reproductive anatomy is almost wholly internal. It comprises ovaries that periodically release mature eggs, collected by the nearby oviducts and transported towards the uterus, the muscular space in which, after successful fertilisation, a baby will grow. The uterus connects, via the cervix, to the vagina, which exits the body at the vulva, incorporating the clitoris and the urethral opening, surrounded by folds of skin called labia.

During intercourse, semen (sperm mixed with water and lubricants from the seminal vesicles and prostate gland) is delivered into the female body via ejaculation. Semen travels to the oviducts, where, should a mature egg be ready, fertilisation occurs. The fertilised egg is transported and then implanted into the uterine wall; at this stage, the female is pregnant. In the absence of a successful fertilisation event, the uterus, having already prepared a blood-rich, spongey lining suitable for implantation, breaks down this lining and expels it via the vagina during menstruation. In humans, gestation—the growing of a baby within the pregnant female—lasts around nine months, after which the female gives birth, typically via the vagina (although surgical interventions like caesarean section may be necessary in negative medical circumstances or as a preference).

Sex determination

The reproductive anatomy of a growing baby develops *in utero* in a series of coordinated anatomical steps. The first step, however, is the determination of the sex of a new embryo: female or male? In humans, sex is genetically determined at fertilisation via the XY determination system of sex chromosomes. Females possess two X chromosomes, while males possess one X and one Y. Given that the paired sex chromosomes, like all other chromosome pairs, are separated when gametes are made, each human egg contains one X chromosome while human sperm contains either an X or Y chromosome. Sex is thus dependent on whether an egg receives, at fertilisation, either an X or Y chromosome from the sperm.

The pattern of chromosomes within an individual is called a 'karyotype'. Like all chromosomes, sex chromosomes carry genes. In humans, a key sex-determining gene is called *SRY* (sex-determining region Y) and it is, in genetically healthy individuals, carried by the Y chromosome (Kashimada and Koopman 2010; Sinclair et al. 1990). The *SRY* gene acts as a 'master switch' for male development, and its presence or absence initiates a cascade of molecular signals that drives the first anatomical step towards a sexed human body: gonad differentiation.

Embryonic development

Gonad differentiation occurs at around six weeks *in utero* when a bipotential pair of gonads—small buds of tissue in the abdominal cavity—are triggered to form ovaries or testes, the gamete-producing tissues in females and males, respectively. XY embryos carrying a functional *SRY* gene will trigger differentiation of testes via a network of molecular signals; in the absence of *SRY* activity, XX embryonic gonads activate distinct molecular signals and begin to differentiate into ovaries (Lecluze et al. 2020; Mamsen et al. 2017). There is feedback between these differentiation pathways; for example, a signal required for ovarian development and the later maturation of eggs also suppresses early testes differentiation (Jaaskelainen et al. 2010).

Gametes do not originate in the growing gonads. Rather, specialised stem cells migrate into the differentiating gonad region where they are embedded as precursor cells that will become eggs or sperm, depending on the gonad type (Magnusdottir and Surani 2014). Ongoing gonad development into mature egg- or sperm-producing tissues relies on sex-specific cell types, a process requiring sex-specific hormone action. Via the sex-specific hormone milieu that each gonad generates, they also drive reproductive anatomy development appropriate for mature gamete type. That is, ovaries fated to produce eggs will direct female anatomical development and testes fated to produce sperm will direct male development. Thus, gonads can be considered as organising tissues, and the absence of future gamete function—infertility—is no barrier to understanding the sex of humans as an anatomical pattern organised around gamete function.

The first embryonic targets of gonadal organisation, from about eight weeks *in utero*, are two pairs of ducts (paramesonephric and mesonephric) alongside the gonads which will grow into female or male internal genitalia respectively. Female and male embryos develop both pairs of ducts in early development; sex-specific hormonal action favours the growth of one pair. Male testes secrete two major hormones that act on these pairs of ducts. Testosterone promotes the growth of the mesonephric duct into male internal genitalia, and secreted anti-Mullerian hormone triggers degeneration of the paramesonephric duct, thus eliminating the duct that would develop into female internal genitalia. There is little testosterone production in females to promote the growth of mesonephric duct structures or anti-Mullerian hormone to trigger the degeneration of paramesonephric duct structures, and the development of the latter into female internal genitalia proceeds.

The second embryonic target of gonadal organisation, from about 10 weeks *in utero*, is the development of external genitalia. The external genitals—vagina, clitoris and labia in females and prostate, penis and scrotum in males—derive from shared precursor tissues. Under the influence of sex-specific hormones, these tissues are moulded into male or female form. Specifically, a testosterone derivative (dihydrotestosterone) is produced locally in the precursor tissues in males, and this derivative is a potent inducer of male external genitalia. Conversely, low testosterone and low dihydrotestosterone in females permit this precursor tissue to develop into female external genitalia. Given that male and female external genitalia develops from the same embryonic tissue under different hormonal influences, analogous structures can be identified: the clitoris and penis share many structural features, while the labia represents an unfused version of the scrotum.

The sex of a baby is routinely and reliably observed at birth by visual and palpable ('touch') assessment of external genitalia. Increasingly, the sex of a baby is identified *in utero* by observation of external genitalia or genetic analysis. These observations are woefully mischaracterised by the term *assignment*, which has been co-opted from medical decision-making in clinical pathologies of the reproductive system (discussed later).

Puberty and secondary sex characteristics

The development of reproductive anatomy *in utero* is called 'primary sex development'. The outcome is a body that has the potential to fulfil the female or male reproductive role. Human sex development undergoes a second phase of development at puberty, around 10–18 years old. This phase of 'secondary sex development' generates divergence between the body shapes of females and males—'sex dimorphism'—that has evolved under selection pressure to increase one's likelihood of mating, following two broad strategies: be the most attractive or the most dominant. Both females and males gain height and bone density and experience typical teenage symptoms like the onset of libido, acne and body odour. Under the influence of the hormone oestrogen, female reproductive anatomy matures, ovulation and menstruation commence, hip width increases and breast tissue develops. As well as experiencing male-typical maturation of reproductive anatomy (increase in testes volume and penile length), males gain greater height than females, grow facial hair, develop deeper voices and broader shoulders, and acquire far larger amounts of skeletal muscle than females.

Atypical sex development

As a system with multiple biological inputs and processes, atypical or pathogenic development of reproductive anatomy can occur; there are many points at which reproductive development can go awry. Collectively, conditions resulting in atypical reproductive development are called disorders (or, in patient-facing language, 'differences') of sex development (DSDs). There are about 40 known DSDs occurring in humans, most a result of mutations in genes required for healthy reproductive development *in utero* (Arboleda et al. 2014); they span simple anatomic and hormone differences in otherwise healthy individuals to disorders with acute clinical sequelae that can cause postnatal harm or even death and that need ongoing management throughout life.

Historically, DSDs have been described by terms such as *hermaphroditism* and—currently falling into disuse—*intersex*. These terms are now deemed clinically inaccurate and stigmatising to patients. Approved nomenclature to categorise DSDs references karyotype and sex. Thus, the overarching categories are sex chromosome DSDs, XY (male) DSDs and XX (female) DSDs. Sex chromosome DSDs are exemplified by Turner syndrome and Klinefelter syndrome, where patients have irregular numbers of sex chromosomes and develop typical reproductive anatomy but experience hormonal issues that compromise sexual maturation and fertility. Other DSDs include conditions in which female embryos are exposed to excessive testosterone *in utero* and develop an enlarged clitoris (an XX DSD called congenital adrenal hyperplasia) or male embryos fail to produce the dihydrotestosterone required for penis growth (an XY DSD called 5 alpha reductase deficiency). Excellent resources on DSDs have been compiled by the UK charity DSD Families and are available on its website (https://dsdfamilies.org).

The frequency of DSDs is the subject of much misinformation. Fausto-Sterling and colleagues define as 'intersexual' any deviation from 'Platonic ideal' bodies and identified a frequency of 1.7 percent of the population (Blackless et al. 2000; Fausto-Sterling 2000). This loose definition of DSDs captures a large number of people with no biologically meaningful ambiguity of sex (most egregiously, the vast majority of this reported frequency are unambiguous females, often mothers who have late-onset adrenal hyperplasia and, at some point post-birth, experience elevated testosterone levels as a result of an adrenal problem). The frequency of 1.7 percent was revised to 0.4 percent by Hull and Fausto-Sterling (2003), after identifying numerous flaws in the original study like failing to account for the sex-specific nature of many DSDs.

When assessing DSD frequency rationally restricted only to individuals with ambiguous reproductive anatomy or a disparity between their reproductive sex and external genitalia, the frequency drops dramatically to approximately 0.018 percent (Sax 2002). Nonetheless, the inflated frequency of 1.7 percent is routinely cited as definitive (e.g. by Amnesty in 2018). But despite atypical sex development, almost all cases are identifiable as either female or male. Within modern medicine, workflows exist to identify sex in ambiguously presenting people (mapping internal genitalia, karyotype and hormonal profiles). Understanding DSDs within typical female and male developmental trajectories aids in diagnosing these clinical disorders and informs prognostic management of specific conditions in terms of sexual function and fertility prospects. When fertility is possible, people with DSDs employ, as for all human beings, either eggs or sperm and do not comprise a novel third sex category.

Sex myths

In a letter published in the *Irish Journal of Medical Science* in 2021 we argued that '[p]ublic discourse around sex increasingly seeks to deny basic facts of human biology' (Hilton and Wright et al. 2021). Gender-identity ideology claims that a privately held identity regarding one's sex defines one's sex: if a person identifies (in some internal, unverifiable sense) as female or male, that person literally is female or male. Accordingly, many seek to undermine the common scientific understanding of sex as a real and important biological phenomenon in favour of a wholly subjective and unfalsifiable categorisation based on one's personal and internal sense of self—gender identity. In this section, we critique emerging misunderstandings around sex.

Myth: sex is a composite score of body parts

Underpinning ideological misrepresentations about sex is the conflation of descriptions anchored in biological function with descriptions, via a checklist of various physical characteristics, of people at the individual level. A *Nature* (2018) editorial asserted sex is 'a classification based on internal and external bodily characteristics' while failing to mention reproductive function and why sexed bodies exist. The obvious follow-up question is: A classification based on internal and external bodily characteristics in which species? Of course, the reference species is human, a peculiarly self-centred view of a biological phenomenon common to almost all complex life. Extending this, given the diversity of physical characteristics associated with sex across the living world, does every species have its own definition of sex? Even if that were the case, the list of characteristics that we know are associated with, for example, male and female hyenas can only be established by anchoring them to sex as a biological function.

In the *Skeptic*, Hearne (2021) accurately defines 'female' as 'organisms whose gametes are . . . ova or eggs' yet asserts that '[u]nless you are a fertility doctor, it's unlikely you will encounter too many ova, so we must be using other definitions in everyday life'. While it is true that gamete type is not directly assessed in strangers, it does not follow that we use alternative 'definitions' when identifying a person's sex; more accurately, we use alternative *markers* of sex: those that arise from the organisational effects of the gonads during development. Hearne acknowledges this: if features like external genitalia—routinely covered—and breast size—plumped by bras—are insufficient to identify a person's sex, we do so by features such as 'amount and distribution of muscle and fat, the length and distribution of hair, the height and so on'. Psychiatrist Nirao Shah, who studies behavioural differences between females and males, considers correct sex identification 'a fundamental decision animals make' (reported in Goldman, 2019). Alongside assessments of body shape like shoulder and hip width, humans are facial experts: sex identification is 'an automatic and effortless aspect of face perception' that triggers differential brain activity (Kaul et al. 2011). Intriguingly, females appear better than males at recognising female faces, even in the absence of gendered cues like hair length (Lewin and Herlitz 2002). Humans also assess movement like walking gait in sex identification (Pollick et al. 2005). However, none of these data points is, as Hearne argues, an alternative 'definition' of sex, merely recognition of sex by morphological characteristics. By analogy, igneous rock is defined as that generated from volcanic lava; we recognise igneous rock by characteristics like texture and density.

Discarding function to define sex as form—explicit in pieces with titles like 'Sex Redefined' (Ainsworth, 2015)—the deconstruction of sex as a biological category begins with claims regarding the variability of physical characteristics. First in line are people with DSDs and atypical reproductive development. Physical descriptions of characteristics in people with DSDs often disaggregate the reproductive system into constituent parts like 'genetic sex' and 'gonadal sex' to better understand incongruent features, clinical management and prognosis (Arboleda et al. 2014). For nearly all DSDs, these constituent parts are aligned or not divergent in any meaningful way. If such disaggregation has utility, it is not in the muddling of definitions of female and male but in the refinement of workflows that generate a complete clinical picture for those people with DSDs. However, since the coining of 'gender identity' by John Money in the 1960s, disaggregated features of sex have occasionally included 'psychological' and 'social' sex (Moore 1968), paving the way for 'gender identity' to be considered not only a sexed characteristic but one that is now argued to supersede the physical and functional.

A related argument evokes sex characteristics that can overlap between the sexes to attempt to demonstrate that 'there is no one parameter that makes a person biologically male or female' (Elsesser 2020). It is true that many females are taller than many males, and that some males have low levels of testosterone more typical of females. However, such arguments fail to acknowledge a point we have already addressed: we only know that males are typically taller and have higher testosterone levels than females if we have a reference characteristic for sex, independent of height and testosterone level, by which to divide and measure people. And it is centuries of study of the anatomic and molecular organisation of the human species around sex as a biological function that serves as the anchor point. Put simply, it would be impossible to claim that low and high testosterone levels are correlated with being female and male, respectively, unless the categories female and male already had established meanings that testosterone levels were being correlated with. The same holds for every other sex correlate.

Myth: sex is not binary

Having remapped the definition of sex from function to form and introduced exceptions to form, commentators move to attack the description of sex as a binary system. They often fail to understand what the term *binary* means in this context. For example, writing for the *Guardian*, Heggie (2015) claims 'binary sex' means 'that there are men and women and they can be clearly distinguished'. The functional system of sex is routinely described as 'binary' (including, on many occasions, by us), meaning 'of, pertaining to, characterised by, or compounded of, two' (*Oxford English Dictionary*). In this context it indicates, simply, a biological system with two components and follows the same etymological pattern by which, for example, a system composed of two stellar masses is described as a binary star.

Rejection of the term 'binary' extends into the rejection of 'two' itself, and the substitution of ideological framings of sex that move the conversation far from biological reality. Many interlocutors posit quantitative descriptions of sex as the necessary alternative to categorical descriptions. The most common quantitative (continuous) distribution evoked is a bimodal distribution, whereby quantifiable traits associated with sex, such as height and testosterone levels, are conceptualised as multiple, overlapping distributions. These overlapping distributions are purported to generate two modes that represent the average or typical female and male (described by a combination of their average or typical sex characteristics). Routinely plotted on a horizontal axis crudely labelled 'sex', this framework necessarily gives rise to the premise that one's sex is a statistical score. For a widely circulated conceptualisation of 'bimodal sex', Hildreth (2022) describes the modes as 'peaks in a graph [that] represent probability clusters'. Furthermore, to claims that sex is bimodal are claims that 'sex is a spectrum', a continuous distribution that replaces modes with, in the words of Brusman (2019), 'unlimited options'. The corollary is that the sex of every human is unique to that individual, or, in the words of Fausto-Sterling (2000), 'sex and gender are best conceptualised as points in a multidimensional space'.

The outcome of this is that every person is scored as some percentage of female or male. The logical progression of such scoring is that a male with lower-than-average testosterone, petite stature or a smaller-than-average penis is scored as 'more female' than male counterparts with average or high testosterone, tall stature and large penises. These damaging judgements equally apply to females with enlarged clitorises, small breasts or increased musculature, who are scored as 'more male' than their larger-breasted and less athletic counterparts. It is opaque how categorical data like gonad type and karyotype are organised on such continuous distributions.

As sex within a continuous framework becomes a matter of sliding people left or right towards and from typical female and male, the middle of this distribution is cast as the no man's land where people with DSDs fit (although supporters fail to recognise that, by their own logic, extremely tall females and extremely short males may equally occupy this 'middle ground'). For those with a false comprehension of DSDs as 'people with both sets of genitals', this is intuitive. However, as we have explained, DSDs do not differ simply by degree: they represent dozens of conditions with unique etiologies that manifest in disparate ways. Attempts to force DSDs into a continuous distribution are, given their qualitative differences, doomed to fail (e.g. Montanez, 2017).

Myth: sex is a social construct

The spider's web of arguments described earlier, and including the occasional reminder that development is very complicated (Sun, 2019)—as if biologists are not well trained in identifying fundamental principles in complex systems—culminates with the premise that sex is a social construct. Butler (1990) writes that '[p]erhaps this construct called 'sex' is as culturally constructed as gender'. While scientists observing the natural world develop language and models to describe that natural world, one cannot credibly argue that the phenomena under observation are human constructions (see Stock, this volume). If that is so, humans have invented not only sex but also gold, clouds and penguins.

The argument that sex is socially constructed settles, once again, on those people with atypical biology who have been framed as category-defying; arguing that the boundary is 'arbitrary' permits the claim that the categories themselves are 'arbitrary', that is, socially constructed. The fact that sex may be ambiguous for some (or even the trivial fact that some females are unusually tall) does not render the categories arbitrary. This argument is like asserting that the two sides of a coin are arbitrary because, occasionally, a coin may land on its edge.

Myth: biologists have alternative understandings of sex

Finally, we challenge the premise that some new scientific consensus on sex has emerged. Writing for *DW*, Sterzik (2021) claims that 'the broad scientific consensus now looks different: sex is a spectrum'. The definitions and understandings of sex we present in this chapter are uncontroversial, appearing in dictionaries, key biology textbooks and medical consensus statements like that issued by the Endocrine Society (Barghava et al. 2021). There is a vast literature which depends, explicitly or implicitly, on these understandings of sex. Searches on the scientific publication database PubMed for 'male' [AND] 'sperm' or 'female' [AND] 'egg' retrieve around 100,000 results each, including numerous and recent publications from Nobel laureates in physiology and medicine and a huge array of biological and medical disciplines.

Searches of the PubMed database (performed on 9 July 2022) for phrases like 'bimodal sex', 'spectrum of sex' or 'sex is a social construct' generate no results in the biological or medical literature, although two close matches for 'sex is a spectrum' are found. The first is a study of how sex (female or male) affects the spectrum of genetic variations acquired in the X chromosome over a lifespan (Agarwal and Przeworski 2019). The second is a study of how foetal sex (female or male) affects the spectrum of placental conditions experienced during pregnancy (Murji et al 2012). Neither study demonstrates any confusion about the nature of sex, and both exemplify the importance of understanding sex in a clinical setting. It seems that claims of a new scientific consensus—or the milder assertion of an academic debate—regarding sex are overblown and manufactured by public commentators to generate an appeal to authority.

Conclusion

We have explained that the most prevalent mechanism of reproduction in complex species has stabilised on a binary system of differential gamete types and the subsequent evolution of body types around this binary system. The majority of species, including humans, are composed of individual females and males, defined by reproductive role, describing their contribution of large, energy-rich gametes (like eggs) or small gametes (like sperm), respectively, to the next generation.

In humans, there are two evolved anatomical body types, each corresponding to one of the two reproductive functions. *In utero*, females and males develop sex-specific primary characteristics pertinent to reproduction, in the first instance, the differentiation of gonad type that will direct future female or male function.

Gonads—ovaries or testes, determined in humans by genetic mechanisms—organise both the development of mature gametes (eggs or sperm) and the coordinated development of the corresponding reproductive anatomy (in males, external testicles, internal genital structures like the vas deferens and an external penis and scrotum; in females, internal ovaries, internal genital structures like a uterus and vagina, and an external vulva incorporating the clitoris).

Finally, we dissected arguments that attempt to challenge these basic understandings of sex. We traced the redefinition of sex from an integrated, anatomical system organised around an evolutionary function to a checklist of human-centred, disaggregated physical characteristics. This redefinition is the foundation on which variability of those physical characteristics (in natural or pathological development) is used to attempt to deconstruct sex as a binary system, further rendering it a construct of the human mind and, if it suits one's political aims, meaningless. We reject such arguments as purely ideological, with no evidence they are taken seriously in the scientific community, lacking explanatory power, and ultimately spurious. Despite these myriad arguments, the foundation of binary function shines through, underpinning the bimodal peaks of traits in a continuous distribution—or, more prosaically, dictating with which other 'point in multidimensional space' a person can successfully reproduce.

References

Agarwal, I. and Przeworski, M., 2019. 'Signatures of replication timing, recombination, and sex in the spectrum of rare variants on the human X chromosome and autosomes'. *PNAS* 116(36): 17916–17924.

Ainsworth, C., 2015. 'Sex redefined'. *Nature* 518: 288–291.

Amnesty, 2018. 'Intersex awareness day: 5 myths [online]'. Available at https://www.amnesty.org/en/latest/news/2018/10/its-intersex-awareness-day-here-are-5-myths-we-need-to-shatter/ [accessed 8th August 2022].

Arboleda, V. A. et al. 2014. 'DSDs: genetics, underlying pathologies and psychosexual differentiation'. *Nat Rev Endocrinol* 10(10): 603–615.

Baresi, M. J. F. and Gilbert, S. F., 2020. *Developmental Biology*. Oxford: Oxford University Press; www.ncbi.nlm.nih.gov/books/NBK9983.

Barghava, A. et al. 2021. 'Considering sex as a biological variable in basic and clinical studies: An endocrine society scientific statement'. *Endocr Rev* 42(3): 219–258.

Becks, L. and Agrawal, A., 2010. 'Higher rates of sex evolve in spatially heterogeneous environments'. *Nature* 468(7320): 89–92.

Bell, G. 1982. *The masterpiece of nature: The evolution and genetics of sexuality*. Berkeley: University of California Press.

Blackless, M. et al. 2000. 'How sexually dimorphic are we? Review and synthesis'. *Am J Hum Biol* 12: 151–166.

Brusman, L. 2019. 'Sex isn't binary, and we should stop acting like it is' [online]. Available at https://massivesci.com/articles/sex-gender-intersex-transgender-identity-discrimination-title-ix/ [accessed 9th August 2022].

Butler, J. P. 1990. *Gender trouble: Feminism and the subversion of identity*. Abingdon, UK: Routledge.

Callier, V. 2019. 'Core Concept: Gene transfers from bacteria and viruses may be shaping complex organisms'. *PNAS* 116(28): 13714–13716.
Carroll, L. 1871. *Through the looking-glass and what Alice found there*. London: Macmillan Publishers.
Casas, L. et al. 2016. 'Sex change in clownfish: molecular insights from transcriptome analysis'. *Sci Rep* 6: 35461.
Charnov, E. L. 1982. *The theory of sex allocation*. Princeton, NJ: Princeton University Press.
Darwin, C. 1859. *On the origin of species by means of natural selection, or, the preservation of favoured races in the struggle for life*. London: John Murray Publishing.
Darwin, E. 1800. *Phytologia: Or, the philosophy of agriculture and gardening*. London: Joseph Johnson Publishing.
Davis, W. M. and Uhrin, M., 1991. 'It has been said'. *Perspect Biol Med* 34(4): 549–552.
Desai, M. M. and Fisher, D. S., 2007. 'Beneficial mutation–selection balance and the effect of linkage on positive selection'. *Genetics* 176(3): 1759–1798.
Elsesser, K., 2020. 'The myth of biological sex'. *Forbes* June 15th.
Fausto-Sterling, A., 2000. 'The five sexes: Revisited'. *Sciences (New York)* 40(4): 18–23.
Fisher, R. A. 1930. *The genetical theory of natural selection*. Oxford: Clarendon Press.
Forstater, M., 2021. 'Sex, gender, and medical data'. *BMJ* 372: n735.
Fu, C. et al. 2019. 'Genetic and genomic evolution of sexual reproduction: Echoes from LECA to the fungal kingdom'. *Curr Opin Genet Dev* 58–59: 70–75.
Goldman, B. 2019. 'Animal magnetism' [online]. Available at https://stanmed.stanford.edu/2019spring/brains-hard-wired-recognize-opposite-sex.html [accessed on 9th August 2022].
Greiner, S. et al. 2015. 'Why are most organelle genomes transmitted maternally?' *Bioessays* 37(1): 80–94.
Hearne, S. 2021. 'Species, Individual, Gender—biology and taxonomy don't deal in black and white' [online]. Available at https://www.skeptic.org.uk/2021/03/species-individual-gender-biology-and-taxonomy-dont-deal-in-black-and-white/ [accessed 9th August 2022].
Heggie, V. 2015. 'Nature and sex redefined – we have never been binary'. *Guardian* February 19th.
Hildreth, C. 2022. 'The gender spectrum: A scientist explains why gender isn't binary' [online]. Available at https://cadehildreth.com/gender-spectrum/ [accessed 9th August 2022].
Hilton, E. et al., 2021. 'The reality of sex'. *Ir J Med Sci* 190(4): 1647.
Hilton, E. and Wright, C., 2020. 'The dangerous denial of sex'. *Wall Street Journal* February 13th.
Hull, C. L. and Fausto-Sterling, A., 2003. 'Response to: How sexually dimorphic are we? Review and synthesis'. *Am J Hum Biol* 15(1): 112–115.
Hurst, L. D. 1996. Why are there only two sexes? *Proc: Biol Sci* 263(1369): 415–422.
Hu, S., Dilcher, D.L., Jarzen, DM., Winship Taylor, D. 2008. 'Early steps of angiosperm pollinator coevolution'. *Proc Natl Acad Sci USA* 150(1): 240–245.
Jaaskelainen, M. et al. 2010. 'WNT4 is expressed in human fetal and adult ovaries and its signaling contributes to ovarian cell survival'. *Mol Cell Endocrinol* 317(1–2): 106–111.
Kashimada, K. and Koopman, P. 2010. 'Sry: the master switch in mammalian sex determination'. *Development* 137(23): 3921–3930.
Kaul, C. et al. 2011. 'The gender of face stimuli is represented in multiple regions in the human brain'. *Front Hum Neurosci* 4: 238.

Kondrashov, A. S. 1988. 'Deleterious mutations and the evolution of sexual reproduction'. *Nature* 336(6198): 435–440.

Lecluze, E. et al. 2020. 'Dynamics of the transcriptional landscape during human fetal testis and ovary development'. *Hum Reprod* 35(5): 1099–1119.

Lehtonen, J. L. and Parker, G. A., 2014. 'Gamete competition, gamete limitation, and the evolution of the two sexes'. *Mol Hum Reprod* 20(12): 1161–1169.

Lessells, C. M. et al. 2009. 'The evolutionary origin and maintenance of sperm: Selection for a small, motile gamete mating type'. In *Sperm Biology: An Evolutionary Perspective*, edited by Birkhead, T. R., Hosken, D. J., and Pitnick, S., pages 43–67. London: Academic Press.

Levin, S. et al. 2019. 'Darwin's aliens'. *IJA* 18(1): 1–9.

Lewin, C. and Herlitz, A., 2002. 'Sex differences in face recognition—women's faces make the difference'. *Brain Cogn* 50(1): 121–128.

Maddrell, S. H., 1998. 'Why are there no insects in the open sea?' *J Exp Biol* 201(17): 2461–2464.

Magnusdottir, E. and Surani, M. A., 2014. 'How to make a primordial germ cell'. *Development* 141(2): 245–252.

Mamsen, L. S. et al., 2017. 'Temporal expression pattern of genes during the period of sex differentiation in human embryonic gonads'. *Sci Rep* 7: 15961.

Maynard Smith, J., 1978. *The evolution of sex*. Cambridge, UK: Cambridge University Press.

McCauley, D. E. and Bailey, M. F. 2009. 'Recent advances in the study of gynodioecy: the interface of theory and empiricism'. *Ann Bot* 104(4): 611–620.

Montanez, A. 2017. 'Visualizing sex as a spectrum' [online]. Available at https://blogs.scientificamerican.com/sa-visual/visualizing-sex-as-a-spectrum/ [accessed 9th August 2022].

Moore, K. L. 1968. 'The sexual identity of athletes'. *JAMA* 205(11): 787–788.

Muller, H. J. 1932. 'Some genetic aspects of sex'. *Am Nat* 66: 118–138.

Muller, H. J. 1964. 'The relation of recombination to mutational advance'. *Mutat Res* 106: 2–9.

Murji, A. et al., 2012. 'Male sex bias in placental dysfunction'. *Am J Med Genet A* 158A(4): 779–783.

Nature. 2018. 'US proposal for defining gender has no basis in science'. *Nature* 563: 5.

Oxford English Dictionary. N.d. 'Binary'. https://www.oed.com/view/Entry/19111??redirectedFrom=binary& [accessed 9th August 2022].

Oyarzun, P. A. et al., 2020. 'Trioecy in the marine mussel Semimytilus algosus (*Mollusca, Bivalvia*): Stable sex ratios across 22 degrees of a latitudinal gradient'. *Front Mar Sci* 7: 348.

Parker, G. A. and Lehtonen, J. L. 2014. 'Gamete evolution and sperm numbers: Sperm competition versus sperm limitation'. *Proc R Soc B* 281: 20140836.

Pollick, F. E. et al. 2005. 'Gender recognition from point-light walkers'. *J Exp Psychol Hum Percept Perform* 31(6): 1247–1265.

PubMed. Available at https://pubmed.ncbi.nlm.nih.gov [accessed 9th August 2022].

Sax, L. 2002. 'How common is intersex? A response to Anne Fausto-Sterling'. *J Sex Res* 39(3): 174–178.

Schaffer, A. 2007. 'Pas de deux. Why are there only two sexes?' [online]. Available at https://slate.com/human-interest/2007/09/why-are-there-only-two-sexes.html [accessed 9th August 2022].

Scharer, L. 2017. 'The varied ways of being male and female'. *Mol Reprod Dev* 84(2): 94–104.

Sinclair, A. H. et al. 1990. 'A gene from the human sex-determining region encodes a protein with homology to a conserved DNA-binding motif'. *Nature* 346: 240–244.

Sterzik, K. 2021. 'Why sex and gender aren't binary issues' [online]. *DW*. Available at https://www.dw.com/en/why-sex-and-gender-arent-binary-issues/a-57062033 [accessed 9th August 2022].

Sun, S. D. 2019. 'Stop using phony science to justify transphobia' [online]. Available at https://blogs.scientificamerican.com/voices/stop-using-phony-science-to-justify-transphobia/ [accessed 9th August 2022].

van Valen, L. 1973. 'A new evolutionary law'. *Evol Theory* 1: 1–30.

Vonnegut, K. 1969. *Slaughterhouse-five, or the children's crusade*. New York: Delacorte Publishing.

Weeks, S. C. et al. 2009. 'Evolutionary transitions among dioecy, androdioecy and hermaphroditism in limnadiid clam shrimp (Branchiopoda: Spinicaudata)'. *J Evol Biol* 22(9): 1781–1799.

Williams, G. C. 1975. *Sex and evolution*. Princeton, NJ: Princeton University Press.

Wizemann, T. M. and Pardue, M. L. 2001. *Exploring the biological contributions to human health: Does sex matter?* Washington, DC: National Academies Press.

World Health Organization. 2022. 'WHO updates its widely-used gender mainstreaming manual' [online]. Available at https://www.who.int/news/item/06-07-2022-who-updates-widely-used-gender-mainstreaming-manual [accessed 9th August 2022].

Wolpert, L. et al. 2019. *Principles of Development*. Oxford: Oxford University Press.

3
SEX AND THE BRAIN
I Still Haven't Found What I Wasn't Looking For

Sophie Scott

Over the last century, there has been an increased interest in the existence and nature of sex differences in the human brain. Studies in the psychological sciences tend to focus on cognitive properties, such as intelligence or spatial abilities, when addressing male/female differences in behaviour and brain function. I argue that these are quite narrow terms of reference when engaging with putative male/female differences in brain and behaviour, both when arguing for sex-based differences and when arguing against them. I demonstrate that while we dispute these rather small effects, we also largely ignore other factors that are associated with brain differences. We often pay less attention to other factors that can affect the brain and behaviour (such as life experience). We also often ignore other, less 'cognitive' sex-based brain/behaviour differences, which show true sexual dimorphism, such as sexual behaviour and aggression. I also argue that the very basis of the effects of testosterone on bodies and brains may not be as simple as we often assume them to be. I finish by addressing some of the studies that claim to find robust differences in the brains of transgender participants and that are interpreted as indicating that in certain aspects of brain structure, transgender women are indistinguishable from those of biological women. I suggest that, as with sex-based brain differences, in the brain, the relationships between brain structure and transgender experience are not yet clear.

Brain sex theory

Male and female bodies have the same basic template, differentiated by the sexual features such as the nature of the gonads and their functions (what kind of gametes they produce), the ability to inseminate or carry live young and the ability to nurse an infant (see Hilton and Wright, this volume). In addition, humans are sexually dimorphic creatures. This means that, like many organisms, the physical adult form

DOI: 10.4324/9781003286608-3

of a human male or female can vary along a number of physical dimensions such that adult females and males can be systematically distinct from one another. Males are, on the whole taller (Department of Health and Human Services, 2000), stronger (Wang et al. 2001), and hairier than females (Giacomoni et al. 2009), while female humans have stronger immune responses than males (Klein and Flanagan 2016; this list is not exhaustive; see de Vries and Forger 2015). All of these differences reflect genetic and hormonal influences on the developing body – exposure to testosterone and oestrogen in utero and in development profoundly change our bodies – and can also reflect environmental interactions with these genetic and hormonal effects. In their simplest form, theories of sex differences in human brains (referring here to biological sex, not gender) posit that as the physical body is affected by sex hormones, testosterone and oestrogen, so is the brain. These influences could be associated with brain structure, brain function or both.

In addition to advancing scientific knowledge, work on male/female differences in brain structure and function can be politically contentious. There is a constant tension, for example, between arguments that females need greater representation in science, technology, engineering, and mathematics (STEM) subjects; arguments that females may simply be less interested or adept at STEM subjects than males; and that their smaller numbers do not necessarily reflect direct sexist policies within STEM subjects. These 'brain sex' arguments can be used, and have been used, to support both sides of this argument.

Gender identity has been suggested to be an important psychological construct, potentially more meaningful than biological sex. However, as we struggle to find the best ways of capturing brain bases of biological sexual differences, it is likely that we will need better techniques and better specific definitions of what is meant by gender identity before we can start to identify any neural bases for gender identity.

In terms of methods, some of the studies I cite here are based on behavioural analyses of female/male differences. Some use magnetic resonance imaging (MRI) techniques to address structural brain differences between the sexes – that is, they are outlining where there are differences in the shape and size of brain areas between men and women. Some are addressing functional differences between females and males, using measures of neural activity to identify differences (such as functional magnetic resonance imaging [fMRI]). These brain imaging techniques can also be related to behavioural measures. Finally, some studies use post-mortem brain analyses that require very detailed microscopy to identify differences in the sizes and neural structure of tiny brain nuclei, that would be too small to be measured with MRI.

The 'normal' distribution and difference

Before I explore a variety of brain sex theories, I need to explain a little about how we describe variation in bodies and brains. A short interrogation of your own experience will reveal that while males are on average taller than females (height is sexually dimorphic in humans), not all females or males are the same height. Indeed, you are probably aware that there is a lot of variation in the heights of males and females. If we look at this variation in detail, you will find that most females in the UK are around the average adult height of 163cm (about 5'4"). If we count females who are a bit smaller than or a bit taller than the average the numbers start to decline as we move away from the average, in either the taller or shorter direction. If we look for yet taller or shorter females, we find that the numbers drop off rather briskly, such that there are very few really tall females and very few really short females. We get to this kind of distribution by plotting the heights of a lot of females, so we could make statistical judgements about the female population, and we plot the number of women that we find of every height, from short to tall. This gives us a 'normal distribution': this means statistically normal, and describes a curve a bit like a bell, that initially increases slowly, then more rapidly increases towards the mean (average), at which point it starts to decline in a symmetrical manner (in fact, this is sometimes known as a bell curve). The curves can be tall or short, wide or narrow, and all points in between. If we were to plot the heights of a lot of males on this same graph, we would see a similar bell curve, now shifted to the right (towards the taller end of the height distribution) and now varying around the average UK male height of 178 cm (about 5'10"). There is some overlap – some males are 5'4"tall, and some women are over 6' tall – but as humans are sexually dimorphic in height, the number of males and females who fall in the overlap between the two distributions is small. When we look at theories of brain sex, it is worth bearing sexual dimorphism in mind – how different do two distributions of sex-based variations in behaviour or brain structure need to be to indicate dimorphism?

Brain sex – the view from the brain

The human brain is a biological entity to marvel at – containing about 86 billion neurones (Azevedo et al. 2009), most of which we are born with, it is a structure of almost bewildering complexity, not least because the pattern of connections between those 86 billion neurons is highly plastic and adaptable – whenever you learn a new skill or encode a new memory, you are changing your brain. Unlike our bodies, visual inspection of the brain tends not to give any information about the sex of the owner of that brain, with the exception of size. Male brains are larger than female brains, even when body size is controlled for (Ruigrok et al. 2014). In contrast, female brains have a relatively thicker layer of grey matter than male brains, and this is often expressed as a higher proportion of grey matter to white matter. Grey matter forms the surface of the human brain, and it contains the cell bodies of the brain cells (neurones), while white matter is made of the long projections of neurones, connecting different brain areas. The projections look white as they have fatty coatings, unlike the cell bodies: this led to the terms white and grey matter, as this is what the tissue looks like in dissection. This greater proportion of grey matter in females may imply that while female brains are smaller, they are fitting comparably more computational processes into this smaller space. Of course, this does not tell us why male brains are bigger – if it is not to fit more computational power in, then we need another explanation. It's also worth bearing in mind that human brains are extremely expensive – both metabolically and physically. Human brains use about 20 percent of the circulating oxygen in our bloodstream, as they are large and the energy required to maintain the potential for the neural systems to work is considerable. The large heads that these large brains need make a big contribution to the considerable physical danger that childbirth constitutes for human females – globally, about 800 females die in pregnancy and childbirth every day. So our big brains – male and female – are expensive, and they need to pay their way.

Brain sex and IQ

There are different varieties of brain sex theory. A historically prominent position argues that intelligence is higher in males than females – a view held without question by the father of IQ studies, Frances Galton (Mackintosh 1996), and many others. However, this pattern is not always found in IQ tests – depending on the subtests used in the IQ test (which can vary a lot), it is possible to find no difference between the sexes on IQ tests or a frequent female advantage (Mackintosh 1996). Even given this variation across studies, studies consistently find that the vast majority of males and females overlap in their IQ distribution – in other words, even when there are sex differences, the differences are small, and IQ does not show sexual dimorphism in the distributions for males and females. A recent brain structure study, which studied the brains of more than 29,000 males and females, found no differences between IQ scores in males and females (Cox et al. 2019). This same study, when investigating how brain structure varied with age, sex and IQ, found a network of brain regions that correlated very consistently with IQ. Notably, this association was identical for male and female brains. The use of big data sets like this really helps emphasise the lack of a behavioural IQ effect between males and females and show that IQ correlates with brain structure in identical ways for male and female participants. Galton was probably wrong.

Brain sex and systematising and empathising brains

Another prominent account argues that there are not male and female brains *per se*, but different kinds of ways that brains can vary, which roughly overlap with male and female categories: brains can vary in the degree to which they are good at systematising, or empathising (Baron-Cohen 2002). The systematising brain is held to be driven to understand rule-based systems and unpack their underlying mechanisms. The empathising brain is driven to attend to other people's states of mind, and to respond to this in an appropriate manner. In this account, male brains tend to follow the more systematising profile, while female brains are typically more empathising. This is a controversial theory – not least because of the political implications of the distinction, which seem to limit those with empathising brains to menial support roles. Notably, although these two distributions (systematising and empathising) are described as normally distributed, a study of these in a large sample of neurotypical adults showed a more complex profile (Greenberg et al, 2018). Male participants showed a normal distribution for both the systematising and empathising scales, with means that the two distributions lie very close to each other – that is, males are not more systematising than they are empathising at the population level. In other words, contrary to Baron-Cohen's main thesis, the data do not suggest that males are less empathising than they are systematising. In contrast, the distributions of the female participants showed a skewed response on the systematising scale, with a distribution tending towards lower scores. In contrast, they showed a skew in the opposite direction for the empathising scale, a shift slightly more towards higher (more empathetic) scores. From this perspective, males do not show a marked difference between the two factors, while females do. It would be intriguing to know if this is in part because many of the questions in the systematising scale address activities that are traditionally considered to be more male-gendered in our culture (cars, trains, do-it-yourself, audio systems, computers), and very few activities that are traditionally considered to be more female-gendered in our culture (there are no questions about knitting, crochet, baking, or dressmaking, all of which are highly technical systems). In contrast, females tend to rate themselves as more agreeable than males do (see the section "Brain sex and personality'), which may relate to the higher mean scores in empathising. Of course, self-rating scales are highly subjective and can be influenced by social expectations.

There are few studies showing how the systematising and empathising dimensions relate to brain structure and function (Baron-Cohen and Lombardo 2017). These data are essential, as the two different variables are independent and orthogonal, such that one could score highly on one, both, or neither. Without a clear model of what that would mean for the relationship with brain structure and function, it is harder to establish the implications for the nature of brain sex differences. One study with adults contrasted brain volumes of participants who score high on systematising and low on empathising with participants who score high on empathising and low on systematising: this revealed great grey matter volumes in the hippocampus, a structure running down the middle of the temporal lobes, and the surrounding parahippocampal areas, the cuneus (in the visual areas of the brain) and the orbitofrontal cortex, at the very front of the brain. The opposite contrast revealed greater grey matter in the inferior temporal cortex, insula and amygdala (Focquaert and Vannette 2015). Notably, these distinctions do not separate in a simple way into 'social brain' regions, which one might expect to be associated more with the empathising brain. A further study on children classified the children into systematisers or empathisers, based on their scores: this study found very different results, with the systematisers showing greater grey matter volumes in the right posterior temporal lobe – another social brain region (Kobayashi et al. 2020). No greater volumes were reported for the empathisers. These inconsistencies could be driven by the fact that these studies involved relatively small numbers of participants: as brains are highly variable, the fewer participants in a study that is trying to delineate differences in brain structure between groups of people, the more likely the study is to report highly noisy data.

Sex and specific cognitive functions

Within psychology and cognitive neuroscience, the two most common cognitive tasks that have been framed as performed differently by males and females are language tasks. There is some controversy associated with this broad area of work (Fine 2010), as many of these studies are small and underpowered, and, of course, showing a difference in performance on a task does not tell us why this is or how has it come about.

Males tend to be better at spatial processing than females, especially on tasks such as spatial rotation, where one has to mentally rotate a complex object in order to determine whether it matches another. Although the differences are not large and vary a lot with task, the general tendency for better spatial processing differences in males and females is reasonably robust (Voyer et al. 1995).

Females often score higher than males on tasks of language processing, although the language advantage for females has been somewhat harder to replicate (Wallentin 2009). It does seem to be the case that at certain developmental stages, younger females do tend to have better language skills (or fewer language problems) than younger males, but this does not translate into consistent adult advantages. Notably, a more recent paper (Martínez et al. 2017) demonstrated that individual differences in brain connectivity predicted ability at language and spatial tasks more than the sex of any one participant.

Brain sex and personality

There are relatively reliable sex differences in personality, where females score more highly on neuroticism, a trait disposition that describes the variance in the tendency to experience negative emotions. Females score higher on extraversion, a measure of variance in how social and outgoing people are. Females score higher on neuroticism, a scale that measures the reported experience of negative emotions, such as anxiety and irritation. Females score higher on agreeableness, which describes variation in traits relating to empathy and kindness (and may relate to the empathising brain measure mentioned earlier), and females also score themselves higher on conscientiousness (which describes traits related to self-discipline and impulse control). Sometimes I worry that females are simply really keen on rating themselves highly in questionnaires, but females and males do *not* differ on measures of Openness/Intellect, a trait which measures variation in imagination and creativity. These data are from a large cross-study looking at sex differences in personality across fifty-five different cultures so these results should not be too distorted by any one set of cultural norms (Schmitt et al. 2008), although they could still be distorted by more universal social norms, especially as people rate *themselves* on these scales. Self-ratings can enable a host of psychological factors to be involved in the ratings people make about themselves. Ratings by other people, for example, can be more predictive of actual performance and behaviour than self-ratings (Oh et al. 2011).

A brain imaging study with around 360 participants (Nostro et al. 2017) found that there were no brain regions where grey matter volume correlated with any personality trait for the whole group. When they studied the two sexes separately, they found an effect in the left praecuneus (lying in front of the cuneus, associated with memory processes) and the parieto-occipital cortex, at the front of the visual areas of the brain, overlapping with somatosensory fields, which correlated with scores on extraversion, neuroticism, and conscientiousness but only in males. This is striking as males rate themselves as *less* neurotic, extraverted, and conscientious than females (Nostro et al. 2017): perhaps further studies will be able to clarify this.

Other kinds of individual differences

There are a few other psychological factors that have been studied. Males and females are often assumed to differ in their ability to multi-task, and one often encounters the assumption that females are better at multitasking than males, but this is not reliably found in studies: this is often because the tasks being used in the multitasking paradigm can greatly affect performance. For example, one study of sex differences in a multitasking paradigm (Tschernegg et al. 2017) found some brain differences in the verbal and spatial elements of the tasks that varied with sex; however, they found no differences in performance between the males and females studied, making the brain differences somewhat harder to interpret.

Males engage in more risky behaviour than females, especially between the ages of 15 to 35, and this can be exacerbated by social contexts such as the presence of females (Pawlowski et al. 2008). While young females can also engage in highly risky behaviour – such as having anything to do with the young males – this is often less socially visible. A brain imaging study with adolescents reported significant differences between males and females, where the females showed greater responses in a subset of brain regions associated with negative outcomes (Korucuoglu et al. 2020).

The story so far

So, there are some behavioural differences that psychology and cognitive neuroscience have identified between males and females, although the scale of these differences is much smaller than for the sexual dimorphism found in our bodies. Some of these differences relate to putative brain differences: many do not. All these accounts enjoy a certain popularity, not least because we have quite a strong cultural interest in male/female differences as ways of explaining the world and the variation within it. Of course, just because something is culturally popular doesn't mean it cannot be true (or false), but it does mean certain accounts can chime with pre-existing biases and beliefs more than others. And it can also provide a helpful diversion from other differences that psychologists (and the rest of our culture) can find more distasteful: when I first saw Baron-Cohen present his systematising/empathising brains theory in the mid-1990s, he made a strong case for the male brain being a systematising brain, based on the overrepresentation of males in maths and engineering departments at universities. I asked why he did not also study the UK prison population, which enjoys a male/female ratio that is even worse than that found in engineering departments, but he did not think that this was a serious question.

To what extent can we explain these differences by looking at the picture from the human brain? Are there really male and female brains? What do we find if we look directly at structural brain differences?

Brain sex anatomy

The UK Biobank project has made it possible for researchers to study brain anatomy at a scale which makes it feasible to start drawing meaningful conclusions about sex differences in brain anatomy. There have been many previous studies, but the small numbers combined with the huge variability in brains mean that the results are very variable. Ritchie and colleagues (2018) collected UK BioBank MRI data from 2750 female and 2466 male adult participants (mean age 61.7 years, range 44–77 years). They used automatic systems to analyse each brain into different anatomical areas, and then compared the size of these statistically.

This very detailed study clearly showed the expected findings of larger brains in males and a relatively thicker grey matter layer in females. They proceeded to address the difference in size of different aspects of brain anatomy in a more detailed way. They identified a range of seven subcortical nuclei (which sit beneath the grey cortical mantle of the brain) and looked for their relative size in males and females in the right and left hemispheres of the brain. While the overall picture was of extensive overlap between the two sexes, there were trends for the subcortical fields in the males to be slightly larger and have a wider range of variance. When they controlled for overall brain volume, meaning that they have controlled out the overall fact that males have larger brains, three of the regions (hippocampus, caudate nucleus, and thalamus) were no longer different between males and females, three more (the amygdala, pallidum, and putamen) were still relatively larger in males, and the nucleus accumbens were larger in females. Note that all these effects were small, as per the overall effects of a large overlap between the male and the female volumes.

In a separate analysis, the different brain area volumes were examined to see if they varied consistently with people's performances on two tests, verbal-numerical reasoning and reaction time tests, that were performed when people came in for the brain scan. There were no significant correlations between performance on these tasks and brain volumes, although when a mediation analysis was performed, some sizes of some brain areas did contribute to performance.

The study also collected 'resting state' data, which means capturing the brain activity while people lie quietly and then doing an analysis of the patterns of connectivity that are seen while people are at rest. This did find clear differences in the overall patterns between females and males, with about a 50:50 split in the networks being dominated by each sex (although both sexes contributed to all patterns seen). However, one significant problem with resting state data is that we do not know what people were thinking about, so it becomes difficult to know what this means, but it may point to overall connectivity differences between females and males.

An important criticism of brain structure studies is that we do not know what the contribution of life experience has been to the patterns of brain structure and function that we see (note – this is also true for all the behavioural differences and brain differences mentioned earlier). Another study used UK Biobank data to ask how the sizes of different brain areas are affected by sex and other factors, that might relate to, for example, the social environments that people are in. Kiesow et al. (2020) took 10,000 brains and examined how the size of different brain areas within the areas associated with social processing was affected by different social factors, in males and females. The social factors were determined from lifestyle questions and fell into the following three categories:

- ***Outer sympathy group:*** *job, friendship satisfaction, belong to a sports club, one romantic partner over lifetime or more than one partner, weekly social activity*
- ***Inner sympathy group:*** *household size; social support; rate self as lonely or not, living alone or not; family satisfaction*
- ***Socio-economic status:*** *income, access to private health care*

Of course, Kiesow and colleagues are stuck with the data that the UK Biobank project has collected, but this is not the finest-grained analysis of people's social lives, and some of the distinctions between outer sympathy group factors and inner sympathy group factors seem a little strange – why is friendship satisfaction an 'outer support group' feature, alongside the total number of romantic partners? All of the male and female participants were classified according to their sex and their scores on these traits (i.e. low or high for each category), and then these categories were analysed to see how they modulated the volume of brain areas within a pre-specified set of social brain areas. Unlike the previous study, they normalised the brains into the same template, so any differences in overall brain size will now be removed from the data from the outset.

One would hope that using this more nuanced approach that looks at sex in combination with social lifestyle markers would shed a little more light on male/female brain differences, but the results were very complex. Living with more family members was associated with increased amygdala volume for females but not males, while living with more family members was associated with a decrease in the volume of the ventromedial prefrontal cortex for males but not females. Increased social support and increased friendship satisfaction is associated with decreases in amygdala volume for females, not males, but for the females, this is going in the opposite direction to the effects of increased family satisfaction and decreased loneliness.

This may be overkill on my part. This study (Kiesow et al. 2020) is a triumph of data analysis and the data are the data. It will be important to consider what this could mean and why the results could be so inconsistent within either sex, as well as between the two sexes. However, the most sobering part of the study is tucked into the supplementary materials: females had a mean age of 61.12 years (SD = 7.42, range = 44.64–77.12 years), and males had a mean age of 62.39 years (SD = 7.56, range = 44.23–76.99 years). The effects of sex accounted for between 1 percent and 3 percent of the R^2 (a measure of the amount of variance in brain volume accounted for by sex). The effects of age accounted for between 20 percent and 39 percent of the overall brain variance. In other words, sex has effects on your brain, but those effects are ten times smaller than the effect of age.

Indeed, when it comes to brain function, for many of the measures that psychologists care about, sex can often be the least interesting part of your brain. For example, Kherif et al. (2009) ran a functional imaging study where 76 adults (who varied in age and handedness) were scanned while they read words aloud. The resulting patterns of brain activity were analysed, and the main source of variance in brain activity was age, followed by how people read (roughly via a 'whole word' or a 'sounding out' strategy). Sex and handedness did not make any significant contribution to the patterns of brain activation.

Of course, the limitations of any science are determined by the questions we ask in the first place, and the significant constraint in the previous paragraph is the phrase 'the measures that psychologists care about'. The vast amount of research into sex differences in human behaviour and human brains is focused on social processing, IQ, spatial cognition, and empathy vs. systematising brains. This means that we rarely even ask questions about the brain basis of other putative sex-based behavioural differences. For example, if we zoom out from these cognitive categories and ask questions about sex differences in human behaviour, the two largest differences between males and females are sexual orientation – males are most commonly sexually interested in females and vice versa (although with a suggestion of more flexibility for females) – and violence and aggression, which are vastly more likely to be associated with males than females. If we apply this lens to theories of human sex–based brain differences, I am not aware of any psychological theory of male and female differences in behaviour that adequately even starts to account for this – theorists often strive to explain male dominance in chess playing or computer programming but not sexual behaviour or violence. We may be back in the territory of more distasteful research questions.

There are some brain imaging studies on aggression showing differences between males and females (Repple et al. 2017; Visser et al. 2014; Herpertz et al. 2017), which all show interesting patterns of brain activation differences across males and females. For example, in a couple of these papers, males show higher aggression-based amygdala activations than females, although, of course, more data are needed.

In terms of sexual responses, when presented with sexual stimuli, heterosexual and homosexual females show a broader, less specific response to sexual stimuli in brain reward networks than heterosexual and homosexual males (Safron et al. 2020), who show a far more focused response to sexual stimuli, consistent with their sexual orientation. There are studies of heterosexual men and sexual orientation, but here the emphasis is often to use them as a control group for looking at bisexual and gay men (Safron et al. 2017) or to contrast between the responses of heterosexual and gay males (Ponseti 2009). When heterosexual and homosexual males and females are studied together, the results remain inconclusive, and the main focus of comparison is not on the heterosexual males and females and how they differ in sexual behaviour (Votinov et al. 2021). More research that starts to unpack these sex differences in sexual responses is likely going to be essential if we want to develop a comprehensive understanding of brain differences based on sex.

Testosterone is not the only sex hormone

As mentioned, studies of aggression implicate the amygdala as showing sex-related functional differences associated with aggression, often being greater in males. This makes sense, as the amygdala does form part of a network in mammalian brains where we know there are hormonally driven effects, which have been shown to modulate differences in behaviour between males and females. However, a truly complicating factor is that in the brain – unlike the rest of the body – testosterone is aromatised into oestrogen, oestradiol, in the sexual behaviour–related regions (Roselli et al 2009). In other words, the masculinising effects of testosterone on the body may be distinctly different in the brain, where testosterone is commonly having its sex-based effects as oestrogen. This complicates matters considerably for the brain sex theory – if testosterone as having its masculinising effects on the brain and behaviour *as an oestrogen,* how does this affect our predictions of the roles of testosterone and oestrogen in the wider range of sex-based behavioural differences that have been hypothesised? Can we separate out the effects that testosterone has via its effects on the body and those that it has on the brain?

From brain scans to microscopes

Finally, what do we see if we frame the question differently? All the studies I have looked at here have started either with brains or with behavioural questions and looked for differences. In another branch of brain sex research, instead of looking for differences in the brains of male and female humans at a whole brain level, people study the human brain in a way that is informed by established sex differences in other mammals – most commonly rats. In mammalian brains, there is a tightly focused set of brain regions where receptors to sex hormones (androgens and oestrogens) are found: these fall largely within the limbic system of the brain. The limbic system is not terribly well defined but includes the accessory olfactory system (including the amygdala), the preoptic area, the hippocampal formation, and the hypothalamus (Madeira and Lieberman 1995). These same regions, especially the accessory olfactory system, and the preoptic area, show marked sexual dimorphism in mammals, in terms of the size and number of brain cells and their connections. Note that there is quite a lot of variation of these structures in mammals and that these do not necessarily generalise to humans, though some studies have found evidence for dimorphism in some of these areas (Garcia-Falgueras et al. 2006). Interrogating some of these regions is possible with techniques like fMRI (Garcia-Falgueras et al. 2006), but many of these structures contain tiny nuclei which need to be examined with microscopy (Madeira and Lieberman 1995). This, in turn, requires working with post-mortem brains, a requirement that dramatically reduces the number of possible brains that can be studied, and means that there is often missing or incomplete data about the participants. However, post-mortem studies with humans do allow direct comparisons with the brains of other mammals.

Much of this work has been carried out in order to address questions about the neural structure of transsexual/transgendered people: putative sexually dimorphic structures within the limbic system were examined in order to determine whether trans people follow a typical male or female pattern (Zhou et al. 1995). In their paper they note: "We searched for a brain structure that was sexually dimorphic.... Our earlier observations showed that the paraventricular nucleus (PVN), sexually dimorphic nucleus (SDN) and suprachiasmatic nucleus (SCN) did not meet these criteria", and they searched until they found the bed nucleus of the stria terminalis (BNST), which *did* show sexual dimorphism, being larger in males. This first study showed a significantly greater volume for the BNST in males than females and found the transsexual volumes were not significantly different from those of the female brains (Zhou et al. 1995). The numbers in this study are very small – 12 males, 11 females, and 6 transwomen. Although the total brain weights vary between the males and females, this does not appear to be corrected for in the analysis – that is, we do not know how much the larger male BNST volumes are due to their having larger brains overall. A further study, looking at the numbers of neurones within the bed nucleus of the stria terminalis in the same brains (Kruijver et al. 2000), reported a similar pattern (although now with fewer control brains, 9 male and 10 female): more neurones in the BNST for the male participants than for the females and the transwomen. This study reported the brain weight data but, again, did not appear to control for this in the analysis.

Both papers report on the same brains, so the latter paper cannot be considered to be a replication of the original paper. The conclusion of both papers is that there is sexual dimorphism in the BNST, being larger and with more neurones in male brains: using this metric, the brains of the transwomen are more similar to those of the female participants than the male participants. This is a finding that has had a lot of impact, but it is worth noting two things. First, using the metric of overall brain size (an extremely robust form of sexual dimorphism in the human brain), the brains of the transwomen (mean = 1368g) are closer in size to the brains of the male participants (mean = 1431g) than the females (mean = 1283g), although they are not statistically different from males or females (with numbers this small, statistical tests are highly unreliable). Second, as the data in neither study are corrected for overall brain volume, it seems at least possible that the BNST in the transwomen is relatively *smaller* than those of the female participants. Furthermore, the BNST is sexually dimorphic in human adults (Allen and Gorski 1990), but a study looking at its development found that there was no significant sex-based difference in the volumes of this structure in infants, children, and adolescents (Chung et al. 2002), suggesting that whatever the role of this sexual dimorphism, it is one that appears relatively late in development. In the original paper (Zhou et al. 1995), the difference in the size of the BNST in males, females and transwomen was identified as showing that 'gender identity develops as a result of an interaction between the developing brain and sex hormones'. If the differences in the size of the BNST across males and females do not appear until adulthood, this implies a later or a more indirect role in the development of gender identity than this claim suggests.

Conclusion

One often hears the suggestion that someone can have a male brain in a female body and that this could lead to gender dysphoria. I accept that this may be a useful metaphor, but does it relate to what we know about brains? Are there really male and female brains?

There certainly are some reliable differences between male and female brains – male brains are bigger; female brains contain proportionally more grey matter (Sowell et al., 2007). There is some less reliable evidence for more specific anatomical differences, although we do not know the functions or causative mechanisms that underlie these differences (e.g. the extent to which they are affected by experience). There are reliable behaviour differences between males and females: male aggression levels are much higher than female levels of aggression, and males and females vary in their sexual behaviour. However, we cannot necessarily relate brain differences to behaviour. For example, we still do not know why male brains are bigger – what the functional role of the larger male brain is. Even with modern techniques, it is hard to find reliable differences in male and female brains at a more granular level and relate them to function. Finally, we typically study sex differences in brains without taking experience into account – and when we do, differences in life experience transpire to have complex effects, and age has been shown to have relatively large effects on brain structure.

We often entertain cultural beliefs about sex differences which are not empirically well-grounded, such as the idea that women talk more than men (Cameron 2010). Similarly, we see a disproportionate focus on sex differences which are empirically minimal and variable, such as those relating to IQ. At the same time, we cheerfully ignore other, very reliable and consistently large differences (e.g. male aggression). As scientists fully immersed in this culture, we are happy to identify certain parameters of behaviour as being sex-linked and rarely try to distinguish how age, experience, and sex might interact to affect this. And as psychologists and cognitive neuroscientists, we have done a very poor job of exploring the very large sex differences found in violence and aggression, and around sexual behaviour, and have failed to address the complex roles of testosterone and oestrogen that underpin these in the brain. The road map from research on sex differences to a better understanding of gender and gender identity is not yet a clear one. However, this chapter suggests that if it can be so hard to show clear effects of biological sex on the brain (beyond the reliable effects of larger brain size in males/more grey matter in females) then whatever gender identity looks like in the brain is going to be yet more complex.

References

Allen LS, Gorski RA (1990) Sex difference in the bed nucleus of the stria terminalis of the human brain. *Journal of Comparable Neurology*, 302(4): 697–706.

Azevedo FAC, Carvalho LRB, Grinberg LT, Farfel JM, Ferretti REL, Leite REP, Filho, Roberto Lent WJ, Herculano-Houzel S (2009) Equal numbers of neuronal and non-neuronal cells make the human brain an isometrically scaled-up primate brain. *Journal of Computational Neurolology*, 513(5): 532–541.

Baron-Cohen S (2002) The extreme male brain theory of autism, *Trends in Cognitive Sciences*, 6(6): 248–254.

Baron-Cohen S, Lombardo MV (2017) Autism and talent: the cognitive and neural basis of systemizing. *Dialogues in Clinical Neuroscience*, 19(4): 344–352.

Cameron, D (2010) Sex and the power of speech. In *Depth Magazine*, March. https://www.aqr.org.uk/a/20100301-speech

Chung WCJ, De Vries GJ, Swaab DF (2002) Sexual differentiation of the bed nucleus of the stria terminalis in humans may extend into adulthood. *Journal of Neuroscience*, 22(3):1027–1103.

Cox SR, Ritchie SJ, Fawns-Ritchie C, Tucker-Drob EM, Deary IJ (2019) Structural brain imaging correlates of general intelligence in UK Biobank. *Intelligence*, 76:101376.

de Vries, GJ, Forger NG (2015) Sex differences in the brain: a whole body perspective. *Biology of Sex Differences*, 6:15.

Department of Health and Human Services (2002). 2000 CDC growth charts for the United States: methods and development. *Vital Health Statistics* 11(246): 1–203.

Fine C (2010) *Delusions of Gender: The Real Science Behind Sex Differences*. Icon Books, London, UK.

Focquaert F, Vanneste S (2015) Autism spectrum traits in normal individuals: a preliminary VBM analysis. *Frontiers in Human Neuroscience*, 9:264.

Garcia-Falgueras A, Junque C, Giménez M, Caldú X, Segovia S, Guillamon A (2006). Sex differences in the human olfactory system. *Brain Research*, 1116(1): 103–111.

Giacomoni PU, Mammone T, Teri M (2009) Gender-linked differences in human skin, *Journal of Dermatological Science*, 55(3): 144–149.

Greenberg DM, Warrier V, Allison C, Baron-Cohen S (2018) Testing the Empathizing–Systemizing theory of sex differences and the Extreme Male Brain theory of autism in half a million people, *Proceedings of the National Academy of Sciences*, 115 (48): 12152–12157.

Herpertz SC, Nagy K, Ueltzhöffer K, Schmitt R, Mancke F, Schmahl C, Bertsch K (2017) Brain mechanisms underlying reactive aggression in borderline personality disorder-sex matters. *Biological Psychiatry*, 82(4): 257–266.

Kherif F, Josse G, Seghier ML, Price CJ (2009) The main sources of intersubject variability in neuronal activation for reading aloud. *Journal of Cognitive Neuroscience*, 21(4): 654–668.

Kiesow H, Dunbar R, Kable JW, Kalenscher T, Vogeley K, Schilbach L, Marquand AF, Wiecki, TV, Bzdok D (2020). 10,000 social brains: sex differentiation in human brain anatomy. *Science Advances*, 6(12): eaaz1170.

Klein S, Flanagan K (2016) Sex differences in immune responses. *Nature Reviews Immunology* 16:626–638.

Kobayashi A, Yokota S, Takeuchi H, Asano K, Asano M, Sassa Y, Taki Y (2020) Increased grey matter volume of the right superior temporal gyrus in healthy children with autistic cognitive style: a VBM study. *Brain and Cognition*, 139:105514.

Korucuoglu O, Harms MP, Kennedy JT, Golosheykin S, Astafiev SV, Barch DM, Anokhin AP (2020), Adolescent decision-making under risk: neural correlates and sex differences. *Cerebral Cortex*, 30(4): 2691–2707.

Kruijver FPM, Zhou JN, Pool CW, Hofman MA, Gooren LJG, Swaab DF (2000) Male-to-female transsexuals have female neuron numbers in a limbic nucleus. *The Journal of Clinical Endocrinology & Metabolism*, 85(5): 2034–2041.

Mackintosh NJ (1996). Sex differences and IQ. *Journal of Biosocial Science*, 28(4): 558–571.

Madeira MD, Lieberman AR (1995) Sexual dimorphism in the mammalian limbic system. *Progress in Neurobiology*, 45(4): 275–333.

Martínez K, Janssen J, Pineda-Pardo JA, Carmona S, Román FJ, Alemán-Gómez Y, Garcia-Garcia D, Escorial S, Quiroga MA, Santarnecchi E, Navas-Sánchez FJ, Desco M, Arango C, Colom R (2017) Individual differences in the dominance of interhemispheric connections predict cognitive ability beyond sex and brain size. *NeuroImage*, 155:234–244.

Nostro AD, Müller VI, Reid AT, Eickhoff SB (2017) Correlations between personality and brain structure: a crucial role of gender. *Cerebral Cortex*, 27(7): 3698–3712.

Oh IS, Wang G, Mount MK (2011) Validity of observer ratings of the five-factor model of personality traits: a meta-analysis. *Journal of Applied Psychology*, 96(4): 762–773.

Pawlowski, B., Atwal, R., & Dunbar, R. I. M. (2008) Sex differences in everyday risk-taking behavior in humans. *Evolutionary Psychology*, 6(1). https://doi.org/10.1177/147470490800 600104

Ponseti J, Granert O, Jansen O, Wolff S, Mehdorn H, Bosinski H, Siebner H (2009) Assessment of sexual orientation using the hemodynamic brain response to visual sexual stimuli, *Journal of Sexual Medicine,* 6(6): 1628–1634.

Repple J, Habel U, Wagels L, Pawliczek CM, Schneider F, Kohn N. (2018) Sex differences in the neural correlates of aggression. *Brain Structure and Function*, 223(9): 4115–4124.

Ritchie SJ, Cox SR, Shen X, Lombardo MV, Reus LM, Alloza C, Harris MA, Alderson HL, Hunter S, Neilson E, Liewald DCM, Auyeung B, Whalley HC, Lawrie SM, Gale CR, Bastin ME, McIntosh AM, Deary IJ (2018) Sex differences in the adult human brain: evidence from 5216 UK Biobank participants. *Cerebral Cortex*, 28(8): 2959–2975.

Roselli CE, Liu M, Hurn PD (2009) Brain aromatization: classic roles and new perspectives. *Seminars in Reproductive Medicine* 27(3): 207–217.

Ruigrok ANV, Salimi-Khorshidi G, Lai MC, Baron-Cohen S, Lombardo MV, Tait RJ, Suckling J (2014) A meta-analysis of sex differences in human brain structure. *Neuroscience & Biobehavioral Reviews,* 39:34–50.

Safron A, Sylva D, Klimaj V, Rosenthal AM, Bailey JM (2020) Neural responses to sexual stimuli in heterosexual and homosexual men and women: men's responses are more specific. *Archives of Sexual Behavior,* 49:433–445.

Safron A, Sylva D, Klimaj V, Rosenthal AM, Li M, Walter M, Bailey, JM (2017). Neural correlates of sexual orientation in heterosexual, bisexual, and homosexual men. *Scientific Reports,* 7:41314.

Schmitt, DP, Realo A, Voracek M, Allik J. (2008). Why can't a man be more like a woman? Sex differences in Big Five personality traits across 55 cultures. *Journal of Personality and Social Psychology,* 94(1): 168–182.

Sowell ER, Peterson BS, Kan E, Woods RP, Yoshii J, Bansal R, Xu D, Zhu H, Thompson PM, Toga AW (2007). Sex differences in cortical thickness mapped in 176 healthy individuals between 7 and 87 years of age. *Cerebral Cortex,* 17(7): 1550–1560.

Tschernegg M, Neuper C, Schmidt R, Wood G, Kronbichler M, Fazekas F, Enzinger C, Koini M. (2017) FMRI to probe sex-related differences in brain function with multitasking. *PLoS ONE* 12(7): e0181554.

Visser TA, Ohan JL, Whittle S, Yücel M, Simmons JG, Allen NB (2014). Sex differences in structural brain asymmetry predict overt aggression in early adolescents. *Social Cognitive and Affective Neuroscience,* 9(4), 553–560.

Votinov M, Goerlich KS, Puiu AA, Smith E, Nickl-Jockschat T, Derntl B, Habel U (2021) Brain structure changes associated with sexual orientation. *Scientific Reports* 11:5078.

Voyer D, Voyer S., Bryden MP. (1995). Magnitude of sex differences in spatial abilities: a meta-analysis and consideration of critical variables. *Psychological Bulletin,* 117:250–270. https://doi.org/10.1037/0033-2909.117.2.250

Wallentin M (2009) Putative sex differences in verbal abilities and language cortex: a critical review. *Brain and Language,* 108(3): 175–183.

Wang ZM, Heo M, Lee RC, Kotler DP, Withers RT, Heymsfield SB. (2001) Muscularity in adult humans: proportion of adipose tissue-free body mass as skeletal muscle. *American Journal of Human Biology,* 13(5): 612–619.

Zhou JN, Hofman MA, Gooren LJ, Swaab DF (1995) A sex difference in the human brain and its relation to transsexuality, *Nature,* 378(6552): 68–70.

4
IS WOMANHOOD A SOCIAL FACT?

Kathleen Stock

Traditionally, analytic philosophy asks 'What is . . .?' questions: What is justice? What is happiness? What is science? and so on. These questions simultaneously concern language, concepts, and the world. When investigating justice, for instance, you do three things: (a) ask what the word *justice* means or refers to, (b) ask under what conditions the concept of justice operates, and (c) investigate the thing in the world we call 'justice' – what kind of thing is it?

These days, previous understandings of womanhood are called into question. New meanings are proposed for an old word. This raises the question: what is a woman? Answering involves investigating language (the word *woman*), concepts (the concept of womanhood) and the nature of womanhood itself, understood as a kind of thing existing in the world.

Let's assume possession of womanhood or manhood can be a fact about a person: a fact picked out by literal, accurate uses of the English sentences '*x* is a woman' or '*y* is a man' and their linguistic equivalents. What sort of fact is it?

A formerly uncontroversial answer is: a natural fact. The categories of human females and males are biological, placing the human species in the natural world alongside other sexually dimorphic species. The divisions between women, girls, men, and boys are also natural divisions, marked by the presence within a sex of developmental maturity or the lack of it. An awareness of these categories allows humans to refer to natural facts about their own kind, as well as to further social facts implicating the natural in various contingent ways. The natural facts referred to are thought of as objective in quite a strong sense. Even if humans collectively lost self-conscious thought and language, changed their sensory apparatus quite radically, or otherwise had very different subjective experiences, there would still be women, men, boys, and girls, albeit alternatively behaved and organised.

DOI: 10.4324/9781003286608-4

Lately, however, it has become somewhat popular to present womanhood as a social and not a natural fact. This is not just the banal claim that being a woman has social effects. It's rather that womanhood is a state whose existence depends on social activity. There are many ways of specifying the natural/social divide, but for our purpose, a social fact is one that 'could only have obtained through the contingent actions of a social group' (Boghossian 2006, 17). Think of euros (social) versus atoms (natural). On this view, a particular kind of social activity is part or even all of what being a woman is. Without that social activity, there wouldn't be any women. Similar points are made for manhood, although not as often – a point that is sociologically interesting in itself.

Another helpful clarification is between *causal* construction and *constitutive* construction. For instance, a person getting a tattoo is causally dependent on the prior existence of certain social expectations, norms, and technologies in a given cultural context (Kõiv 2019, 78). Such social factors partly cause tattoos to come into existence. But this doesn't yet establish that tattoos are constitutively socially constructed. For someone who thinks tattoos are constitutively social, the existence of patterned ink marks on skin isn't sufficient to produce a tattoo. A certain social world is also required to maintain them.

In this chapter, I focus on the claim that womanhood, constitutively, already is something social. (This should be distinguished from so-called amelioriative attempts to engineer the existing concept of womanhood towards a social fact. See Bogardus 2020b). A moderate version says that being an adult human female is a necessary but not yet sufficient condition for womanhood and that social facts are additionally required. On some, although not all interpretations of Simone De Beauvoir ([1949] 2011), what is required for womanhood is, first, being female and, second, being inculcated into a sociocultural practice of femininity. Young females meet a particular feminising culture, which teaches them what it is to be a woman there. Assuming with other commentators (e.g. Moi 1999, 73–84) that this process can only happen to human females, on at least one reading, womanhood then emerges as a hybrid of natural and social facts.

A more radical view is that certain social facts are both necessary and sufficient to constitute womanhood, and there's no role for natural facts at all. A currently popular example says that womanhood is constituted, necessarily and sufficiently, by the fact of some people psychologically identifying with some ideal or stereotype of femininity – colloquially known as having a 'female gender identity' (Stock 2021, chap. 4). According to this version, womanhood is constituted by the social fact that certain people have a particular psychological attitude. If there were no such attitudes, there would be no women, and wherever there are such attitudes, there are women. According to a different version, historically popular amongst feminists, what it is to be a woman is to occupy a certain oppressed social role.

Much of the interest in social construction concerns its apparent promise of possibilities of change (Hacking 1999, 6–7). What had previously seemed inevitable now looks only contingent. The moderate version says that women must always be female, but females need not always be women. The more radical version says that women need not always be female. It's the more radical claim that tends to be used in support of the claims that transwomen are women, not men, and that transmen are men, not women.

In this chapter, I focus a critical lens on the claim that womanhood is constitutively a social fact. I examine and dismiss arguments seeking to establish this, using the methodology standard of analytic philosophy. More specifically, I address three argumentative routes:

a. Womanhood is identical to adult human femalehood. Adult human femalehood is social.
b. *Woman* has at least two meanings. One of these refers to adult human femalehood. Another refers to a social fact.
c. *Woman* has only one meaning. It doesn't refer to adult human femalehood at all but to a social fact.

Before we get to those, here's an argument to get quickly out of the way. Let's agree that *names, concepts, ideas, and theories* of womanhood are human-made representations. I accept that these are all constitutively social entities. But, as has been pointed out by many, it doesn't follow that the *things that the names, concepts, ideas, and theories describe* are constitutively social (Hacking 1999, 21–22; Haslanger 2012, 152–157; Mallon 2019). Human-made representations can describe natural things. This is what, for instance, many scientific theories do. For all we yet know, the best theories of womanhood might be like this.

Another preliminary is this. An ostensibly quick route to the claim that womanhood was a social fact would simply point to the existence of a contemporary linguistic practice saying that 'transwomen are women' (etc.) and argue that on its own, it's evidence that there's at least one sense in which womanhood is social, not natural. But this is sub-optimal, not least because claims that transwomen are women (etc.) are highly contested. The assertion that womanhood is social, not natural, is often brought in, precisely, to bolster the impression of the truth of such claims. If womanhood is to be convincingly established as social, in a way that might help establish claims like 'transwomen are women', independent grounds must be found.

a. <u>Womanhood is identical to adult human femalehood. Adult human femalehood is social.</u>

i. Adult human femalehood is constitutively social because everything is constitutively social.

Here are two radically different approaches to the relationship between concepts and the world. On the first view, concepts – understood as mental representations – are cognitive tools, refined over time. They are developed, refined, or abandoned by humans, usually collectively, in response to pre-existent mind-independent features of the world. Sometimes concepts fail to represent what is there or fail to represent it in a sufficiently fine-grained way. But we can be confident that at least some concepts are responsive to the way the world is and help give us knowledge of it.

This approach to concepts is naturalistic, in the sense of taking reality to determine representation and not the other way around for at least some domains of representation. It's compatible with a variety of further positions on truth, reality, and justification. All it requires is that a mind-independent reality can make a systematic difference in the concepts humans develop so that knowledge of that reality is potentially produced.

This approach is also compatible with discovering that some objects at a local level are socially constructed: race, for instance, or certain mental health conditions. But this limited version of social constructionism can be contrasted with a second approach, which operates at a much wider level – a global one. At base, this says that everything humans can think about is socially constructed. Human conceptual schemes and associated social practices determine all there is in a metaphysically primitive, irreducible way (Mallon 2016, 156). The idea of a concept as a cognitive tool does not apply here. And unlike in the last case, the existence of particular socially constructed entities is not retrospectively identified via empirical investigation. Rather, their ubiquitous presence is inferred from highly abstract claims about the nature of language and thought. (So, in this approach, there are no hybrid, part-natural, part-social facts. All is social, at least insofar as we can intelligibly think about it.)

Doyens of this global approach to social construction include Thomas Kuhn, Michel Foucault, Nelson Goodman, Richard Rorty, Hilary Putnam, and Judith Butler. In particular, Butler (1990, 1993) has been influential in popularising the idea that womanhood, understood as adult human femalehood, is a social fact. But Butler's view, like that of other global constructionists, is scaffolded by a totalising metaphysical and linguistic worldview that applies to far more than womanhood. She makes clear that her suspicions about a distinction between natural biological sex and sociocultural 'gender' that is inextricably linked to a more general distrust of the distinction between nature, understood as something prelinguistic and ahistorical, and culture, understood as something social and imposed upon a natural base (1990, 50–51). Although she sometimes balks at the explicit claim that there is nothing but discourse – and although others (e.g. Ásta 2018, chap. 3) unconvincingly defend her from this – time and again, she implies there's nothing intelligible or articulable before discursive (social) construction of it and certainly nothing ahistorical or non-contingent to which we could confidently refer. Clearly, this point must apply to far more than womanhood. She concedes there is an 'outside' to discourse but only in the sense of what is excluded and made 'unthinkable' via the arbitrary placing of a boundary as part of a 'hegemonic position' (1993, 8–12). Effectively, then, what is 'outside' is produced by construction too.

This is not the place to subject global constructivism to detailed critique. What we can do is identify a well-known problem: its incoherence. I will use Boghossian's

(2006, 52–57) formulation. Effectively, global constructivism says that there are no facts that exist independently of our concepts or theories of them. It asserts this claim as a knowable fact. So – using parentheses to make sense clearer – the question arises: Is the fact that (all facts are socially constructed) supposed to be an absolute fact or a socially constructed one? It can't be an absolute fact on pain of making the global thesis false. However, the second option is also problematic. For it can't be a socially constructed fact on pain of an infinite regress. If it were a socially constructed fact that (all facts are socially constructed), then we could also ask, What would make *this* a fact? Assuming that socially constructed facts are all there are, presumably the answer would have to be that the fact that (there is a social construction, according to which there is a social construction, according to which all facts are socially constructed). And what would make *this* construction a fact? The fact that (there is a social construction, according to which there is a social construction, according to which there is a social construction . . .), and so on, *ad infinitum*. As Boghossian (2006) puts it, 'it is absurd to propose that, in order for our utterances to have any prospect of being true, what we must mean by them are infinitary propositions that we could neither express nor understand' (56).

A better and more interesting claim, then, would be that *some not all* objects are socially constructed. We must therefore ask: Is there any plausible way in which womanhood – understood as adult human femalehood – emerges as constitutively social for relatively local and not global reasons?

ii. Adult human femalehood is constitutively social because it is an interactive kind and so constitutively social.

According to Hacking (1999) many human kinds are 'interactive kinds' that exhibit 'looping effects'. That is: the way that the kinds are classified enables members of the kind to conceive of themselves differently and so act differently, which then causes revisions in the conditions of membership of the kind. Interactive kinds are contrasted with 'indifferent' kinds: kinds that are indifferent to classification and relatively stable in the attributes of members as a result.

An example of an interactive kind discussed by Hacking (1995) is that of people with "multiple personality disorder", known these days as dissociative identity. As the possibility of this diagnosis became better known in the 1980s, there were more diagnoses of multiple personality disorder, which, in turn, altered the prototype and what was looked for by clinicians and sufferers. Contemporaneous social trends also changed understanding, such as feminism's interest in uncovering suppressed histories of child abuse. Over time, the prototype of a person with multiple personalities shifted from 'double personalities' grounded in 'hysteria' to people conceived of as potentially having hundreds of personalities and personality fragments, usually accompanied by amnesia, and typically caused by child abuse.

Here then is a possible argument. If you possess womanhood, you are a member of womankind. Womankind – understood as adult human femalekind – is an interactive kind, and interactive kinds are social kinds. So womankind is a social kind, and womanhood is a social fact.

But womankind – in the sense of adult human femalekind – is not an interactive kind. All or nearly all natural languages, historical and actual, have a concept corresponding to the division between adult human males and females (Goddard 2001) – something that is not the case with the concept of 'multiple personalities'. It's reasonable to take the cross-cultural ubiquity of the concept *woman* as evidence that the category it refers to is stable and indifferent to classification (Tsou 2007, 339). A further point is that women and men also seem relatively easy for non-specialists to *perceptually* identify as such, most of the time (unsurprising, given that this is required for the reproduction of the species and is presumably hardwired). This again is a disanalogy with a multiple personality diagnosis.

In fact, it's arguable that multiple personality disorder is a good example of an interactive kind, partly because it is at most only weakly associated with a biological basis. In contrast, when a mental disorder – for instance, depression – is firmly associated with a biological or other physiological basis, there is less inclination to call it interactive in any way that makes it unstable (Tsou 2007). (In contrast, the claim that 'trans' is an interactive social kind looks much more promising.)

It's true, of course, that some male people describe themselves as 'women' or 'not men', that some female people describe themselves as 'men' or 'not women', and that both facts apparently influence some other people to follow suit, so that within certain sub-cultures womanhood is no longer described as related to human biology at all. We have already ruled out such contested practices as primary sources of evidence with respect to womanhood. In any case, even in the case of genuinely interactive kinds, it would be unusual to count every ascription as inevitably accurate. And in fact, this scenario is compatible with other explanations than interactivity. On one plausible explanation, such usage is non-literal (Stock 2021, chap. 6).

iii. Womanhood is constitutively social because human femalehood is social, not biological.

For many, an apparently irresistible reason to think womanhood is constitutively social is that human femalehood, generally, is constitutively social. For instance, Dembroff (2021) writes that 'binary classification of bodies as female and male is socially motivated' (997). This is best understood as saying that experts have discovered *a posteriori* that necessarily, femalehood is social, not biological, despite previous understandings of it (Mallon 2019). But why should we accept this?

One reason offered by Dembroff (2021) is that sex 'classifications . . . are historically and contextually variable' (997). But the fact a classification has a history doesn't make it social not natural (Byrne 2021, 20). Natural kind classifications have histories too. Nor does the fact that sex classifications are, in Dembroff's (2021) words, 'typically vague, underdetermined, and ambiguous' (997) make them social.

On many standard accounts of natural kinds, a natural kind's boundaries are vague and underdetermined (Bird and Tobin 2018; Ludlow 2014, 65; Bogardus 2020a). For instance, within a given chemical reaction, it can be indeterminate at a given point whether there is an acetic acid molecule or an ethanol molecule (Hawley and Bird 2011, 214). But there is no temptation therefore to say these molecules are social, not natural, kinds.

By far, the most popular reason offered for the conclusion that femalehood is social is the existence of so-called intersex conditions, more recently described as disorders or differences of sexual development (DSDs). For instance, Barnes (2020) writes:

> The prevalence of intersex conditions seems to be enough to show that our gender terms are not simple synonyms for biological sex terms – even if ordinary speakers often take them to be. Research increasingly shows a spectrum of sex variation between the male and female binaries. (719)

Similar thoughts have attracted Butler (1990, 144–150), Stoljar (1995, 273), Saul (2012, 198), Ásta (2018, 72), Dembroff (2021, 999), and others. Yet whether the existence of DSDs threatens the idea of a sex binary depends on what sex, and a binary, is taken to be. Being a human female or a human male is plausibly understood in one of two ways, each of which accommodates nearly all DSDs unproblematically. On the first of these, being female essentially involves being a member of a species on a developmental pathway to the production of large gametes (as opposed to being a member of a species on a developmental pathway to the production of small, motile gametes, which would make an entity male; Byrne 2018). This is a cross-species account of being female, and alongside its complementary account of being male, can account for over 99.9 percent of humans as male or female, including nearly all DSDs (Stock 2021, chap. 2). A second account of sex is a human-specific one, which views femalehood and malehood as homeostatic property clusters of endogenous human sex characteristics, with no particular characteristic as necessary or sufficient. This can also account for nearly all humans as either male or female (Stock 2021, chap. 2).

Both accounts leave very few people with rare DSDs whose sexed status is genuinely ambiguous. However, the fact of sexual ambiguity for very few shows nothing about the allegedly social nature of femalehood and malehood unless it shows something similar for any concept where there is ambiguity at its 'edges' – which is very many concepts and possibly even all of them. A 'binary' in biology always comes with the expectation of small amounts of variation. Indeed, *human being* is arguably indeterminate when it comes to *Homo erectus* versus *Homo sapiens*. It's also arguably in the nature of concepts generally to be indeterminate when it comes to peripheral hard cases (Ludlow 2014, chap. 4). Admitting indeterminacy at the edges is compatible with the continued usefulness of natural concepts generally, and of *female* and *male* in particular, in causal inference, prediction, and explanation. Viewed in these terms, then, the sex binary is about as stable and as natural as it gets. (See Byrne [2020] and Bogardus [2020a] for related discussions.)

iv. Womanhood is constitutively social because the concept of human femalehood is essentially normative. Wherever a concept X is essentially normative, then X is constitutively social.

As part of her argument that human femalehood is socially constructed, Butler (1990, xi) argues that sexed categories for humans are essentially normative and constructed by reference to an idealised heterosexuality. For instance, you're a woman to the extent you're attractive to men, sexually desirous of men, reproductively fertile, and so on. For Butler (1993, 8), sexed categories create a hierarchy, empowering those who fit neatly within the norms for the categories, and disempowering those outside. Meanwhile, those outside the binary become illegible, inarticulable, even inhuman.

Let's accept that wherever a concept X is essentially normative – where social approval or disapproval is built into its meaning – then X is constitutively social, at least partly. We still need a good reason to accept that the concepts *woman* and *female* (etc.) are inevitably normative. A standard distinction within analytic philosophy is between descriptive and prescriptive concepts: between describing and evaluating. Descriptive concepts, when applied by a thinker, imply no positive or negative evaluation but neutrally refer to aspects of the world. The concepts of science – *atom, species, chemical element, gene*, and so on – are usually thought of as paradigmatically descriptive. In the traditional view of womanhood – which has yet to be dislodged – the concepts *woman* and the more general *human female* describe, not prescribe.

Butler (1990, xxi) rejects the whole distinction between description and prescription. In rejecting this distinction, Butler (1990, 125–145) is apparently appealing to a picture inspired by Foucault, according to which discursive categorisation of humans into groups can only ever be a means of creating contingent, normative hierarchies of political dominance and subordination, rather than reflecting what was antecedently there. In other words, her collapse of the descriptive into the prescriptive seems motivated not by special concerns about sex categories but by a more global constructionist stance. But what we are looking for is a *specific* reason to think that the concept of woman, understood as adult human femalehood, is essentially normative. (For further discussion, see Bogardus 2020a.)

The prospects don't look great. One specific reason offered is the fact of people with DSDs who, Butler (1990) writes, 'implicitly challenge the descriptive force of the available categories of sex' (148). However, as I just argued, at least two plausible accounts of the human sexes as natural kinds are available, both compatible with such variation. A different move would be to appeal to how the West deals with sexual variation culturally to try to somehow motivate the idea that notions of human femaleness and maleness are arbitrary and prescriptive. Is the fact that some people with DSDs are subject to invasive surgery in early childhood good evidence that sexed categories generally are normative? No. Such surgeries are guided by an aesthetic norm, perhaps perniciously. That norm appeals approvingly to what is standardly or stereotypically found. However, this doesn't show that our concepts of sex themselves, designed to help us describe the structures found in nature, are intrinsically normative.

v. Womanhood is constitutively social because adulthood is constitutively social.

Both Dembroff (2021, 996) and Heartsilver (2021) attempt to argue that womanhood is social, partly on the grounds that adulthood is allegedly social. This looks strange, assuming that adulthood pertains to the moment of reaching sexual maturity. The advent and completion of sexual maturity, albeit vague in its precise timing, looks paradigmatically natural. (Recall that natural categories can be vague). In fact, it isn't just natural but visually detectable in many cases, due to the presence of secondary sex characteristics.

But Dembroff and Heartsilver suggest that people typically considered women and men are not 'adult' in the sense of being sexually mature – although they may be – but are 'adult' in a different, arguably stipulated and wholly social sense, pertaining to legal personhood. Sexual maturity typically tends to come too early to grant womanhood and manhood, they argue. Heartsilver (2021) adds: 'There is a wide range of ages at which girls complete puberty, but we do not, on that basis, recognize a wide range of ages at which girls become women' (4).

However, if Dembroff and Heartsilver were denying that 'adult' *ever* pertained to sexual maturity, they would surely be mistaken. In a recognisable sense, there are – if not a wide range, then at least, a range – of 'ages at which girls become women'. Around the world, a range of social arrangements are structured around adulthood, in the sense of the achievement of sexual maturity, for one or both sexes – the possibility of marriage being an obvious one in many cultures and culturally specific rites of passage to adulthood being another. The linking of adulthood to sexual maturity gives sense to the phrase 'young adults', who may not yet have met legal majority requirements but are nonetheless correctly described as a kind of adult (Byrne [2021] makes a related point). Attempts to pin down the legal majority in various societies are often inextricably linked to sexual maturity; in many cases, they are designed to track it, at least roughly, by defining a relatively arbitrary cut-off point within a range. The point may be arbitrary, but the range is not.

I turn now to a different overall strategy.

b. *Woman* has at least two meanings. One of these refers to adult human femalehood. Another refers to a different social fact.

On this sort of view, *woman* is lexically ambiguous. One meaning is presumed to refer to adult human females – although in practice, those who adopt this approach tend to combine it with doubts about the naturalness of this category. A different meaning refers to something else which is social. Those who hold this view include Stone (2007), Bettcher (2013), and Laskowski (2020). It should be noted that this view does not show that *woman* is *not* identical to *adult human female*, as is sometimes implied (e.g. by Stone 2007, 141). The most it shows is that in one sense of *woman*, women are identical to adult human females, and in another sense, they are something else.

The prospects for lexical ambiguity here look limited, however. As Byrne (2020) notes, lexical ambiguity (roughly – two words with the same form or one word with two senses, depending on your theory) tends to persist in natural language only where the context makes clear what exactly is being referred to. Where disambiguation is hard to do from context alone, new forms of words tend to be found to make communication easier. If, *ex hypothesis*, *woman* referred to something natural and, separately, to something 'social', then context alone presumably wouldn't be enough for disambiguation, and we should expect at least some pressure to rename one of the referents.

A further objection is that arguably *woman* achieves unproblematic conjunction reduction, where a failure to achieve this is a standard test for ambiguity. With a term 'N' that is genuinely ambiguous between meanings N1 and N2, then 'N is *x*' can be true (because N1 is *x*) and 'N is *y*' can be true (because N2 is *y*), but 'N is *x* and *y*' will produce discordant and perhaps even comic zeugmatic effects. For instance, 'some banks are good for mortgages' is true of banks that, by definition, deal with money, and 'some banks are good for catching fish' is true of banks that, by definition, border rivers; but 'some banks are good for mortgages and catching fish' sounds discordant. In contrast, when we conjoin a predicate attached to a natural understanding of the term *woman* (e.g. 'some women have ovaries') and one attached to a supposedly social understanding of that term (e.g. 'some women have female gender identities'), arguably we don't get discordant effects: 'some women have ovaries and female gender identities' sounds fine. Similar failures seem to occur with other standard tests for ambiguity: ellipses, contradiction, and so on (Sennet [2021] summarises these).

Despite this lack of promise, we should still consider the reasons offered to think *woman* is ambiguous. Two can be discounted quickly. Bettcher (2013) relies on a background picture where existing definitions of *woman* are inevitably in the service, not of reflecting pre-existing reality, but of 'distributions of power and the capacity to enforce a way of life' (242). Laskowski (2020) meanwhile just assumes that *prima facie* the word *woman* is used to refer to two different kinds of entity, one natural and one social; what is treated as in dispute by the paper is how best to explain this.

Another gambit says that, in one sense of *woman*, although not the one that refers to adult human femalehood, cultural notions of femininity are part of its semantic content. An attempt to establish this point is made by Bettcher (2009), who makes an inference from adjectives like 'womanly' and 'girly' to *woman* and *girl*:

> adjectives such as "womanly," "manly," "girly," and the like . . . have cultural traits packed right into their meaning. When somebody says, "Well, no. That's a bit too girly for me, I'm afraid," we shouldn't expect them to be complaining about having to dig ditches. (104)

The challenge here, however, is to establish the relevance of such denominalised adjectives to the nouns *woman* and *girl*. Although it's true that a stereotyped set of characteristics is built into the meaning of *womanly*, it's easy to find analogous cases of adjectives, identifying some restricted set of social attributes, which don't retrospectively alter either the intention or extension of the noun to which they are related, either way. 'Childish', 'presidential' and 'bushy' are three. Not all children are childish or presidents presidential or all bushes bushy, and not all women are womanly. (For discussion, see Bogardus 2020a, 887–90).

A different attempt is made by Stone (2007), who writes:

> Consider that in everyday language, 'woman' not only suggest[s] a female human being. It also suggests someone who occupies a specific social role, as in the phrase "a woman's place is in the kitchen" and it suggests someone with a specific set of psychological traits such as being liable to cry (hence the phrase 'boys don't cry'). (141)

This is also unconvincing. Claims like 'a woman's place is in the kitchen' and 'boys don't cry' are known as normative generics and either function to describe general empirical tendencies in behaviour or place normative expectations on that behaviour. Either way, they characteristically admit of exceptions, and it would be odd to take these as claims about what it is, necessarily, to be a woman (or boy). (For related discussion, see Hesnia 2021).

A third argument might be pursued by way of remarks by Beauvoir ([1949] 2011, 3). Does the fact that language users sometimes talk about some females as 'real women' or, alternatively, talk of other females as 'not women' (etc.) suggest that there is a social – presumably normative – meaning to *woman* in addition to the natural one? No, not unless it shows something about any concept subject to similar constructions, which is many of them. As was pointed out by J.L. Austin (1962, 70), whether something is counted as 'real' or not depends on what's effectively being excluded as uninteresting by way of the contrast in the current conversational context. (See also Hall 1959.)

Take, for instance, the concept of a diamond – a natural one, referring to a carbon allotrope with four covalent bonds. A jeweller might still say of a huge, clear, sparkly diamond, 'Now, that's a real diamond!' or to a seller of a small, dull one, 'Call that a diamond?' although both jeweller and seller both know that it is. Similar moves can be made for almost any concept which identifies a kind of entity in which we have a specific social interest, in terms of some limited properties.

As competent speakers, we easily adapt and understand others' adaption of our use of nouns on the fly, to communicate the fact that an entity, understood by all parties as unproblematically falling under a noun, exemplifies a certain set of contingent expectations of that sort of thing really well – or doesn't. Relatively easily, we temporarily invent or adapt concepts to suit present conversational purposes (Ludlow 2014). In claims about who is 'still very much a woman' or what's 'not a real diamond', for instance, there's what we might call a temporary escalation, whereby concepts plus attributive qualifiers such as 'real', 'not real', and/or certain emphases and tones of voice are used by speakers to draw attention to particular contingent properties of objects, currently of interest, or the lack of them. In the case of diamonds, this doesn't establish that generally *diamond* means something other than a carbon allotrope with four covalent bonds. And *a fortiori* nor does it establish that *diamond* refers, not to that form of carbon at all but to the set of its socially valued properties, such as being clear, sparkly, and large. Similar points go, *mutatis mutandis*, for *woman*. Whatever is said to fall, or fail to fall, under a concept in temporarily escalated usage, falls under it unproblematically in a de-escalated one. Hence, there is no great temptation to hive off the escalated use from the de-escalated one and somehow make it a separate normative referent of the concept.

For every proposed case of ambiguity, we should check whether evidence can be accommodated to avoid semantic proliferation. Although, of course, our examination here hasn't been exhaustive, so far we have seen no compelling reason to accept that *woman* is ambiguous.

I turn now to a final sort of approach.

c. *Woman* has only one meaning. It doesn't refer to adult human femalehood at all but to a social fact.

This approach, like the last, can accept that there is something real and natural called adult human femalehood but argues that *woman* does not refer to that fact, even ambiguously. Instead, *woman* exclusively refers to something constitutively social.

As in the previous section, I start by objecting to the conclusion. Were it true that the concept of woman referred only to something social and not to adult human femalehood, then – quite apart from the fact that we would need one heck of an error theory – the concept of woman could not perform the functions that it currently performs. That is, it would disconnect the concept from hundreds of causal-explanatory discourses in which it has – at least until recently – been easily and fruitfully located, for instance, in discussions about women's distinctive medical needs, women's economic situation as related to their reproductive capacity, women's susceptibility to distinct forms of violence such as vaginal rape, women's involvement in heterosexual prostitution and surrogacy, women's sporting capacities as opposed to men's, women's position within religious movements, women's position within education, women's position within workplaces, and so on.

Each of these issues is inflected by the presence of adult human femalehood, understood as a natural state with multiple causal effects in a given social context. Nothing we have reviewed thus far has given us cause to doubt the real existence of adult human femalehood, or its social effects. If *woman*, despite appearances, somehow referred to something other than adult human femalehood, we should not expect these discourses to work successfully. In fact, were the concept *woman* ever to go this far off-piste, it would seem urgent to re-engineer it immediately, re-orienting it straight back towards adult human femalehood.

I turn now to three bad arguments for the conclusion.

i. Womanhood is constitutively social, because gender is constitutively social and womanhood is a gender.

It's sometimes assumed that womanhood is constitutively social because gender is constitutively social and womanhood is a gender, not a sex. But this is to trade illegitimately on an ambiguity in the word *gender*.

In one sense, gender is social, because it's unambiguously defined as such. In this sense, popularised from the 1960s onwards, 'gender' is the contingent set of sociocultural stereotypes, norms, and expectations surrounding biological sex; what is often referred to as femininity and masculinity. For instance, Gayle Rubin (1975) writes that 'the "sex/gender system" is the set of arrangements by which a society transforms biological sexuality into products of human activity, and in which these transformed sexual needs are satisfied' (159). In this sense, then, gender is constitutively social, but womanhood itself is not a gender (or, at least, we have not yet been given reason to think that it is). In another sense, womanhood *is* a 'gender' – but only because *gender* is being used as a polite synonym for *biological sex*. In Elizabeth Gaskell's novel *Cranford*, for instance, one character refers to the 'masculine gender', meaning men but not the set of social stereotypes and norms around malehood (Gaskell 1986, p. 42).

The upshot is that we can't quickly get from saying, 'Gender is socially constructed', to saying, 'Womanhood is not adult human femalehood but some further social fact'. Surprisingly, this basic point is often overlooked by philosophers (for instance, Hacking 1999). If *gender* means the sociocultural aspects of sex, then it's tautological that gender is socially constructed but womanhood can still be thought of as identical to adult human femalehood, unproblematically. However, if *gender* means *woman*, then the claim that womanhood is non-identical to adult human femalehood, but rather is something else that is social, needs to be argued for independently.

ii. Womanhood is non-identical to adult human femalehood and is constitutively social, because this avoids biological determinism.

A frequently cited motive for the claim that womanhood is a social fact separate from the fact of adult human femalehood goes as follows:

> '[S]ex' denotes human females and males, and depends on biological features. . . . Then again, 'gender' denotes women and men and depends on social factors. . . . The main feminist motivation for making this distinction was to counter biological determinism: the view that one's sex determines one's social and cultural traits and roles.
>
> *(Mikkola 2016, 21)*

In other words, womanhood is social, not biological, because if womanhood were social, not biological, it would avoid the politically difficult claim that women are biologically determined to be domestic, submissive, and so on (see also Saul 2012, 96; Bach 2012, 4). This is a bad argument, viewed from any position which takes seriously the project of apolitical, true description of the world. The fact that certain descriptions, were they true, would help women avoid politically difficult claims has no bearing on whether those descriptions are actually true. Equally, if biological determinism did turn out to be true, choosing to avoid understanding womanhood in terms of biology wouldn't save us from it. (For further criticism, see Alcoff 2006, 160–162; Bogardus 2020a, section 1.2; Stock 2021, 15).

Perhaps surprisingly, this argument form is not a historical anomaly in academic feminism, even from those methodologically distant from Judith Butler. On a currently popular view within analytic philosophy, the semantics of *woman* are contextual; they refer, broadly speaking, to something social, although the specific referent changes from context to context, depending on background social variation of some kind. For Saul (2012), the relevant variation is in local standards governing judgements of similarity to femalehood; for Diaz Leon (2016), the relevant variation is in local 'normative standards'; for Barnes (2020) the term *woman* is used flexibly, and 'there aren't any deep, language-independent facts about which people are women' (720). In all cases, these authors start with the conviction that it is a desideratum of any account of womanhood to be (what they think of as) politically strategic or ethically just. Yet, as we have just seen, against a naturalistic picture, this argument form is terrible. Philosophers have often argued that 'you can't derive an "ought" from an "is", but this is manifestly worse: an attempt to derive an "is" from an "ought"'.

iii. Womanhood is constitutively social, because womanhood is essentially subjective. Adult human femalehood is not essentially subjective. Essentially subjective states are constitutively social.

In relatively recent history, some academic feminists have assumed that womanhood is a state essentially grounded in subjectivity, not objectivity, from which it would seem to follow that an account of womanhood cannot be an account of adult human femalehood, since it is not essentially subjective. From this starting point, plus the additional assumption that the human subject or self is constitutively social, it's a short step to saying that womanhood is also constitutively social. Authors who have argued for something like the second step here – that the human subject or self is constitutively social – include Butler, once again, alongside Heidegger, Sartre, Foucault, Derrida, and many others. But we need not engage here with the second stage, because the conclusion about womanhood can be undermined at an earlier stage. Namely, there is no good reason to think that womanhood is a state essentially grounded in subjectivity. Of course, most women are also subjects and have subjectivity, but women are not *essentially* subjects. To put it brutally, there are deceased women, unconscious women, and women in comas or vegetative states. None of these have subjectivity, but they don't stop being women.

Why has this obvious point been overlooked? One reason is the influence of global versions of social constructivism on academic feminism (Warnke 2018). If nothing intelligible exists prior to discourse, then, in a sense, everything intelligible is subjective (or, at least, intersubjective). But this can't help us bolster a more local claim that womanhood in particular is constitutively subjective.

Another influence seems to be the fact that, as a political project, feminism has been primarily focused on women's experiences and (latterly) their identities, both of which are essentially subjective. However, the fact that feminism reasonably focuses on subjective aspects of womanhood obviously doesn't entail that womanhood itself is essentially subjective. And in any case, it would be bizarre to pretend that the only discourse in which the concept of woman usefully featured was feminism. The concept is also essential to medicine, law, sport, criminal justice, education, leisure, and many other social contexts.

Whatever the motive, an obvious problem quickly emerges for any feminism that thinks of womanhood as essentially subjective: what is sometimes called 'the commonality problem'. As Warnke (2018) puts it, 'What experiences does a black Sudanese Muslim woman displaced by ethnic cleansing in Darfur share with the Queen of England?' There are no particular experiences that all women share, except couched at the most general of levels, and in trying to find some, feminists have often ended up privileging a narrow, self-regarding set. This isn't a problem for feminism *per se*, construed only as a political movement for women, since it would be both demanding and arbitrary to ask that feminism attended only to those experiences all women shared. But it *is* a problem for any version of feminism attached to a theory of womanhood as a subjective state, and it is also a problem for any such theory of womanhood itself. The many authors who have taken the commonality problem seriously include Spelman (1988), Young (1994), Bach (2012), and Mikkola (2016). Sometimes, as in the case of Spelman and Mikkola, the two challenges have been taken as partly indicating the futility of trying to offer a coherent concept of *woman* at all. Yet, a rather more obvious solution to the commonality problem is to deny that the concept of woman refers to anything subjective.

Conclusion

My concluding summary can be swift. In some quarters, including many feminist ones, it has become popular to say that womanhood is a social fact. Prolonged examination of this claim has established no good reason to agree. Womanhood is a natural fact, if any is.

Acknowledgements

Grateful thanks for the helpful comments to Sophie Allen, Tomas Bogardus, Alex Byrne, John Collins, Donovan K. Cleckley, John Divers, Cordelia Fine, Simon Glendinning, Michael Jordan, James Ladyman, Holly Lawford-Smith, Mary Leng, Peter Ludlow, Katharina Rietzler, Paul D. Smart, David Wallace, and anyone else I've forgotten over the course of a very long writing period.

References

Alcoff, Linda Martín. 2006. *Visible Identities: Race, Gender, and the Self.* Oxford: Oxford University Press.
Ásta. 2018. *Categories We Live By.* New York: Oxford University Press.
Austin, John L. 1962. *Sense and Sensibilia.* Edited by G. J. Warnock. London: Oxford University Press.
Bach, Theodore. 2012. Gender is a natural kind with a historical essence. *Ethics* 122 (2): 231–72.
Barnes, E. 2020. Gender and Gender Terms. *Noûs,* 54: 704–730.
Bettcher, Talia Mae. 2009. Trans Identities and First-Person Authority. In *You've Changed: Sex Reassignment and Personal Identity*, edited by L. Shrage, pp. 98–121. Oxford: Oxford University Press.
Bettcher, Talia Mae. 2013. Trans Women and the meaning of "woman". In *Philosophy of Sex: Contemporary Readings*, 6th ed., edited by A. Soble, N. Power and R. Halwani, pp.233–250. Lanham, MA: Rowan & Littlefield.
Bird, Alexander and Emma Tobin. 2018. Natural Kinds. In *The Stanford Encyclopedia of Philosophy* (Spring 2018 ed.), edited by Edward N. Zalta. https://plato.stanford.edu/archives/spr2018/entries/natural-kinds/
Bogardus, Tomas. 2020a. Evaluating Arguments for the Sex/Gender distinction. *Philosophia* 48: 873–892.
Bogardus, Tomas. 2020b. Some Internal Problems with Revisionary Gender Concepts. *Philosophia* 48: 55–75.
Boghossian, Paul. 2006. *Fear of Knowledge: Against Relativism and Constructivism.* New York: Oxford University Press.
Butler, Judith. 1990. *Gender Trouble.* New York: Routledge.
Butler, Judith. 1993. *Bodies That Matter.* New York: Routledge.
Byrne, Alex. 2018. Is Sex Binary? *Arc Digital*, 2 November. https://arcdigital.media/is-sex-binary-16bec97d161e
Byrne, Alex. 2020. Are Women Adult Human Females? *Philosophical Studies* 177: 3783–3803.
Byrne, Alex. 2021. Gender Muddle: Reply to Dembroff. *Journal of Controversial Ideas* 1(1): 5.

De Beauvoir, Simone. (1949) 2011. *The Second Sex*. Translated by Constance Borde and Sheila Malovany-Chevallier. New York: Vintage.

Dembroff, Robin. 2021. Escaping the Natural Attitude about Gender. *Philosophical Studies* 178: 983–1003.

Diaz Leon, Esa. 2016. 'Woman' as a Politically Significant Term: A Solution to the Puzzle. *Hypatia* 31(2): 245–258.

Gaskell, Elizabeth. 1986. *Cranford/Cousin Phillis*. London: Penguin Classics.

Goddard, Cliff. 2001. Lexico-Semantic Universals: A Critical Overview. *Linguistic Typology*, 5(1): 1–65.

Hacking, Ian. 1995. *Rewriting the Soul: Multiple Personality and the Sciences of Memory*. Princeton, NJ: Princeton University Press.

Hacking, Ian. 1999. *The Social Construction of What?* Cambridge, MA: Harvard University Press.

Hall, Roland. 1959. Excluders. *Analysis* 20(1): 1–7.

Haslanger, Sally. 2012. *Resisting Reality*. New York: Oxford University Press.

Hawley, Katherine and Bird, Alexander. 2011. What Are Natural Kinds? *Philosophical Perspectives* 25(1): 205–221.

Heartsilver, Maggie. 2021. Deflating Byrne's "Are Women Adult Human Females?" *Journal of Controversial Ideas* 1(1): 1–16.

Hesnia, Samia. 2021. Normative Generics: Against Semantic Polysemy. *Thought* 10(3): 218–225.

Kõiv, Riin. 2019. Causal Social Construction. *Journal of Social Ontology*, 5(1): 77–99. https://doi.org/10.1515/jso-2019-0006

Laskowski, N.G. 2020. Moral Constraints on Gender Concepts. *Ethical Theory and Moral Practice* 23: 39–51.

Ludlow, Peter. 2014. *Living Words*. Oxford: Oxford University Press.

Mallon, Ron. 2016. *The Construction of Human Kinds*, Oxford: Oxford University Press.

Mallon, Ron. 2019. Naturalistic Approaches to Social Construction. In *The Stanford Encyclopedia of Philosophy* (Spring 2019 ed.), edited by Edward N. Zalta. https://plato.stanford.edu/archives/spr2019/entries/social-construction-naturalistic/

Mikkola, Mari. 2016. *The Wrong of Injustice: Dehumanization and Its Role in Feminist Philosophy*. Oxford: Oxford University Press.

Moi, Toril. 1999. *What Is a Woman?* Oxford: Oxford University Press.

Rubin, Gayle. 1975. The Traffic in Women: Notes on the "Political Economy" of Sex. In *Toward an Anthropology of Women*, edited by Rayna R. Reiter, pp. 157–210. Monthly Review Press.

Saul, Jennifer. 2012. Politically Significant Terms and the Philosophy of Language: Methodological Issues. In *Out from the Shadows: Analytical Feminist Contributions to Traditional Philosophy*, edited by Sharon L. Crasnow and Anita M. Superson pp.195–214. Oxford: Oxford University Press.

Sennet, Adam. 2021. Ambiguity. In *The Stanford Encyclopedia of Philosophy* (Fall 2021 ed.), edited by Edward N. Zalta. https://plato.stanford.edu/archives/fall2021/entries/ambiguity/

Spelman, Elizabeth.1988. *The Inessential Woman: Problems of Exclusion in Feminist Thought*. Boston: Beacon Press.

Stock, Kathleen. 2021. *Material Girls: Why Reality Matters for Womanhood*. London: Fleet.

Stoljar, Natalie. 1995. Essence, Identity, and the Concept of Woman. *Philosophical Topics* 23: 261–293.

Stone, Alison. 2007. *An Introduction to Feminist Philosophy*. Cambridge UK: Polity.

Tsou, Jonathan Y. 2007. Hacking on the Looping Effects of Psychiatric Classifications: What Is an Interactive and Indifferent Kind? *International Studies in the Philosophy of Science,* 21(3): 329–344. https://doi.org/10.1080/02698590701589601

Warnke, Georgia. 2018. Intersections Between Analytic and Continental Feminism. In *The Stanford Encyclopedia of Philosophy* (Fall 2018 ed.), edited by Edward N. Zalta. https://plato.stanford.edu/archives/fall2018/entries/femapproach-analy-cont/

Young, Iris Marion. 1994. Gender as Seriality: Thinking about Women as a Social Collective. *Signs,* 19(3): 713–738.

5
THE HISTORY OF SEX
Sex Denial and Gender Identity Ideology

Jane Clare Jones

The contemporary trans rights movement emerged in the early 1990s on both sides of the Atlantic through a blend of legal activism and academic theorisation (Jones 2020). The present movement is distinguished by a belief system we will call here 'gender identity ideology' or 'trans ideology,' the core claim of which is that being a man or a woman is a matter of gender identity rather than biological sex. Stephen Whittle, a transman, legal scholar and co-founder of Press for Change – the first major transgender lobby group in the UK – has expressed this idea by asserting that '[t]o be a man or a woman is contained in a person's gender identity' (Whittle [1999] 2002, 6). This thought is also encapsulated in the central slogan of contemporary transactivism, 'Trans Women are Women, Trans Men are Men.'

If 'Trans Women are Women' is a true statement, then the concept 'woman' must refer to something *other* than biological sex, because transwomen are, by definition, not female. Given that UK law defines 'woman' as 'a female of any age' (Equality Act 2010, s.212), this constitutes a radical redefinition of the concept. Over the last two decades the trans rights movement has effectively disseminated this redefinition throughout public institutions in the Anglophone world and beyond through a process of 'policy capture' (Murray and Blackburn 2019). The impact of this has been a systematic replacement of biological sex designations with gender identity categories in law, language, public policy, data collection and the organisation of public space, subjects dealt with by other chapters in this volume. I have called this process 'the political erasure of sex' (Jones and Mackenzie 2020).

The aim of this chapter is to examine the intellectual development and cogency of the sex-denialist ideas that have underpinned this process of political erasure. In the discussion that follows, I distinguish between sex (biological and immutable), gender (roles and behaviours that are socially and politically constructed) and gender identity (the notion that each human has an innate sense of their own gender).

The thought that 'gender identity trumps sex' rests on two core beliefs. The first, which we shall call 'gender-identity essentialism,' is that humans have an innate 'gender identity': an internal sense of whether they are a man or a woman, which is not determined by their sex and may not be aligned with it. Gender-identity essentialism relies on analogy with the generally accepted innateness of homosexuality, and much of the success of trans rights discourse depends on the intuitive appeal of the idea that people should be free to express their innate 'authentic' selves. For example, the strapline for the lobby group Stonewall (2022) reads, 'We imagine a world where all LGBTQ+ people are free to be ourselves.' While in many ways this is a laudable sentiment, it needs to be underlined that, with respect to contemporary transgender identity, 'being yourself' implies a claim about the pre-eminence of gender identification over one's sex.

The second belief that underpins the trans-ideological conviction that gender identity should trump sex can be understood as 'sex denial,' that is, the effort to persuade people that biological sex is not a meaningful material phenomenon, and that the categories of 'male' and 'female' are social or historical constructs. This chapter focuses on examining the development of these sex-denialist arguments and subjecting them to interrogation and critique. The first section outlines three of the most common arguments used by gender identity advocates to undermine the material reality of sex and trace the intellectual history of these arguments. The second section examines whether these arguments stand up to scrutiny and elaborates a critique of sex denial from my perspective as a radical materialist feminist.

Sex-Denialist Arguments

Sex denial attempts to demonstrate that the natural phenomenon of biological sex is actually a cultural construct that serves the interests of 'power.' In this respect, trans-ideological sex denial apparently conforms to the classical critique of ideology, which may account for why it resonates with many academics and people who consider themselves 'progressives.' The classical Marxist critique is that 'ideology' presents socially constructed phenomena as if they are 'natural' or 'God-given' and, hence, propagates the idea that they cannot be changed. This idea influenced many twentieth-century rights movements, including the second-wave feminist critique of 'biological determinism,' that is, that 'masculine' and 'feminine' gender roles do not arise 'naturally' from biological sex but are, rather, social constructs which serve male interests in exploiting women's bodies and labour (see Todd, this volume).

Tracing a genealogy of concepts is a method deployed to demonstrate that a purportedly natural phenomenon is actually historically constructed. *Genealogy* is a significant term because much contemporary sex denial has been influenced by Michel Foucault's (1978) claim that 'the notion of 'sex' functions to 'group together' in a 'fictitious unity' a variety of disparate phenomena, including 'anatomical elements, biological functions, conducts, sensations and pleasures' (154). Foucault's (1994) genealogical method emphasised 'the complex course of descent' of concepts and suggested that they do not express a fundamental empirical reality but arise, rather, from historical 'accidents' (374). According to Judith Butler (1990) – Foucault's most influential heir – Foucauldian genealogy undermines the 'naturalness' of our sex and gender concepts and works to 'expose the foundational categories of sex, gender, and desire as effects of a specific formation of power' (xxxi). This is the vein in which the British sociologist Sally Hines has recently argued that sex and gender categories should be 'historicised.' Hines (2020) draws on Foucault's work on 'how bodies come into being through historical processes' (704), anthropological studies indicating 'great historical divergence' in the understanding of 'male' and 'female' (700), and third-gender cultures to ground the claim that 'rather than biology, it is social, cultural, political and economic factors that bring into being distinct ways of understanding sex, gender, and their relationship' (701).

There are two observations to be made about arguments such as that made by Hines. First, while trans ideology often appeals to Foucault to buttress the claim that 'sex' is a historical artefact, it does not apply Foucault's relativising historicism to its own discourse. Hines (2020) observes that 'the heart of the current debates' between transactivists and gender-critical feminists lies in 'divergent understandings of the ontology of the categories of 'sex' and 'gender'' (700). However, she clearly does not consider her ontology to be just one possibility among others and implicates her 'conservative' opponents in 'transgender moral panics' (Hines 2020, 699) and 'bigotry' (Hines 2019). This belief in a 'right' vs 'wrong' ontology is untenable from a strict Foucauldian perspective that would deny any empirical reality one might be right or wrong about. It is, moreover, ironic that by demonising critics, gender identity advocates are propagating a Foucauldian 'regulatory regime' that functions to discipline thought towards one normatively approved conclusion.

There is also a second Foucauldian paradox in the relation between the 'gender identity essentialist' and 'sex denialist' aspects of contemporary trans ideology. In direct contradiction to the Foucauldian thought that concepts are historically arbitrary artefacts of power, gender-identity essentialism makes grand claims about the universal and timeless nature of trans identity. Trans ideology's selective application of Foucauldian historicism is therefore a politically strategic gesture. The claim is not that there is no underlying reality at all but, rather, that there is no empirical reality to sex, while gender identity is real, innate and 'has always existed.' The chapters in this volume suggest that this is precisely the reverse of the case: that sex is an empirical reality, while gender identity is a recent historical concept. Sex denial itself is also a recent historical phenomenon. This chapter traces the intellectual genealogy of sex denial to demonstrate how, over the last half century, the concept of sex has been constructed as historical. We examine three main sex-denialist arguments: that 'sex is a spectrum,' that 'gender constructs sex,' and that 'colonialism created the gender binary.'

Sex-is-a-spectrum arguments first developed in the context of transgender legal activism in the early 1990s. In August 1992, transwoman, lawyer, and tech-entrepreneur Martine Rothblatt delivered an address at the first annual meeting of the International Conference on Transgender Law and Employment Policy (ICTLEP) in Houston, Texas. The function of the address was to outline the 'emerging paradigm' of transgender health law, which should aim, Rothblatt (1992) argued, 'to redefine sex itself as a continuum of lifestyle behaviors' (246). By 'lifestyle behaviour,' Rothblatt meant '[g]ender,' or the 'classification . . . into masculine and feminine based . . . on role-playing behaviour' (252), and was hence claiming 'sex' should be legally redefined as gender roles. However, another part of Rothblatt's speech proposed a different conception of sex, suggesting it be redefined as a 'continuum of male and female anatomical . . . and biological characteristics' (263), a formulation which approached the claim that biological sex itself is a 'continuum.'

This is exactly the claim made a year later in Anne Fausto-Sterling's 'The Five Sexes' (1993), a widely recognised source of the now common trans-ideological assertion that sex is a spectrum. Fausto-Sterling suggested that 'the intersexual body' means that 'biologically speaking, there are many gradations running from female to male' and that 'sex is a vast, infinitely malleable continuum' (21). Later that year, at ICTLEP's second annual meeting, Rothblatt (1993) explicitly cited Fausto-Sterling's notion of an 'infinitely malleable continuum' (A5–5). The following year, Rothblatt (1994) asserted that 'science is really coming to the conclusion that there is no natural dividing line between the sexes,' that the distinction between male and female is rather just 'a continuum of different possibilities,' and that as such, there is 'no logical, no objective . . . reason for labelling people as either male or female' (110).

This claim was quickly picked up in academic literature. In 1996, drawing on both Rothblatt and Fausto-Sterling, Ruth Hubbard suggested that 'sex differences are not all that clear-cut' and questioned the 'binary paradigm that, biologically speaking, there are only . . . two sexes' (158). In 2002, Stephen Whittle noted that 'medicine recognises an ever-growing number of intersex syndromes' (10) and that 'individuals are now scientifically regarded as living on a continuum, with female characteristics at one extreme and male at the other' (7). Over the last decade, the idea that sex is a spectrum has been commonly asserted in more popular publications, especially following Claire Ainsworth's 2015 article 'Sex Redefined' in the journal *Nature*. A write-up of Ainsworth's article in *The Guardian* noted that 'rather than being simply male or female . . . all of us exist across several spectrums of sexual identity.' According to the article's author, Vanessa Heggie (2015), no test of any dimension of sex will yield a "male or female' binary answer,' and '[r]esults will always depend on . . . arbitrary cut-off points.' This particular genealogy offers some insight into how sex-denialist arguments developed from political lobbying into academic thought and then influenced public discourse.

Heggie's article is a good illustration of how 'sex is a spectrum' arguments work by suggesting there are no differences in *kind* between males and females and that such differences are merely quantitative differences of *degree*. It then seems to follow that any line drawn on the 'continuum' between male and female is simply 'arbitrary.' From here, it is a short walk to the thought that this 'arbitrary' line is simply 'socially constructed' or produced by systems of 'power.' In the opening chapter of *Sexing the*

Body, Fausto-Sterling (2000a) argued that because the reality of 'the body's sex is simply too complex,' with too many 'shades of difference' to be made 'either/or,' it follows that 'labelling someone a man or a woman is a social decision' (3).

One prominent version of this 'social decision' claim suggests that it is the registration of sex at birth that creates a system of two sexes, which exists only in the interests of power. In 1995, Rothblatt claimed that 'a rigid apartheid of sex' is created by 'the law . . . starting with the birth certificate' (37) while Fausto-Sterling (1993) has argued that although it is 'in defiance of nature' sex registration is required by 'modern Anglo-Saxon legal systems' to determine questions of 'inheritance, legitimacy, paternity' (23). In 1998, Christine Burns – a key activist for the UK trans lobby group Press for Change – called for the total elimination of birth sex registration, arguing that the 'fourth column of the British birth certificate is the root of the most enduring and entrenched systems [*sic*] of discrimination in modern society,' In 2017, the Yogyakarta Principles Plus 10 – often held up as international human rights 'best practice' regarding sexual orientation and gender identity (SOGI, and see Auchmuty and Freedman, this volume) – encoded this by calling to 'end the registration of the sex and gender of the person in . . . birth certificates, identification cards, passports and driver licences' (Principle 31).

Closely related to sex-is-a-spectrum arguments that deny there is a clear 'dividing line' between the sexes are those that look at variation *within* the categories of male and female. They suggest that because there is no 'essential' defining characteristic shared by *every single member* of the category, then the categories are arbitrary or socially constructed. The most common form of this argument relies on the fact that some humans are infertile to claim that sex cannot refer to reproductive capacity (Rothblatt 1995, 36; Whittle [1999] 2002, 5). Recently, Sally Hines (2020) has argued that because 'some men are born without testicles and some women without a uterus; some men do not produce sperm as some women do not produce eggs,' there can be no 'essential' criteria which define sex, and it is therefore historically constructed (708).

The second group of sex-denialist arguments are based on this thought that ideas about sex are 'arbitrarily' created by 'power,' centring on the claim that it is gender norms that *construct* sex. One of the earliest sources of this argument is Suzanne J Kessler and Wendy McKenna's (1978) *Gender: An Ethnomethodological Approach*. Their work asserted that gender *produces* 'a world of two "sexes"' (vii) over a decade before Judith Butler (1990) made the same claim in her more renowned work *Gender Trouble*. Kessler and McKenna (1978) argue that the identification of sex in humans results from the 'gender attribution process.' They note that 'the natural attitude' of most people is that 'genitals are the essential insignia of gender' (154) but that decisions about whether someone is a man or a woman cannot rely on genitals, because they cannot usually be seen. Instead, they suggest, we attribute what they call 'cultural genitals,' which are those that are 'assumed to exist' (154). They dismiss the idea that this is a usually accurate inference made on the basis of secondary sexual characteristics, because humans are 'far from being dichotomous, at least when compared to those markers in other species (e.g., plumage in birds)' (155–156). What is happening, Kessler and McKenna suggest, is that we decide whether someone is a man or a woman on the basis of 'the socially constructed signs of gender,' including 'dress and accessories, and nonverbal and paralinguistic clues' (157). We are not, therefore, observing biological sex but rather socially constructed gender.

Another set of arguments that gender constructs sex relies on the treatment of infants with differences of sexual development (DSDs) – often previously referred to as 'intersex' conditions (see Hilton and Wright, this volume). In 'The Medical Construction of Gender,' Kessler (1990) discusses the process of surgical intervention on infants with ambiguous genitalia – now often referred to as 'infant genital mutilation.' Kessler claims that the 'very idea of gender' resides in thinking 'it consists of two exclusive types: female and male' (25) and that the process of surgically 'assigning' a sex to infants 'reveal the model for the social construction of gender generally' (4). In *Sexing the Body*, Fausto-Sterling (2000a) echoed Kessler, characterising sex assignment in infants with DSDs as a 'literal tale' of the 'social construction . . . of a two-party system of sex' (32). By this time, Fausto-Sterling was blending her 'sex is a spectrum' arguments with probably the most influential argument that 'gender constructs sex': Judith Butler's (1990) claim in *Gender Trouble* that 'sex' is *produced* by the 'regulatory regime' of heteronormative gender. Fausto-Sterling's (2000a) appeal to the alleged empirical reality of sex as a spectrum is, in fact, incompatible with *Gender Trouble*'s thoroughgoing constructivism. But she nonetheless approvingly nodded towards Butler's thought that 'bodily materiality' is 'constructed through a 'gendered matrix"' (22).

The central claim of *Gender Trouble* is that the 'very binary frame for thinking about gender' (Butler 1990, xxx) *constructs* 'ideal dimorphism, heterosexual complementarity of bodies' and 'ideals . . . of proper . . . masculinity and femininity' (xxiv–xxv). For Butler, gender is not only a social system which ascribes 'masculinity' and 'femininity' to certain sexed bodies but is *also* the assumption that there are two 'ideal' sets of bodies. This assumption is informed, Butler thinks, by a 'gendered' or 'heteronormative matrix' which then *produces* the belief in sex-as-dichotomous, an argument that *subsumes sex under gender* in the thought now commonly denoted as 'the gender binary.' As Butler (2000a) writes, the 'institution of . . . naturalised heterosexuality requires . . . gender as a binary relation' (31), and 'the categories of female and male, woman and man, are similarly produced within the binary frame' (32).

For Butler (2000a), therefore, 'the immutable character of sex' should be 'contested,' and we should ask whether 'this construct called "sex"' is as culturally constructed as gender; indeed, perhaps it was always already gender with the consequence that the distinction between sex and gender turns out to be no distinction at all' (9–10). While Butler is the thinker most often cited as providing an intellectual foundation to trans ideology, it is notable that neither Fausto-Sterling nor Rothblatt reference Butler in their earliest formulations of sex-denialist arguments. It was only in the mid-1990s that Fausto-Sterling and Butler started being linked by other scholars keen to promote the idea that sex is not a material reality and that the 'bipolar' categories of male and female should be understood as 'the effect of . . . compulsory heterosexuality,' or of gendered norms (Bem 1995, 59).

The third group of sex-denialist arguments also relies on the idea that sex is constructed by 'power' and aims to show that 'the gender binary' was created by colonialism. As we just saw, the gender binary is a concept which evolved out of Butler's thought that gender constructs sex. As such, it conflates sex with gender and suggests that the perception of human sexual difference is *created* by the existence of binary gender roles. The first version of the argument about colonialism's role in the construction of sex originated in Leslie Feinberg's (1992) political pamphlet *Transgender Liberation*. Feinberg's analysis centred on her discovery that Native American cultures recognised 'Two-Spirit' people and honoured a type of 'sex/gender' diversity which was destroyed by European colonisation. Feinberg was working at the same time as Rothblatt and Fausto-Sterling and acknowledged their support in her 1996 book *Transgender Warriors*.

Another important source of this argument is Maria Lugones's (2007) 'Heterosexualism and the Colonial/Modern Gender System,' which claims that 'naturalising . . . sexual difference' was a product of the system that she calls the 'coloniality of power' (195). Lugones's account uses important scholarship which details how Western patriarchal gender systems were imposed on indigenous communities in the course of colonisation. However, her suggestion that this involved the imposition of 'sexual dimorphism' depends on subsuming sex under gender using the Butlerian thought of the gender binary. We also see an example of this in another recent article examining the 'imposition of binary *sex/gender* as part of the European colonialist project' (Costello 2020, emphasis added). While 'third gender' cultures evidently exist, there is no evidence that such societies do not understand that humans are divided into two sexes (Joyce 2021, 63). Such a reading is produced by imposing a contemporary notion of trans identity – and its idea that gender constructs sex – onto other cultures and other histories. It is therefore ahistorical and culturally imperialist.

A Radical Materialist Feminist Critique of Sex Denial

The critiques outlined here are informed by my perspective as a radical materialist feminist. Radical materialist feminism synthesises a materialist analysis of women's exploitation with a radical feminist analysis of the cultural, psychological and ontological infrastructure of male dominance. Patriarchy is understood here as a system of sex-based oppression, in which male people *as a class* benefit from the exploitation of the bodies and labour of female people *as a class*. According to radical materialist feminism, patriarchy is a socio-cultural system which developed historically in the course of the transition to agrarian societies and functions by converting both the bodies and labour of women into an exploitable resource. Women's oppression is firstly based on their reproductive capacities, because it is these capacities that mean they can be turned into a reproductive resource. Women's oppression is not, however, biologically *determined* by these capacities, because the socio-cultural system which treats women as an appropriable resource is a historical development and is, therefore, contingent rather than necessary. In the effort to escape the spectre of biological determinism, it is therefore misguided to assert that women's oppression is unrelated to the fact that women are female (Jones 2021).

My radical materialist analysis of the cultural, psychological and ontological infrastructure of male dominance is derived from a synthesis of radical feminism and ecofeminism, with French psychoanalytic and deconstructive feminism. Patriarchal gender is a system which maintains male dominance, and functions by positing a default male subject, while the image of 'Woman as Other' is created by male projection, in a manner that serves male interests. The male default subject allocates to himself all the characteristics he considers 'properly' human, while the gendered projection of Woman as Other is constructed, by negation, from his perspective. Patriarchal masculinity is hence associated with mind/reason/idea/culture, while the devalued characteristics of body/emotion/matter/nature are allocated to the feminine. This hierarchical devaluation is a crucial part of the cultural apparatus which facilitates the erasure, and appropriation, of the bodies of women and the historically associated exploitation of the earth. According to Luce Irigaray, and many ecofeminist thinkers, positioning Woman as Other is hence interlaced with a system of philosophical thinking which privileges mind over body, idea over matter, and culture over nature.

This kind of philosophical idealism is most significantly outlined in the Platonic Theory of Forms, which still influences many people's everyday assumptions about how concepts work. Platonic essentialist accounts of meaning propose that concepts depend on absolute similarities and absolute differences. It posits that members of a particular category must *all* share exactly the same 'essential' defining characteristics and must be absolutely differentiated from members of other categories. While sex-denialist arguments often style themselves as 'anti-essentialist,' they nonetheless assume that concepts *must* work on the basis of perfectly identical essences and that, hence, by reversal, anomalies or edge cases prove that a concept does not refer to any empirical reality and is an 'arbitrary' artefact of power. This effectively issues in an idealist belief that human categorisation makes the world materialise. The fact is, however, that you can play as many definitional games with the concepts of 'male' and 'female' as you like – male and female organisms will carry on existing, regardless. The subjugation of material reality to the imperious sovereignty of human concepts is, from a radical materialist perspective, simply an expression of the structure of patriarchal dominance: a manifestation of idealist ontological assumptions which facilitate the subjugation and appropriation of matter and earth and the exploitation of the bodies and reproductive capacities of women.

With this in mind, we now turn to critiquing the various sex-denialist arguments we have encountered so far. As we have seen, sex-is-a-spectrum arguments work by instrumentalising people with 'intersex' conditions to posit sex as a continuum which is only arbitrarily divided into the discrete categories of male and female. It is often supported by overinflated claims about the incidence of DSDs, which Fausto-Sterling (1993, 21) first estimated to be as high as 4 percent, a figure later revised to 1.7 percent (Blackless et al. 2000), and then to 0.4 percent (Hull and Fausto-Sterling 2003). As Hilton and Wright discuss in this volume, the incidence of DSDs has been estimated to be as low as 0.018 percent by Leonard Sax (2002). Hull (2005) has attributed Fausto-Sterling's over-inflation of the incidence of DSDs to a 'philosophy' that is 'too deeply invested in uncovering high rates of sexual nondimorphism' (68).

Fausto-Sterling (2000b) is invested in this 'uncovering' because she takes herself to be battling against 'the idealised, Platonic, biological world,' in which 'human beings are divided into two kinds: a perfectly dimorphic species' (19–20). This reveals the Platonic assumptions underpinning sex-denialist thought. Fausto-Sterling thinks she is refuting Platonism, but her argument depends on the assumption that meaningful empirical differences between 'two kinds' must manifest with absolutely 'perfect' regularity. Sex-denialist literature is littered with claims like 'the physical distinction between men and women is not absolute' (Whittle [1999] 2002, 7) or we cannot 'draw a hard line between the sexes' (Hines 2020, 709). This flies in the face of the fact that most empirical phenomena exhibit edge cases. We cannot 'draw a perfect line' between, say, day and night or hot and cold, but we do not therefore conclude there is no meaningful distinction between them or they were created by power. Empirical phenomena are usually fuzzy, and human concepts work perfectly well with fuzzy edges all the time.

It is not, moreover, the case that, as Whittle ([1999] 2002) argued, human sex is 'a continuum, with female characteristics at one extreme and male at the other' (7). A situation with more than 99 percent of people at either 'extreme' and only a tiny number of ambiguous cases is not 'a spectrum.' It's a dichotomous physical difference with a small number of irregularities caused by the fact that sex is the outcome of a complex developmental pathway. Furthermore, while the outcome of these developmental pathways may show a tiny degree of irregularity, human sexual development has only two pathways, which evolved to produce an organism capable of fulfilling one of two reproductive functions. The difference between ovaries and testes is not a quantitative matter of degree but a qualitative difference in kind, and each structure evolved to produce one of the two types of gametes necessary for fertilisation throughout the plant and animal kingdoms (Hilton and Wright, 2020).

It is important to emphasise here that the concept of sex denotes 'the two main categories (male and female) into which . . . many . . . living things are divided on the basis of their *reproductive functions*' (*Oxford English Dictionary*; my emphasis). The distinction in humans between the 'can produce sperm and inseminate' function, and the 'can produce eggs and get pregnant' function is not a difference in degree. Sex denotes reproductive function, and reproductive function is a *difference in kind*. Human sexual morphology evolved to fulfil particular reproductive functions, and the fact some people with a particular morphology can't fulfil that function due to developmental anomalies, illnesses, or accidents does not mean they cease to be a member of the category or cannot be identified (Bogardus, 2022). Moreover, individuals who exhibit ambiguity in sexual characteristics are not capable of performing some third or fourth type of reproductive function because *there are only two possibilities*. That is, there are not 'more than two sexes.'

As we have seen, some sex-denialist arguments use human infertility to claim 'sex' does not denote reproductive function. This argument is again dependent on a Platonic essentialism which holds that every single member of a category must exhibit *all* the essential defining characteristics of that category and thinks, by reversal, that anomalies fatally undermine the category or can't be categorised. This is manifestly untrue. An albino zebra doesn't stop being a zebra. A mug with a broken handle is still identifiable as a mug. The fact humans are bipedal does not become untrue because some humans lose a leg, and one-legged humans are still human. This type of mistake is caused by confusing *post hoc* definitions and *theories* about how we categorise, with both the existence of things in themselves, and how we actually categorise. Humans are remarkably good at categorisation and remarkably bad at explaining how we do it, but it is evidently far more complicated than a simple Platonic story about perfect distinctions and 'essential' defining properties, because otherwise, we couldn't identify anomalous members of categories, which we do, with great facility, all the time.

The various arguments that gender constructs sex we've encountered all conflate dichotomous sexual differences and gendered social norms under the thought of the gender binary. These arguments depend on effacing the material differences between males and females and subsuming them under social norms by denying that humans can cognise sex independently of 'that very binary frame for thinking about gender' (Butler 1990, xxx). The starkest illustration here is Kessler and McKenna's (1978) facile dismissal of the human ability to sex other humans to a high degree of reliability on the basis of our secondary sexual characteristics, because humans are not as sexually dimorphic as, say, peacocks. The suggestion that we should be the one animal incapable of sexing other members of our species without relying on cultural cues is an absurd denial of our biological evolution and a politically suspect form of human exceptionalism. Moreover, the fact we are animals who have developed surgical techniques, and dubiously used them to 'assign' sex to infants with ambiguous genitalia, is not, as Fausto-Sterling (2000a) claims, a 'literal tale' of the 'social construction' of *all* sex designation. As we saw earlier, the vast majority of human infants are unambiguously male or female. In such cases, sex is inferred, perfectly correctly, from observation of genitalia and then recorded.

Butler's (1990) argument fundamentally depends on conflating sex and gender and, following Foucault, is grounded on the *assumption* that the concept of sex includes within it 'sex, gender,' *and* 'desire' (xxxi). It is true that patriarchal Western culture has normatively assumed only two gender roles, which follow 'naturally' from sex and conform to one of the two roles in heterosexual pairing. It does not follow from this, however, that the concept of sex inherently contains patriarchal and heteronormative gender assumptions or that such assumptions are biologically determined by the existence or cognition of sex. There is evidently a liminal zone of interaction between sex and gender, but they are, nonetheless, analytically different concepts. While it is eminently reasonable to talk about the construction of gender roles and their relation to sexuality, it is far less reasonable to maintain, as Butler does, that the regularity of human sexual difference is 'as constructed' as gender. Indeed, in *Gender Trouble*, Butler (1990) gives no coherent argument for this claim. She grounds her analysis in Foucault's conflation of biology, behaviour and sexuality and on that basis wonders whether sex was 'always already gender,' and hence, 'the distinction . . . turns out to be no distinction at all' (9–10).

This is rhetoric masquerading as a philosophical demonstration (a common Butlerian technique) and is manifestly circular. If you start by assuming that the concept of sex contains the concept of gender, then you have not, in fact, *demonstrated* that there is no distinction between them. In *Bodies That Matter*, Butler (1993) tries to justify her elision of the materiality of the body using the type of Platonic argument we've already discussed, which suggests that meaningful empirical difference demands absolutely clear delineation. The 'moderate critic might concede,' she writes, 'that some part of 'sex' is constructed, but some other is certainly not, and then, of course, find . . . herself . . . under some obligation to draw the line between what is and is not constructed' (Butler 1993, 11). This claim again depends on the thought that liminality confounds the possibility of meaningful difference. As with the difference between males and females, my contention is that it does not (cf. Jones 2018).

While it has been woven into trans-ideological sex denial, Butler's conflation of sex and gender emerged originally in the context of feminist debates about how to understand the relation *between* these key concepts. Starting in the 1980s, feminists became increasingly divided about the sex/gender distinction, with some socialist feminists concerned that radical feminist accounts of patriarchy as sex-based oppression were 'ahistorical' and biologically determinist (see Todd, this volume). This concern was echoed by post-structural feminists like Joan Scott (1986), whose influential 'Gender: A Useful Category of Historical Analysis' dismissed the view that patriarchy arises from 'male appropriation of . . . reproductive labour' because it 'rests on the single variable of physical difference' (34). To Scott's mind, sex-based analysis assumed the 'ahistoricity of gender itself' and could not account for its 'social or cultural construction' (34).

This fundamentally misunderstands that patriarchal gender is a system of norms and cultural values which developed to enable men to appropriate women as a reproductive and sexual resource. That is, gender is a *historical* mechanism of resource extraction. This mechanism does not arise by *necessity* from the existence of the resource, any more than the international oil trade arises by necessity from the existence of oil. That does not mean, however, that the motive for appropriating a resource is unrelated to its material properties. Males want to control women's bodies because women are female, and females have the reproductive capacities males *need* to produce offspring. Patriarchal gender is the mechanism that developed *historically* to enable men to control that resource (Jones 2021).

This seems entirely lost on Foucauldian feminists, who assume that if sex is related to gender, then it must normatively determine it. In *Sex, Gender and the Body*, Toril Moi (2005) analyses a 1993 interview in which Butler argues that claims about the 'materiality of the body' necessarily involve 'a discursive enforcement of a norm' about 'the social institution of reproduction' (41). Moi notes that Butler apparently believes that if one understands 'sexual difference' as defined by 'the potential reproductive function of the body' one 'must be caught up in repressive sexist ideology' (41), a determinist assumption also shared by the view that believing 'there were only two sexes . . . must be heterosexist' (38). This type of assumption is also expressed in the common transactivist claim that anyone who believes women are female is guilty of 'bioessentialism' and must think only female people can behave in 'feminine' ways. What seems to be going on here is confusion between the *philosophical* idea that human categories work by Platonic 'essence' (which is false), with the *feminist* use of 'essentialism' to mean 'biological determinism.' As Moi writes: 'Because they think that to speak about biological facts is . . . to speak about essences . . . many poststructuralists believe that . . . to avoid biological determinism one has to be a philosophical nominalist,' which is 'obviously absurd' (43). There is, she notes, 'no good reason to assume' that anyone asserting the material reality of sex is 'being essentialist in the bad . . . political sense' (36). Indeed, 'to avoid biological determinism all we need to do is to deny that biological facts justify social values' (43).

However, because Foucauldian feminists assume that facts about biological sex will necessarily create gendered social norms, they have concluded that the only way to avoid biological determinism is to deny there are biological facts at all and subsume those facts under the social construct of gender. This reasoning is legible throughout sex-denialist literature, which is often extremely explicit that its aim is erasing gendered social conventions and hierarchies. As Kessler and McKenna (1978) write, 'once a physical dichotomy has been constructed it is almost impossible to eliminate sociological and psychological dichotomies' (164). They continue, in a passage worth quoting at length:

> As long as the categories female and male present themselves to people in everyday life as external, objective, dichotomous, physical facts, there will be scientific and naive searches for differences and differences will be found. Where there are dichotomies it is difficult to avoid evaluating one in relation to the other, a firm foundation for discrimination and oppression. Unless and until gender, in all of its manifestations *including the physical*, is seen as a social construction, action that will radically change our incorrigible propositions cannot occur. (164, emphasis in the original)

'Incorrigible propositions' is ethnomethodological jargon for certain basic assumptions or 'unquestionable axioms' (4) about the world, the most basic of which,

Kessler and McKenna tell us, is 'the belief that the world exists independently of our presence, and that objects have an independent reality and a constant identity' (4). This is a startling admission of the extent to which sex denial is grounded on an idealist dismissal of a material world beyond our own cognition. While this is an untenable form of narcissistic solipsism, there is something extremely seductive about such forms of radical constructivism. First, they strike some as unfathomably sophisticated as opposed to the purportedly 'naïve' or 'simplistic' belief that our concepts are grasping real phenomena (to some degree or other). Second, they seem to offer the possibility of social change entirely controlled by human mastery and ideals and unconstrained by any natural or material limits.

Fausto-Sterling (2000a), for one, is clear that her commitment to 'challenging ideas about the male/female divide' (79) is driven by a vision of 'a world in which sexes have multiplied' and 'all those oppositions . . . would have to be dissolved as sources of division' (1993, 24). Similarly, Rothblatt's (1992) 'genderpioneers' will free us from 'the pernicious fiction of separate male and female classes . . . with associated separate gender roles . . . which has been especially unfair to women since time immemorial' (268). Butler dedicates the 1999 preface of *Gender Trouble* to the 'collective struggle' of 'increasing the possibilities for a liveable life for those . . . on the sexual margins' (xxviii), a clear indication that her concern in *Gender Trouble* is not women's oppression. There is absolutely nothing wrong with this *per se* – everyone is entitled to be concerned with political causes that matter most to them. The problem here is that Butler's intervention is probably the defining text of third-wave feminism and has generated massive normative censure of the materialist analysis of women's oppression *within* feminism.

Indeed, there are totalitarian implications of all this utopian imagining. For if sex denial is the one true path to freeing us from oppressive hierarchies, then anyone asserting the material reality of sex could only be motivated by the desire to enforce such oppression. In 'progressive' circles, this has contributed to the disciplinary frame used to justify the widespread vilification of gender-critical feminists, who are, without evidence, often indicted for being 'privileged' agents of the status quo. What most gender-identity activists will not grant is that there are decent, justice-minded people who simply think sex denial is wrong, believe the material world exists and can be cognised to a high degree of reliability, and consider effective political intervention should be based on how the world actually works rather than on wish fulfilment. What will also never be recognised is that many feminists are genuinely committed to a materialist analysis of women's oppression and are unwilling to abandon that analysis for an account that does not stand up to either common sense or logical scrutiny, has no ability to explain *why* gender exists in the first place, and demands we all believe patriarchal oppression will simply evaporate if we pretend sex isn't real. Indeed, I would argue that the fact that gender-identity ideology cannot withstand interrogation is, moreover, heavily implicated in why its advocates are so fond of vilifying and censuring their critics.

The last set of sex-denialist arguments we encountered are those that claim that the gender binary was created by the process of European colonisation. As we've seen, the thought of the gender binary developed out of Butlerian arguments that gender constructs sex and conflates the perception of human sexual difference with the 'binary' structure of patriarchal gender. This conflation is a necessary part of these arguments, because, while it is more than plausible to suggest that Western patriarchal conventions changed gender roles, the acceptance of homosexuality, and the social structures around gender non-conformity, there is no basis for asserting that Native Americans, or any other third gender cultures, did not understand biological sexual differences. Indeed, many people might think it historically myopic, and an artefact of racialised hierarchy between the 'civilised' and the 'primitive,' to suggest that colonised peoples couldn't accurately sex humans and didn't understand the mechanics of sexual reproduction until white people arrived.

The motive for this argument, I'd argue, is partly explicable by the disciplinary structure of trans ideology. Convincing people that humans are not sexed is actually quite a hard sell. If you can persuade people that 'sex' is an artefact of colonial white supremacy and is thus inherently racist, you strengthen the appeal of your argument to people who see themselves as progressives. This is also how 'colonialism invented the gender binary' comes to circulate in trans-ideological discourse in concert with the suggestion that understanding the reality of biological sex is characteristic of 'white feminism' (e.g. see Upadhyay 2021). This claim is made despite the fact that there are many black women who also reject sex denial, from high-profile figures like Chimamanda Adiche to notable gender-critical activists such as Allison Bailey or Raquel Rosario Sánchez. Nor do such narratives take into account the fact that bell hooks' (1984) original critique of 'white feminism' was focused on liberal feminist capitulations to capitalist patriarchy and had nothing whatsoever to do with the human ability to recognise sex.

These arguments also relate to the deliberate misconstrual of the black feminist thinking of 'intersectionality,' which rightly highlighted how feminism privileges the experience of white middle-class women as universal when it does not attend to the axes of race and class. This has now been interpreted to mean that the very concept of 'woman' denotes only 'white bourgeois femininity' (another sex/gender conflation) and that black women have been historically excluded from the class of women. This then buttresses the claim that if black women are women, then so, too, are transwomen. While posing as anti-racism, a claim that comes down to 'if black women are women, then males are women' invokes the historic masculinisation of black women and is, in fact, racist. Patriarchal white supremacists may have coded black women as insufficiently 'feminine' to be considered women, but there is no earthly reason to collude with their logic. Black women are female, and being female is the only qualification for being a woman. As Lugones points out, in the course of colonisation, ideas of gender were inextricably interlaced with racialised hierarchy. But 'women' are not 'white bourgeois femininity.' Defining them as such *repeats* a system of thinking that is racist, sexist, and classist.

Conclusion

Gender-identity ideology emerged during the early 1990s and depends on two belief complexes: 'gender identity essentialism' and 'sex denial.' As we have seen, sex denial is grounded in a series of arguments developed over the last half century which claim that sex is a spectrum, conflate sex and gender, and aim to posit the cognition of human sexual dimorphism as an oppressive historical artefact of power. We have explored the history of sex denial to understand how these arguments attempt to construct sex as historical and examined the ways they do not stand up to empirical or logical scrutiny. While contemporary sex denial therefore considers itself to be conforming to the traditional critique of ideology and 'unveiling' the way historical norms pose as 'natural,' I would argue that it is actually a distinctive reversal aimed at convincing people that a billions-of-years-old evolved biological mechanism is actually a recent historical invention, impelled by clear political motives.

Radical materialist feminists, by contrast, retain second-wave feminism's distinction between the material reality of sex and the cultural construction of gender. We argue that women's subjugation by the social norms and cultural values of patriarchal gender is a historical development which functions by converting women's reproductive capacities and domestic labour into an appropriable resource. Sex is not a historical artefact, although the way humans socially organise reproduction, and the wider work of reproductive labour is historically contingent and open to social transformation. Because radical materialist feminists believe women's oppression is grounded in the material appropriation of women's bodies and labour, we do not think it can be ameliorated by simply playing games with concepts or mandating the non-existence of sex. Rather, a more just world for women requires a material transformation of the *conditions* of women's reproductive and domestic labour. Sex denial hampers such transformation by undermining the concepts needed to describe women's oppression and politically organise to challenge it. It is not, therefore, in the material interests of women as a sex class.

References

Ainsworth, Claire. 2015. 'Sex Redefined.' *Nature* 518, pp. 288–291. https://doi.org/10.1038/518288a

Bem, Sandra Lipsitz. 1995. 'Dismantling Gender Polarization and Compulsory Heterosexuality: Should We Turn the Volume Down Or Up?' *Journal of Gender Studies* 17(2). Available at https://www.digitaltransgenderarchive.net/files/h702q645g

Blackless, Melanie, et al. 2000. 'How Sexually Dimorphic Are We?,' *American Journal of Human Biology*, Mar 12(2), pp.151–166. https://doi.org/10.1002/(SICI)1520-6300(200003/04)12:2<151::AID-AJHB1>3.0.CO;2-F

Bogardus, Tomas. 2022. 'How Our Shoes Can Help Explain the Biology of Sex.' *Reality's Last Stand*, August 9. https://www.realityslaststand.com/p/how-our-shoes-can-help-explain-the

Butler, Judith. 1990. *Gender Trouble: Feminism and the Subversion of Identity*. New York and London: Routledge Classics.

Butler, Judith. 1993. *Bodies that Matter: On the Discursive Limits of 'Sex.'* New York and London: Routledge.
Burns, Christine. 1998. 'Fourth Column Revolutionary.' *Press for Change Blog*, January 10. Available at https://www.webarchive.org.uk/wayback/archive/20060124120000/http://www.pfc.org.uk/gendrpol/4th-col.htm
Costello, Cary Gabriel. 2020. 'Beyond Binary Sex and Gender Ideology.' In *The Oxford Handbook of the Sociology of Body and Embodiment*, edited by Natalie Boero and Katherine Mason, pp. 199–220. Oxford: Oxford University Press. Abstract available at https://www.oxfordhandbooks.com/view/10.1093/oxfordhb/9780190842475.001.0001/oxfordhb-9780190842475-e-14
Fausto-Sterling, Anne. 1993. 'The Five Sexes: Why Male and Female are Not Enough.' *The Sciences,* March/April, 33(2), pp. 20–24.
Fausto-Sterling, Anne. 2000a. *Sexing the Body: Gender Politics and the Construction of Sexuality*. New York: Perseus Books.
Fausto-Sterling, Anne. 2000b. 'The Five Sexes Revisited.' *The Sciences,* July/August, 40(4), pp. 18–23.
Feinberg, Leslie. 1992. *Transgender Liberation: A Movement Whose Time Has Come*. New York: World View Forum
Feinberg, Leslie. 1996. *Transgender Warriors: Making History from Joan of Arc to Dennis Rodman*. Boston: Beacon Press.
Foucault, Michel. 1978. *The History of Sexuality, Volume 1*. New York: Pantheon Books.
Foucault, Michel. 1994. 'Nietzsche, Genealogy, History.' In *Aesthetics, Method, and Epistemology: Essential Works of Foucault 1954–1984*, pp. 369–391. London: Penguin Classics.
Heggie, Vanessa. 2015. 'Nature and Sex Redefined – We Have Never Been Binary.' *The Guardian*, 19 February. Available at https://www.theguardian.com/science/the-h-word/2015/feb/19/nature-sex-redefined-we-have-never-been-binary
Hilton Emma N., and Colin M. Wright. 2020. 'The Dangerous Denial of Sex.' *Wall Street Journal*, February 13. Available at https://www.wsj.com/articles/the-dangerous-denial-of-sex-11581638089
Hines, Sally. 2019. "Spoiler: So to conclude, . . .' Twitter, April 2. https://twitter.com/sally_hines/status/1113072399304527872?s=20
Hines, Sally. 2020. 'Sex Wars and (Trans) Gender Panics: Identity and Body Politics in Contemporary UK Feminism.' *The Sociological Review Monographs,* 68(4), pp. 699–717.
hooks, bell. 1984. *Feminist Theory: From Margin to Center*. Boston, MA: South End Press.
Hubbard, Ruth. 1996. 'Gender and Genitals: Constructs of Sex and Gender.' *Social Text* (46/47), pp. 157–165.
Hull, Carrie. 2005. *The Ontology of Sex*. London and New York: Routledge.
Hull, Carrie, and Fausto-Sterling, A., 2003. 'Response to: How Sexually Dimorphic Are We? Review and Synthesis.' *American Journal of Human Biology* 15(1), pp. 112–115.
Jones, Jane Clare. 2018. 'Post-structuralism, Butler and Bodies Part III: All that trouble with gender.' *Jane Clare Jones*, July 18. Available at www.janeclarejones.com/2018/07/18/part-3-all-that-trouble-with-gender/. Reprinted in Jane Clare Jones, *The Annals of the TERF-Wars and Other Writing*. 2022. Willingdon, East Sussex: Radical Notion Publishing.
Jones, Jane Clare. 2020. 'A Brief History of Transgender Ideology.' Appendix to *The Political Erasure of Sex*. University of Oxford and Woman's Place UK. Available at https://thepoliticalerasureofsex.org/
Jones, Jane Clare. 2021. 'Woman as Resource: Towards a Radical Materialist Feminism.' *The Radical Notion,* 3, pp. 4–12.

Jones, Jane Clare, and Lisa Mackenzie. 2020. *The Political Erasure of Sex: Sex and the Census*. University of Oxford and Woman's Place UK. Available at https://thepoliticalerasureofsex.org/

Joyce, Helen. 2021. *Trans: When Ideology Meets Reality*. London: Oneworld Books.

Kessler, Suzanne J. 1990. 'The Medical Construction of Gender: Case Management of Intersexed Infants.' *Signs* 16(1), pp. 3–26.

Kessler, Suzanne J and Wendy McKenna. 1978. *Gender: An Ethnomethodological Approach*. Chicago and London: The University of Chicago Press.

Lugones, Maria. 2007. 'Heterosexualism and the Colonial/Modern Gender System.' *Hypatia* 2(1), pp. 186–209.

Moi, Toril. 2005. *Sex, Gender and the Body: The Student Edition of 'What is a Woman?'* Oxford: Oxford University Press.

Murray, Kath and Lucy Hunter Blackburn. 2019. 'Losing Sight of Women's Rights: The Unregulated Introduction of Gender Self-Identification as a Case Study of Policy Capture in Scotland.' *Scottish Affairs*, 28(3), pp. 262–289. https://www.euppublishing.com/doi/full/10.3366/scot.2019.0284

Oxford English Dictionary. 1989. 'Woman.' Available online at https://www.oed.com/oed2/00286737

Rothblatt, Martine (as Marla Aspen). 1992. 'Report of the Health Law Committee.' In *Proceedings of the First International Conference on Transgender Law and Employment Policy*, pp. 245–275. Houston, TX: International Conference on Transgender Law and Employment Policy. Available at https://www.digitaltransgenderarchive.net/files/bc386j278

Rothblatt, Martine. 1993. 'Second Report on the Health Law Project.' In *Proceedings of the Second International Conference on Transgender Law and Employment Policy*, Appendix 5, pp. A5-1–A5-16. Houston, TX International Conference on Transgender Law and Employment Policy. Available at https://www.digitaltransgenderarchive.net/files/gq67jr234

Rothblatt, Martine. 1994. 'Your Heath Report Project.' In *Proceedings of the Third International Conference on Transgender Law and Employment Policy*, pp. 107–117. Houston, TX: International Conference on Transgender Law and Employment Policy. Available at https://www.digitaltransgenderarchive.net/files/kw52j810t

Rothblatt, Martine. 1995. 'The Apartheid of Sex' at 'Keynote Luncheon.' In *Proceedings of the Fourth International Conference on Transgender Law and Employment Policy*, pp. 33–41. Houston, TX: International Conference on Transgender Law and Employment Policy. Available at https://www.digitaltransgenderarchive.net/files/kw52j813n

Sax, Leonard. 2002. 'How Common Is Intersex? A Response to Anne Fausto-Sterling.' *Journal of Sex Research* 39(3), pp. 174–178. https://doi.org/10.1080/00224490209552139

Scott, Joan. (1986) 1988. 'Gender: A Useful Category of Historical Analysis' [reprint]. In *Gender and the Politics of History*, pp. 28–50. New York: Columbia University Press.

Stonewall. 2022. 'About Us.' Available at https://www.stonewall.org.uk/about-us. Accessed on January 16, 2022.

Upadhyay, Nishant. 2021. 'Coloniality of White Feminism and Its Transphobia: A Comment on Burt.' *Feminist Criminology* 16(4), pp. 539–544. https://doi.org/10.1177/1557085121991337

Whittle, Stephen. (1999) 2002. 'Disembodied Law.' In *Respect and Equality: Transsexual and Transgender Rights*, pp. 1–18. London: Cavendish Publishing.

Yogyakarta 2017. 'The Yogyakarta Principles Plus 10.' Available at https://yogyakartaprinciples.org/wp-content/uploads/2017/11/A5_yogyakartaWEB-2.pdf

6

SEX AND GENDER IN SECOND-WAVE FEMINISM

Selina Todd

Between the late 1960s and the end of the 1980s feminists transformed women's lives. 'Second-wave' feminism (a term used to distinguish it from the first wave of feminism, which took place between the late nineteenth and early twentieth centuries) aimed to achieve women's equality with men in all spheres of society. One of the second wave's most important achievements was to develop an important distinction between sex – in the words of British sociologist Ann Oakley (1972) 'the biological differences between male and female' – and gender, which she described as 'the social classification into "masculine" and "feminine"' (16). Oakley was the first British feminist to assert this in print, but her understanding of sex and gender was shared by many second-wave feminists. This chapter examines how this understanding underpinned many of their achievements.

Decoupling sex from gender enabled feminists to successfully argue that women required certain rights and services by virtue of their sex *and* challenge the sexist assumptions that justified women's inequality with men. They explained that women's biology, particularly their ability to bear children, means they require specific rights and resources. But they used gender to argue that women's biology does not make them inferior to men. They recognised that women's specific needs were neglected by policymakers and medical practitioners not because women's needs were inevitably less important than men's but because the world was male-dominated. They also showed that women's inequality is often justified by the claim that women are best suited to perform 'feminine' roles. Feminists demonstrated that there was no evidence to substantiate this notion that gender is innate. They also showed that masculinity and femininity are not simply different from one another but also inherently unequal (which explained why, for example, 'women's' work was paid less than men's). As Angela Philips (1974) wrote in the feminist magazine *Spare Rib*, ending women's oppression relied on creating a new relationship between the sexes 'which is not built

DOI: 10.4324/9781003286608-6

out of domination [commonly perceived as masculine] and submission [widely defined as feminine]' (31). Feminists therefore critiqued and sought to eradicate gender.

This chapter focuses on the Women's Liberation Movement (WLM), which was the activist core of second-wave feminism. Not all feminists were activists, but the WLM captured and developed aspirations that most of them shared. The emphasis on 'liberation' asserted that feminists wanted more than equality with men in the existing status quo. Many of them aspired to a wholesale transformation of the world. They argued that designating care, nurture and compassion as 'feminine' roles deemed them less valuable than the 'masculine' activities of competition, making a profit or fighting wars. They believed that creating a more egalitarian and collectivist society in which everyone was encouraged to embrace so-called feminine values would be better for everyone. But feminism focused absolutely and exclusively on women, whose specific needs had long been neglected or ignored and whose capabilities and horizons were most constrained by gender.

Historical scholarship on second-wave feminism is surprisingly limited and, as Bruley and Forster argue (2016), many scholarly assessments rely on assumption rather than evidence. This chapter challenges the claim that a feminism which acknowledges biological sex as a material reality is biologically essentialist (Stryker 2007). It also challenges assumptions that feminists were exclusively concerned with the white middle class (Waters 2007) and that women's diversity doomed the movement to failure (Caine 1997). Second-wave feminists were not exclusively white or middle class, and many of those who were nevertheless campaigned for rights and transformations from which all women could benefit. Understanding that women shared some important political interests by virtue of their sex and that they were constrained by gender was integral to this project. However, feminists never argued that women shared a singular cultural identity.

This chapter focuses on Britain, one of the wealthy Western countries where the WLM was prominent. Feminists exchanged ideas with activists across the world, including the Middle East and Africa, where many feminists were focused on fighting colonialism and establishing independent states (Ahmed 1992; Davis 2007). However, national political and legal distinctions affected feminists' priorities and strategies.

The rest of this chapter is divided into two periods: before and after 1978, when the final annual WLM conference was held. This did not mark the end of second-wave feminism, but the increasing prominence of radical feminism and the rise of the political right changed priorities and activities. A short final section examines the backlash against second-wave feminism after 1990.

1968–1978

Aims and Organisation

The WLM owed much to older campaigns for women's equal pay (achieved for many female public sector workers by the late 1960s) and their reproductive rights:

in 1967, the National Health Service (NHS) was allowed to prescribe the contraceptive pill to unmarried women for the first time, and the Abortion Act of the same year gave women the right to terminate a pregnancy if two doctors agreed that it endangered the mother's health or that of the foetus. The Equal Pay Act of 1970 (which took effect in 1975) and the Sex Discrimination Act of 1975 were victories for feminist campaigners of the 1950s and 1960s.

Many of the instigators of the British WLM were inspired by these campaigns (Stevenson 2019, ch. 1), but most were too young to have been involved. They belonged to the first generation to benefit fully from the social democratic reforms introduced by Western governments after the Second World War. In Britain, these included free and compulsory secondary education and near-full employment. Many feminists were university students or in professional jobs, but they came from a range of socio-economic backgrounds and were often the first in their families to have such opportunities (Bunkle 2016). Most feminists were white – as was 97 percent of Britain's population (Peach et al. 2000, 138) – but black feminists were involved in the WLM from the start (Thomlinson 2016, 65–66).

Women were frustrated to find that, despite the post-war reforms, they remained unequal because of their sex. They were paid less than men and had fewer job opportunities. Many teachers, parents, employers and husbands expected them to be entirely fulfilled by marriage and motherhood (Bruley 2017). Inspired by the anti-imperialist and socialist movements of the 1960s, some young women started groups to fight for women's liberation – the first British groups appeared in 1968 (Coote and Campbell 1982, 14–20).

The WLM did not have a formal structure: there was no central organising committee and no party line. Women's groups developed organically across Britain (Bruley 2016). Many initially focused on 'consciousness-raising' (CR), described by one Scottish feminist as 'a process of sharing and examining our experience as women . . . and the social and political obstacles to the development of [our] potential' (Breitenbach 1990, 209). CR embodied the second-wave feminist assertion that the 'personal is political', which declared that private and domestic life should be the target for political action. While some feminists questioned the political value of focusing solely on CR (as some WLM groups did), many believed that personal experience was an important starting point for developing political priorities. The British Asian feminist Pragna Patel recalled that '"[i]t was CR that taught us: women can do it . . . women will do it . . . and women are doing it"' (quoted in Hague 2022, 70).

In 1970 feminists organised the first annual WLM conference at Ruskin College in Oxford. The location – a trade union college in a university city – embodied the activists' belief that their movement was of the political left and was for women of all classes. The annual conferences, the feminist press – notably *Spare Rib* magazine which ran from 1972 until 1993 – and initiatives like feminist theatre groups and bookshops enabled activists across Britain to forge networks and share ideas and introduced yet more women to the WLM (Wonders, 2020). 'Discovering women's bookshops . . . reading *Spare Rib* . . . attending conferences; joining women's groups' enabled Kim Clancy (1997), a working-class woman, to connect her own experience to that of other women: 'What bliss to be alive and to discover that my feelings, emotions, confusions were shared, and that there appeared to be a culprit for them all – patriarchy!' (48). In 1977, 3,000 women attended the WLM conference (Rees 2010, 345).

The annual conferences formulated increasingly radical demands which aimed to transform women's lives in all spheres. In 1970, the first conference agreed on four: equal pay, equal education and job opportunities, free contraception and abortion on demand and free twenty-four-hour nurseries. In 1974, came the demand for women's financial and legal independence and for an end to discrimination against lesbians and the right to a self-defined sexuality (including same-sex attraction). The 1978 conference separated this sixth demand into two and underlined the importance of women's right to a self-defined sexuality by turning it into a declaration that prefaced the demands. This conference also introduced the final, seventh demand: freedom from violence and sexual coercion.

These priorities reflected feminists' understanding that women's reproductive capacity (their sex) necessitated specific rights to grant them control over their bodies *and* that women's abilities were not inferior to men's. Rather than define equality as simply gaining legal parity with men, feminists argued that specific measures were required to address women's biological needs *and* counteract the social, political and economic discrimination that women were subjected to. The seventh demand, for example, recognised that women are more likely to be the victims of sexual assault and coercion than men and that the vast majority of the perpetrators of such abuse are male. But it also recognised that women were not *inevitably* subordinate to men – they should be able to live free of domination.

Like all political alliances, 'sisterhood' was not easy to create or sustain. Some black, working-class and lesbian feminists complained that many white middle-class women failed to appreciate the importance of class, race or sexuality, and feminists differed among themselves about working with the state or in political parties. But feminists found ways of working together across these divisions. Some women preferred to meet frequently with others who shared their particular experience of oppression – lesbian groups and black feminist groups existed across Britain – but united with other feminists to pursue particular campaigns at local and national level (Lockyer 2016; Thomlinson 2016). Local groups, national WLM conferences and correspondents to feminist periodicals debated such questions as the place of black women in the movement and whether feminist events should exclude men. These debates could be tense, but they enabled women to raise questions that weren't explored in wider society – like the experience of lesbians – and express their opinions without being silenced or dismissed by men (Rees, 2010; Wonders, 2020). The point was not to reach consensus but to uncover the diversity of women's experiences, enable the 'airing of conflict' and analyse issues through 'a feminist lens' (Wonders, 2020, 113). Many women agreed with the working-class feminist Jo Stanley (1997) that 'at least the [WLM] nominally understood the extra oppression of class and race (even if some members carried on being clueless about it)' (182).

Sex and Gender

Feminists believed that while sex is determined by biology, gender is socially and politically constructed. This set them apart from most psychologists and policymakers of the 1950s and 1960s, who argued that because women bear children, they should also take primary responsibility for their upbringing (Birmingham Feminist History Group 1979).

The influential clinicians John Money and Robert Stoller agreed with feminists that sex and gender were distinct. But unlike feminists, they believed that gender was a core part of a person's being which existed independently of biological sex (although they did not present convincing evidence of this). Money and Stoller believed it was important that a person's sex aligned with their gender, and that it was preferable to change a person's sex through surgery than to seek to change their gender identity (Stock 2021, 16–18; and see Matthews, this volume). By contrast, feminists understood that sex is immutable and gender is constructed – conclusions upheld by biology and sociology (see Hilton and Wright, this volume; Oakley, 1972).

Feminists' understanding of sex and gender was grounded in their own experiences of childhood socialisation, education and employment and in their recognition – gained through CR – that these experiences were shared by other women. They concluded that sex and gender were distinct yet connected. Most agreed with the radical feminist Sandra McNeill (1982) that women are 'products both of our conditioning by our culture from birth and of our conditioning by our bodies' (82). For Sheila Rowbotham (1973), a socialist feminist, 'this does not mean that we are not more than our biology . . . [b]ut . . . our consciousness as women is inseparable from our relation to . . . our anatomy' (36).

Women's reproductive power was the foundation on which their oppression was constructed, but feminists believed this was neither inevitable nor desirable. Many feminists read *Our Bodies Ourselves*, a self-help manual first produced in 1971 by the Boston Women's Health Collective in the USA; British feminists (Philips and Rakusen) issued a British edition in 1978. Women's health was the focus of discussion in the feminist press and in women's groups. Feminists focused on those experiences that a large majority of women shared and which *no* man could have: menstruation, pregnancy and menopause among them. They considered the distinct experiences of lesbian and heterosexual women, the choice over whether to bear children (which legal contraception had made possible) and the experience of female infertility. Their own experiences of motherhood led feminists to argue that women's ability to bear children did not make them innately suited to full-time parenthood (Coote and Campbell 1982, 16; Crook 2018, 1156). They explored how some symptoms of puberty and menopause might be caused or exacerbated by context – such as depression in menopausal women who were no longer able to fulfil stereotypes of 'feminine' beauty (Philips and Rakusen 1978, 33–35, 523, 529). Being born female *and* being socialised as feminine were important shared experiences.

Feminists sought to eradicate gender. Some researched women's history and showed how constructions of femininity and masculinity differed to suit the interests of men or capitalism in a given place and time (Alexander 1976). Feminists were particularly concerned with childhood socialisation. The limited job opportunities for graduate women meant that many feminists became schoolteachers and learned first-hand how education reproduced gender roles (Deem 1978).

Feminists differed over *why* women were oppressed and by whom. Socialist feminists argued that women were oppressed by capitalism. Radical feminists argued that men, regardless of their class position, benefitted from women's exploitation. Radical feminists called this system 'patriarchy'. Most feminists did not align themselves with either group but took on elements of each argument, as the WLM's demands demonstrated. By the late 1970s, a significant number of feminists clearly agreed that men's behaviour was a chief cause of women's exploitation. However, they also believed that the state should provide more services for women, and they wanted to challenge sexism in mixed schools, workplaces and heterosexual relationships rather than live entirely separately from men.

By the mid-1970s, almost all feminist groups were single sex. Some initially included men but stopped doing so because they dominated discussion or inhibited women (Coote and Campbell 1982, 34–35). In 1972, men were barred from WLM conferences for the same reasons. Some black women's groups were more amenable to mixed-sex activities, recognising that black men also experienced racism, but they held women-only meetings as well as mixed-sex ones (Owen 2013, 812). Some of the first women-only spaces were created for the victims of domestic violence (WLM groups established the first women's refuges). But most feminists came to believe that all women should have access to single-sex spaces and places, not just the most vulnerable. This enabled women to take on leadership roles and jobs considered 'masculine' in wider society, like carpentry and printing (Hague 2022, 70; Murphy 2021). And single-sex space fostered – in the words of the working-class feminist Val Walsh (1997) – deep 'friendship, affection and love between women' (166).

Strategies and Achievements

The sisterhood that Walsh described underpinned the feminist networks which instigated political and social change. The WLM has been represented as a militant movement, defined by iconic actions like the storming of the Miss World television final in 1970 to protest against the objectification of women's bodies. Playful protests consciously shattered gendered stereotypes of submissive femininity. 'Part of the power was . . . in the physicality of being with a gang of women like me in a public site', recalled Jo Stanley (1997). 'We entered – took swaggering possession of – universities and City Halls for our conferences. I'd never been in one before . . . This was where power was: and we – anyone – could enter it, organize in it, shout in it, laugh at cabaret skits on gender in it' (182). Giving women this strength and confidence was one of the WLM's key achievements.

But feminists used a range of strategies to achieve their aims. Many successful campaigns were localised, at a time when municipal councils provided education, housing and a wide range of social services. Feminists began providing services that women required and then lobbied the state to fund these. This tactic helped establish more than 40 women's centres across Britain by the end of the 1970s (Bruley 2016, 729). And feminists established women-only housing cooperatives, some specifically for lesbians, at a time when women found it hard to rent a property or get a mortgage without a male guarantor (Egerton 1990). They were committed to collective ways of working; women's centres, cooperatives and refuges, arts groups and educational projects were characterised by imaginative 'experimental practices' that were 'breath-taking' in their audacity and, often, in their achievements (Hague 2022, 97, 68).

Feminists also worked within existing institutions and sought to persuade colleagues and municipal councillors to help them. Feminist teachers created curricula and activities that challenged gender stereotyping and persuaded many schools to adopt these (Deem 1978). Feminists supported women workers' strikes for better conditions and greater control over their working lives (Moss 2019) and feminist trade unionists agitated for maternity leave, achieved by the Employment Protection Act of 1975. They did not get the twenty-four-hour nurseries they demanded, but their campaigns contributed to a 30 percent increase in nursery places between 1965 and 1979 (Todd 2014, 308).

Feminism was decentralised and grassroots. The few national initiatives grew out of local campaigns. In 1975, the National Women's Aid Federation (NWAF) was established to coordinate the establishment of women's refuges: by 1977, Britain had almost 200 (Byrne 1996, 59). In the same year, feminists founded the National Abortion Campaign (NAC) to oppose a Conservative member of parliament's attempt to overturn the 1967 Abortion Act. The NWAF pointed out that women as a sex were likely to be subjected to male violence and that women's political and economic inequality meant that, without refuges, they were unable to escape violent relationships (Hague 2022). The NAC asserted that a woman could only achieve liberation if she had the ability to control and plan her reproductive life (Knight and Gorton 1976). In this way, the NAC linked women's right to control their bodies to their political and economic rights. Feminists used this reasoning to argue that women's reproductive rights should be a priority for the labour movement, which championed political and economic equality. In 1979, the NAC and the Trades Union Congress jointly organised a pro-choice demonstration that attracted 100,000 participants (Byrne 1996, 60), and the Abortion Act remained intact.

1979–1989

Aims and Organisation

At the beginning of the 1980s, the WLM was 'still . . . a growing, developing movement, with enormous potential' (Breitenbach 1990, 215). Black feminists instigated some of the most exciting developments. The Organisation of Women of African and Asian Descent (OWAAD) was founded in 1978 and, in 1979, became an umbrella for black women's organisations. In 1979, Asian women in Southall established Southall Black Sisters (SBS), which became nationally known for its campaigns against domestic violence and its advocacy for black British and migrant women.

But the women's movement was weakened. The 1978 WLM conference was the last, partly because it had been engulfed by an acrimonious debate about separatism instigated by revolutionary feminists (Rees 2010). These internal divisions weakened the movement. However, a far bigger crisis was heralded by the election of Margaret Thatcher's Conservative government in 1979. The Tory governments of 1979–1997 made swingeing public-sector cuts and reduced workers' rights and emphasised 'traditional' family values. This forced many feminist groups onto the defensive, with many spending the 1980s fighting to preserve the rights and resources women had already won. Cuts to council budgets forced many women's centres to close, and some feminist groups became preoccupied with filling the gaps left by threadbare social services rather than with campaigning (Griffin 1995).

Nevertheless, feminists continued to successfully campaign for the original seven demands. In workplaces and trade unions, they focused on the implementation and, where necessary, expansion of sex-equality legislation. The provision of anti-sexist education remained a priority, and feminist lecturers joined schoolteachers in campaigning for the teaching of women's history and women's studies (Evans 1982; Weiner 1985). Youth work became an important site of feminist activity, often instigated by working-class women who used council funding to broaden the horizons of girls in Britain's poorest areas and challenge sex stereotyping (Somerset 2018).

Much feminist activism focused on the seventh demand: freedom from violence and sexual coercion. The murder of thirteen women and girls in northern England between 1975 and 1980 by Peter Sutcliffe (dubbed the 'Yorkshire Ripper') and the inept and sexist response of the police (Smith 1993, 163–205) provoked radical feminists in Yorkshire to form Britain's first Women Against Violence Against Women (WAVAW) groups. WAVAW groups mushroomed in the 1980s, campaigning for the criminalisation of marital rape, fairer police treatment of rape victims and better policing of male violence against women (Bindel et al. 1995, 66). Radical feminists also spearheaded campaigns against pornography and for the criminalisation of men who used prostitutes.

Some feminists pursued freedom from violence in the peace movement. The arms race between East and West escalated in the early 1980s and, with it, the threat of nuclear war. When the British government agreed that the United States could station nuclear weapons in the UK, feminists collaborated with peace activists to establish camps close to the bases at Greenham Common in England (in 1981) and Faslane in Scotland (in 1982). In February 1982, Greenham became a women-only peace camp. At a time when the world beyond Greenham was an increasingly difficult place for feminists, the protestors 'created "a model of how people could live differently in society"' through democratic debate, tolerance of conflicting views, cooperative living and direct action against the base (quoted in Roseneil 2000, 124).

Towards the end of the 1980s, new signs of feminist solidarity emerged in response to emergent or growing threats. Many feminists were concerned by the global rise in religious fundamentalism and the dangers this posed to women's rights. In 1989, Iran's Ayatollah Khomeini issued a fatwa (Islamic legal pronouncement) condemning Salman Rushdie to death for his book *The Satanic Verses*. In response, some members of SBS, in cooperation with Labour Party activists, established Women Against Fundamentalism (WAF). WAF argued that women's shared experience of oppression by religious fundamentalists was more vital than the religious or ethnic differences between them. For many participants, including co-founder Gita Saghal, the internationalist and anti-racist dimensions of WAF were also important in connecting the British women's movement with the global women's struggle. '[W]e were defending our secular traditions', wrote Saghal (2014), 'an important emphasis since most people think secularisation is a product of western thinking rather than having its source in nationalist, anti-colonialist struggles' (89), and being a priority for many Asian feminists. This was a direct riposte to 'multiculturalism', a strand of thought on the British liberal left which had gained in popularity in the 1980s and suggested that attacking different cultures and religions was racist. Against this, WAF declared that women's rights were universal. Clara Connolly (2014), another WAF activist, recalled that

> [w]hen WAF was invited to speak [at meetings] . . . we tried to stick to the principle of travelling in pairs, from different ethnic or religious backgrounds. This provided surprises for the audience, and underlined our commitment to fight fundamentalism in all religions. . . . My role . . . was usually to speak about the privileged role of Christianity in a supposedly secular Britain. (76)

WAF's work was underpinned by the WLM's demands for women's financial and legal independence and for equal rights. However, the group's critique of religion and multiculturalism contributed another dimension to understandings of women's liberation.

Sex and Gender

Feminists increasingly discussed the relationship between sex and gender, but the vast majority of them continued to understand sex as biological and gender as constructed. In 1979, some revolutionary feminists accused heterosexual women of sleeping with the enemy (Leeds Revolutionary Feminist Group 1981). Some socialist feminists attacked this stance, which they argued presumed that men's oppression of women was an inevitable result of male biology (Segal 1989, 14–15). But very few feminists believed that biology determined women's exploitation; most were interested in exploring the relationship between different factors that may help explain women's inequality and, more pressingly, advance their liberation. Even revolutionary feminists tended to agree that women's oppression could not be solely explained by 'biology, economics, psychology, or sexuality per se' (Friedman 1982, 19).

In the 1980s, feminists increasingly clashed over pornography and prostitution. Some adopted a libertarian stance, arguing that women and men should freely pursue their sexual desires (Segal 1987, 37). By contrast, many radical feminists proposed that the equation of pleasure with heterosexuality, the objectification of women and the commodification of sex were worth interrogating, given that feminists believed that the personal is political (Garthwaite, 1984). These radical feminists believed that if gender was constructed, sexuality and desire may be constructed, too.

Some feminists began to ask whether a 'women's movement' was a realisable political project. In 1978, a small group founded the periodical *m/f*, which argued that 'the category of woman is not a pre-given unity'. The *m/f* group asserted that the act of organising *as women* treated womanhood as 'a fixed and unchanging essence', determined by biology and therefore unresponsive to reform (Adams et al. 1978, 2).

In the 1980s, this stance gained more popularity. Thatcherism led many on the left (including some second-wave feminists) to believe that their agency was now limited to choices over consumption and cultural practices, not the redistribution of political and economic power. This encouraged a new stress on personal and cultural identities. Together with ongoing tensions about class, homophobia and racism in the WLM, this led some black and Jewish feminists to question whether the category 'woman' ignored important differences between women (Carby 1982).

But other feminists (including black and Jewish women) questioned the value of this new form of identity politics. They argued that women shared some important injustices and experiences that bridged ethnicity, class or religious differences. They also challenged the presumption that belonging to a particular ethnic or religious group meant holding a specific set of beliefs. Feminists had long argued that women should have the right to act in a variety of ways, unconstrained by gender stereotypes. Many of them now also argued that black or Jewish people should not be expected to conform to particular behaviours or customs that were often devised or upheld by conservative male religious or 'community' leaders. SBS faced 'immense hostility' from some other black feminists when the group objected to police neglect of male violence within black and Asian communities (Patel 2014, 58). Their opponents argued that state intervention in black communities was inherently racist because it failed to respect distinct ethnic or religious values. Against this, SBS contended that freedom from violence and freedom of expression were universal rights.

Much second-wave feminist politics focused on tackling issues and interests that transcended women's diverse cultural identities. Consciousness-raising had encouraged women to explore their identities as well as other aspects of their lives, but many British feminists agreed with the black American feminist June Jordan that identity "'may be enough to get started on but not enough to get anything finished'" (quoted in Parmar 1989, 61). In deliberately challenging gendered stereotypes through their assertive demands, militancy and intervention in traditionally masculine fields, feminists argued that socialisation could be overcome and cultural norms overturned. The notion that some cultural practices were beyond political critique, and some cultural identities immutable, sat uneasily with the second wave's recognition that gender was socially and politically constructed.

By the late 1980s, some feminists, including the founders of WAF, criticised 'identity politics' for treating certain religious and cultural practices as sacrosanct, rather than examining whose interests they served (a question feminists had long asked of gender; Bard 2014). By contrast, WAF's 'sisterhood' was rooted in 'a politics of solidarity that both recognises difference and also unites round common political values' (Patel 2014, 59). WAF, like so many second-wave campaigns, developed from a political analysis of women's exploitation, not from the presumption that women shared a cultural identity.

During the 1980s, feminists in Britain and further afield began to interrogate the extent to which aspects of womanhood were 'natural'. Psychoanalysis, which increased in popularity in the 1980s, and the development of new reproductive technologies – the first baby to be conceived using in vitro fertilisation (IVF) was born in Britain in 1978 – raised questions about how far brains and bodies were malleable (Alexander 1991; Rowbotham 1989). Rapid advances in computing and robotics raised further questions about how far human biology could be transformed (Haraway 1987). These new perspectives led a minority of feminists to wonder whether certain sexed aspects of womanhood were more historically contingent than had earlier been assumed. In subsequent decades, these discussions would be taken in new directions by postmodernist feminism and the trans rights movement (see Jones, this volume).

The impact of these discussions should not be over-estimated. They were almost entirely confined to academic research, and most of the feminists involved reflected on the relationship between sex and gender, rather than concluding that sex was unimportant or nonexistent. Most feminists believed that women's reproductive and bodily autonomy was essential, and therefore, being able to name and understand sex was important – but they did not see biology as destiny. This informed the limited discussion provoked by the very small number of male-to-female transsexuals ('transgender' identity in its twenty-first-century sense did not yet exist). Feminists did not see male-to-female transsexuals as women, because transsexuals neither had female bodies nor had they experienced female socialisation – a distinction that the small number of British transsexuals tended to accept (Morris 2018). Feminists viewed transsexuality as a response to repressive gender roles. They encouraged men who were uncomfortable with masculine roles to collectively reject these rather than seeking identification as women, pointing out that sex was distinct from gender and that women should not be defined by femininity or men by masculinity (McNeill

1982, 83–84). But this was not an issue that most feminists encountered, because the number of transsexuals was so tiny.

Most feminists remained committed to single-sex space. In 1982, the decision by women at Greenham Common Peace Camp to exclude men was motivated both by men's attempts to dominate the camp and by the women's positive experience of living and organising together (Harford and Hopkins 1984, 32–33). The 'principle of separate space' was the guiding objective for feminist youth workers, because this meant activities and workers' training were shaped entirely by women's needs, whereas mixed-sex youth work tended to be dominated by boys and men. The provision of time and resources helped both the workers and the young women they served to "'believe in themselves'" (quoted in Somerset 2018, 89), leading many to try new activities and encouraging some to return to education or escape abusive relationships (Somerset 2018, 89). Feminists worked hard to maintain women-only refuges and women's centres. And WAF, like many earlier feminist initiatives, was committed to women-only organisations and some exclusively female activities while cooperating with sympathetic mixed-sex groups.

Strategies and Achievements

Despite the travails of the 1980s, feminists used direct action, pragmatic alliances with like-minded groups and lobbying to achieve some important victories. Mikhail Gorbachev, secretary general of the Soviet Union, credited the Greenham women's campaign with helping bring about the 1987 Intermediate-Range Nuclear Forces Treaty between the USSR and the US, which paved the way for cruise missiles to leave Greenham in 1991 (Pettit, 2006, 8, 193). At Greenham and in other single-sex campaigns, women shattered their own preconceptions of their capabilities. They discovered they could be "'brave'" in the company of like-minded women: "'It dragged me . . . out of doing as I was told'", one Greenham protestor recalled (quoted in Roseneil 2000, 120). Gendered identities, far from being innate, could be jettisoned – sometimes swiftly.

Feminists' hard and often unpaid work increased the number of Women's Aid groups and refuges, despite public spending cuts (Breitenbach 1990, 221). Grassroots campaigners raised awareness of male violence against women by organising Reclaim the Night marches (the first in 1977), public meetings and protests: SBS adopted a tactic of Indian feminists by publicly protesting outside the homes of victims (Patel 2014, 59). And feminist researchers and campaigners worked with police forces and councils to improve the treatment of rape victims and contributed to women's greater willingness to report rape. The number of recorded cases in England and Wales rose from 1,842 in 1985 to 5,930 in 1996 (D'Cruze 2001, 210). In 1989 the Scottish courts ruled that marital rape was a crime, and two years later, marital rape was criminalised in England and Wales. However, the rise in the number of women reporting rape was not matched by an increased conviction rate: 24 percent of reported rapes led to a conviction in 1985 but less than 10 percent in 1996. Experts attribute this to the police and Crown Prosecution Service dropping cases in which the victim knew the man who raped her (Gregory and Lees 1991, 91).

Feminists had a tangible impact in both schools and universities. They persuaded schools and local authorities to devise and implement policies to tackle sex discrimination (Leonard 2006). By the 1990s, 50 percent of university entrants were women, and an increasing minority enrolled on science and engineering courses (Dyhouse 2001, 130). By the 1990s, approximately 100 British universities offered women's studies courses (Coate 1999, 17). Feminist campaigners also thwarted attempts by religious fundamentalist groups opposed to women's equality to take over some of Britain's state schools (Patel 2014, 62).

Feminists helped to advance lesbian and gay rights. In 1988 the Conservative government introduced Section 28 to prohibit local authorities in England, Scotland and Wales from 'promoting' and teaching about homosexuality. In the following year, lesbian feminists were among the founders of Stonewall, the lesbian and gay rights organisation. Stonewall's campaign against Section 28 eventually achieved its repeal in 2000 in Scotland and 2004 in England and Wales. But feminists also recognised that lesbians had distinct needs. In the 1970s, lesbian mothers generally lost custody battles for their children. The tenacity of some of these mothers and the work of feminist lawyers changed this. In 1994, the Court of Appeal ruled that lesbianism did not make a woman an unfit mother (Radford, 1995).

Women made less progress economically. In 1971, women composed 38 percent of the workforce. Sex equality legislation, and campaigns to extend and enforce this, meant that by 2001, women composed 45 percent of the workforce, and a growing proportion were in the professions (Scott et al. 2008, 4–5, 10–12). In 1980, women were paid on average 30 percent less than men; by 2001, they were paid 18 percent less, although this gap was far higher – 40 percent – among part-time workers. These were qualified victories: women workers remained disproportionately concentrated in low-paid, insecure jobs (Scott et al. 2008, 9–10). Nevertheless, women's increasing employment opportunities and rights provided them with a greater degree of financial independence from men.

The Backlash against Second-Wave Feminism

The questions about womanhood raised by identity politics were being debated in universities – especially in the North American academy – by the mid-1980s. Scholars such as historian Joan Scott and philosopher Judith Butler argued that there were no universal truths and that womanhood was a social construction (Scott [1986] 1988; Butler 1990). In the 1990s, this argument gained wider purchase in higher education. It owed something to second-wave feminists' demonstration that *gender* was a social construction. But it was antithetical to the second-wave feminist understanding that the relationship between sex and gender was vital to understanding women's oppression and fighting for their liberation. This postmodern version of womanhood failed to recognise that women were united by some important shared experiences and that recognising the commonality of their sex actually enabled feminists to challenge gender stereotypes while identifying women's specific needs. By contrast with the second-wave activists' call for women's liberation, postmodernist feminism – sometimes called 'third-wave' feminism – focused on a much more academic and less ambitious task: problematising, or 'queering', the linguistic categories of sex and gender (Jones, this volume).

The WLM's legacy came under sustained political attack in the 1990s. As neoliberal governments continued to cut back public services, women's resources suffered. Charitable and religious groups – some of them hostile to feminism – stepped in to fill the gaps. As the space for feminist activism shrank, the influence of ideas antithetical to the WLM grew. Liberal feminism gained popularity in workplaces, in the media and among policymakers. Liberal feminists had more limited ambitions than second-wave activists had espoused, focusing on women's ability to 'empower' themselves individually rather than campaigning for political and economic equality. This was never the whole picture: women's networks did develop in politics and business and challenged the 'glass ceiling' there, but they were confined to a small, mostly affluent minority (Moss 1995).

Both liberal and postmodern versions of feminism drew attention away from structural inequalities and the value of collective challenges to the status quo. In universities, budget cuts resulted in the closure of some women's studies courses; postmodernism meant that others were replaced by gender studies (Davis et al. 2006). This new emphasis on 'gender' reflected a wider trend in civic institutions and workplaces, away from centring women in policy and research towards an emphasis on 'gender blindness' or 'diversity'. This approach emphasised toleration of difference rather than redistribution of power (Mirza 2006; Patel 2011). In education, it meant shifting the spotlight from girls' continued alienation from traditionally 'masculine' subjects and boys' long-standing domination of classroom discussion to improving boys' performance in those subjects in which girls did better (Leonard 2006).

Yet many of the ideas and strategies of the second wave survived. Some groups, including SBS and Justice for Women, continued to work in the twenty-first century. And new groups emerged, such as Woman's Place UK (WPUK), founded by socialists and trade unionists in 2017 to campaign for women's sex-based rights. WPUK's conscious debt to the second wave is evidenced by their 'Five Demands' (WPUK 2018), and their distinction between sex as biological – which underpins their emphasis on women's bodily autonomy – and gender as a restrictive construction that feminists must challenge.

Conclusion

Second-wave feminists' achievements transformed women's lives and rights. These feminists based their activism on the understanding that while sex is biological, gender is a social construct. In the early 1970s, this was a radical idea; by the 1990s, it was widely accepted. Some postmodernist thinkers have challenged this understanding, but it remains embedded in British equality law.

'Sisterhood' never meant sameness or harmony. Feminists did not believe that women shared an innate identity; rather, they mobilised around a set of shared political principles, honed by debate. By using female networks, direct action, research, lobbying and strategic alliances, they enacted lasting social and political change. Their actions explain why women's participation in education and employment expanded and their legal rights increased in the late twentieth and early twenty-first centuries (Scott et al. 2008; Patel 2011).

The argument that 'woman' is not a useful category for analysis or activism was initially confined to university seminar rooms. It entered the political mainstream in the early twenty-first century (see Jones, this volume). But the achievements of second-wave feminists undermine its premise. By arguing for the importance of sex, second-wave feminists drew attention to women's specific needs. They recognised the importance of women's bodily autonomy as a foundation for achieving equality with men. In the absence of this recognition that sex matters, women's bodies and choices can be treated as less important than male desire.

But feminists also showed that biology is not destiny. They both asserted women's right to have their sex-specific needs met and challenged gendered assumptions about women's abilities. In this way, second-wave feminists mounted a sustained, ambitious, wide-ranging attack on women's oppression and exploitation. Their arguments, and the myriad strategies that they used to pursue their goals, increased women's political and economic rights and influenced social attitudes. The creation of single-sex space enabled women to challenge gender stereotyping and forge sisterhoods that fought campaigns, offered mutual support and pioneered new ways of living. Yet as the backlash against their achievements shows, women can never take these rights and opportunities for granted.

References

Adams, Parveen, Rosalind Coward, Elizabeth Cowie. 1978. 'Editorial'. *m/f 1* (1): 3–6.
Ahmed, Leila, 1982. 'Feminism and Feminist Movement in the Middle East, a Preliminary Exploration'. *Women's Studies International Forum 5* (2): 153–168.
Alexander, Sally, 1976. 'Women's Work in Nineteenth-Century London: A Study of the Years 1820–60s'. In *The Rights and Wrongs of Women*, edited by Juliet Mitchell and Ann Oakley, 59–111. Harmondsworth, UK: Penguin.
Alexander, Sally, 1991. 'Feminist History and Psychoanalysis'. *History Workshop Journal 32* (1): 128–133.
Bard, Julia, 2014. 'Learning to Question'. In *Women Against Fundamentalism: Stories of Dissent and Solidarity*, edited by Sukhwant Dhaliwal and Nira Yuval-Davis, 154–166. London: Lawrence and Wishart.
Bindel, Julie, Kate Cook and Liz Kelly, 1995. 'Trials and Tribulations – Justice for Women: A Campaign for the 1990s'. In *Feminist Activism in the 1990s*, edited by Gabriele Griffin, 65–76. London: Taylor and Francis.

Birmingham Feminist History Group, 1979. 'Feminism as Femininity in the 1950s?' *Feminist Review 3* (1): 48–65.

Breitenbach, Esther, 1990. '"Sisters Are Doing It for Themselves": The Women's Movement in Scotland'. In *Scottish Government Yearbook*, edited by Alice Brown and Richard Parry, 209–225. Edinburgh: Paul Harris Publishing.

Bruley, Sue, 2016. 'Women's Liberation at the Grass Roots: A View from Some English Towns, c.1968–1990'. *Women's History Review 25* (5): 723–740.

Bruley, Sue, 2017. '"It Didn't Just Come Out of Nowhere, Did It?": The Origins of the Women's Liberation Movement in 1960s Britain'. *Oral History 45* (1): 67–78.

Bruley, Sue and Laurel Forster, 2016. 'Historicising the Women's Liberation Movement'. *Women's History Review 25* (5): 697–700.

Bunkle, Phillida. 2016. 'The 1944 Education Act and Second Wave Feminism'. *Women's History Review 25* (5): 791–811.

Butler, Judith. 1990. *Gender Trouble*. London: Routledge.

Byrne, Paul, 1996. 'The Politics of the Women's Movement'. *Parliamentary Affairs 49* (1): 55–70.

Carby, Hazel, 1982. 'White Women Listen! Black Feminism and the Boundaries of Sisterhood!' In *The Empire Strikes Back: Race and Racism in 70s Britain*, edited by the Centre for Contemporary Cultural Studies, 211–234. London: Hutchinson.

Caine, Barbara. 1997. *English Feminism, 1780–1980*. Oxford: Oxford University Press.

Clancy, Kim, 1997. 'Academic as Anarchist – working-class lives into middle-class culture'. In *Class Matters: Working-Class Women's Perspectives on Social Class*, edited by Pat Mahony and Christina Zmroczek, 44–52. London: Taylor and Francis.

Coate, Kelly. 1999. 'The History of Women's Studies as an Academic Subject Area in Higher Education in the UK: 1970–1995'. PhD thesis, University of London.

Coote, Anna and Beatrix Campbell. 1982. *Sweet Freedom. The Struggle for Women's Liberation*. London: Pan.

Crook, Sarah, 2018. 'The Women's Liberation Movement, Activism and Therapy at the Grassroots, 1986–1985'. *Women's History Review 27* (7): 1152–1168.

Davis, Kathy. 2007. *The Making of Our Bodies, Ourselves. How Feminism Travels Across Borders*. London: Duke.

Davis, Kathy, Mary Evans and Judith Lorber, 2006. 'Introduction'. In *The SAGE Handbook of Gender and Women's Studies,* edited by Kathy Davis, Mary Evans and Judith Lorber, 1–10. London: Sage.

D'Cruze, Shani, 2001. 'Crime'. In *Women in Twentieth-Century Britain*, edited by Ina Zweiniger-Bargielowska, 198–213. Harlow, UK: Pearson.

Deem, Rosemary. 1978. *Women and Schooling*. London: Routledge.

Dyhouse, Carol, 2001. 'Education'. In *Women in Twentieth-Century Britain*, edited by Ina Zweiniger-Bargielowska, 119–133. Harlow, UK: Pearson.

Egerton, Jayne, 1990. 'Out but not Down: Lesbians' Experience of Housing'. *Feminist Review 36* (1): 75–88.

Evans, Mary, 1982. 'In Praise of Theory: The Case for Women's Studies'. *Feminist Review 10* (1): 61–74.

Friedman, Scarlet, 1982. 'Heterosexuality, Couples and Parenthood: a "Natural" Cycle?' In *The Problem with Men*, edited by Scarlet Friedman and Elizabeth Sarah, 5–20. London: Women's Press.

Garthwaite, Al, 1984. 'All You Never Wanted to Know about Sex . . . But Were Forced to Learn'. In *Sweeping Statements: Writings from the Women's Liberation Movement 1981–83*, edited by Hannah Kanter, Sarah Lefanu, Shaila Shah and Carole Spedding, 24–36. London: Women's Press.

Gregory, Jeanne and Sue Lees. 1999. *Policing Sexual Assault*. London: Routledge.
Griffin, Gabriele. 1995. 'Introduction'. In *Feminist Activism in the 1990s*, edited by Gabriele Griffin, 1–10. London: Taylor and Francis.
Hague, Gill. 2022. *History and Memories of the Domestic Violence Movement: We've Come Further Than You Think*. Bristol: Policy Press.
Haraway, Donna, 1987. 'A Manifesto for Cyborgs: Science, Technology, and Socialist Feminism in the 1980s'. *Australian Feminist Studies 2* (4): 1–42.
Harford, Barbara and Sarah Hopkins. 1984. *Greenham Common: Women at the Wire*. London: Women's Press.
Knight, R. and A. Gorton. 1976. *Abortion. Where We Stand*. National Abortion Campaign pamphlet. London: Rye Press.
Leeds Revolutionary Feminist Group. 1981. *Love Your Enemy? The Debate Between Heterosexual Feminism and Political Lesbianism*. London: Onlywomen Press.
Leonard, Diana, 2006. 'Gender, Change and Education'. In *The SAGE Handbook of Gender and Women's Studies*, edited by Kathy Davis, Mary Evans and Judith Lorber, 167–182. London: SAGE.
Lockyer, Bridget, 2013. 'An Irregular Period? Participation in the Bradford Women's Liberation Movement'. *Women's History Review 22* (4): 643–657.
Malik, Kenan. 2023. *Not So Black and White: A History of Race from White Supremacy to Identity Politics*. London: Hurst.
McNeill, Sandra, 1982. 'Transsexualism: Can Men Turn Men into Women?' In *The Problem with Men*, edited by Scarlet Friedman and Elizabeth Sarah, 82–87. London: Women's Press.
Mirza, Heidi Safia, 2006. 'Transcendence over Diversity: Black Women in the Academy'. *Policy Futures in Education 4* (2): 101–113.
Morris, Jan. 2018. *Conundrum*. London: Slightly Foxed.
Moss, Frances, 1995. 'Making the Invisible Visible: The Rise of a Professional Women's Network in the 1990s'. In *Feminist Activism in the 1990s*, edited by Gabriele Griffin, 171–181. London: Taylor and Francis.
Moss, Jonathan. 2019. *Women, Workplace Protest and Political Identity in England, 1968–1985*. Manchester, UK: Manchester University Press.
Murphy, Gillian, 2021. '"Balancing on a Razor's Edge": Running the radical feminist lesbian Onlywomen Press'. *Women: A Cultural Review 32* (3–4): 442–456.
Oakley, Ann. 1972. *Sex, Gender, and Society*. London: Temple Smith.
Owen, Nicholas, 2013. 'Men and the 1970s British Women's Liberation Movement'. *The Historical Journal 56* (3): 801–826.
Parmar, Pratibha, 1989. 'Other Kinds of Dreams'. *Feminist Review 31* (1): 55–65.
Patel, Pragna, 2011. 'Women Migrants and Faith Organisations: Changing Regimes of Gender, Religion and Race in London'. *Feminist Review 97* (1): 142–150.
Patel, Pragna, 2014. 'Flying by the Nets of Racism, Patriarchy and Religion'. In *Women Against Fundamentalism: Stories of Dissent and Solidarity*, edited by Sukhwant Dhaliwal and Nira Yuval-Davis, 52–66. London: Lawrence and Wishart.
Peach, Ceri, Alisdair Rogers, Judith Chance and Patricia Daley, 2000. 'Immigration and Ethnicity'. In *Twentieth-Century British Social Trends*, edited by Albert H. Halsey with Josephine Webb, 128–178. Basingstoke, UK: Macmillan.
Pettit, Ann. 2006. *Walking to Greenham*. Dinas Powys, UK: Honno.
Philips, Angela, 1974. 'Rape'. *Spare Rib 20*: 30–31.
Philips, Angela, and Jill Rakusen. 1978. *Our Bodies Ourselves*. London: Penguin.
Radford, Jill, 1995. 'Rights of Women'. In *Feminist Activism in the 1990s*, edited by Gabriele Griffin, 51–64. London: Taylor and Francis.

Rees, Jeska, 2010. 'A Look Back at Anger: The Women's Liberation Movement in 1978'. *Women's History Review* 19 (3): 337–356.

Roseneil, Sasha, 2000. *Common Women, Uncommon Practices: The Queer Feminisms of Greenham*. London: Cassell.

Rowbotham, Sheila, 1973. *Women's Consciousness, Man's World*. Harmondsworth, UK: Penguin.

Rowbotham, Sheila, 1989. 'To Be or Not to Be: The Dilemmas of Mothering'. *Feminist Review 31*: 82–93.

Scott, Joan. (1986) 1988. 'Gender: A Useful Category of Historical Analysis' [reprint]. In *Gender and the Politics of History*, 28–52. New York: Columbia University Press.

Scott, Jacqueline L., Shirley Dex and Heather Joshi, 2008. 'Introduction'. In *Women and Employment: Changing Lives and New Challenges*, edited by Jacqueline L. Scott, Shirley Dex and Heather Joshi, 1–15. Cheltenham, UK: Edward Elgar.

Segal, Lynne, 1987. *Is the Future Female? Troubled Thoughts on Contemporary Feminism*. London: Virago.

Segal, Lynne, 1989. 'Slow Change or No Change?: Feminism, Socialism and the Problem of Men'. *Feminist Review 31* (1): 5–21.

Smith, Joan, 1993. *Misogynies. Reflections on Myth and Malice*. 2nd ed. London: Faber and Faber.

Somerset, Jo, 2018. 'Pushing the Boundaries of Feminism in a Northern English Town'. *Northern History 55* (1): 76–91.

Stanley, Jo, 1997. 'To Celeb-Rate and Not to Be-Moan'. In *Class Matters: Working-Class Women's Perspectives on Social Class*, edited by Pat Mahony and Christina Zmroczek, 175–189. London: Taylor and Francis.

Stevenson, George. 2019. *The Women's Liberation Movement and the Politics of Class in Britain*. London: Bloomsbury.

Stock, Kathleen. 2021. *Material Girls*. London: Fleet.

Stryker, Susan, 2007. 'Transgender Feminism: Queering the Woman Question'. In *Third Wave Feminism: A Critical Exploration*, edited by Stacey Gillis, Gillian Howie and Rebecca Munford, 59–70. Basingstoke, UK: Palgrave.

Thomlinson, Natalie, 2016. *Race, Ethnicity and the Women's Movement in England, 1968–1993*. Basingstoke, UK: Palgrave.

Todd, Selina, 2014. *The People: The Rise and Fall of the Working Class, 1910–2010*. London: John Murray.

Walsh, Val, 1997. 'Interpreting Class: Auto/Biographical Imaginations and Social Change'. In *Class Matters: Working-Class Women's Perspectives on Social Class*, edited by Pat Mahony and Christina Zmroczek, 152–174. London: Taylor and Francis.

Waters, Melanie, 2007. 'Sexing It Up? Women, Pornography and Third Wave Feminism'. In *Third Wave Feminism: A Critical* edited by Stacey Gillis, Gillian Howie and Rebecca Munford, 250–265. Basingstoke, UK: Palgrave.

Weiner, Gaby, ed. 1985. *Just a Bunch of Girls: Feminist Approaches to Schooling*. Milton Keynes, UK: Open University Press.

Woman's Place UK. 2018. 'Our 5 Demands'. July 23. https://womansplaceuk.org/our-5-demands.

Wonders, Bec. 2020. 'Mapping Second Wave Feminist Periodicals: Networks of Conflict and Counterpublics, 1970–1990'. *Art Libraries Journal 45* (3): 106–113.

7
WHY DO WE NEED DATA ON SEX?

Alice Sullivan, Kath Murray and Lisa Mackenzie

Data on sex has been collected by health scientists, social scientists, and public bodies for centuries. Sex is recognised as a fundamental variable, which affects health and social and economic outcomes. This chapter explains why collecting data on sex is important and documents some examples of public bodies and surveys moving away from data collection on sex. We address the reasons why we are losing data on sex and examine the arguments that have been used to oppose data collection on sex. In conclusion, we argue that accurate data on sex is essential for the human sciences, for policymaking, and to tackle sexism.

Sex matters

Why do we collect data on sex? The reason is that differences between the sexes are an important factor for analysis in most, if not all, of the areas that social and health scientists address. We outline a few examples below.

Demography: Sex, alongside age, is a fundamental demographic variable, vital for projections regarding fertility and life expectancy (Grundy and Murphy 2015). In some parts of the world, sex-selective abortion leads to substantially more male than female births, due to a preference for sons (Chao et al. 2019).

Physical health: Sex has systematic effects on physical health (Koblinsky et al. 2018). Some conditions only affect males or females. Only females experience pregnancy, menstrual periods, and menopause. Only males suffer testicular cancer, and only females experience gynaecological cancers. Other conditions are more prevalent in one sex or the other; for example men are more likely to have heart attacks, whereas women are more likely to suffer osteoporosis. Health behaviours also vary according to sex, with men typically engaging in more 'risky behaviours' such as smoking and excessive alcohol consumption.

DOI: 10.4324/9781003286608-7

Mental health: Women report higher rates of depression and anxiety than men, although men are more likely to commit suicide (Ploubidis et al. 2017).

Crime: Men commit more crime than women, a pattern that holds over time and internationally (Smith 2014). Violent and sexual crime is particularly rare among women (Phoenix, this volume).

Education: Historically, women and girls were excluded from advanced education. In much of the world, such discrimination is still prevalent (Benjamin, this volume). In recent decades, women in advanced industrialised societies have surpassed male attainment on indicators such as the likelihood of gaining a university degree. However, substantial variation in the field of study persists; for example males are more likely to study science, technology, engineering and maths, while females are over-represented in languages and humanities subjects (Cassidy et al. 2018).

Employment: Women have traditionally been excluded from many occupations and still face barriers in the workplace, some of which are due to maternity and being the primary carers for children and other family members. Social scientists have analysed the 'gender pay gap', meaning the gap in pay between the sexes, and documented sex differences in entry and progression in different fields of employment (Bryson et al. 2020).

Religion: Women are more likely than men to be affiliated with a religion and to express religious beliefs (Voas et al. 2013).

Social and political attitudes: Women were traditionally more likely to vote for right-wing parties than men, but this pattern has reversed over time (Shorrocks 2018).

In research in all of these areas, sex is not examined in isolation but in conjunction with other important characteristics such as socio-economic position, ethnic group and age. The ability to understand the intersections between these variables is important.

The biological cannot be neatly parcelled off from the social, since human beings are both biological and social animals. The term *biosocial* describes the interaction between biological and social factors, an important focus in multidisciplinary research across the health and social sciences.

Losing data on sex: UK surveys and administrative data

Despite its importance as an explanatory variable, many UK public bodies have ceased collecting data on sex, often replacing it with data on self-declared gender identity, or with a fudge between gender identity and sex. This is despite the fact that public bodies are bound by the Public Sector Equality Duty within the Equality Act 2010 (EA2010) to monitor and publish data on the protected characteristic of sex. The EA2010 defines sex in binary terms: a 'woman' is a 'female of any age', and a man is a 'male of any age'.

The Office for National Statistics (ONS) sought to redefine sex to encompass gender identity for the purposes of the 2021 England and Wales census and was only prevented via a legal challenge (Sullivan 2021). In Scotland, the guidance for the 2022 census allowed people to answer the sex question according to their gender identity.

The loss of data on sex is an international phenomenon. Scotland's chief statistician has stated that collecting data on biological sex is justifiable only 'in a small number of instances . . . on an individual basis for a very specific purpose' (Scottish Government 2021, 11). Statistics Canada (2021a) and Statistics New Zealand (2021: 8) advise that asking about gender rather than sex should be the default approach.

In this section, we provide further examples from the UK.

Gender pay gap (UK Government Equalities Office)

Since 2017, UK public authorities and private sector employers with headcounts of 250 or more have been required by law to report annually on their 'gender pay gap' – the difference between the average earnings of men and women. However, UK government guidance states that employers 'should be sensitive to how an employee identifies in terms of their gender' and that 'where the employee does not self-identify as either gender, an employer may omit the individual from the gender pay gap calculation' (Government Equalities Office 2021). This means that gender identity is recorded rather than sex, and employees who identify as non-binary are excluded from the data, making it impossible to assess whether non-binary males may have different labour market experiences from non-binary females. It is not obvious why employers would be less likely to discriminate against a woman simply because she identifies as non-binary. For example, employers may still discriminate based on the perceived risk of pregnancy and maternity, irrespective of self-defined gender identity.

Crime

Crime statistics rely on reporting by the police. Many police forces record crimes by male suspects as though they were committed by women at the request of the perpetrator. The Criminal Justice Act 1991 requires the secretary of state for England and Wales to publish relevant information for the purpose of avoiding discrimination, including sex and race discrimination. To meet this requirement, the Ministry of Justice publishes 'Statistics on Women and the Criminal Justice System', which compiles statistics from a range of data sources, including the police, courts and prisons (Ministry of Justice 2020a). The accompanying Technical Guide states that the publication is aimed at understanding 'trends in the CJS [criminal justice system] in England and Wales, and how these vary between the sexes and over time' (Ministry of Justice 2020b, 4). However, it explains further that 'given the range of recording practices throughout the CJS, it is likely that most recording includes a mixture of physiological and personal identity' (Ministry of Justice 2020b, 6). These variously include sex as 'self-identified', 'self-reported', 'officer identified', and a mix of the above (Ministry of Justice 2020b, Table G.01).

In 2021, Police Scotland confirmed that in cases of rape or attempted rape 'if the male who identifies as a woman were to attempt to or penetrate the vagina, anus or mouth of a victim with their penis, Police Scotland would record this as an attempted rape or rape and the male who self-identifies as a woman would be expected to be recorded as a female on relevant police systems.' (Hunter Blackburn et al. 2021).

National Health Service

Over the past twenty years, there has been a gradual shift away from recording and analysing sex in National Health Service (NHS) data sets. Patient data sets have replaced data fields denoting biological sex with fields denoting self-declared gender identity. In 2002, the NHS introduced a 'Person Sex' data field, with two sub-fields: 'Gender at Registration' (sex registered at birth) and 'Gender Current' (self-identified). Around 2016, the NHS replaced these subfields with 'Person Phenotypic Sex' (observed sex) and 'Person Stated Gender', respectively. However, the former is only used in three NHS national data sets (relating to maternity services and neonatal outcomes) and is missing entirely from the NHS patient demographic database (Fair Play for Women 2021).

The NHS's failure to record biological sex on patient records has led to trans patients not being called in for screening for conditions which may affect them due to their sex (Richards 2018). This has potentially fatal consequences for trans people. Administrative data based on patient records is also a vital resource for health research. Throughout the UK, individuals can change their NHS 'gender' marker on request. In Scotland, NHS National Services Scotland (2014) confirmed that '[n]o evidence is required; the patient simply needs to advise either their GP practice or Practitioner Services that they wish to change their gender' (1).

Higher Education Statistics Authority

The role of the Higher Education Statistics Authority (HESA) is to 'collect, assure and disseminate data about UK Higher Education' (HESA 2022a). Higher education institutions return data to HESA on both their staff and students. Data on sex are collected alongside other characteristics such as age, ethnicity and institution. For students, the information includes the subject of study, and for staff, it includes salaries. For staff records, in 2017/8 HESA replaced the binary 'legal sex' variable with a variable labelled 'sexual identification'. The variable description stated: 'This field records the sex of the member of staff' and provided three response categories: male, female and 'other'. The 'other' category included 'people who associate with the terms intersex, androgyne, intergender, ambigender, gender fluid, polygender and genderqueer' (HESA 2018). Yet in reality, being androgynous or otherwise gender non-conforming in no way implies that one lacks a sex.

Student records followed the same structure, with an 'other' option. For tax-reporting purposes, there are only two sex categories, male and female. HESA guidance stated:

> It is therefore no longer possible to ask staff one question about sex, as staff who select 'Other' cannot be reported to the HMRC (Her Majesty's Revenue and Customs). We would recommend that providers ask staff about sex in two separate surveys at two separate points in time to avoid any confusion.
>
> *(HESA 2019)*

Yet the confusion lay entirely with the HESA if they imagined that the sex binary only existed for tax purposes.

The number of students reported as identifying their sex as 'other' has increased more than tenfold over a five-year period, from 510 individuals in 2014/15 to 5,505 in 2020/2021 (HESA 2022b). While many universities have no students at all who claim that their sex is 'other', some have a surprising number of such students. According to the HESA, the University for the Creative Arts had 285 other-sexed students in 2019/20, 4 percent of its student body.

The HESA dropped its guidance on the definition of the 'other' sex category in 2021 and, in 2022, issued amended guidance in line with the England and Wales Census so that the sex variable reverts to legal sex, and the 'other' category is only intended for use in the case of non-UK nationals for whom an additional category is legally recognised by their country of citizenship (HESA 2022c). Thus, the HESA no longer treats gender non-conformity as a third sex.

Athena Swan Charter

The Athena Swan Charter was established in 2005, initially to encourage commitment to advancing the careers of women in STEMM (science, technology, engineering, maths and medicine) subjects in higher education. Monitoring gaps between men and women in recruitment and career progression was an essential feature of the scheme. Yet, in 2016, Athena Swan recommended that data collection should be based exclusively on gender identity, not sex: 'Asking questions about gender is more inclusive than asking questions about sex' (Equality Challenge Unit, 2016).

By 2021, the recommended question on 'gender' included non-binary identities (AdvanceHE 2021):

'How would you describe your gender?

- Man
- Non-binary
- Woman
- In another way (specify, if you wish)
- Prefer not to say'.

If higher education institutions collected data on gender identity in addition to sex, this would provide useful insights into the experiences of trans and non-binary people of each sex. Yet Athena Swan explicitly recommended against asking about both sex and gender identity, as they claimed this could lead to people who identify as trans being outed.

Athena Swan's embrace of 'the wider definition of gender beyond male and female' (Advance HE 2020) meant that sex had been jettisoned.

Following critical commentary which attracted media coverage (Sullivan and Armstrong 2021) Advance HE took down their data collection advice in December 2021. Subsequent guidance (AdvanceHE 2022) recommended asking 'What is your sex?' with options 'Male', 'Female', and 'Prefer not to Say'. A separate question on gender identity was also recommended.

Why are we losing data on sex?

It is difficult to think of an area of life where sex is not an important dimension for analysis, and few quantitative social scientists today would question the central place of sex as an analytic category. So why are surveys and administrative data collection exercises moving away from asking about or observing sex?

The erasure of sex in data collection has been driven by quiet lobbying and has often gone under the radar (Sullivan 2020, 2021). Gender-identity lobbyists have campaigned to remove sex as a protected characteristic in law and to replace sex with gender identity in data collection (Jones and Mackenzie 2020). Much of this campaigning has occurred without public debate, due process or democratic scrutiny, a process termed 'policy capture' (Murray and Hunter Blackburn 2019). The removal of sex-based data collection is part of a wider supranational political project, aimed at replacing sex with self-defined gender identity in law and policy (Murray et al. 2020).

Adding to these dynamics, the gender identity lobby is marked by intolerance of dissent and has waged a remarkably successful campaign to shut down debate, making it difficult to challenge the loss of data on sex. Academics have faced harassment simply for asserting the reality and social salience of sex (Suissa and Sullivan 2021). This has a chilling effect, meaning that normal open and rigorous discourse is effectively suspended.

The arguments against collecting data on sex

Arguments against data collection using a conventional binary sex variable typically confuse sex, gender and gender identity and aim to problematise the concept of sex. Many of the public bodies and organisations influenced by such arguments may be unaware of their intellectual provenance, rooted in 'a set of inter-locking fallacies about sex which derive from a strand of postmodernist queer theory' (Sullivan 2020, 520).

We address the main arguments against collecting data on sex, and related conflations and fallacies, next.

Conflating sex, gender, and gender identity

The gender-identity movement uses the term *gender* to refer to both gender (a social construct) and gender identity (an individual self-perception; Todd and Sullivan, this volume). Yet, whereas gender is rooted in sex and how others treat us based on our sex, gender identity derives its meaning in opposition to sex. A male may 'identify as' a woman, whereas a female simply is a woman.

Statistics Canada's definition of 'gender of person' illustrates the lack of clarity regarding what gender refers to. This definition includes gender identity, 'which refers to the gender that a person feels internally and individually', and gender expression, 'which refers to the way a person presents their gender, regardless of their gender identity, through body language, aesthetic choices or accessories (e.g., clothes, hairstyle and makeup), which may have traditionally been associated with a specific gender' (Statistics Canada, 2021b). So, does gender refer to 'identity', or is it 'expression'? And what is the basis of the 'specific gender' with which certain gender expressions have traditionally been associated?

Attempts to capture some combination of sex, gender and gender identity in a single survey item fall foul of basic principles of questionnaire design, including that multiple-choice response options requiring a single answer must be *mutually exclusive*. The 2021 NHS Staff Survey provides an example of a set of response categories which breaks this principle, asking 'What of the following best describes you?: Female; Male; Non-Binary; Prefer to Self-describe; Prefer not to say' (NHS 2021, 7). The question's wording leaves it unclear what the target of the question is, that is, what information is actually sought. The categories are not mutually exclusive, because non-binary people have a sex – they are either male or female. If the question is intended to record sex, the 'prefer to self-describe' category is both redundant and mysterious. A person's identity may be non-binary or any other preferred description, but this should be captured in a separate question on gender identity, not be confused with sex. Confusing the two concepts leads to poor-quality data on both.

The sex question in the Australian 2021 census includes a 'non-binary sex response category' for 'people who wish to report their sex as other than male or female' (Australian Bureau of Statistics 2021a). Statistical standards from the Australian Bureau of Statistics (Australian Bureau of Statistics 2021b) state that 'a person's reported sex can change over the course of their lifetime and may differ from their sex recorded at birth'. The same claim is made by Statistics New Zealand (2021, 17). At a Scottish High Court Appeal hearing on the definition of sex in Scotland's 2022 census, counsel for the Scottish Government claimed: 'It may once have been thought that sex at birth is immutable. It is no longer so' (MurrayBlackburnMackenzie 2022). Yet sex is immutable – what may actually change is gender identity.

Are sex categories oppressive?

Judith Butler ([1990] 2007) is the most influential theorist behind the denial of the material reality of sex. Butler understands gender as a performance rather than a social structure (Jones, this volume). Butler asserts that sex and gender cannot be distinguished, and argues that sex is socially constructed, in the radical sense that sexed bodies do not exist prior to the categories that people use to describe them in language and law. In other words, sex categories do not describe the sexes but rather create them. This claim seems incredible. Lacking both linguistic and legal categories, can a dog not recognise a bitch when he meets one or vice versa?

For Butler, the categories themselves are responsible for social hierarchy and oppression: 'The "naming" of sex is an act of domination and compulsion, an institutionalised performative that both creates and legislates social reality by requiring the discursive/ perceptual construction of bodies in accord with principles of sexual difference' (Butler 1990, 2007, 157). Sex categories are described as 'violent'. This idea that categories are violent is taken quite literally by Butlerians. For example, Lloyd (2013, 828) claims that the 'constant and unrelenting violent (re-) production of bodies as sexed operates to uphold the norm of compulsory heterosexuality that requires this binary designation of the sexes in the first place' and draws an analogy between such categorisation and a brutal murder. This view underpins the vitriolic response of gender-identity activists to sex-based data collection.

But if categories are responsible for oppression, rather than helping us to describe it, why not apply this logic to other categories? For example, we could abolish poverty simply by ceasing to categorise people as poor. The belief that categories are violent implies that empirical social science is an inherently thuggish pursuit.

A further claim is that sex categories 'deny the existence' of trans people. The claim that asking people their sex denies their existence appears odd, given that the concept of being transgender does not make sense without the existence of a disparity between sex and identity, which, in turn, implies that sex is real. Yet the assertion that 'Trans Women Are Women' is taken to imply that any acknowledgement of biological sex is a denial of trans people's identities, whereas if we distinguish between identity and material factors, it is clear that we can acknowledge everyone's identities without denying their sex.

Are there more than two sexes?

Data standards produced by Statistics New Zealand (2021, 21) suggest that it is incorrect to view sex as a fixed binary variable. They reference Gender Minorities Aotearoa, which define the 'sex binary' as follows:

> An incorrect system of viewing sex as consisting solely of two categories, termed male and female. . . . This system is oppressive, and is a cause of marginalisation for people who do not fit within the sex binary, including many trans and intersex people.
>
> *(Gender Minorities Aotearoa, 2020, 6)*

The claim that sex is 'assigned' rather than observed at birth appears regularly in official documents, for example, Statistics Canada's 2018 guidance refers to 'sex at birth ... typically assigned based on a person's reproductive system and other physical characteristics'.

The claim that there are more than two sexes, and the related idea that sex is 'assigned at birth', is associated with the influential queer theorist Anne Fausto-Sterling. Fausto-Sterling (1993) initially posited the existence of five sexes, later sliding into the claim that sex is a continuous variable: 'Indeed, I would argue further that sex is a vast, infinitely malleable continuum that defies the constraints of even five categories' (21). She then dialled back from such bold claims, in favour of the more nebulous notion that 'sex and gender are best conceptualised as points in a multidimensional space' (Fausto-Sterling 2000, 22). No one has yet attempted to operationalise such a view of sex empirically.

In an attempt to problematise the concept of binary sex, Fausto-Sterling grossly exaggerated the number of people with 'intersex' conditions, now known as differences of sex development (DSDs). DSDs are a group of rare conditions which lead to sex development which differs from the norm (Hilton and Wright, this volume). Fausto-Sterling (2000, 20) claimed that 1.7 percent of the population has an intersex condition. Going further, Judith Butler (1990) has claimed that 'a good ten percent' (146) of people have chromosomal variations outside of the XX/XY norm. Butler attributes this statement to a scientific paper in the journal *Cell* which, in fact, contains no such claim (Page et. al. 1987). In reality, conditions in which chromosomal sex is inconsistent with phenotypic sex or in which the phenotype is not classifiable as either male or female account for only 0.018 percent of births (Sax 2002).

It is clearly a fallacy to suggest that the existence of a small minority of anomalous cases invalidates the existence or usefulness of a categorical variable. As an ethical principle, general data collection exercises should not request information on rare conditions, because this would be intrusive and may potentially identify individuals. Nor can it be justified, since there will not be enough cases for any useful analysis. The appropriation of DSD conditions in the service of a distinct ideological cause is deemed insensitive by many individuals and families affected by DSDs (DSD Families 2021).

Does gender identity always trump sex?

Is it possible that it is really gender identity, and not sex, which affects people's lives? This argument suggests that sex is a mere proxy for gender identity as the true underlying explanatory variable. The claim that gender identity should replace sex is very different from the claim that gender identity matters in addition to sex.

For some outcomes, such as the risk of becoming pregnant or contracting testicular cancer, the evidence against the assertion that gender identity is always the salient variable is overwhelming. In others, such as patterns of criminality, empirical evidence also suggests that sex trumps identity (Dhejne et al. 2011; Fair Play for Women 2020). The hypothesis that sex is never a relevant variable is an extraordinary one and would require extraordinary evidence to support it. No such evidence has yet been put forward.

The hypothesis that gender identity is a more powerful predictor than sex for any particular outcome cannot be tested without data on both sex and gender identity. Those who use the claim that gender identity trumps sex as a justification for not collecting data on sex seek to make it impossible to test their assumptions. This demonstrates a radically anti-scientific approach to evidence.

Has sex changed over time?

The Office for National Statistics stated in 2017 that '[w]ithin today's society the traditional view of gender as a binary classification, male or female, is changing'. No one would deny that gendered roles have changed over time. But does that really imply that humans no longer have just two sexes, male and female? Or that sex is no longer relevant to our lives?

It is certainly the case that demographic variables can change over time. For example, the ethnic group categories used in a society at any given time will tend to reflect the groups that are numerous enough to capture meaningfully and so will change in line with migration flows and fertility. Occupational categories and social-class schemas are revised due to changing labour markets. New questions are added, for example the addition of questions on sexuality and gender identity as these categories have become politically visible. No one has argued against collecting data on gender identity, however. The contested issue is the attempt to remove sex via redefinition in terms of gender identity.

Categories like race and social class are socially constructed. These categories change as society changes. But sex is different. The social implications of being male or female have certainly changed over time and differ between cultures. But the biological categories remain constant and have been recognised in all societies throughout history for the simple reason that they are the basis for human reproduction.

Is asking people's sex a violation of their privacy?

The view that collecting data on sex may constitute an unlawful violation of privacy has gained wide traction. The Government Equalities Office (2021) advice to employers on reporting the gender pay gap suggests that collecting data on sex would be unduly intrusive. Public Health England told sexual health and HIV clinics to stop collecting data on the sex of service users after advice from the LGBT Foundation that it may be unlawful to do so (Newman and Bindel 2021). A similar position has been put forward by the Equality and Human Rights Commission, although it has subsequently changed its view (MurrayBlackburnMackenzie 2021).

Surveys ask about many aspects of people's lives which may be deemed sensitive, from a person's salary to their sexuality. So it is odd that asking about something which is, in the vast majority of cases, readily observable, should be deemed a privacy violation. Moreover, both survey and administrative data sets are typically anonymised so that analysts cannot identify individuals.

In the case of surveys, participation is voluntary, and participants also have the option of not responding to particular questions which they do not want to answer. A 'prefer not to say' option is often explicitly provided.

One data collection exercise which compels respondents to provide data on sex is the census. There is a legal obligation to respond to the census and its required particulars, including sex. However, even in this case, it is clear that requiring data on sex is lawful. Justice Swift, addressing this point in the judicial review of the sex question in the England and Wales Census, ruled that it was unlikely that there was any privacy breach in requiring information on a person's sex but that if it were, it would be justified, as the question would be posed in pursuit of a legitimate objective. He further noted the careful and confidential way in which census information is used (Sullivan 2021).

We recognise that there are sensitivities here because some respondents may prefer not to acknowledge their natal sex. Nevertheless, the purpose of data collection is to provide accurate data which can be used to identify and address social problems. Data collection must always treat respondents with respect but should not lose sight of its function.

Has sex always been self-identified?

Items in surveys are typically self-reported, which means that people are asked to report various facts about themselves and their lives, such as their sex, age, who they live with, how much they earn and so on.

The argument is sometimes made that, since sex has typically been self-reported, it has therefore always been a self-identified measure, implying that it has always referred to gender identity rather than sex. For instance, in relation to the sex question in Scotland's census, the National Records of Scotland (2021) stated that 'the self-completion nature of the survey, combined with there being no previous guidance can be seen as having enabled respondents to reach their own conclusions on how to complete the sex question i.e. self-identification'. Similarly, following changes to the Scottish Household Survey (SHS) in 2018, which saw the longstanding binary sex question replaced with a gender-identity question, the Scottish government claimed that the survey had never collected data on sex:

> As the questions have always reported gender based on what respondents tell interviewers, there has been little change to the concept behind the question being asked. Biological sex is not collected and has never been asked in the SHS.
> *(Scottish Government 2019, 300)*

This conflation of self-reported sex and gender self-identification is misleading. Self-reported data and self-identification are different things. Self-report means that an individual provides their own information, whereas self-identification implies that the information is about the individual's subjective identity rather than their material reality. Social scientists ask people to provide information about both their subjective identities, attitudes and opinions and their objective conditions, and sometimes the interest lies precisely in comparing the two. For example, the British Social Attitudes survey asks people whether they identify with a particular social class and if so which one (Evans and Mellon 2016). It also asks people to report what job they do, and an occupational class variable is derived from this information. As Evans and Mellon (2016) show, many people in professional and managerial jobs identify as working class.

Competing social class schemas exist, and the concept of social class is clearly socially constructed. Yet it is reasonable to make a distinction between an individual's social-class identity and their material conditions, such as the earnings and labour market conditions associated with the kind of job they actually do. Both of these variables, social-class identity and occupation, are self-reported – but only the former concerns identity. 'Self-report' simply refers to the fact that the respondent provides the information. So, if sex is determined via a survey item asking 'what is your sex', it is self-reported. This is distinct from a survey item on self-defined gender identity, where respondents are asked to report their subjective identity rather than their sex.

Are the numbers too small to make a difference?

It is sometimes assumed that the proportion of the population who may not identify with their biological sex is so small that the effects on data quality of asking for gender identity in place of sex must be negligible. However, at the time of writing, we await reliable data on the size of the trans, non-binary and 'gender diverse' population, and international estimates of gender diversity among youth vary widely (MurrayBlackburnMackenzie 2020). Crucially, it is impossible to predict how the prevalence of diverse gender identities may change in the future.

The trans population is unlikely to be evenly distributed, for example by age, sex and geography. This means that the effects on data reliability are likely to be greater at the sub-group level. This can have extreme consequences for particular subgroups. For example, in 2019/2020, a survey by HM Chief Inspector of Prisons (2020, 43) reported that one in 50 prisoners in the men's prison estate described themselves as trans.

The trans population is growing rapidly, particularly among young females (Littman 2018, Cass 2022). Education data may be particularly affected by relatively high numbers of youth, especially girls, identifying outside of their natal sex. The Tavistock and Portman NHS Trust states that between 1.2 percent and 2.7 percent of children and young people are 'gender-diverse' (National Institute for Health and Care Research 2019). A representative population study in Sweden found that, among people aged 22 to 29, 6.3 percent would like to 'live as or be treated as someone of a different sex' (Åhs et al. 2018). A 2018 survey of an urban school district in Pennsylvania found that nearly 10 percent of high school students surveyed reported a gender-diverse identity (Kidd et. al. 2021). The American College Health Association (2021, 2) have reported that in 2008, one in 2,000 female undergraduates in the US identified as transgender, but by 2021, this had risen to one in 20 (5%). Non-standard gender identities are most prevalent among highly educated, relatively affluent youth (Whyte et al. 2018).

In the context of understanding outcomes for 'gender diverse' populations, research suggests that questions on both sex and self-defined gender identity are needed (Reisner et al. 2014). In order to improve both demographic survey data and the health care provided to trans people, clinicians have recommended that information on both natal sex and gender identity should be collected (Mays et al. 2018; Wylie et al. 2016). The experiences of people who identify as trans or non-binary are likely to vary substantially according to their sex. We certainly cannot assume that natal males and females who identify as trans or non-binary or otherwise 'gender diverse' will have the same or similar experiences in any social domain where sex is a factor, such as education, the labour market or experiences of domestic violence or sexual assault. Thus, without accurate data on sex, we cannot adequately monitor the differing experiences of males and females who identify as gender diverse, including those who have the protected characteristic of gender reassignment.

Many people find the idea that small numbers of misclassified cases can be substantively important in statistical analysis counter-intuitive. However, small numbers of people identifying as the opposite sex can, in fact, have substantive implications for research findings and for assessing policy interventions.

Small errors can make a big difference when the baseline category is also small. One instance where this is likely to make a difference is data on gay, lesbian and bisexual people. The removal of sex as a category risks erasing lesbians and gay men as meaningful categories for analysis. For example, in data from more than 40,000 people responding to the UK Household Longitudinal Study 'Understanding Society', 2 percent said that they were gay, lesbian or bisexual. Of the 482 people who stated they were gay/lesbian, 183 were recorded as female (Booker et al. 2017). Given the small size of the gay and lesbian categories, it only takes a small number of people to switch sex categories to skew the data. Heterosexuals are by far the dominant category, and when opposite-sex-attracted people identify as the opposite sex, they are also likely to reclassify as same-sex-attracted. If 1 percent of male Understanding Society respondents identified as lesbians, they would slightly outnumber the current lesbian category. If just 40 males were classified as lesbians, they would represent 18 percent of the lesbian category, which would clearly represent a major skew in the sex composition of the lesbian category. Such a skew in the data would risk significant distortion of research findings on gay and lesbian people. Both sex and sexuality may be associated with outcomes of interest. For example, economists have established that women cohabiting in same-sex couples earn more than women in heterosexual couples, whereas men in co-habiting same-sex couples earn less than men who co-habit with a female partner (Aksoy et al. 2018).

Education researchers often assess phenomena with large sex differentials to help inform policy. For example, there have been various educational initiatives aimed at increasing the proportion of women among higher education students who take degrees in physical science or engineering, although the growth is slow. Table 7.1 shows the HESA figures of first-year students in these subject areas in 2016 and 2018.

Plausible numbers of men self-identifying as women could swamp these trends. In Table 7.1, if there were, in 2018, in reality, the same number of women and men as in 2016, but 6.3 percent of men were misclassified as women (based on Åhs et al. 2018), then the number of students ostensibly classified as women would be 10,908 in physical science and 9,158 in engineering, that is, greater than the number of women actually recorded in 2018. In other words, it is quite possible that plausible rates of misclassification based on gender self-identification could account for the entire growth in female participation in these subjects of study. Even a rate of self-identification of males as female as low as 1.5 percent (instead of the 6.3 percent postulated here) would be enough to account for the whole natural growth between 2016 and 2018. Replacing biological sex with gender identity makes it impossible to reliably assess the impact of policies aimed at increasing female participation in these subjects.

The potential for substantial errors due to small levels of misclassification according to sex increases as the baseline sex ratio increases. Given the very small numbers of women committing violent and sexual crimes, misclassifying even small numbers of males as women leads to a substantive increase in the proportion of these crimes attributed to women. Arrest data for England and Wales show that women typically account for about 15 percent of arrests annually, compared to 85 percent of men (Home Office 2022, Table A.01a). This difference is most marked in relation to

TABLE 7.1 First-Year Undergraduates in Physical Science and Engineering

Physical science

	Female	Male	% Female
2016	10,075	13,215	43.3
2018	10,265	12,475	45.1

Engineering

	Female	Male	% Female
2016	6,855	36,555	15.8
2018	7,280	36,555	17.0

Source: Higher Education Statistics Agency: https://www.hesa.ac.uk/data-and-analysis/students/table-40. Analysis from Professor Lindsay Paterson's contribution to the 2020 Census Judicial Review.

sexual offences, where women accounted for just two percent of arrests annually between 2017/18 and 2020/21 (Home Office 2022, Table A.01a). These low figures mean that a small number of males recorded as women can skew the figures substantively. For example, there were 733 female arrests for sexual offences in 2020/21, compared to 28,307 males arrested for sexual offences in the same year. If just 1 percent (283) of these male offenders were classified as female, this would imply a 39 percent increase in reported sexual offences attributed to female perpetrators.

We know that the possibility of male perpetrators identifying into the female category is not hypothetical, but the prevalence of this phenomenon is impossible to establish precisely because of the lack of data. For example, Crown Prosecution Service (CPS) data for England and Wales shows that, between 2012 and 2018, the proportion of rape defendants classified as women varied between 1.2 percent and 1.8 percent (Crown Prosecution Service 2018, Table 1). During this seven-year period, 436 individuals prosecuted for rape were recorded as women. Rape is classified as a male crime in England and Wales, requiring non-consensual penetration with a penis, and females can only be charged with rape as an accomplice. A Freedom of Information request established that it is not possible to state how many of those 436 individuals who faced prosecution were biological females, due to police policies that allow for gender self-identification in crime recording.

Conclusion

This chapter has explained that sex matters in social statistics. Sex has a powerful influence on a wide range of outcomes at every stage of life, from the risk of selective abortion to life expectancy.

We have documented the rapid loss of data on sex in recent years. This has not been driven by scientific concerns but by highly effective lobbying by groups advocating for the removal of sex as a category in data, policy and law.

Sex and gender identity are distinct concepts. Arguments against collecting data on sex typically depend on muddling the two and attempting to problematise the concept of sex. The intellectual underpinnings of these beliefs are incompatible with scientific approaches to understanding the world.

We have addressed the arguments against data collection on sex. These include that sex categories are oppressive, that there are more than two sexes, that gender identity is always more important than sex, that sex categories are socially constructed and have changed over time, that asking people's sex is a violation of privacy, that data on sex has always been self-reported and is therefore really data on gender identity, and that the number of people with identities incongruent with their sex is too small to make any difference to data analysis.

The arguments against collecting data on sex are unconvincing. In order to fully understand outcomes for people of either sex and any self-defined gender identity, we need data on both variables. As we have argued, concerns about the loss of sex-based data are often brushed aside, as it is assumed that the numbers of people whose gender identities are incongruent with their sex are so low that they will not make a difference to statistical results. While this seems intuitive, we have shown that statistical results may be distorted for at least two reasons. First, the prevalence of trans and non-binary identities is higher in some population sub-groups, for example young people, than in the general population. Second, small levels of misclassification can have a large effect where the baseline category is also small. When both considerations apply, the issue will be compounded. A lack of data on sex will therefore have particularly negative effects on research addressing outcomes for trans people. It also risks erasing lesbians and gay men as meaningful categories for analysis.

We need data on sex in order to understand differences in the lives of women and men, girls and boys, and to monitor and tackle sexism. Striving to collect accurate data on sex is therefore both a scientific and an ethical imperative. Rather than removing data on sex, we should collect data on both sex and gender identity in order to develop a better understanding of the influence of both of these factors, and the intersection between them, on people's lives.

In the UK, there are signs that we are starting to reverse the trend away from sex-based data collection. The ONS was obliged by a judicial review verdict to define the sex question in the England and Wales 2021 Census in terms of legal sex rather than gender identity (Sullivan 2021), although a Scottish court reached a different decision regarding Scotland's 2022 Census. As described earlier, higher education data collected by both the HESA and Advance HE have reverted to including sex. The UK Statistics Authority (2021) has recently published guidance that recommends that 'sex, age and ethnic group should be routinely collected and reported in all administrative data and in-service process data, including statistics collected within health and care settings and by police, courts and prisons'. These gains reflect the combination of quantitative data experts expressing a clearly evidenced view that sex matters; activism and legal cases brought by feminist campaigners, notably Fair Play for Women; and guidance from the Equality and Human Rights Commission reasserting the status of sex as a protected characteristic in law. While much remains to be done, it seems the tide is turning.

References

AdvanceHE. 2020. 'Athena SWAN strengthened and fit for the future'. AdvanceHE. 19 March. https://www.advance-he.ac.uk/news-and-views/athena-swan-strengthened-and-fit-future

AdvanceHE. 2021. 'Gender'. AdvanceHE, 22 August. https://web.archive.org/web/20210822195453/https://www.advance-he.ac.uk/guidance/equality-diversity-and-inclusion/using-data-and-evidence/monitoring-questions/gender

AdvanceHE. 2022. 'Guidance on the collection of diversity monitoring data'. AdvanceHE, 26 April. https://s3.eu-west-2.amazonaws.com/assets.creode.advancehe-document-manager/documents/advance-he/Advance%20HE%20Guidance%20on%20the%20collection%20of%20diversity%20monitoring%20data_1650986130.pdf

Åhs, J., Dhejne, C., Magnusson, C., Dal, H., Lundin, A., Arver, S., Dalman, C., and Kosidou, K. 2018. 'Proportion of adults in the general population of Stockholm County who want gender-affirming medical treatment'. *PLoS One* 13 (10): e0204606.

Aksoy, C.G., Carpenter, C.S. and Frank, J. 2018. 'Sexual Orientation and Earnings: New Evidence from the United Kingdom'. *Industrial and Labor Relations Review* 71(1): pp. 242–272.

American College Health Association. 2021. 'American College Health Association-National College Health Assessment III: Undergraduate Student Reference Group Data Report Spring 2021'. Silver Spring, MD: American College Health Association. https://www.acha.org/documents/ncha/NCHA-III_SPRING-2021_UNDERGRADUATE_REFERENCE_GROUP_DATA_REPORT.pdf

Australian Bureau of Statistics. 2021a. 'ABS Statement on sex and gender questions and the 2021 Census'. Australian Bureau of Statistics, 15 May. https://www.abs.gov.au/media-centre/media-statements/abs-statement-sex-and-gender-questions-and-2021-census

Australian Bureau of Statistics. 2021b. 'Standard for sex, gender, variations of sex characteristics and sexual orientation variables'. Australian Bureau of Statistics. 14 January. https://www.abs.gov.au/statistics/standards/standard-sex-gender-variations-sex-characteristics-and-sexual-orientation-variables/latest-release#sex

Booker, C.L, Rieger, G., and Unger. J.B. (2017). 'Sexual orientation health inequality: Evidence from Understanding Society, the UK Longitudinal Household Study'. *Preventative Medicine* 101: pp. 126–132.

Bryson, A., Joshi, H., Wielgoszewska, B. and Wilkinson, D. 2020. 'A short history of the gender wage gap in Britain'. *Oxford Review of Economic Policy* 36 (4): pp 836–854.

Butler, J. (1990) 2007. *Gender trouble*. New York: Routledge.

Cass, H. 2022. 'Independent review of gender identity services for children and young people: Interim report'. *The Cass Review*, February. Cass Review – Independent Review of Gender Identity Services for Children and Young People

Cassidy, R., Cattan, S. and Crawford, C. 2018. 'Why don't more girls study maths and physics?' Institute for Fiscal Studies, 22 August. https://www.ifs.org.uk/publications/13276

Chao, F., Gerland, P., Cook, A. R., and Alkema, L. 2019. 'Systematic assessment of the sex ratio at birth for all countries and estimation of national imbalances and regional reference levels'. *Proceedings of the National Academy of Sciences* 116 (19): pp. 9303–9311.

Crown Prosecution Service. 2018. 'Sexual offending: Crown Prosecution Service appendix tables'. Office for National Statistics, Crown Prosecution Service, 13 December. https://www.ons.gov.uk/peoplepopulationandcommunity/crimeandjustice/datasets/sexualoffendingcrownprosecutionserviceappendixtables

Dhejne, C., Lichtenstein, P., Boman, M., Johansson, A. L., Långström, N., and Landén, M. 2011. 'Long-term follow-up of transsexual persons undergoing sex reassignment surgery: cohort study in Sweden'. *PLoS ONE* 6 (2): e16885.

DSD Families. 2021. 'Submission to Gender Recognition Reform (Scotland) Bill'. 2 September. Edinburgh: Scottish Government. https://www.gov.scot/binaries/content/documents/govscot/publications/consultation-analysis/2021/08/organisation-responses-to-gender-recognition-consultation-scotland-a-g/documents/dsdfamilies/dsdfamilies/govscot%3Adocument/dsdfamilies.pdf

Equality Challenge Unit. 2016. 'Trans staff and students in HE and colleges: improving experiences'. Equality Challenge Unit, November. https://www.qub.ac.uk/directorates/HumanResources/hr-filestore/Filetoupload%2C866819%2Cen.pdf

Fair Play for Women. 2020. 'Transgender women exhibit a male-type pattern of criminality: Implications for legislators and policy makers'. Fair Play For Women, 12 December. https://fairplayforwomen.com/transgender-male-criminality-sex-offences/

Fair Play for Women. 2021. 'How does the NHS record information about sex and gender identity?' Fair Play For Women, 16 June. https://fairplayforwomen.com/how-does-the-nhs-record-data-about-sex/

Evans, G., and Mellon, J. 2016. *Social class: Identity, awareness and political attitudes: Why are we still working class?* British Social Attitudes, vol. 33. London: National Centre for Social Research.

Fausto-Sterling, A. 1993. 'The five sexes: Why male and female are not enough'. *The Sciences* 33 (2): pp. 20–24.

Fausto-Sterling, A. 2000. 'The five sexes, revisited'. *The Sciences* 40 (4): pp. 17–23.

Gender Minorities Aotearoa. 2020. *Trans 101: Glossary of trans words and how to use them.* 4th ed. Wellington, Aotearoa New Zealand: Gender Minorities Aotearoa. https://genderminorities.com/wp-content/uploads/2021/08/Glossary-2020.pdf

Government Equalities Office. 2021. Who needs to report their gender pay gap'. London: UK Government. Updated 1 November 2021. https://www.gov.uk/guidance/who-needs-to-report-their-gender-pay-gap#gender-identity

Grundy, E. and Murphy, M. 2015. 'Demography and public health'. In *Oxford Textbook of Global Public Health*, edited by R. Detels, M. Guilliford, Q. A. Karim, and C. C. Tan, pp. 718–735. Oxford: Oxford University Press.

Higher Education Statistics Authority. 2018. 'Staff 2017/18: Fields required from institutions in all fields: Sexual identification'. Higher Education Statistics Authority. https://web.archive.org/web/20220719162824/https://www.hesa.ac.uk/collection/c17025/a/sexid

Higher Education Statistics Authority. 2019. 'Staff 2019/20. Fields required from institutions in All fields: Sex identifier'. Higher Education Statistics Authority. https://web.archive.org/web/20220721171801/https://www.hesa.ac.uk/collection/c19025/a/sexid

Higher Education Statistics Authority. 2021. 'Sex identifier (SEXID)'. Higher Education Statistics Authority. https://web.archive.org/web/20220719165446/https://www.hesa.ac.uk/collection/student/datafutures/a/student_sexid

Higher Education Statistics Authority. 2022a. 'About HESA'. Higher Education Statistics Authority. 14 July 2022. https://web.archive.org/web/20220719170511/https://www.hesa.ac.uk/about

Higher Education Statistics Authority. 2022b. 'Who's studying in HE? Higher Education Statistics Authority'. 10 February 2022. https://web.archive.org/web/20220719172202/https://www.hesa.ac.uk/data-and-analysis/students/whos-in-he

Higher Education Statistics Authority. 2022c. 'Sex identifier amended'. https://web.archive.org/web/20220719162143/https://www.hesa.ac.uk/definitions/sex-identifier-amended-12-may-2022

HM Inspectorate of Prisons. 2020. 'HM Chief Inspector of Prisons for England and Wales. Annual Report: 2019 to 2020'. 20 October. London: UK Government.

Home Office. 2022. 'Arrest Statistics: Police powers and procedures, stop and search and arrests, 2020/21'. 6 May. London: UK Government. https://assets.publishing.service.gov.uk/government/uploads/system/uploads/attachment_data/file/1072832/arrest-police-powers-procedures-mar21-tables-2e.ods

Hunter Blackburn, L., Mackenzie, L. and Murray, K. 2021. 'Petitioner submission of 7 June 2021'. Scottish Parliament Citizen Participation and Public Petitions Committee. https://www.parliament.scot/chamber-and-committees/committees/current-and-previous-committees/session-6-citizen-participation-and-public-petitions-committee/correspondence/2021/pe1876_a-petitioner-submission-of-7-june-2021

Jones, J. and Mackenzie, L. 2020. 'The political erasure of sex: Sex and the census'. Oxford: University of Oxford. https://thepoliticalerasureofsex.org/wp-content/uploads/2020/10/The-Political-Erasure-of-Sex_Full-Report.pdf

Kidd, K.M., Sequeira, G.M., Douglas, C., Paglisotti, T., Inwards-Breland, D.J., Miller, E., and Coulter, R.W. 2021. 'Prevalence of gender-diverse youth in an urban school district'. *Pediatrics* 147 (6): e2020049823.

Koblinsky, M.A., Campbell, O. and Harlow, S. 2018. 'Mother and more: A broader perspective on women's health'. In *The Health of Women*, edited by M. Koblinsky, J. Timyan, and J. Gay. pp. 33–62. New York: Routledge.

Littmann, L. 2018. 'Parent reports of adolescents and young adults perceived to show signs of a rapid onset of gender dysphoria'. *PLoS One* 14 (3): e0214157.

Lloyd, M. (2013). 'Heteronormativity and/as Violence: The "Sexing" of Gwen Araujo'. *Hypatia* 28 (4): pp. 818–834.

Mays, J.A., Greene, D.N., Metcalf, R.A., and Pagano, M.B. 2018. 'Transfusion support for transgender men of childbearing age'. *Transfusion* 58 (3): pp. 823–825.

Ministry of Justice. 2020a. 'Statistics on Women and the Criminal Justice System 2019'. Ministry of Justice. https://assets.publishing.service.gov.uk/government/uploads/system/uploads/attachment_data/file/938360/statistics-on-women-and-the-criminal-justice-system-2019.pdf

Ministry of Justice. 2020b. 'A Technical Guide to Statistics on Women and the Criminal Justice System, 2019'. Ministry of Justice. https://assets.publishing.service.gov.uk/government/uploads/system/uploads/attachment_data/file/938460/technical-guide-to-women-and-the-CJS-2019.pdf

MurrayBlackburnMackenzie. 2020. 'International evidence and the risks of reframing the sex question in the census'. MurrayBlackburnMackenzie, 30 November. https://murrayblackburnmackenzie.org/2020/11/30/international-evidence-and-the-risks-of-reframing-the-sex-question-in-the-census/

MurrayBlackburnMackenzie. 2021. 'Diminishing the value of public sector data: How the Chief Statistician's guidance lost sight of biological sex'. MurrayBlackburnMackenzie, 4 November. https://murrayblackburnmackenzie.org/2021/11/04/diminishing-the-value-of-public-sector-data-how-the-chief-statisticians-guidance-lost-sight-of-biological-sex/

MurrayBlackburnMackenzie. 2022. 'Gender recognition reform and data collection'. MurrayBlackburnMackenzie, 5 June. https://murrayblackburnmackenzie.org/2022/06/05/gender-recognition-reform-and-data-collection/

Murray, K. and L. Hunter Blackburn. 2019. 'Losing sight of women's rights: the unregulated introduction of gender self-identification as a case study of policy capture in Scotland'. *Scottish Affairs* 28 (3): pp. 262–289.

Murray, K., Blackburn, L. and Mackenzie, L. 2020. 'Reform "under the radar"? Lessons for Scotland from the development of gender self-declaration laws in Europe'. *Edinburgh Law Review* 24 (2): pp. 281–289.

National Records of Scotland. 2021. 'Sex question recommendation report'. 29 April. https://www.scotlandscensus.gov.uk/documents/sex-question-recommendation-report/html/

Newman, M. and Bindel, J. 2021. '"Viruses do not recognise pronouns": Use of gender identity by sexual health clinics causes confusion and concerns over data'. *Lesbian and Gay News*, 1 October. https://staging.lesbianandgaynews.com/2021/09/use-of-gender-identity-as-descriptor-by-sexual-health-clinics-causes-confusion-and-concerns-over-data/

NHS National Services Scotland. 2014. 'Requirements for processing a change of gender and title. Reference: 2014–000084'. NHS National Services Scotland, 25 June. https://www.ngicns.scot.nhs.uk/wp-content/uploads/2021/04/2014-06-25-Requirements-for-Processing-a-Change-of-Gender-and-Title-NSS-FOI.pdf

NHS. 2021. 'National NHS Staff Survey 2021'. NHS. https://www.nhsstaffsurveys.com/static/5051c9bf4e3622339dc41f581d4739e7/Core-questionnaire-2021.pdf

National Institute for Health and Care Research. 2019. 'Outcomes and predictors of outcome for children and young people referred to UK gender identity development services:

A longitudinal investigation'. National Institute for Health and Care Research. https://fundingawards.nihr.ac.uk/award/17/51/19.

Office for National Statistics. 2017. 'Gender identity update'. Office for National Statistics, January. https://www.ons.gov.uk/methodology/classificationsandstandards/measuringequality/genderidentity/genderidentityupdate

Page, D., Mosher, R., Simpson, E., Fisher, E., Mardon, G., Pollack, J., McGillivray, B., Chapelle, A. and Brown, L. 1987. 'The sex-determining region of the human Y chromosome encodes a finger protein'. *Cell* 51 (6): 1091–1104.

Ploubidis, G., Sullivan, A., Brown, M. and Goodman, A. 2017. 'Psychological distress in mid-life: evidence from the 1958 and 1970 British birth cohorts'. *Psychological Medicine* 47 (2): pp. 291–303.

Reisner, S.L., Conron, K.J., Tardiff, L.A., Jarvi, S., Gordon, A. and Austin, S. 2014. 'Monitoring the health of transgender and other gender minority populations: Validity of natal sex and gender identity survey items in a U.S. national cohort of young adults'. *BMC Public Health* 14: Article 1224.

Richards, A. 2018. 'Trans men not offered NHS routine screening for cancers'. *Evening Standard*, 15 January. https://www.standard.co.uk/news/health/trans-men-not-offered-nhs-routine-screening-for-cancers-a3740586.html

Sax, L. 2002. 'How common is Intersex? A response to Anne Fausto-Sterling'. *Journal of Sex Research* 39 (3): pp. 174–178.

Scottish Government. 2019. *Scottish Household Survey 2018: Annexes.* Edinburgh: Scottish Government. https://www.gov.scot/binaries/content/documents/govscot/publications/statistics/2019/09/scotlands-people-annual-report-results-2018-scottish-household-survey/documents/annexes/annexes/govscot%3Adocument/annexes.pdf

Scottish Government. 2021. *Data collection and publication guidance: Sex, gender identity, trans status.* Edinburgh: Scottish Government.

Shorrocks, R. 2018. 'Cohort change in political gender gaps in Europe and Canada: The role of modernization'. *Politics & Society* 46 (2): pp. 135–175.

Smith, G. 2014. 'Long term trends in female and male involvement in crime'. In *The Oxford Handbook of Gender, Sex and crime*, edited by R. Gartner and B. McCarthy, pp. 139–157. Oxford: Oxford University Press.

Statistics Canada. 2018. 'Sex of person'. Statistics Canada. Updated 1 October 2021. https://www23.statcan.gc.ca/imdb/p3Var.pl?Function=DEC&Id=467214

Statistics Canada. 2021a. 'Sex at birth of person'. Statistics Canada. Updated 2 November. https://www23.statcan.gc.ca/imdb/p3Var.pl?Function=DEC&Id=24101

Statistics Canada. 2021b. 'Gender of Person. Statistics Canada. Updated 1 October 2021. https://www23.statcan.gc.ca/imdb/p3Var.pl?Function=DEC&Id=1326692

Statistics New Zealand. 2021. *Statistical standard for gender, sex, and variations of sex characteristics.* April 2021. https://www.stats.govt.nz/assets/Methods/Data-standards-for-sex-gender-and-variations-on-sex-characteristics/downloads/Data-standard-for-gender-sex-and-variations-of-sex-characteristics.pdf

Suissa, J. and Sullivan, A. 2021. 'The gender wars, academic freedom and education'. *Journal of Philosophy of Education* 55 (1): pp. 55–82.

Sullivan, A. 2020. 'Sex and the census: Why surveys should not conflate sex and gender-identity'. *International Journal of Social Research Methodology* 23 (5): pp. 517–524.

Sullivan, A. 2021. 'Sex and the Office for National Statistics: A case study in policy capture'. *The Political Quarterly*. Published ahead of print 24 June 2021. https://doi.org/10.1111/1467-923X.13029

Sullivan, A. and Armstrong, J. 2021. 'Has Athena Swan lost its way?' British Educational Research Association, 30 November. https://www.bera.ac.uk/blog/has-athena-swan-lost-its-way

UK Statistics Authority (2021). *Inclusive Data Taskforce recommendations report: Leaving no one behind – How can we be more inclusive in our data?* London: ONS.

Voas, D., McAndrew, S. and Storm, I. 2013. 'Modernization and the gender gap in religiosity: Evidence from cross-national European surveys'. *Kölner Zeitschrift für Soziologie und Sozialpsychologie* 65: pp. 259–282.

Whyte, S., Brooks, R.C., and Torgler, B. 2018. 'Man, woman, "other": Factors associated with nonbinary gender identification'. *Archives of Sexual Behaviour* 47: pp. 2397–2406.

Wylie, K., Knudson, G., Khan, S.I., Bonierbale, M., Watanyusakul, S., and Baral, S. 2016. 'Serving transgender people: clinical care considerations and service delivery models in transgender health'. *The Lancet* 388 (10042): pp. 401–411.

8
SEX AND GENDER IN LAW

Rosemary Auchmuty and Rosa Freedman

This chapter considers the concepts of sex and gender in relation to law and particularly in relation to claims for self-identification of legal sex and the replacement of 'sex' as a protected characteristic under equality law by the concept of 'gender identity'. To date, discussions about self-identification of legal sex have taken place amongst a relatively small group of mainly global North states (e.g. in Europe, North America and Australasia), often with very different legal approaches to the overarching topic and to the individual legal issues within their jurisdictions. Those debates often centre on human rights, referencing human rights mechanisms in the international arena but with limited understanding or discussion of how those mechanisms work, the powers they hold, or how their jurisprudence influences the creation and interpretation of domestic law. At the national level in the United Kingdom, there has been misinterpretation, misunderstanding and misrepresentation of the law by lobbying groups and other bodies that is only now beginning to be addressed and corrected by legal authorities. This chapter sets out the current position and history of sex and gender in English and international law to demonstrate not only that, in both jurisdictions, 'sex' and 'gender' have been treated as two distinct concepts, but also that they should remain so. In doing so, we aim to contribute to greater knowledge and understanding of what the law is and how it should be applied.

Our sexed heritage

That men and women enjoy a largely equal status in law today is due to the efforts of feminist campaigners who sought to separate the inevitability of the sexed body from the socially-imposed gender norms that had been built upon it (Levine 1987; Smith 1990; Caine 1997; Rackley and Auchmuty 2019). By identifying and peeling back the layers of gendered norms and socialisation into those norms from their association with particular sexed bodies, feminists tried to remove the restrictions on women's access to rights enjoyed by men as well as the mechanisms which gave men rights and power *over* women.

Much of first-wave (nineteenth-century) feminist energy was devoted to showing that women's supposedly 'natural' predisposition to domestic life and their 'natural' inability to compete intellectually, creatively or physically with men were not due to an innate nature at all but the product of a sustained process of socialisation that began with the arrival of a female baby (e.g. Cobbe [1881] 2010). Only by challenging the assumption that women's biological make-up meant that their role should be confined to marriage, homemaking and rearing children – an argument developed in response to the separation of work and home after the Industrial Revolution – could feminists hope to change the legal customs that barred women from public life and disqualified them from participating in lawmaking as voters, Members of Parliament and lawyers. They realised they had to show that possession of a female body did not mean that a woman could not function in what were seen to be masculine fields of activity. It is the great achievement of first-wave feminism that they succeeded. Having managed to gain admission to an academic education, they quickly showed themselves intellectually the equal of men; and from there, they made their way into the professions. With the achievement of the vote for some women in the Representation of the People Act 1918 and the removal of the barrier of sex from the ability to work in any profession (except the church) in the Sex Disqualification (Removal) Act 1919, they achieved a measure of formal equality that went a long way towards breaking the link between sex and appropriate social roles for women.

The other goal of first-wave feminism was to expose and dismantle coverture, the doctrine that denied married women legal independence and failed to protect them (although it purported to do so) from their husbands. Through their research and writings, feminists demonstrated how coverture facilitated men's exploitation and abuse of their wives at every level – financial, physical, sexual and psychological (Norton 1854; Bodichon [1854] 1987; Cobbe [1868] 1995; Cobbe [1878] 1995). Feminist campaigning led to reforms granting married women control over their property (Married Women's Property Acts 1870 and 1882), rights to their children (Custody of Infants Acts 1839 and 1873) and some relief from male violence (Matrimonial Causes Act 1878). The clearest example of legal injustice being justified by 'nature' and biology was the sexual double standard that made every allowance for men's sexual 'needs' and desires while punishing female exercise of an independent sexuality and even the victims of men's licentiousness. Men's abuse was tolerated, even expected, because of men's physical make-up; women, being innately moral, were not supposed to be sexual at all. Here, too, first-wave feminists were active: in a rare example of cross-class protest against the sex bias in the law, first-wave feminists achieved the repeal of the Contagious Diseases Acts, which exposed prostitutes to forced medical examinations and imprisonment while their male clients were left unmolested (Butler [1870] 1984).

History shows that there is always a backlash after feminist gains. The idea that women's 'natural' place was in the home was quickly restored after the upheavals of the First World War (1914–18) and again after the Second (1939–45; Wilson 1980). While the pressure was largely social, remnants of coverture assured a legal basis for the ideology: husbands remained legal guardians of a couple's children until the Guardianship of Children Act 1975 and heads of the household for the purposes of the Census until 2001; couples were jointly taxed, in *his* name, until the Finance Act 1988; domestic violence was considered by police and courts alike to be a 'private' matter, not requiring legal intervention until 1976 (Domestic Violence and Matrimonial Proceedings Act); husbands could not be charged with rape of their wives until 1991 (*R v R* [1991] 3 WLR 767). Discrimination against women was freely permitted, allowing banks and building societies to refuse loans to women or require a male guarantor and lawyers to insist on conveying the marital home to the husband alone. Equal pay only existed in one or two professions, and there were still advertisements for 'Jobs for men and boys' and 'Jobs for women and girls'.

So, when the Women's Liberation Movement (second-wave feminism) emerged at the end of the 1960s, once again aided by an expanding economy that required the presence of married women in the workplace, it faced the task, yet again, of breaking down the association between women's reproductive role and their social role as wives and mothers (Todd, this volume). The Sex Discrimination Act 1975 outlawed discrimination against women (and also against men) in employment, education, goods, facilities, services and premises. Jobs could no longer be sex-specific unless sex was a 'genuine occupational requirement' for the post. While the Act was hugely important in shifting attitudes and opening opportunities for both women and men to work in fields from which they had formerly been excluded and for women to progress to levels hitherto sacred to men, feminists knew all too well that formal equality measures were not going to be enough to ensure women's *substantive* equality. What was also needed were sex-specific measures to *recognise women's sexed difference* from men and to *compensate for their historical disadvantage*. From this realisation came the hard-fought rulings on pregnancy and maternity rights (Atkins and Hoggett 1984, ch. 2; Horton 2018; Morris 2019), the campaigns around sexual harassment in the workplace and violence and abuse at home (Atkins and Hoggett 1984, ch. 7) and positive action policies in politics and at work (Atkins and Hoggett 1984, ch. 3).

As this brief history shows, women's current formal equality masks a legal heritage of inequality, discrimination and exploitation derived from, and justified by, our physical difference from men – our biology – against which feminists have always had to fight and which persists in both the public sphere (unequal pay, for example, usually being explained by reference to women's reproductive role) and the private (in the statistics of violence and abuse of women by men).

Definitions

Law starts from the proposition that male and female human beings are physically different. Sex is defined on the basis of reproductive function, and 'woman' has always been understood in English law by reference to female biology. So far as we know, the word has never been defined in statute – not in itself an unusual feature of English law, which does not even have a written constitution – because it has been taken for granted that it meant 'adult human female'. (The word *man*, in contrast, has caused many problems, as the law sometimes includes women within it and sometimes not, leading to a century of litigation in what were known as the 'persons' cases – see Sachs and Hoff Wilson 1978.)

This understanding of law and biology was confirmed in the case of *Corbett v Corbett* [1970] 2 All ER 33 which concerned a well-known transsexual model, April Ashley. Born George Jamieson, Ashley had been a sailor as a young man before embarking on a course of hormone treatment and genital surgery and living as though she were a woman. She married Arthur Corbett, 3rd Baron Rowallen, who was well aware of her background. The case centred on their mutual desire to end their marriage. He said it should be annulled on the basis that April Ashley remained a man despite being transsexual. (Marriage was then defined in law as the union of one man and one woman.) She sought divorce on the ground of non-consummation. The court looked in great detail at what 'sex' is for the purposes of law. The judge, Mr Justice Ormerod, who had a medical background and demonstrated deep understanding of the issues, ruled that sex is about chromosomes, endogenous gonads and genitalia, and that the sex of a person is determined by at bare minimum two of those three markers. This meant that even when a person such as April Ashley altered their external genitalia, their sex remained that defined by their chromosomes and endogenous gonads. While deeply sympathetic to those who experienced gender dysphoria, Ormerod made it clear that sex is about biology. The case received much press attention at the time.

Although this case is more than 50 years old, it remains good law. The English doctrine of precedent ensures that, unless or until overturned by subsequent case law or statute, a decided case must be followed. None of the cases since that time have challenged the definition of sex as biology, nor have any statutes overturned the law set out by Ormerod in his judgment. So, we adopt that definition as the current law.

As for 'gender', in spite of efforts by second-wave feminists to use it to distinguish between the *biological* and the *social* characteristics associated with each sex (Oakley 1972), in the last decades of the twentieth century the word came to be used as a synonym for 'sex' in expressions such as 'gender pay gap'. We see it used in that sense in Parliamentary debates and case law, but it was not until 2004 that it entered the *legislative* discourse. The Gender Recognition Act 2004 (GRA) allows the law to treat a person as someone of the other sex if they have obtained a Gender Recognition Certificate (GRC). Possession of such a certificate enables the person to change their statement of sex on all official documentation, such as birth certificate, driving licence and passport. To obtain a GRC, a person must be at least 18, have lived as if a member of the opposite sex for two years, intend to remain permanently in that gender, and have a medical diagnosis of gender dysphoria. Surgical modification of the body is not required. The GRA creates a legal fiction whereby the person is thenceforth treated as a member of the opposite sex from their birth sex for many but not all purposes. Legal fictions exist in areas where something known not to be true in reality is treated as truth for the purposes of law: for example, the personhood of companies (Schane 1986; Fagundes 2001).

Nevertheless, people in possession of a GRC retain characteristics of their birth sex that distinguish them from persons born into the acquired sex. One obvious distinction is biological so that a transgender woman's medical needs will not map on to the gynaecological or obstetrics provision in a hospital, while a trans man's might. The law also recognises some situations where the person with a GRC will not be encompassed within the new sex (see the next section). For example, the Equality Act 2010 (EA) allows for 'sex' as well as 'gender re-assignment' to be a protected characteristic in order to preserve some spaces, such as changing rooms and refuges, for those with female (or male) bodies alone. This is a balancing exercise, which also takes into account the intersection of sex with other protected characteristics such as religion. For example, an argument for sex-specific changing rooms is that several faiths do not permit women to undress in the presence of male bodies or vice versa. Separate spaces are also justified in the interests of the social goal of women's protection, for example to allow sex-specific refuges set up for women escaping male violence.

The rights of any particular group are not absolute and, as with all rights, courts may be called upon to decide whether the right of a member of one protected group should have precedence in a given situation over the right of a member of a different protected group. For example, in *Lee v McArthur and Ashers* ([2018] UKSC 49), the Supreme Court (the highest court in the UK) ruled that it was lawful for bakers to turn away the custom of a client because he had asked them to produce a cake with the message 'support gay marriage', something that was contrary to their religious beliefs. The court emphasised that the bakers had not discriminated against Mr Lee on the basis of his sexual orientation but rather that they could not be compelled to promote a message with which they profoundly disagreed because of their protected characteristic of freedom of religion or belief. The ruling was even supported by some prominent LGBT+ activists who pointed to the ruling as being important to protect the hypothetical gay baker who might in the future be asked to create a cake with a message against gay marriage. The issue of belief as a protected characteristic was further discussed in *Maya Forstater v CGD Europe*: UKEAT/0105/20/JOJ, in which the Employment Appeal Tribunal found that Forstater's comments and gender-critical beliefs were shared by others and 'statements of neutral fact', not expressions of antipathy towards trans persons or transphobic. Her views met the threshold of being a 'philosophical belief', that is that the belief is 'worthy of respect in a democratic society, not incompatible with human dignity and not in conflict with the fundamental rights of others'.

Unfortunately, courts and the government have so far avoided making a clear and unequivocal statement that, while for most purposes possession of a GRC allows a person to be treated as a member of the other sex, this does not mean that they *are* a person of the other sex or will be so treated in every situation. Further, they have failed to define 'gender reassignment', still less 'gender identity', making it difficult for courts to interpret and apply current statutes. In the 2020 case of *Elan-Cane* [2020] EWCA Civ 36, where a person who self-defined as 'non-binary' lost an action against the Home Office for failing to allow an 'X' option as a third 'gender' option on a passport, a person's gender was described by the Court of Appeal (where appeals against first-instance judgments are heard) as 'a matter of self-perception'. If this is so, then definition becomes impossible and, with it, enforcement of any discrimination legislation, both because the courts cannot determine how a person perceives him- or herself and because any definition cannot deal with the long – and constantly increasing – list of gender categories set out by organisations such as Stonewall (Stonewall n.d.).

Domestic Law and Human Rights

The main cause of the conflict in England and Wales over sex and gender in law is the tension between two key pieces of legislation: the GRA and the EA. Both Acts protect the human rights of minority groups, but the fact that they were created for very different reasons, seemingly without due consideration as to how they might interact with one another, has caused significant problems in theory and in practice, leading to competing interpretations as to how they ought to be applied.

The background to the GRA is as follows. In 1998, Parliament passed the Human Rights Act, which brought into domestic law the European Convention on Human Rights to which the UK had been a signatory for almost half a century. (In a dualist state, domestic legislation is required in order to give effect to international laws.) Article 8 of the Convention assures the right to a private and family life and Article 12 the right to marry. A case was soon taken through the domestic courts and then on appeal to the European Court of Human Rights about whether the right to a private and family life of a transsexual named Christine Goodwin had been violated by the law's failure to recognise her as a transsexual *woman* (*Goodwin v. United Kingdom*, Application no. 28957/95, Council of Europe: European Court of Human Rights, 11 July 2002). Goodwin argued that by not being able to change her birth certificate, her employer knew of her transsexual status (which she would have preferred to keep private) and also that she was not able to marry a man because same-sex marriage was not allowed at that time. She also objected to having to wait until she was 65 to receive her pension, rather than 60, which, as a woman, she was then entitled to (at that time there were different retirement ages for men and women). The European Court of Human Rights ruled that this violated her Article 8 and 12 rights.

This ruling obliged the state to bring domestic law into line with the Convention, so in 2004 the UK Parliament enacted the GRA. The Act states that for a person to change their *legal sex* they must have a medical diagnosis and have lived meaningfully as though they were a person of the other sex for two consecutive years. And while this provision does not change the fact of someone's *biological sex* – chromosomes, gonads and genitalia – it provides a mechanism that allows the law to treat a person as though they were the other sex. It is important to note, however, that it *allows*, rather than *mandates*, the law to do so and that there are some exceptions where the law treats such individuals as members of their biological sex. Where a person meets the legal test, s/he receives a Gender Recognition Certificate that allows her/him to change their birth certificate and be treated in law as a person of their preferred sex.

The EA replaced and brought together all the earlier equalities legislation, including that related to sex, race, disability and sexuality, into one piece of law (Hepple 2010). Under the Act, discrimination is unlawful on the basis of nine protected characteristics, among them 'sex' and 'gender reassignment'. 'Gender reassignment' was included because of the Gender Recognition Act 2004 while 'sex' was there both to carry forward the protections enacted under the Equal Pay Act 1970 and the Sex Discrimination Act 1975 and also to recognise the need for sex-segregated services set up specifically for women's protection, such as separate accommodation in prisons, medical facilities and youth hostels, or introduced after feminist campaigning, such as refuges and rape crisis centres (Kaganas 2019; Diduck 2019). Inclusion of 'sex' as a protected characteristic also provided a mechanism for redressing the historical imbalance of power between men and women in the public arena, permitting the provision of separate women's sports and all-women shortlists for political parties or prizes in business (Atkins 2019; Devine, this volume).

Sex is defined in law by s.212(1) EA to mean that a woman is a female, while a man is a male. 'Male' and 'female' in this context relate to biological sex classifications. Section 9(1) of the GRA, however, allows a biological male to be legally considered female on acquisition of a GRC. There are therefore two ways to be a man or woman in law: biologically by birth or legally by acquisition of a GRC.

The EA introduced exemptions to protect single-sex services. There are nine specific provisions allowing direct sex discrimination: Separate- and single-sex services (Schedule 3 ss. 26, 27 and 28), Occupational requirement (Schedule 9), Communal accommodation (Schedule 23), Charities (Section 193), Associations (Schedule 16) and Single sex schools (Schedule 11). These exemptions can be used to exclude from female-only services men and also, in some circumstances, males with the protected characteristic of gender reassignment. As the Equality and Human Rights Commission (EHRC, 2021) – the country's national human rights institution – explained:

> If you are accessing a service provided for men-only or women-only, the organisation providing it should treat you according to your gender identity. In very restricted circumstances it is lawful for an organisation to provide a different service or to refuse the service to someone who is undergoing, intends to undergo or has undergone gender reassignment.

The statute provides at s.28 to Schedule 3 that

[a] person does not contravene section 29, so far as relating to gender reassignment discrimination, only because of anything done in relation to a matter within sub-paragraph (2) if the conduct in question is a proportionate means of achieving a legitimate aim.

The matters are:
(a) the provision of separate services for persons of each sex;
(b) the provision of separate services differently for persons of each sex;
(c) the provision of a service only to persons of one sex.

What happens then when someone holds a GRC and wants to access single-sex services that fall under the EA exemptions? The EHRC had previously stated that it was unlawful to exclude trans women with a GRC from single-sex services. Following the consultations on self-identification for the purposes of obtaining a GRC in the autumn of 2018, that guidance was changed to '[a] business may have a policy about providing its service to transsexual users, but this policy must still be applied on a case-by-case basis' and that a birth certificate proves legal sex. That approach appears to leave each situation to the discretion of the service-provider, with limited guidance on how to apply the law to each individual case. This approach of a 'case-by-case basis' was adopted in *R v AEA and EHRC* [2021] EWHC 1623 (Admin) in which the court ruled that the EHRC's approach was lawful. In that same case, the EHRC acknowledged that some service providers had misinterpreted the EA and had adopted unlawful policies that did not uphold single sex exemptions and therefore called on the government for clearer guidance to be provided in this area.

The government's 2018 consultation on proposed reforms to the GRA was expected to be relatively non-controversial, with an estimate of 700 expected responses. But more than 100,000 responses were submitted, thanks to information sharing and campaigning from grassroots organisations concerned about women's and/or trans rights and the resulting significant media attention. The most contested proposal was one that would allow individuals to obtain a GRC simply by self-identifying their legal sex, without any further requirements. Discussions about self-identification brought to the fore the conflict of rights between the GRA and the EA and the failure of courts and policymakers to clarify the exemptions for single-sex spaces under the EA. The public became more aware that trans rights activists and organisations such as Stonewall had been advising organisations that maintained single-sex spaces – such as the National Health Service, schools, the Girl Guides, prisons and sports teams – that they must include any person who self-identified as women or men whether or not they held a GRC. This is legally incorrect. The EA specifically allows for these exceptions to the terms of the GRA, and self-identification is not yet recognised in law. There had also been legally incorrect advice given that a GRC *always* allows a holder to access single-sex spaces. The threat to natal women has been starkly exposed by revelations of male sexual offenders without GRCs asserting that they are trans women in order to serve their time in the female prison estate, some of whom have gone on to assault female prisoners (Phoenix, this volume). It has been argued that we should not judge the motives of trans activists by the actions of this small group. But laws exist to protect us against the small minority who offend.

Discussions about law reform and self-identification in England and Wales did not take place in a vacuum. Other countries had or have been grappling with similar issues, each with its own context for such discussions, and different approaches have been adopted (Burt, this volume). In England and Wales, the government decided to shelve the reform proposals after the consultations but failed to provide any clarity on the issues that had arisen regarding the conflicts between the different GRA and EA provisions and the exemptions in the EA.

Human rights issues relating to sex and gender identity have been raised in other domestic legal contexts over recent years. Three particularly high-profile cases are worth noting. In 2020, the Court of Appeal refused to allow Freddy McConnell, a trans man, to be registered as the father on his child's birth certificate (*R v McConnell* [2020] EWCA Civ 559). The Supreme Court refused an application to hear a final appeal in the UK, and McDonnell is seeking leave to appeal to the European Court of Human Rights, claiming that his human rights have been violated by the UK government's insistence that he be registered as the mother on the birth certificate of the child he gestated and gave birth to. In 2021, the UK Supreme Court ruled, in the case of *Elan-Cane* [2021] UKSC 56, that there is no obligation for a state to provide a third ('X') gender marker on passports. The Court examined the UK's human rights obligations and found that there is no requirement under international human rights law to provide a neutral sex/gender category. In the same year, Keira Bell applied for leave to appeal to the Supreme Court to overturn a Court of Appeal ruling [2021] EWCA Civ 1363 that children under the age of 16 are able to consent to taking puberty blockers to prevent puberty until such time as they are old enough to consent to cross-sex hormones.

As the discussion above shows, human rights law is frequently invoked in these cases and sometimes in competing ways. As things stand at present, the European Convention on Human Rights is incorporated into domestic law through the Human Rights Act 1998, but a right of appeal exists to the European Court of Human Rights (which is quite separate from the European Court of Justice, the court of the European Union). This means that it is crucial to understand the international human rights law frameworks on sex and gender (including other international conventions to which the UK is a signatory) when discussing human rights law at the domestic level. The next section explains the operation of international human rights law on issues of sex and gender.

International Human Rights Law

When the Universal Declaration of Human Rights (UDHR, 1948) was being drafted, there were discussions about whether to have specific protections for women

(Gaer 2009). The decision not to have separate provisions was made because the entire point of the Declaration was to enshrine in law that *every* individual has every right by virtue of being born human. It was decided that having specific protections for particular groups would undermine the universality of the human rights project. Ultimately, however, trying to mainstream women's rights into human rights left significant and problematic gaps in terms of women's rights. At that time, one third of United Nations member states did not grant political rights to women, and women remained subjugated in many ways, often in the name of 'religion' or 'culture'.

In 1967, the UN Commission on the Status of Women took the groundbreaking step of adopting the Declaration on the Elimination of Discrimination against Women, followed in 1979 by the Convention on the Elimination of All Forms of Discrimination against Women. Thus was created an accountability mechanism to review and implement that Convention in those States that signed up to it (Englehart and Miller 2014). There has certainly been progress in advancing women's rights but, despite much focus on ending discrimination and achieving equality for women, and despite increasing concern about violence against women and girls, women are still denied their fundamental rights in many parts of the world both in law and in practice. Some forms of human rights abuses and discrimination against women are based on their sex – for example denying access to reproductive rights, or permitting child brides. Others are based on gendered constructs, such as denying girls the right to education, or men's violence against women and girls (although this is enacted in sex-specific ways).

As in domestic law, in international human rights law the word *women* has always been defined as referring to biological sex. This definition was adopted in many international human rights treaties and discussions. For example, the 1998 Statute of Rome, which created the International Criminal Court, states that the word *gender* refers to the two biological sex classes of male and female. At the UN Committee on the Elimination of Discrimination Against Women, some states, including New Zealand, recently opted to report on trans women as part of their periodic reporting, but there is no requirement to do so. Scholars such as Sandra Duffy (2021) have documented the number of times that trans-inclusive language has been used at the Committee, but this practice is not adopted by most Committee members, most states party to the treaty or, indeed, most of global civil society. Rather, it generally comes from a small group of global North states. Elsewhere, other treaty-based bodies have rejected the conflation of sex and gender identity; the UN Committee Against Torture, for example, has considered these issues in relation to trans women in prisons and, in doing so, made it clear that sex is biological. And at the UN Human Rights Council, a political body based on proportionate geographic representation of UN members, these issues are not even discussed.

The fight for women to have specific protections paved the way for other vulnerable groups to do the same. Once the idea of having specific protections for groups who face particular risk was no longer viewed as undermining the nature of human rights, similar steps could be taken for children, persons with disabilities, racial minorities, and migrant workers. There is now clear understanding that the risks faced by members of such groups means that they require specific protection in law and practice. Of course, just because such an understanding exists, and states formally accept obligations by ratifying treaties, changes on the ground do not necessarily follow. But these international law provisions have given those groups tools for lobbying for effective change, which is at the heart of human rights advocacy and work.

Yet while many vulnerable groups have now received specific protections from the UN human rights system, attempts to protect sexual orientation and gender identity (SOGI, the UN umbrella term for LGBT+) minorities have been less successful. Efforts to protect SOGI minorities are almost always done independently of the protection of women's rights, with members of those groups seen as suffering separate disadvantage. In the 1990s, a pivotal time for human rights with the end of the Cold War and a new commitment to advancing human rights in the international arena, there were moves to include SOGI minorities in the declarations and plans of action for human rights. These moves were blocked by the 75 countries that still criminalise, discriminate against, or oppress LGBT persons, with even the most basic attempts to protect SOGI individuals from being killed by their governments, as in the UN resolutions on extrajudicial killings in the early 2000s, being fiercely resisted by a sizeable minority of countries.

In response to this refusal to recognise the need to protect SOGI minorities within the UN, in 2006 a group of international human rights law experts and SOGI activists devised the Yogyakarta Principles at a workshop. These Principles set out rights which the workshop participants advocated that gender identity minorities ought to have, although like many other similar texts from campaigning organisations they do not include adequate definitions of terms like '*gender identity* and *sex characteristics*. Some commentators mistakenly claim that these principles have international law status and even that they have overturned international law on sex. This is wrong: international law continues to define sex as biological. We must remember that the Yogyakarta Principles were aimed at kick-starting discussions to develop much-needed protections for SOGI minorities. But they are *not* law, and they were not promoted as anything other than a starting point. While they have occasionally been referred to by academics, or even (very rarely) by a court, they are not discussed even as 'soft law' (Chinkin 1989). And since they have hardly been discussed by UN member states, they have gained little traction.

A key reason why the Yogyakarta Principles were not taken forward was that in 2011 the UN Human Rights Council passed the UN's first resolution on protecting and promoting the human rights of SOGI minorities (UN Human Rights Council 2019). This marked a significant turning point after years of attempts to discuss SOGI rights had been blocked by coalitions of states that criminalise or oppress SOGI minorities. Since 2011, there have been significant steps taken within the UN human rights system to protect and promote rights of SOGI minorities, including the creation in 2016 of a Special Procedures mandate holder on violence and discrimination against SOGI minorities. Attention from SOGI activists, including those who created the Yogyakarta Principles, turned to how to advance SOGI rights within the UN human rights system. As such, despite the claims of some proponents of those Principles, they do not represent international law but rather remain a representation of the views of the self-selecting group of academics and activists who created them. The issues that have been raised about the Principles, including lack of definitions and expansion of rights beyond the fundamental ones enshrined in the UDHR and codifying covenants, have not been addressed.

Unfortunately, at the UN level, steps taken to protect and promote the fundamental rights of SOGI minorities have also failed to define transgender or gender reassignment in a uniform manner. 'Gender identity' has been defined tautologically ('the gender with which someone identifies') or as an umbrella term in much the same way that Stonewall does (Stonewall n.d.). At the international level, therefore, the problem is similar to that at the domestic level: sex, being defined as biological, can be protected as a class in law, but the absence of a clear legal definition of gender identity makes it near-impossible for the law to be effective in this area.

Conclusion

This chapter has surveyed the history and current state of English and international laws on sex and gender. It has shown that, where laws relating to sex have been enacted, they have been intended to remedy the disadvantages suffered directly and indirectly by *women*. These disadvantages have always been based on women's biology as females and on the social constructs built upon their biology. In consequence, the law has defined women as *females* and has provided rights and protections to counter the historical and continuing restrictions imposed by these. Where once biology was invoked to justify the denial of rights to females, today it provides the rationale for the rights and protections the law offers. As this chapter has explained, without a clear definition of the class requiring protection, the law cannot protect it. If we erase sex as a legal category and replace it by gender identity, we not only end up with a category that has so far not been adequately defined in either national or international law, and so cannot be properly enforced, but we will also dilute – even sabotage – those efforts to protect women from the wrongs they suffer as biological females.

We note that much of the support for conflating sex and gender identity comes from those claiming to be allies of feminism and of females. This can only be understood if we assume that these people believe that the sexes are already equal and that women do not need special protections based on their biology any more. This is plainly not true. Attempts to restrict and control women's reproductive rights remain widespread; existing gender pay gaps are exacerbated by economic downturns around the world; the COVID-19 pandemic has demonstrated the disparities in healthcare provision and research between men and women, let alone women of colour or with disabilities; and more than two women a week are killed by their male partners or relatives in the UK alone.

Our conclusion is that there are just too many situations – those envisaged in the Equality Act exemptions being prime examples – where removal of the protected category of sex will reduce, and possibly remove, the very protections that were enacted to help natal women and redress their historical disadvantage. It is for this reason we argue that we need to retain the protected characteristic of sex in the EA, since its replacement by 'gender identity' would obliterate its historical and continuing basis in biology, cut women off from our heritage (women's lives matter, just as black lives do) and blur the distinction between people who have been discriminated against because of their bodies and those discriminated against because of their identities.

References

Atkins, Susan. 2019. 'Sex Discrimination (Election Candidates) Act 2002'. In *Women's Legal Landmarks: Celebrating the History of Women and Law in the UK and Ireland,* edited by Erika Rackley and Rosemary Auchmuty, 511–17. Oxford: Hart Publishing.

Atkins, Susan and Brenda Hoggett. 1984. *Women and the Law*. Oxford: Basil Blackwell; reprinted London IALS, 2018.

Bodichon, Barbara Leigh. (1854) 1987. 'A Brief Summary, in Plain Language, of the Most Important Laws Concerning Women: Together with a Few Observations Thereon'. In *Barbara Leigh Bodichon and the Langham Place Group*, edited by Candida Ann Lacey, 23–35. London: Routledge and Kegan Paul.

Butler, Josephine. (1870) 1984. 'The Ladies' Appeal and Protest against the Contagious Diseases Acts'. In *Strong-Minded Women and Other Lost Voices from 19th-Century England*, edited by Janet Horowitz Murray. Harmondsworth, UK: Penguin.428–32.

Caine, Barbara. 1997. *English Feminism 1780–1980.* Oxford: Oxford University Press.

Chinkin, Christine M. 1989. 'The Challenge of Soft Law: Development and Change in International Law'. *International & Comparative Law Quarterly* 38, 850.

Cobbe, Frances Power. (1868) 1995. 'Criminals, Idiots, Women, and Minors'. Reprinted in *Criminals, Idiots, Women, & Minors: Nineteenth-Century Writing by Women on Women*, edited by Susan Hamilton, 108. Peterborough, ON: Broadview Press.

Cobbe, Frances Power. (1878) 1995. 'Wife Torture in England'. Reprinted in *Criminals, Idiots, Women, & Minors: Nineteenth-century writing by women on women*, edited by Susan Hamilton, 132. Peterborough, ON: Broadview Press.

Cobbe, Frances Power. (1881) 2010. *The Duties of Women*. London: Williams and Norgate, reprinted Cambridge University Press.

Diduck, Alison. 2019. 'First Rape Crisis Centre, 2019'. In *Women's Legal Landmarks: Celebrating the history of women and law in the UK and Ireland,* edited by Erika Rackley and Rosemary Auchmuty, 321. Oxford: Hart Publishing.

Duffy, Sandra. 2021. 'Contested Subjects of Human Rights: Trans and Gender-variant Subjects of International Human Rights Law'. *Modern Law Review* 84, 1041.

Englehart, Neil A. and Melissa K. Miller, 2014. 'The CEDAW Effect: International Law's Impact on Women's Rights'. *Journal of Human Rights* 13, 22.

Equality and Human Rights Commission. 2021. 'Gender Reassignment Discrimination'. https://www.equalityhumanrights.com/en/advice-and-guidance/gender-reassignment-discrimination, accessed January 19, 2022.

Fagundes, Dave. 2001. 'Note, What We Talk about When We Talk about Persons: The Language of a Legal Fiction'. *Harvard Law Review,* 114 (6), 1745–68.

Gaer, Felice. 2009. 'Women, International Law and International Institutions: The Case of the United Nations'. *Women's Studies International Forum* 32, 60.

Hepple, Bob. 2010. 'The New Single Equality Act in Britain'. *Equal Rights Review* 5, 11.

Horton, Rachel. 2018. 'Employment/Labour Law'. In *Great Debates in Gender and Law*, edited by Rosemary Auchmuty, ch 10. London: Palgrave.

Kaganas, Felicity. 2019. 'First Women's Refuge, 1971'. In *Women's Legal Landmarks: Celebrating the History of Women and Law in the UK and Ireland,* edited by Erika Rackley and Rosemary Auchmuty, 301. Oxford: Hart Publishing.

Levine, Philippa. 1987. *Victorian Feminism 1850–1900.* London: Hutchinson.

Morris, Debra. 2019. '*Webb v EMO Air Cargo (UK) Ltd (No 2)* (1994)'. In *Women's Legal Landmarks: Celebrating the History of Women and Law in the UK and Ireland,* edited by Erika Rackley and Rosemary Auchmuty, 463. Oxford: Hart Publishing.

Norton, Caroline. 1854. 'English Laws for Women in the Nineteenth Century'. London: Privately printed. http://www.digital.library.upenn.edu/women/norton/elfw/elfw.html, accessed January 19, 2022.

Oakley, Ann. 1972. *Sex, Gender, and Society.* London: Temple Smith.

Rackley, Erika and Rosemary Auchmuty, eds. 2019. *Women's Legal Landmarks: Celebrating the History of Women and Law in the UK and Ireland.* Oxford: Hart Publishing.

Sachs, Albie and Joan Hoff Wilson. 1978. *Sexism and the Law: A study of Male Beliefs and Judicial Bias.* Oxford: Martin Robertson.

Schane, Sanford A. 1986. 'Corporation Is a Person: The Language of a Legal Fiction'. *Tulane Law Review* 61, 563.

Smith, Harold L., ed. 1990. *British Feminism in the Twentieth Century.* Aldershot, UK: Edward Elgar.

Stonewall. n.d. 'List of LGBTQI+ Terms'. https://www.stonewall.org.uk/help-advice/faqs-and-glossary/list-lgbtq-terms, accessed January 19, 2022.

UN General Assembly, Universal Declaration of Human Rights, 10 December 1948, 217 A (III).

UN Human Rights Council, 2019. UN Doc. A/HRC/Res/17/19.

Wilson, Elizabeth. 1980. *Only Halfway to Paradise: Women in Postwar Britain 1945–68.* London: Tavistock.

9
SEX, GENDER, AND EQUALITY IN THE UNITED STATES

Confusion, Conflict, and Consequences

Callie H. Burt

> The Equality Act is quite literally a life-saving bill that addresses some of the fundamental inequalities that still exist in the American legal system. . . . We are on the right side of history.
> —Democrat Representative David Cicilline (RI)

> This bill may have 'equality' in its title, but it does not serve all people. . . . Its vague and circular definitions of gender identity will lead only to uncertainty, litigation, and harm to individuals and organizations that will be forced to comply with a law the authors don't even seem to understand. This is a classic example of passing something now and figuring out what it actually means later. We have been here before. If the Devil is in the details, we are in for a lot of devilish surprises.
> —Republican Representative Virginia Foxx (NC)

> Today, with passage by this House of H.R.5, the Equality Act, we bend [the moral] arc even more in the direction of justice. I am proud to be an original cosponsor of this life-changing and life-affirming legislation . . .
> —Democrat Representative Jackson Lee (TX)

In the wake of marriage equality, transgender or trans rights issues have moved to the forefront of LGBT activism. Recent years have seen the trans rights movement gain unprecedented momentum, arguably 'faster progress than any movement in American history' (Keisling 2016; see also Taylor et al. 2018). This success is due in no small part to the efforts of LGBT+ organisations, which leveraging their existing reputations as progressive groups acting on behalf of a well-defined, marginalised demographic ('the LGBT community'), have fostered a view of 'trans rights' as a natural extension of LGB rights. These prominent, very well-funded LGBT+ organisations, such as the Human Rights Campaign (HRC) and GLAAD in the

DOI: 10.4324/9781003286608-9

U.S., like the UK's Stonewall, now, in practice if not in explicit policy, prioritise the T over the LGB (Biggs n.d.). Democrat politicians, perhaps still regretting their previous opposition to gay marriage and aiming to be on what is the 'right side of history' this time around, align themselves with the position of these LGBT groups, adopting their slogans and endorsing their demands. Indeed, during his campaign, Democrat president Biden called the trans rights movement 'the civil rights movement of our time' (Biden 2020).

In the United States, the Equality Act (H.R.5, S.393) represents the culmination of these efforts. The Equality Act (hereafter EA) is a prominent piece of legislation, which would amend the Civil Rights Act of 1964 (CRA) and other core civil rights statutes to prohibit discrimination on the basis of sexual orientation and gender identity (like age, race, etc.). At present, LGB and/or trans people in more than half of U.S. states can be legally discriminated against in housing, for example. The EA addresses this deficiency of federal discrimination protections by expanding anti-discrimination statutes to include LGB and transgender people. The bill would also widen the scope of protections in public accommodations 'to include places or establishments that provide (1) exhibitions, recreation, exercise, amusement, gatherings, or displays; (2) goods, services, or programs; and (3) transportation services' (CRS 2021).

The EA is a prominent piece of Democrat legislation, which passed the House (as H.R.5) in 2019 and again in 2021 with unanimous Democrat support. As of this writing (July 2022), the Senate companion bill (S.393) still awaits consideration.

As with most sociopolitical issues in the U.S. at present, debates around the EA tend to flop along left–right party lines with little debate on substance, including the gender-identity ideology implicitly endorsed by the bill (Burt 2020). The Congressional discussion of the EA in the House, illustrated in the introductory quotes, consisted of Democratic lawmakers lauding the bill (e.g., as 'literally a life-saving bill') and Republicans condemning 'the deep flaws' in the legislation (CRS 2019, 2021). Most Democrats appear content to adopt party-line positions without discussion or critical scrutiny, such that the bulk of the political left supports, even champions, the EA. After all, some might think, what leftist would oppose LGBT equality or a so-called Equality Act?

Unfortunately, statements by supporters of the EA, including some politicians, suggest that many are uninformed about the details of this legislation and its implications, including the sweeping change it would institute from sex-based to gender-identity-based protections (Burt 2020). As I discuss, the bill would eliminate sex-based provisions for females while undermining the protected nature of women's provisions. First, I provide a brief overview of the current 'trans rights debate' in the U.S., and I critique the prevailing leftist view of trans rights as equivalent to LGB rights.

LGB and the T Rights: One of These Is Not Like the Others

The contemporary movement for 'LGBT' equality, which informs the EA, frames trans rights as inextricably linked to, and no different from, LGB rights, such as marriage equality (achieved in the U.S. in 2015) and the decriminalisation of same-sex sex (in 2003). However, this framing obscures some important differences between LGB rights and current trans rights demands. Most significantly, the rights extended to LGB people—for example, to marry or to have (legal) consensual same-sex sex—do not infringe on the rights or protections of others. That is, no one is required to have same-sex sex or marry a same-sex partner; they are merely required to allow others to do so. To be sure, marriage equality changed the definition of marriage from one man and one woman to one adult to another adult; however, this change in definition does not alter the protections afforded to married people (or any other people, for that matter). Quite simply, opposite-sex marriages are not altered by allowing same-sex couples to participate in the institution of marriage. Similarly, opposite-sex sex is not modified by allowing others to legally engage in same-sex sex. In short, these hard-won LGB rights do not take away from the rights or provisions of another group, nor do they require the adoption of a particular set of beliefs.

In contrast, current trans rights activism includes—in addition to rights that all deserve, such as employment, housing, and equal treatment as humans of equal value—demands for *opposite-sex* provisions. This follows from the current—now orthodox on the left—gender-identity ideology, undergirding the EA, which includes the mandate that society treat people on the basis of their self-declared gender identity regardless of their sex for all purposes, no exceptions, including access to (previously) sex-separated female provisions.

Prominent in this debate are trans activists' demands for females to relinquish hard-won sex-separated provisions to transwomen because, on the gender-identity ideology view, 'transwomen are women'. The definition of what is a woman is currently debated, and under the traditional definition of a woman as an adult human female, transwomen are not women (e.g., Byrne 2020; Bogardus 2020). The implicit (and occasionally explicit) motivation for this shift appears to be the belief that the suffering of transwomen justifies their being treated as females, regardless of the implications for females, including safety considerations. Such demands are thus not for equality but for special treatment—an exemption from the sex-based requirements for access and eligibility based on a distinct characteristic: gender identity.

This is no minor quibble. Females have hard-won separate provisions justified by biological differences, such as males' greater average size, strength, metabolism, and oxygen utilisation as well as the primary labour of reproduction, and social disadvantages due to women's historical exclusion and subordination (e.g., being male property, denied the right to education, employment, and the vote) and ongoing disadvantages (e.g., Lawford-Smith 2019). Separate women's spaces are also justified by the existing threat of male violence and harassment and exist as a place of felt security and respite from males (Burt 2020, 2021). Some provisions, such as sports, are explicitly sex-separated due to biological differences and justified by the individual and social benefits of female social involvement such provisions facilitate (Coleman, 2017). In general, sex-based provisions continue to be crucial to females' well-being and equal participation in society (e.g., Lawford-Smith 2019; Lorber 1994).

For these reasons, trans activist demands for special access to opposite-sex provisions are distinct from LGB demands for equal treatment and protection. The prevailing knee-jerk leftist support for 'LGBT rights'—manifest by ostensibly unthinking support for whatever LGBT+ organisations demand without reflection or consideration—while no doubt well intended, disregards important differences between LGB and T 'rights' demands as well as associated conflicts and potential negative consequences. Although the slogan 'trans rights are human rights' is catchy and compelling, many of the 'rights' they seek are opposite-sex provisions, and there is no human right to provisions set aside for the other sex. Thus, we find ourselves at an impasse. Effective solutions require deep discussion, negotiation, and ongoing dialogue between various affected groups in our society, including those who represent (in all their diversity) the interests of transgender people and females.

Tragically, such dialogue is lacking. The discourse vacillates between eerie silence and cacophony. On the right, calls for recognising sex and supporting women and girls come from a Republican party that historically (and for some still to the present) opposes equal human rights to LGB people and attempts to curtail women's rights in other domains (birth control, equal pay, etc.). Among Democrats, political discussion has been replaced by sloganeering and mantras ('Trans women are women'), explicit calls for 'No Debate', and puerile name-calling rather than engagement and respectful dissent.

Yet, far from being monolithic, there is viewpoint heterodoxy on the left, with LGB and even T activists and other left-leaning individuals objecting to the unqualified extension of opposite-sex rights to those identifying as transgender. Although among the most heated and vitriolic political debates at present, this 'transgender debate' is a microcosm of the current cultural climate of the left, which can be openly intolerant of dissenting ideas, including recognition of competing interests and protections. The progressive ethos of lifting all marginalised people up through public policies that promote a public good has been splintered by a burgeoning identity politics where marginalised groups are mired in an 'oppression Olympics' with a winner-take-all mentality. The influence of the trans lobby along with the marginalisation and suffering of transgender people has positioned them atop this hierarchy of victimhood, which has contributed to their power to castigate, even censor, dissenting viewpoints as 'hateful', 'harmful', 'prejudiced', and 'bigoted' (Suissa & Sullivan 2021). Consequently, a façade of leftist consensus exists because dissenting viewpoints are increasingly unaired because of censorship, especially self-censorship.

At present, the transgender debate in the U.S. (as elsewhere) is not characterised by open discussion, democratic input, and balanced, thoughtful deliberation. Nuanced descriptions of the current situation are scarce and inadequate. The actual situation of trans people is distorted, important public discussions are silenced, and misguided and shortsighted public policies are crafted to ameliorate the suffering of transgender people without adequate consideration for the impacts on other groups (especially females) and unintended negative consequences. In addition to censorship, this situation is also due to the failure of the democratic process due to policy capture (see Murray & Hunter Blackburn 2019, also Burt 2020). As Republicans have lamented, the EA was brought to the House without going through full committee hearings under a closed rule with no amendments (CRS 2019, 2021).

The U.S. EA—a flawed piece of legislation with good intentions—is a product of this noxious sociopolitical climate in which one is either 'for' or 'against' LGBT rights, and if 'for', then—according to this shallow reasoning—one supports the EA. The debate over the EA is depicted in the media and public discussion as between Democrats who support LGBT+ rights and conservative Republicans who oppose LGBT+ rights for religious reasons. Political critics of the EA, exclusively Republicans, raise concerns about women's safety and rights, women's sports, and religious freedoms. Democratic politicians portray themselves as supporting equality and life-affirming rights and characterise those in opposition to the EA as being conservative and anti-LGBT, and no doubt some are—but not all.

Objections to the EA's from feminists, LGB and event T activists, and others who support LGBT+ equality but have concerns about the legal and social erasure of sex to protect transgender people are largely ignored. Heeding these concerns, in this chapter, I interrogate the EA from a left-of-center gender-critical feminist perspective—an often censored, censured, or misrepresented perspective. As I discuss, one can (and I do) support the aims of the EA—extending federal nondiscrimination protections to both LGB and transgender people—while opposing the act given its current form.

In what follows, I discuss the legislative background, including the existing social problems the EA aims to address, as well as a brief overview of the historical background of the bill. I then describe the form of the EA, including its terminological imprecision and prioritisation of in-the-moment gender self-identification over biological sex for access to (currently) sex-based provisions. This is followed by a more in-depth discussion of the flaws of the bill, including foreseeable negative consequences. Such consequences are, I explain, avoidable through reformulations, which I briefly sketch out. Reformulated, the EA could extend federal anti-discrimination protections to LGBT+ people without eliminating sex-based provisions and the protected nature of women's spaces.

The Legislative Backdrop

The Problem: Insufficient Discrimination Protections

Over the past two decades, a variety of U.S. states have passed nondiscrimination laws on the basis of sexual orientation as well as, although less commonly, gender identity. Yet at present, fewer than 25 states prohibit discrimination against LGBT individuals. There is a patchwork of state protections, such that individuals in more than half of U.S. states can be legally discriminated against in, for example, housing, public accommodations, or jury service because they are LGB or transgender. The exception is in employment, as the recent Supreme Court ruling in *Bostock v. Clayton County* (2020) clarified that firing someone for being LGB or transgender was a violation of Title II of the CRA (see discussion in Byrne & Burt 2020).

There is thus a deficit in discrimination protections for LGBT+ people. The U.S. EA aims to remedy this deficit by federally prohibiting discrimination on the basis of sexual orientation and gender identity.

Historical Setting of the U.S. Equality Act

The EA, which has passed the U.S. House (as H.R. 5) and awaits consideration in the Senate (as S. 393), is designed to 'prohibit discrimination on the basis of sex, gender identity, and sexual orientation' in employment, public accommodation, housing, education, federally funded programs, jury service, and credit by amending the U.S. CRA (including Titles II, III, IV, VI, VII, and IX). The bill also expands the definition of public accommodations, thereby increasing the scope of protections for all groups protected in the CRA (e.g., race, colour, religion, and national origin). Notably, the current EA is not the first 'Equality Act' proposed to Congress to expand the CRA to protect additional groups, although it has been revised substantially from its earlier form. In the mid-1970s, two Democratic representatives from New York, feminist Bella Abzug and Ed Koch introduced an Equality Act to revise the CRA to extend protections on the basis of sex, marital status, and sexual orientation in housing, federal assistance programs, and credit. The bill never came up for a vote.

In 1994, a narrower successor bill, known as the Employment Non-Discrimination Act (ENDA), which would prohibit employment discrimination against individuals on the basis of sexual orientation, was introduced but failed to pass. The bill was re-introduced without passing in each Congress from 1994 to 2013, save one, largely unchanged until 2007, when the debate around transgender inclusion in the bill became salient. In 2007, gender identity was added and then dropped at the cost of support from activist organisations and lobby groups. Subsequently, ENDA included both sexual orientation and gender identity; the bill never passed both Houses.

In 2015, efforts to pass nondiscrimination protections shifted back to a broader Equality Act. Spearheaded in the U.S. House by David Cicilline, H.R.5 as the 'Equality Act' was introduced in 2015 and 2017 but never came up for a vote. In May 2019, H.R.5 passed the House on a largely a party-line vote (all but one Democrat was a co-sponsor of the bill) before dying in the Senate (i.e., not being brought to a vote). Most recently, in February 2021, H.R.5 again passed the House, largely on a party-line vote (all Democrats in favour, all but three Republicans against). The Senate companion bill (S. 393), also introduced in February 2021 and referred to the Judiciary Committee, awaits consideration.

For those unfamiliar with the context of U.S. lawmaking, the House and the Senate can (and often do) pass non-identical bills. If a different version of a bill passes the House and Senate, this initiates a process known as 'conference committee', where members of both Houses work to reconcile differences in the passed bills. The resulting compromise or consolidated bill (known as the 'conference report') then goes back to both the House and Senate for final approval (as an up or down vote). If approved, the U.S. president has 10 days to sign or veto the bill. Presently, the versions of the EA in the two Houses of Congress (H.R.5 and S. 393) are equivalent; however, changes can be made in the Senate version of the bill, and if it passes, these changes could be negotiated in conference committee. As noted, President Biden strongly supports the EA, in contrast to President Trump before him, who indicated he would veto the bill. All evidence suggests that if the EA passes the House and Senate, Biden will sign the bill into law with fanfare.

The Legislation: Sex-Based Protections Regardless of Sex

The EA is designed to prohibit discrimination against LGBT+ people and provide redress for such discrimination when it occurs. Although its aims are laudable and, as currently constituted, the bill would accomplish those nondiscrimination aims, it would do so with an unnecessary, unjustified, and self-defeating cost: eliminating sex-based protections and the protected nature of women's provisions. The EA is thus a well-intended, yet flawed, piece of legislation, which has foreseeable negative consequences for vulnerable groups. There are three main flaws, which are distinct but interrelated: terminological imprecision, clash of rights, and in-the-moment gender self-identification.

Terminological Imprecision

The most obvious flaw in the EA is its terminological precision. The EA would extend federal nondiscrimination protections to LGB and T groups not by creating two new protected classes (i.e., sexual orientation and gender identity) alongside sex and other protected classifications (e.g., race, age, religion), but by redefining 'sex' in civil rights law to 'include sexual orientation and gender identity' (see statutory redefinition in Figure 9.1). Additionally, where 'sex' appears as a protected category in the CRA, the EA changes sex to 'sex (including sexual orientation and gender identity)'. The bill would also add 'sex (including sexual orientation and gender identity)' where previously sex was not a protected characteristic (as in public accommodations).

Obviously, neither sexual orientation nor gender identity is, in fact, sex. Sex (male, female) is not sexual orientation (defined as 'heterosexuality, homosexuality, or bisexuality') or gender identity. Indeed, defining one's sexual orientation requires a working definition of sex (Stock 2019). Likewise for defining a transwoman or a transman; a female cannot be a transwoman because of sex. Thus, departing from our creditable legal tradition of conceptual clarity, by redefining sex to include non-sex categories, the EA is terminologically inaccurate.

Self-Identification

This redefinition of sex is not only problematic in its imprecision but also in its vagueness. As shown in Figure 9.1, which shows the text of the redefinition in the bill, gender identity is amorphously and circularly defined.

Impractically, gender is not defined at all. Without a working definition of 'gender', the definition of gender identity is not just circular (as Representative Lesko noted during House floor discussions) but incomprehensible, amounting to 'the []-related identity, appearance, mannerisms or other []-related characteristics of individuals, regardless of the individual's designated sex at birth'. Gender identity is thus only knowable through simple self-identification: what one says one is in the moment.

To be sure, self-identification is not always problematic; we self-identify as brown- or blond-haired, blue- or brown-eyed, and even gay or straight on doctors' forms, driver's licenses, and dating profiles. However, self-identification for access to protected provisions or rights is widely recognised to be problematic in the U.S. We do not allow self-identification for access to gatekept provisions, including for 'disabled' parking permits, driving, voting, air travel, and even purchasing alcohol

---

"SEC. 1101. DEFINITIONS AND RULES.
   "(a) DEFINITIONS.—In titles II, III, IV, VI, VII, and IX (referred to individually in sections 1106 and 1107 as 'covered title').

      "(1) RACE, COLOR; RELIGION; SEX; SEXUAL ORIENTATION; GENDER IDENTITY; NATIONAL ORIGIN.—the term 'race', color', 'religion', 'sex' (including 'sexual orientation and 'gender identity'), or 'national origin', used with respect to an individual, includes—

         "(A) the race, color, religion, sex (including sexual orientation and gender identity), or national origin, respectively, of another person with whom the individual is associated or has been associated; and

         "(B) a perception or belief, even if inaccurate, concerning the race, color, religion, sex (including sexual orientation and gender identity), or national origin, respectively, of the individual.

      "(2) GENDER IDENTITY.—The term 'gender identity' means the gender-related identity, appearance, mannerisms, or other gender-related characteristics of an individual, regardless of the individual's designated sex at birth.

      "(3) INCLUDING.—The term 'including' means including, but not limited to, consistent with the term's standard meaning in Federal law.

      "(4) SEX.—The term 'sex' includes—

         "(A) a sex stereotype;

         "(B) pregnancy, childbirth, or a related medical condition;

         "(C) sexual orientation or gender identity; and

         "(D) sex characteristics, including intersex traits.

      "(5) SEXUAL ORIENTATION.—The term 'sexual orientation' means homosexuality, heterosexuality, or bisexuality.

   "(b) RULES.—In a covered title referred to in subsection (a)—

      "(1) (with respect to sex) pregnancy, childbirth, or a related medical condition shall not receive less favorable treatment than other physical conditions; and

      "(2) (with respect to gender identity) an individual shall not be denied access to a shared facility, including a restroom, a locker room, and a dressing room, that is in accordance with the individual's gender identity." and

FIGURE 9.1 Text from the Equality Act (H.R. 5); Definitions

Source: See https://www.congress.gov/bill/117th-congress/house-bill/5/text.

(which is why last week I, a 42-year-old, arrived home from grocery sans wine for my wife because I left my driver's license in my car. The fact that I am manifestly older than the legal age of purchasing alcohol [21] and I said as much was not sufficient). Viewing truth in self-identification as ineffective for safeguarding policies—that some people will take advantage of self-identification—the U.S. gatekeeps protected divisions by requiring proof of status for access. This EA's adoption of self-identification, which is a curious departure from normal gatekeeping procedures, is rooted in the prevailing gender-identity ideology and its emphasis on the individual right of sex/gender self-definition. (As we all know, this is not the case for age, race/ethnicity, or other demographic characteristics.)

At the heart of these problems is the clash between sex and gender identity. In particular, there is an inherent contradiction in the effort to include members of a group (males) purposely excluded from women's provisions based on a different characteristic (gender identity).

Conflict of Rights

The EA's conflation of sex with gender identity creates a blatant clash of rights (Jeffreys 2014). One can separate provisions based on sex or based on gender identity but not both. Once males are given access to provisions set aside for females, those provisions are no longer separated by sex, obviously. Rather than negotiating this conflict of rights, for example, by seeking to balance the hard-won provisions of female people with rights demands and protections for transgender people, the EA simply prioritises transgender people over females. This prioritisation of transgender people over females is undoubtedly influenced by the success of the LGBT lobby in situating transgender people at the top of the victimhood hierarchy and by censoring debate and slandering those who disagree as 'transphobic bigots' whose concerns can be dismissed.

Manifestly recognising this conflict of rights, the Democrat authors of the bill explicitly and repeatedly clarified that gender identity takes precedence over sex for access to formerly sex-separated provisions. For example, the act amends unlawful employment practices to specify that when 'sex is a bona fide occupational qualification, individuals are recognised *as qualified in accordance with their gender identity*' (emphasis added; see Sec. 701A, H3932). Thus, under the EA, for example, not hiring a male who identifies as a woman in a women's rape crisis shelter (which was formerly female only) or as an exotic dancer in a club for men would be federally prohibited discrimination.

Similarly, Democrats added a rule in Section 1107: '(with respect to gender identity) an individual shall not be denied access to a shared facility, including a restroom, a locker room, and a dressing room, that is in accordance with the individual's gender identity'. Thus, a policy prohibiting access to a women's spa, where women are nude, to a bepenised male who identifies as a woman would be deemed impermissible discrimination. Under the EA, any male who says, 'I identify as a woman'—whether or not this identification is sincere—must be given access to female provisions (and so, too, for females identifying as men). Democrats rejected several Republican efforts to amend the bill to include exceptions for sex-separated spaces where people undress, as well as amendments to maintain the sex separation of sport for fairness. This prioritisation of gender identity over sex, without exception, contrasts with the approach of other countries, such as the UK, which allows the use of sex-based distinctions when doing so 'is a proportionate means to a legitimate aim', such as safety and fairness.

In sum, by defining sex to include gender identity and defining gender identity as something 'gender-related' that exists, 'regardless of sex', the EA eliminates the legal distinction between (biological) sex and gender identity. (Although the EA defines gender identity as 'sex', here and throughout I employ the commonly accepted definition of sex as biological sex, observed at birth [correctly >99% of the time] and immutable.) Consequently, the EA eliminates sex-based provisions. That is, currently de facto sex-separated provisions would become de jure gender identity–separated provisions, such that access to formerly opposite-sex spaces is granted through simple self-declaration about one's gender identity—no sincerity or presentation style required. There are expectable negative consequences.

Foreseeable Negative Consequences of the EA

As articulated, the EA would replace sex-based provisions with in-the-moment gender self-identification rights for all purposes, no exceptions, including female-only rape crisis and domestic violence shelters, locker rooms, sports, events, and so on. Shockingly, this sweeping legislation was developed in the absence of policy impact evaluation. Government-funded studies have assessed the difficulties that transwomen experience in sex-separated spaces, for example, and how this affects their safety and psychological well-being. Yet, no studies have been conducted to examine how vulnerable females in prisons and shelters might be affected by gender self-identification (Burt 2020). These studies are needed because the voices of these women are rarely heard. The physical and psychological well-being of these women—who are disproportionately poor and minority and who have experienced high rates of male sexual violence—matter. The persistent sociopolitical failure to consider the policy impact on females follows from the subordination of their needs to that of transgender people, a wholly unnecessary and objectionable move, as I discuss more later. First, I highlight three domains that the EA as currently formulated would undermine for females: safety and felt psychological security, fairness and equal opportunity, and solidarity and collectivism.

Notably, here, as elsewhere, I focus on the clash of rights created by prioritising the protection of one group (transwomen) over another protected group (females). This does not imply that transmen are less important, only that women's spaces were created after lengthy feminist campaigning to provide a protected space for women and girls as a protected class. Allowing females to identify into male spaces does not create a clash of rights with protected groups or threaten male safety and well-being. That is not to say, of course, that males may not wish for females to enter their spaces, only that this is not my focus.

Undermining Safety

A well-intended concern for the safety of transgender people has blinded many to the foreseeable negative consequences of the EA, including the erosion of the protected nature of women's spaces. The fact that women's provisions will no longer be 'women's' or 'protected' due to gender self-identification seems to be widely misunderstood, but it is actually quite straightforward. For a provision to be a protected one, access must be restricted. If anyone can opt into a protected space on a say-so, it is no longer a protected space (Burt 2022). Male rapists can self-identify into the women's prison, sex offenders can self-identify into women's spas, adolescent boys can self-identify into the girls' locker rooms for a joke or on a dare, and girls and women—however defined—cannot do anything about it. Thus, the EA would eliminate women's protected spaces in order to protect and validate transgender people, especially transwomen, at the cost of the safety and privacy of both.

That the EA would eliminate the protected nature of women's provisions is neglected or dismissed by Democrat supporters of the bill. This neglect takes the form of simply ignoring or denigrating those who protest, while dismissals are more insidious and disturbing and take one of several forms. One response by supporters of the EA is to disparage those who raise concerns about the safety implications as being motivated by transphobia and their concerns as 'transphobic trans panic' (i.e., concerns about 'devious, dangerous, deceitful' transwomen as predators). This is confused and/or disingenuous. The safety concern that I and others have raised about the EA is that it would allow predatory males to self-identify into women's spaces without any gatekeeping or challenge (Burt 2020). To be clear, the point is not that women are particularly endangered by and should thus fear transwomen. The point is that women are, in general, vulnerable to males and made less safe by a policy that would allow any male to access formerly protected spaces on a say-so. Indeed, this gender self-identification aspect of the EA would threaten the safety of everyone in women's spaces (females and transwomen).

Others also misunderstand the concerns about self-identification and argue that it is absurd or unlikely that men would identify as women to gain access to women's spaces. Unfortunately, not only is it not absurd, it has already happened in various places around the world with gender self-ID policies (see Burt 2020). More important, whether men will increasingly present as women to access women's spaces is irrelevant, because under the EA, *they don't have to*. Say-so is enough. Under the EA, with the intent of voyeurism or even sexual assault, males can self-identify into women's spaces and wait for the right opportunity for predation, and women (however defined) cannot do anything about their presence. Failure to consider the threat self-identification poses to women and girls is a manifestation of an abject failure of democratic policymaking and a disregard for the reality of male violence, especially sexual violence, which is an ever-present threat in the lives of many women and girls. Under the EA, licence to enter into women's sex-separated protected spaces—including prisons, rape crisis shelters, refuges—to prey on them is a simple self-utterance, which cannot be verified or challenged.

As I have noted, and it bears repeating, this reliance on 'truth in self-identification' is at odds with almost all public policy (and all policies to my knowledge that concern safety). The U.S. is not a society that operates on trust and self-identification, which is why obvious adults have to show government identification to buy a beer and manifestly differently abled persons have to procure and display a special parking permit to avail themselves of the spaces set aside for them. Importantly, available policy evaluation from other protected spaces suggests that self-identification does not work for protected provisions; gatekeeping is necessary.

Among the best evidence comes from Sharon Dolovich's (2011) research on the Los Angeles (LA) County Jail's K6G unit. The K6G unit (previously K11) is a segregated protected unit in the LA County Jail set aside for gay men and transwomen given their vulnerability to male predation in the general population. As Dolovich explains, 'L.A. County has managed to create a surprisingly safe space for the high-risk populations K6G serves' (p.5). The not-secret success of the K6G unit is its gatekeeping policies (as 'tight control over admission', p.88). Previously, entry into the K6G unit was based on self-identification; however, as administrators learned, self-identification policies undermined the safety of residents housed there—because predatory males would 'falsely claim to be gay' to gain access to the unit, which defeated the purpose. To be clear, some incarcerated males falsely claimed to be gay—a highly stigmatised identity in the extremely masculine prison/jail context—to gain access to and thus prey on gay males and transwomen in the 'protected' unit. Under self-identification, the K11 unit, like the segregated unit in New York's Rikers Island, was not actually protective (Dolovich 2011; von Zielbauer 2005).

Indeed, remarking on the close of the Rikers Island Protective Unit, City Commissioner Horn noted: "'It was the only area of the department where inmates could choose where they wanted to live,'" irrespective of the security classification each inmate receives on entering the jail system. "'What we ended up with was this housing unit where people were predatory and people were vulnerable. The very units that should be the most safe, in fact, had become the least safe'" (see von Zielbauer 2005). Thus, despite clear and compelling evidence that gatekeeping is necessary for (even defining of) protected spaces, the EA would eliminate sex-based criteria for the ostensible benefit of transgender people.

To be sure, my argument is not that we will see a sweeping epidemic of male violence against women in formerly sex-separated spaces after the passage of the EA. Rather, I argue that *some* predatory males will use gender self-identification to prey on women and girls and that 'some', whatever the count may be, is an unnecessary and therefore morally objectional cost given alternatives (such as gender-neutral third spaces, protected special united, like the K6G), which can provide safety to transwomen without undermining the protected nature of women's spaces.

Undermining Felt Security and Psychological Well-Being

Probably the most pervasive cost of allowing any male to self-identify into women's spaces will be the erosion of felt security in women's spaces. Given the realities of male violence and harassment and women's recognition that predatory males may enter a formerly female space—shower, locker room, rape crisis shelter, or other space—at any time based on a simple self-declaration, one can reasonably suspect that this will undermine felt security and psychological well-being. Women have no way of ascertaining which males pose a threat and which do not. Furthermore, many women have learned to treat men who violate rules and customs around sex separation (e.g., who enter women's locker rooms and expose their male genitalia) as a threat because until recently that was a crime and widely recognised as threatening.

From a young age, many girls are taught to be alert to the possibility of male predation, and sexed spaces provide respite from this threat, a place of felt psychological and physical safety where women and girls have a right to exclude male entrants (Lawford-Smith 2019). Not only are women socialised to be wary of the presence of male bodies in sex-separated spaces, especially where they are vulnerable, such as when undressing or sleeping, but given the reality of male sexual violence against women, a substantial number of women have prior violating experiences with male victimisation. Indeed, based on U.S. population, estimates and rates of sexual assaults of females (approximately 20%), for every one transwoman (<0.5% prevalence in the population), there are *at least* 40 women who have been victims of attempted or completed sexual assault (see Black et al. 2011). Research suggests an 'alarmingly high rate of PTSD [post-traumatic stress disorder] in survivors of sexual assault', with a lifetime prevalence of PTSD after sexual assault of 50% (Chivers-Wilson 2006, p.111). For women suffering from PTSD from male assaults, especially sexual assaults, the presence of males in their intimate spaces can trigger a cascade of PTSD symptoms, which can involve debilitating psychological discomfort and uncontrollable terror (Ullman et al. 2007). More frequent exposure to such cues, outside of a therapeutic environment, is associated with the worsening of PTSD symptoms, depression and hopelessness, and downregulated immune system functioning.

Thus, for a non-trivial proportion of women, the presence of males in formerly protected female-only spaces may cause severe anxiety and distress due to PTSD. Yet, quoting Representative Gohmert (R-TX), with whom I do not usually agree: 'We are just going to say to those women: You know what? You have just got to get over your trauma [to help transgender people]' (CRS, 2021). To suggest this is imbalanced legislation is an understatement; a compelling case could be made that the EA displays a callous, even sexist, disregard for the well-being of females.

Fairness and Equal Opportunity

Finally, the EA would also undermine fairness and equal opportunity. That females have different physiologies, including the reproductive burden (the capacity to get pregnant, a menstrual cycle, which combined is seven years of a woman's life menstruating, all going well) and, on average, lesser size, strength, lung capacity, and skeletal structure (relevant for most sports) is well established. Females, unlike transwomen, are treated from birth as girls and socialised as female, which often involves encouragement to be selfless, deferent, caregiving, concerned with appearances, and so on, whereas males are socialised to be assertive, outgoing, self-promoting, and the like. Evidence suggests that this socialisation matters for personality, opportunity, styles of interaction, and many other social-psychological traits relevant to numerous domains.

In part to deal with a world where females have different physiological and social experiences, women and girls have created sex-separated events, meetings, communities, even colleges. This is not because they hate males or think themselves superior to them but rather to come together—as other historically disadvantaged groups do—with others so situated (socialised, treated) and with similar experiences and concerns (e.g., pregnancy, birth control, breastfeeding, menstruation, even sexual pleasure). One male—however presenting or identifying—in a women's meeting about any of these female/women's issues can alter group dynamics, significantly, and this is especially true in this new world where discussing female sex-related characteristics is deemed 'transphobic genital fetishism' and 'exclusionary'. Under the EA, females could not legally exclude males from women's groups even when the discussion is about female issues (menstruation, childbirth, breastfeeding).

This will also affect sports; the EA would prohibit the sex separation of sports. Any male—without undergoing any treatment of any kind—would be able to self-identify into female sports. We have sex-separated sports to allow females a chance at winning and pro careers because mediocre elite males can crush even the best females in most sports. This is why men's elite sports (e.g., pro soccer, football, basketball, tennis, cycling) need not explicitly limit participation to males because no female can make those teams. When it comes to transwomen in sports, the available evidence suggests that we can have fairness (and exclude males from women's sports) or inclusivity, not both (Harper et al. 2021; Hilton & Lundberg 2021; Devine, this volume). We all know competitive sports categories are not about inclusivity. If sports categories are meant to be about inclusivity (i.e., not excluding people on the basis of excluded group characteristics—age, sex, weight class, etc.), we are doing it all wrong, and we need to change much more than simply allow gender self-identification.

Reformulating the EA

The problems with the EA are glaring and significant, but we can revise the EA to address the lack of federal nondiscrimination protections for LGBT+ people, without eliminating sex-based provisions, erasing the distinction between sex and gender identity, and initiating an unchallengeable policy of gender self-identification. I, along with others, have suggested proposals to revise the act (see Burt 2020; Women's Human Rights Campaign 2020; Feminists in Struggle [FIST], 2019). The key to these reformulations is recognising and maintaining the distinction between sex and gender identity. We can, and should, protect transgender people as transgender people, who are of equal worth, value, and dignity as any other human, without denying the reality of sex. Transwomen are not female—by definition, transwomen are natal males—and this recognition implies no more and no less than the fact that the recognition that a same-sex marriage is composed of two wives or two husbands. Just as we needn't act as if one member of a same-sex marriage was the opposite sex to protect them, we needn't deny the reality of biological sex and the distinction between females and transwomen to provide the latter with safety and nondiscrimination protections in a manner that also protects the former.

A truly 'equal' EA would not require that females deny the reality of their sex or relinquish their hard-won sex-based provisions. It would not tell a woman in a rape crisis shelter with PTSD that her feelings about male bodies after her assault matter less than that of the transwoman with whom she is required to share a room or conduct her post-rape gynaecological examination.

In my view and that of others, amending the EA to protect sexual orientation and gender identity as two new protected classes, alongside sex and other existing protected categories, is necessary to promote equality. Balancing rights between different groups with different interests—including when sex distinctions serve a legitimate purpose and how to accommodate and protect transgender people when they do—will require discussion, negotiation, and policy impact evaluation. This situation evades facile solutions, which is why the expertise of social scientists who study the distinctions between sex, gender, sexual orientation, and gender identity; of criminologists and sociolegal scholars who can bring to bear evidence on the effects of these different characteristics on behaviour and law; and of policy scholars who can evaluate the manifold outcomes of social policy changes are needed. In the meantime, a variety of alternatives to the EA that will provide human rights protections to LGBT people without compromising women's rights are available and should be on the policy table for discussion and debate.

If the EA passes as currently constituted, gender self-identification will supersede sex for all formerly sex-based rights, no exceptions. Once passed, subsequent revisions or a reversion to sex-based protections will be exceptionally difficult. History is replete with examples of flawed legislation, with good intentions and insufficient consideration of broader impacts, having negative and/or collateral consequences that could have been foreseen with due diligence and widespread democratic input into decision-making and policies. We shall see if this is the case with the EA.

References

Biden, J. 2020. 'Let's be clear: Transgender equality is . . .'. Twitter thread, 25 January. https://twitter.com/JoeBiden/status/1221135646107955200?s=20

Biggs, M. n.d. LGBT Facts and Figures. http://users.ox.ac.uk/~sfos0060/LGBT_figures.shtml.

Black, M., Basile, K., Breiding, M., Smith, S., Walters, M., Merrick, M., . . . Stevens, M. 2011. 'National Intimate Partner and Sexual Violence Survey: 2010 summary report'. National Sexual Violence Research Center. https://www.nsvrc.org/publications/NISVS-2010-summary-report.

Bogardus, T. 2020. 'Some internal problems with revisionary gender concepts'. *Philosophia, 48*(1): 55–75.

Bostock v. Clayton County, No. 17–1618, 590 U.S. ___ (2020).

Burt, C. H. 2020. 'Scrutinizing the U.S. Equality Act 2019: A feminist examination of definitional changes and sociolegal ramifications'. *Feminist Criminology, 15*(4): 363–409.

Burt, C. H. 2022. 'Discounting females, denying sex, and disregarding dangers from self-ID— A reply and a defense of open debate'. *Journal of Controversial Ideas, 2*: 15. https://journalofcontroversialideas.org/article/2/1/179.

Byrne, A. 2020. 'Are women adult human females?' *Philosophical Studies, 177*(12): 3783–3803.

Byrne, A., & Burt, C. 2020, August 20. 'Biological sex and the legal protection of transgender people'. *Aero.* https://areomagazine.com/2020/08/20/biological-sex-and-the-legal-protection-of-lgbt-individuals/.

Coleman, D. L. 2017. 'Sex in sport'. *Law & Contemporary Social Problems, 80*: 63–126.

Creamer, M., Burgess, P., & McFarlane, A. 2001. 'Post-traumatic stress disorder: Findings from the Australian National Survey of Mental Health and Well-being'. *Psychological Medicine, 31*(7): 1237–1247.

CRS (Congressional Research Service). 2019. https://www.congress.gov/bill/116th-congress/house-bill/5/text.

CRS (Congressional Research Service). 2021. https://www.congress.gov/bill/117th-congress/house-bill/5/text.

Dolovich, S. 2011. 'Strategic segregation in the modern prison'. *American Criminal Law Review, 48*: 1–55.

Feminists in Struggle. 2019. 'Feminists in Struggle (FIST) launches campaign for feminist amendments to the Equality Act'. https://feministstruggle.org/2019/10/19/feminists-in-struggle-fist-launches-campaign-for-feminist-amendments-to-the-equality-act/.

Harper, J., O'Donnell, E., Khorashad, B. S., McDermott, H., & Witcomb, G. L. 2021. 'How does hormone transition in transgender women change body composition, muscle strength and haemoglobin? Systematic review with a focus on the implications for sport participation'. *British Journal of Sports Medicine, 55*(15): 865–872.

Hilton, E. N., & Lundberg, T. R. 2021. 'Transgender women in the female category of sport: Perspectives on testosterone suppression and performance advantage'. *Sports Medicine, 51*(2): 199–214.

Jeffreys, S. 2014. 'The politics of the toilet: A feminist response to the campaign to 'degender' a women's space. *Women's International Forum, 45*: 42–51.

Keisling, M. 2016. *Statement from Mara Keisling on the election of Donald Trump* [Press release]. National Center for Transgender Equality. https://transequality.org/press/releases/statement-from-mara-keisling-on-the-election-of-donald-trump.

Lawford-Smith, H. 2019, July 8. *Women-only spaces and the right to exclude* [Paper presentation]. Australasian Association of Philosophy Conference, Wollongong, Australia.

Lorber, J. 1994. *Paradoxes of gender*. Yale University Press.

Murray, K., & Hunter Blackburn, L. 2019. 'Losing sight of women's rights: The unregulated introduction of gender self-identification as a case study of policy capture in Scotland'. *Scottish Affairs, 28*(3): 262–289.

Stock, K. 2019. 'Sexual orientation: What is it?' *Proceedings of the Aristotelian Society*, *119*(3): 295–319.

Suissa, J., & Sullivan, A. 2021. 'The gender wars, academic freedom and education'. *Journal of Philosophy of Education, 55*(1): 55–82.

Taylor, J. K., Daniel, C. L., & Donald, P. H.-M. 2018. *The remarkable rise of transgender rights*. University of Michigan Press.

Ullman, S. E., Filipas, H. H., Townsend, S. M., & Starzynski, L. L. (2007). Psychosocial correlates of PTSD symptom severity in sexual assault survivors. *Journal of traumatic stress, 20*(5): 821–831.

von Zielbauer, P. 2005, December 30. 'City Prepares to Close Rikers Housing for Gays'. *New York Times*. Section B, p. 9.

Women's Human Rights Campaign. 2020. 'The Equality for All Act'. https://womens-declaration.com/documents/104/WHRC_Equality_for_All_Act.pdf.

10
PSYCHOSOCIAL FACTORS AND GENDER DYSPHORIA
Emerging Theories

Lisa Littman

Over the past 15 years, there have been striking changes in the numbers and characteristics of individuals seeking care for gender dysphoria (GD). The number of adolescents, particularly natal female adolescents, has rapidly increased. The sex ratio of the adolescent patient population shifted from one that was predominantly natal males to one that was predominantly natal females. And a new presentation of GD has emerged in which natal females who lacked observable signs of GD during their childhoods became gender dysphoric and transgender-identified during or after puberty. Gender clinics have documented that their recent patients with GD have higher than expected rates of psychological, social, and developmental problems often predating the onset of GD. Online, parents report that their teens became gender dysphoric in the context of friend-group clusters in which multiple or even all members of a friend group became transgender-identified around the same time. The reported changing demographics, psychological complexities, and friendship group clusters suggest that psychological and social factors may play an essential role in this cohort. This chapter reviews the basics of GD, highlights recent demographic changes, and explores, through two studies, the potential role of psychosocial factors in the development of GD.

GD

Definitions and context

GD, broadly defined, is a person's distress or discomfort associated with the feeling that their physical body and biological sex do not match their perception of themselves in terms of masculinity and femininity. The term *transgender* (or transgender-identified) is used to describe a person whose perception of themselves does not

DOI: 10.4324/9781003286608-10

match their physical body and biological sex. In previous decades, GD and identifying as transgender were closely aligned. However, recent cohorts have started to claim that GD is not necessary to identify as transgender (Jacobsen, Devor & Hodge, 2022). Furthermore, not all individuals with GD identify as transgender. So while the concepts of GD and transgender identification have significant overlap, individuals may experience one without the other.

GD is a diagnosis given by health professionals when a patient meets the specific criteria as defined in the *Diagnostic and Statistical Manual of Mental Disorders, Fifth Edition* (*DSM-5*; American Psychiatric Association, 2013). The diagnosis first appeared in the *DSM-III* (American Psychiatric Association, 1980) as Gender Identity Disorder (GID) in 1980 and was called GID in subsequent *DSM* versions (III, III-TR, IV, and IV-TR; American Psychiatric Association 1980, 1987, 1994, 2000, respectively) until the name of the diagnosis was changed to GD in 2013 with the publication of the *DSM-5*. The diagnoses of GD (and GID previously) should not be confused with *gender nonconformity*, which is simply having the interests, personality, behaviours, preferences, aesthetics, fashion sense, and so on that are not consistent with the stereotypes associated with one's sex.

GD can be temporary or long term (Ristori and Steensma 2016; Singh et al. 2021; Wallien and Cohen-Kettenis 2008; Zucker 2018). When a person has GD and then the GD resolves, it is called *desistance*. That is, the GD desisted, resolved, or ceased to be present. *Persistence* is the continuation of GD. Although there is no formal threshold for how long GD needs to continue in order to be called persistent, many use the term to refer to GD that continues from childhood through adolescence and into early adulthood.

There are several different types (typologies) of GD, and it is important to distinguish them from one another because different types of GD have different expected trajectories and outcomes (Blanchard et al. 1989; Ristori and Steensma 2016). One aspect of GD is the timing relative to puberty. In *early-onset GD*, symptoms begin in childhood before the start of puberty (Zucker et al. 2016). In *late-onset GD* the symptoms of GD begin with the onset of puberty or later (Zucker et al. 2016). When late-onset GD occurs during adolescence, it is sometimes called adolescent-onset GD. Another distinguishing attribute of GD is the sexual orientation of the individual involved (Blanchard 1985, 1989).

According to the best available evidence, the most likely outcome for children with early-onset GD who are allowed to experience natural puberty is that their GD will spontaneously resolve (they will desist) without medical interventions, and they will grow up to become mostly lesbian, gay, and bisexual (LGB), non-transgender adults (Ristori and Steensma 2016; Wallien and Cohen-Kettenis 2008). Childhood GD is more predictive of LGB adulthood than it is of transgender adulthood (Ristori and Steensma 2016; Wallien and Cohen-Kettenis 2008; Zucker, 2018). Thus far, at least 10 studies in which GD youth were evaluated as children and then evaluated again as adolescents or young adults found that the majority of these children (50 percent to 97.8 percent) desisted (American Psychiatric Association 2013;

Singh, Bradley & Zucker, 2021; Zucker 2018). Because the youth in desistance studies received diagnoses during the time that GD was referred to as GID, the discussion about desistance in this chapter uses GID/GD to refer to the diagnosis.

Studies of desistance often mix data from children who met the full diagnostic criteria for GID/GD with children who met only partial criteria for the diagnosis. Zucker (2018) carried out a reanalysis of the data separating children who met the full *DSM* diagnostic criteria and those who didn't. He found that 67.2 percent of the children who received a full childhood *DSM* diagnoses for GID/GD desisted and that 92.9 percent of the children who only met a partial diagnosis desisted (Zucker 2018). Some have argued against the validity of the desistance evidence, claiming that, because of changes to the *DSM*, the children who desisted after receiving diagnoses of GID/GD prior to 2013 were likely to have been just gender non-conforming (Rafferty et al. 2018; Temple Newhook et al. 2018). However, because every version of the DSM that contains a chapter about GID or GD explicitly instructs clinicians that the diagnosis should *not* be used for individuals who are just gender non-conforming (American Psychiatric Association 1980, 1987, 1994, 2000, 2013), the argument that the individuals who desisted in desistance studies were just gender non-conforming can be dismissed as specious.

The scientific literature about desistance, prior to 2010, is based on gender-dysphoric children who did not receive puberty blockers. Studies after 2010, those that follow children who received puberty blockers, find that very few (less than 5 percent) desist and that most will proceed to taking cross-sex hormones (Brik et al. 2020; Carmichael et al. 2021; de Vries et al. 2011; see Biggs, this volume). The stark difference between most gender-dysphoric youth without puberty blockers desisting and most gender-dysphoric youth with puberty blockers persisting invites explanation. Several maturational events are associated with desistance, including experiencing sexual attraction, falling in love, and finding that the physical changes that occur with puberty were not distressful (Steensma et al. 2011). Some professionals are concerned that puberty blockers, by preventing the maturational events associated with desistance, could prevent desistance and cause an iatrogenic persistence of GD (D'Angelo et al. 2021; Korte et al. 2008). In other words, there is concern that the treatment produces the persistence of the condition. Additionally, because LGB individuals often experience temporary GD during their normal development before the consolidation of a homosexual identity has occurred, there is concern that administering puberty blockers during this process could derail the development of young people who would otherwise grow up to be LGB adults (Korte et al. 2008; Wallien and Cohen-Kettenis 2008).

Adolescents with GD are a unique population. As recently as 2012, only two speciality gender clinics in the world (one in Toronto, Canada, and one in Amsterdam, the Netherlands) had sufficient experience with gender-dysphoric adolescents to provide any conclusions about this cohort (Byne et al. 2012). The clinicians from both clinics agreed that there were two categories of adolescents (those with early-onset GD and those with recent late-onset GD) and that the teens with late-onset

GD were more complicated and more likely to have psychiatric problems than the early-onset teens (Byne et al. 2012). When evaluating adolescents with GD, it is imperative to identify whether their GD is early-onset GD or late-onset GD because, in addition to having different complexities and likelihoods of associated comorbidities, only one group of adolescents (those with early-onset GD) has been studied for persistence, desistance and treatment with puberty suppression, cross-sex hormones, and surgery (de Vries et al. 2014, 2011; Delemarre-van de Waal and Cohen-Kettenis 2006; Singh et al. 2021; Wallien and Cohen-Kettenis 2008). Adolescents who had a late-onset of GD and who lacked obvious signs of GD before puberty would not have been eligible for the studies that are used to justify medical transition in youth, and therefore, the results of these studies are not applicable them (de Vries 2020; de Vries et al. 2011, 2014; Delemarre-van de Waal and Cohen-Kettenis 2006).

Many individuals with GD will *transition* by taking medical and surgical steps to change their bodies to more closely align with their perceptions of themselves. Cross-sex hormones (providing testosterone to natal females and oestrogens to natal males) are used to make natal female bodies more masculine and natal male bodies more feminine. The effects of testosterone on natal females include the lowering of their voices, increasing facial and body hair, increasing muscle mass, and clitoral enlargement (Hembree et al. 2017). The effects of oestrogens on natal males include the development of breasts, redistribution of fat stores, and skin softening (Hembree et al. 2017). Surgical procedures can include mastectomy (removal of the breasts), hysterectomy and oophorectomy (removal of the uterus and ovaries) and genital surgeries for natal females and breast augmentation, orchiectomy (removal of the testes), and genital surgeries for natal males (Hembree et al. 2017).

Detransition is when an individual who was gender dysphoric or identified as transgender took steps to transition and subsequently stops or reverses those steps. The reasons that individuals detransition are diverse and include becoming comfortable identifying with their birth sex, finding that other conditions were related to (or caused) their GD, concerns about potential medical complications, developing or having a non-binary gender identification, discrimination, and external pressures to detransition (Guerra et al. 2020; Littman 2021; Turban et al. 2021; Vandenbussche 2021).

It is challenging to estimate the prevalence of detransition as a transition outcome. Historically, studies reported small numbers of individuals who regret their transitions and returned to living as their birth sex, ranging from less than 1 percent to, more recently, 9.8 percent (Boyd et al. 2022; Dhejne et al. 2011; Hall et al. 2021; Murad et al. 2010; Wiepjes et al. 2018). However, these studies are limited by high rates of patients who are lost to follow-up, short durations of follow-up after transition, and the use of a very high bar to determine regret (Dhejne et al. 2011; Hall et al. 2021; Murad et al. 2010; Wiepjes et al. 2018). Furthermore, only a small percentage of detransitioners return to the clinics that facilitated their transitions, so clinic reports on detransition rates are likely to be underestimated (Littman 2021).

Recently, there has been an increase in the visibility of people who have detransitioned, and in response, clinicians have called for additional research into this area (Butler and Hutchinson 2020; D'Angelo et al. 2021; Marchiano 2020).

Conceptualising GD

There are currently two distinct conceptual models for GD—a developmental, biopsychosocial model and an innate gender identity model. These models differ in their views about the causes for (etiologies of) GD, whether underlying psychological conditions can lead to gender dysphoria, whether GD can desist, and the role of a thorough evaluation before considering medical and surgical transition.

In a developmental, biopsychosocial model (a model that considers biological, psychological, and social contributors), GD can emerge in the context of a variety of psychological, social, and cognitive situations (such as being bullied for having gender-non-conforming interests, in the aftermath of rape, or due to difficulty accepting oneself as lesbian, gay, or bisexual); can be temporary; and can be the result of underlying psychological conditions (Churcher Clarke and Spiliadis 2019; D'Angelo 2020; D'Angelo et al. 2021; Spiliadis 2019; Zucker, Wood, et al. 2012). Treatment approaches are specific to the type of GD and the context in which it arose. In other words, there are multiple causes for GD and multiple treatments. Medical and surgical transition are not appropriate treatments for all types of gender dysphoria (Churcher Clarke and Spiliadis 2019; D'Angelo 2020; D'Angelo et al. 2021; Zucker, Wood, et al. 2012). Because there can be multiple causes for GD, the approaches associated with a developmental model employ thorough evaluations to identify the causes of distress and a judicious use of medical and surgical transition so that each patient receives the correct treatment for their situation (Churcher Clarke and Spiliadis 2019; D'Angelo 2020; D'Angelo et al. 2021; Spiliadis 2019; Zucker, Wood, et al. 2012). The approaches consistent with a developmental perspective include the developmentally informed, biopsychosocial approach, and exploratory approaches (Churcher Clarke and Spiliadis 2019; D'Angelo 2020; D'Angelo et al. 2021; Spiliadis 2019; Zucker, Wood, et al. 2012).

In contrast, the innate gender identity model is based on gender identity theory and may be referred to as a gender-affirmative model. From an innate gender identity perspective, every person has an innate soul-like gender identity that represents their 'true self', and this entity can either match or not match one's biological sex (Ehrensaft 2012; Rafferty et al. 2018; Wagner et al. 2019). In this model, GD has one cause (a mismatch between a person's gender identity and their physical body) and one treatment: changing the physical body to align with the innate gender identity (Ashley 2021). Proponents of this model support an approach where once a person expresses a gender identity that differs from their biological sex, the stated gender identity is reinforced without question or delay, and transition interventions are made available to them according to any of several protocols (Hembree et al. 2017; Rafferty et al. 2018). The assumptions supporting this approach are that when transition interventions are provided to gender-dysphoric individuals, the benefits will usually exceed the risks and that delaying these interventions will usually cause harm. The clinical approaches that are related to an innate gender identity model include the gender-(identity-)affirming approach and the informed consent model of care which employ minimised or eliminated evaluations and a liberal use of medical and surgical transition (Rafferty et al. 2018; Schulz 2018).

From the perspective of the innate gender-identity model, the desistence evidence is rejected, and if a person has GD and psychological issues, it is believed that the psychological issues cannot be underlying conditions for the GD (Rafferty et al. 2018; Temple Newhook et al. 2018; Wagner et al. 2019). However, the existence of people who desist after experiencing GD, people who have been harmed by transition, detransitioners who regret transitioning, and people who have had underlying psychological conditions for their GD contradict the assumptions and beliefs associated with the innate gender-identity model. While the developmental model prioritises making the correct diagnosis and providing the correct treatment to the gender-dysphoric patient, the innate gender-identity model prioritises quick access to transition. These differences in priorities contribute to the current contentious public debate surrounding the topics of GD, transition, and detransition.

Recent changes

Demographic change in patients seeking care for GD

Over the past 15 years, there have been monumental changes in the population of patients seeking care for GD, notable for a striking increase in adolescent patients and a steeper increase in natal female adolescents, so much so that the teen patient populations that used to be predominantly natal male shifted to predominantly natal female. This change is referred to as an *inversion* or reversal of the sex ratio. The rapid increase in teen patients and the inversion of the sex ratio from natal male to natal female was documented by specialty gender clinics in Canada, the Netherlands, and the United Kingdom (Aitken et al. 2015; de Graaf et al. 2018). In Finland, a speciality gender clinic serving adolescent patients documented that in their first two years of experience (2013–2015), it received higher than expected numbers of teen referrals, far more natal female teens than natal male teens, and the patients often had severe psychological or developmental issues that occurred before their GD symptoms began (Kaltiala-Heino et al. 2015). The clinicians in Finland suggested that their findings may represent several additional developmental pathways of GD (Kaltiala-Heino et al. 2015). Another recent change is the emergence of a new presentation of GD: late-onset GD in females. Prior to 2012, this type of presentation was nearly absent from the scientific literature (Steensma et al. 2013; Zucker, Bradley, et al. 2012), and by 2018, a gender clinic in the United Kingdom reported that 'this rapid onset of gender dysphoria in assigned females post puberty is indeed a worrying phenomenon we are observing more and more at the clinic' (Bonfatto and Crasnow 2018, p. 43).

It is currently unknown why these demographic and clinical changes have occurred, but several explanations have been considered. Some have hypothesised that decreases in stigma, increases in the visibility of transgender people, and expanded access to information and medical interventions may explain the observed changes (Aitken et al. 2015; de Graaf et al. 2018). Although these factors could increase the overall number of patients seeking care, they do not explain why the increase is concentrated in adolescents, why the sex ratio reversed, or why there is a new presentation of GD (late-onset GD in females). Some researchers have hypothesised that if stigma around transgender identification decreased more for natal females than it did for natal males, then the difference in stigma could result in more natal females seeking care (Aitken et al. 2015; de Graaf et al. 2018). But although sex-based reductions in stigma could explain the increase in natal female patients relative to natal male patients, this doesn't explain the new presentation of late-onset GD in natal females or why the sex ratio reversal occurred for teens but not for older adults (Zucker 2017). Explanations related to changes in stigma and access cannot fully explain the dramatic demographic and clinical changes observed. It's plausible that there could be multiple factors contributing to these changes. But because these demographic shifts could indicate a new type of GD with different etiologies, trajectories, and responses to interventions, it is imperative to explore why these changes might be occurring and study this new cohort of gender-dysphoric individuals.

Online observations

Around 2015, parents started reporting on social media forums that their adolescent and young adult children, mostly daughters, became gender dysphoric and transgender-identified in the context of belonging to a friend group in which multiple or even all the friends in the group became transgender-identified in a similar time frame (Marchiano 2017). Parents reported that around the time that their children became transgender-identified, they had become immersed in social media, binging on Reddit and YouTube transition videos. A review of social media sites popular with teens (YouTube, Reddit, Tumblr) revealed advice and messages that encouraged youth to believe that vague symptoms and common adolescent emotions were signs of being transgender and that transitioning as soon as possible was the only way that they could feel better and provided youth with instructions about how to deceive their parents and doctors to obtain cross-sex hormones (Littman 2018).

Psychosocial factors

Why explore social influences and psychological factors?

The demographic changes raise the concern that published results on treatment for people presenting with GD may no longer apply and other approaches may need to be considered. Because the shift in patients seeking care for GD has been driven by an unprecedented surge in adolescent patients, it's logical to examine factors that are especially salient to adolescence. Adolescence is the life stage during which individuals are most susceptible to peer influences (Chein et al. 2011; Dishion and Tipsord 2011; Steinberg and Monahan 2007). Peer influences, including peer contagion, have been associated with depressive symptoms, disordered eating, aggression, and bullying (Dishion and Tipsord 2011; Prinstein 2007). The pattern of new transgender identifications occurring in clusters of pre-existing friendship groups, although not definitive, is suggestive that peer influence may be relevant to this phenomenon. Furthermore, the social media content that urges transition and instructs individuals on how to deceive parents and health professionals parallels the types of content found on pro-eating disorder websites (Harshbarger et al. 2009). Clinicians have documented that the most recent cohort of youth seeking care for GD has higher than expected rates of psychological and developmental issues often emerging before the onset of GD, strengthening the case for investigating these factors (de Graaf et al. 2018; Kaltiala-Heino et al. 2015).

Let's look in detail at two studies that explored these factors. The first, the parent-report study, recruited parents of gender-dysphoric youth in 2016 to collect information about youth who became gender dysphoric and transgender-identified as adolescents and young adults (Littman 2018). Building on the preliminary findings of the parent-report study, a second study, the detransition study, recruited participants from 2016 to 2017 and collected first-hand information from detransitioners about their experiences with GD, transition, and detransition (Littman 2021).

The parent-report study

The purpose of the study was to collect data from parents about their adolescent or young adult children who seemed to become gender dysphoric and transgender-identified suddenly during or after puberty and to generate hypotheses to explain the recent demographic changes in gender-dysphoric patients seeking care. The study was designed as a descriptive study that employed an anonymous, online survey to collect data from parents about their observations of their children's development, mental health history, friendship group, social media use, and interactions with clinicians.

At the time of study recruitment, there were only a few existing websites that had reported on this phenomenon, so these websites were selected as sites to post the recruitment information about the study. To expand the reach of the project, snowball sampling was used so that any person viewing the recruitment information could share it with any community where there might be people eligible for the study. In the first week, there were four websites sharing the study information. Three of the websites could be described as parent-support sites for parents of gender-dysphoric children or professional sites that seemed supportive about evaluating gender-dysphoric children for other conditions and cautious or negative about medical and surgical transition for gender-dysphoric teens and young adults

(4thwavenow, transgendertrend, youth trans critical professionals). The fourth website was a private Facebook support site for parents of gender-dysphoric children and seemed to be supportive of facilitating medical and surgical transition for teens and young adults (parents of transgender children).

Parent-participants were eligible for the study if they indicated that (1) their child exhibited a sudden or rapid onset of GD, (2) the youth's GD first began during or after puberty (not before), and (3) prior to puberty, the child would not have met diagnostic criteria for GD (as calculated by parent report about the number of observed GD indicators the youth had prior to puberty). After cleaning the data, there were 256 eligible participants. The parent-participants were predominantly White (91 percent), female (92 percent), 45 to 60 years of age (66 percent), and resided in the United States (72 percent), the United Kingdom (15 percent), and Canada (7 percent). Most of the parents held liberal views about LGBT rights, with 90 percent favouring the rights of lesbian and gay couples to marry and 88 percent reporting that they believe transgender individuals deserve the same rights and protections as others. The adolescents and young adults described by their parents were predominantly female (83 percent), and 41 percent had expressed a non-heterosexual sexual orientation prior to identifying as transgender. The young people had a mean age of 15 years when they announced a transgender identification and a mean age of 16 years at the time their parents completed the surveys.

The young people described in this survey had several psychological, emotional, and social vulnerabilities that existed before they became gender dysphoric. Prior to the onset of observed GD symptoms, 63 percent had been diagnosed with one or more psychiatric disorders or neurodevelopmental disabilities, 48 percent had experienced a traumatic event, and 45 percent were engaged in non-suicidal self-injury. More than half of the young people (56 percent) had very high expectations that transitioning would solve their problems.

Parents provided detailed information about their children's friendship groups and the behaviours that they (the parents) witnessed. At the time when the youth became gender dysphoric and transgender-identified, most of the young people (69 percent) belonged to a friendship group in which one or more members became transgender-identified around the same time. In more than a third of the friendship groups (37 percent), the majority of the friends became transgender-identified. At the time that recruitment for this study was active, the expected prevalence for transgender-identified young adults was 0.7 percent (Flores et al., 2016). Thus, a friendship group with 50 percent or more people becoming transgender-identified was more than 70 times the expected rate of transgender-identified individuals in the general population.

Parents described intense friend group dynamics where individuals who identified as transgender were highly praised and those who were not transgender-identified were ridiculed. Most of the parents (61 percent) who reported on the details of the friendship groups indicated that their child's popularity increased within the group when they announced a transgender identification, and 60 percent of the groups were observed to mock people who were not transgender or LGBT. The quality and type of mocking activities can be illustrated in the following quotes. One parent stated, 'If they aren't mocking "cis" people, they are playing pronoun police and mocking people who can't get the pronouns correct'. Another parent explained, 'New vocabulary includes "cis-stupid" and "cis-stupidity"'. There were two cases in which teens spent time away from their primary friendship group and desisted. These young people were so concerned about returning to school and informing their friends that they no longer identified as transgender, that they, with the help of their parents, transferred to new schools.

Most of the parents (65 percent) reported that their child's use of social media increased before the young person announced a transgender identification. Parents indicated which types of advice their child had seen online, which included how to tell if they were transgender (54 percent), reasons that they should transition right away (35 percent), what to say and not say to clinicians to obtain cross-sex hormones (22 percent), the acceptance of lying to clinicians to get hormones (18 percent), and the use the topic of suicide in transgender people should be used to convince reluctant parents to take them for hormones (21 percent).

When asked to select which sources parents felt were most influential in their child's becoming gender dysphoric, the most frequently cited were YouTube transition videos (64 percent), Tumblr (62 percent), a group of friends they knew in person (45 percent) and a community of people they met online (43 percent). One parent offered the following perspective: 'We believe the biggest influence was the online pro-transition blogs and YouTube videos. We feel she was highly influenced by the "if you are even questioning your gender you are probably transgender" philosophy'. Another parent reported, 'I believe my child experienced what many kids experience on the cusp of puberty—uncomfortableness!—but there was an online world at the ready to tell her that those very normal feelings meant she's in the wrong body'.

The findings from this study generated several hypotheses about the development of GD. One hypothesis is that the described cases may represent a new subcategory of gender dysphoria (preliminarily called rapid-onset gender dysphoria or ROGD). The presentation of ROGD is characterised by a lack of observed signs of GD sufficient for a diagnosis of GD before puberty and a new onset of GD or transgender identification that occurs during or after puberty in adolescence or young adulthood. A second hypothesis is that social influences may contribute to the development of GD in some individuals. And a third hypothesis is that maladaptive coping mechanisms for a variety of psychosocial stressors (such as psychiatric disorders, sex- or gender-related trauma, internalised homophobia, etc.) may underlie the development of GD for some individuals. These hypotheses can be referred to collectively as the ROGD hypotheses or the psychosocial hypotheses. Although ROGD is not an official diagnosis in the *DSM* or the International Classification of Diseases, it is a useful construct as it speaks to the specifics of the presentation (lack of observed signs of GD before puberty, new onset of GD or transgender identification during or after puberty in teens and young adults) and connects it to the proposed hypotheses about the mechanism of psychosocial factors as underlying conditions or contributory factors for GD.

Strengths of this study include that it is the first study to empirically explore a phenomenon that has been observed by parents and clinicians and that the study examined the social and psychological context in which youth first announced a transgender identification (Zucker 2019). As with all studies, the limitations should be kept in mind when interpreting the results. The methods used in this study (parent report, targeted recruitment and convenience samples, anonymous surveys, cross-sectional design) are common research methods and have both advantages and weaknesses. Parent reports have the advantage of collecting data from adults who are knowledgeable about the youth's full developmental history and who possess a mature understanding of events that the youth may not be able to recollect or fully comprehend. A weakness of parent report is that there are details of the young person's life to which the parent does not have access. Targeted recruitment and the use of convenience samples are beneficial as they allow researchers to find hard-to-reach populations but have the weakness that they introduce selection bias, which limits the generalisability of the findings. Although anonymous surveys protect the privacy of participants, the identities of the participants cannot be verified. And finally, conclusions about cause and effect cannot be made in research using a cross-sectional design. The methods used in this research are consistent with methods used in other GD research including James et al. (2016; targeted recruitment, convenience sample, anonymous survey, cross-sectional design) and Olson et al. (2016; parent report, targeted recruitment).

After the publication of this research, several clinicians who work with gender-dysphoric youth published editorials noting that the findings of the research were consistent with what they are seeing in their own patient populations (Hutchinson et al. 2020; Zucker 2019). And individual detransitioners publicly stated that the research was consistent with their own experiences with gender dysphoria (Pique Resilience Project 2019). The next steps for exploring the hypotheses generated from this work and further exploring the potential role of psychosocial factors in the development of GD should include surveying individuals who experienced GD and recruitment efforts to reach a broader and more diverse population of potential respondents.

The detransition study

In the detransition study, detransitioners aged 18 years and older were surveyed about their own experiences with gender dysphoria, transition, and detransition. Efforts were made to reach out to communities with strongly pro-transition perspectives (sharing recruitment information on electronic mailing lists from the World Professional Association for Transgender Health and the American Psychological Association) and communities where individuals may be more inclined to hold the view that transition isn't always beneficial for everyone (sharing recruitment information in private detransition groups and blogs that had covered the topic of detransitioning). To date, very few, if any, research studies in this area have reached out to communities with strong pro-transition views and communities who question the pro-transition paradigm. Participants were eligible for the study if they indicated that, for the purpose of transitioning, they had taken or had one of more or the following: puberty blockers, cross-sex hormones, anti-androgens, or surgery, and for the purpose of detransitioning, they stopped taking the medications or had surgery to reverse the changes from their transition. The sample of 100 detransitioners was predominantly natal female (69 percent), White (90 percent), and resided in the United States (66 percent), the United Kingdom (9 percent), Canada (9 percent), Australia (4 percent), and other countries (12 percent). Most participants had no religious affiliation (68 percent), and the vast majority (93 percent) supported the rights of gay and lesbian couples to marry legally. The age of respondents at the time they completed the survey ranged from 18 years of age to more than 60 years of age, with a mean age for females of 26 years and a mean age for males of 37 years. On average, females were 20 years of age when they sought care to transition and 24 years of age when they decided to detransition. Males were older at the average age of seeking transition (26 years) and deciding to detransition (33 years).

Before becoming gender dysphoric, more than half of the respondents had been diagnosed with one or more psychiatric disorders or neurodevelopmental disabilities. Depression, anxiety, and attention-deficit/hyperactivity disorder (ADHD) were the most common diagnoses. Nearly half of the female participants had experienced trauma less than one year before the onset of their GD. Trauma preceding GD was rarer for males (13 percent). Slightly more than half of the participants (56 percent) could be categorised as having early-onset GD (their GD began during childhood), and slightly less than half (44 percent) experienced late-onset GD (their GD began at the onset of puberty or later). More than half (55 percent) of the female participants fell into the relatively recent new category of late-onset GD in natal females. Participants wanted to transition for reasons including wanting to be perceived as the target gender (77 percent), believing that transition was their only option to feel better (71 percent), and having the sense that their bodies felt wrong to them the way that they were (71 percent). Most participants believed that transitioning would reduce (63 percent) or eliminate (65 percent) their GD.

There was a wide range of experiences related to detransitioning. The most frequently endorsed reason for detransitioning was that the participant's personal definition of male and female changed and they became comfortable identifying with their birth sex (60 percent). Other reasons included being concerned about potential medical complications (49 percent) and transitioning did not improve the participant's mental health (42 percent), as well as many others. Experiences were captured by a combination of open-text and multiple-choice questions and tallied into narratives. Narratives included coming to the view that the participant's GD was caused by a mental health condition or trauma (58 percent), detransitioning because the participant faced discrimination and external pressures to detransition (29 percent), and experiencing GD and the drive to transition because of internalised homophobia and difficulty accepting themselves as LGB (23 percent). Other narratives included social pressure to transition (20 percent), discovering or maintaining a non-binary identification (16 percent), and misogyny (7 percent of natal females).

Findings suggest that a subset of participants experienced social influences around the interpretation of their symptoms, the belief that transitioning would be beneficial to them, and being pressured to transition. Specifically, participants were asked how they feel currently about having identified as transgender in the past. More than a third of the participants (35 percent) endorsed the response, 'Someone else told me that the feelings I was having meant that I was transgender and I believed them', suggesting that social influence played a substantial role in the interpretation of symptoms and coming to the conclusion that they were transgender. Some participants belonged to friendship groups where one or more friends transitioned before the participant decided to transition (36 percent). These friendship groups engaged in mocking people who weren't transgender-identified (22 percent), and some participants experienced an increase in their popularity within their friend group when they announced their plans to transition (20 percent). Respondents identified sources that encouraged them to believe that transitioning would help them. The most commonly endorsed sources of transition encouragement were social media sources including YouTube transition videos (48 percent), blogs (46 percent), Tumblr (45 percent), and online communities (43 percent). Several in-person social sources were also identified including therapists (37 percent), a person (28.0 percent), or group of friends (27 percent). These findings support the psychosocial (ROGD) hypotheses regarding the potential for social influences to contribute to the development of GD and transgender identification.

Also supporting the psychosocial (ROGD) hypotheses about social influence was the finding that 37 percent of the participants felt pressured to transition at some point. One fifth of the participants (20 percent) indicated that they felt pressured to transition and provided additional information that specified they were pressured to transition by a person or group of people – specifically their clinicians, partners, friends, online communities, and society. Natal female participants were statistically more likely to report that they felt pressured to transition than natal male participants. The following quotes illustrate how they were pressured and by whom. One respondent who felt pressured by their clinician wrote, '[My] [d]octor pushed drugs and surgery at every visit'. Other participants wrote about feeling pressured by societal messages and online sources as shown in the following quotes: 'Everyone says that if you feel like a different gender . . . then you just are that gender and you should transition', and 'The forums and communities and internet friends'. Examples of pressure from friends included the following quote: 'A couple of later trans friends kept insisting that I needed to stop delaying things'.

The findings that support a role for psychological factors contributing to GD include 58 percent of the participants expressing that their GD was caused by trauma or a mental health condition and 51 percent reporting that they felt that the process of transitioning delayed or prevented them from dealing with their underlying conditions, which suggests that maladaptive coping mechanisms could be relevant for some participants. Additionally, participants expressed how internalised homophobia was salient to their experience of gender dysphoria as seen in the following quotes. In response to a question about why participants transitioned, respondents added the following: 'I didn't want to be a gay man', and 'Transitioning to male would mean my attraction to girls would be "normal"'.

There were several strengths of this study, including the use of a precise definition for detransition, recruitment from communities with different perspectives about transition and detransition, and the collaboration with individuals who detransitioned to help create survey questions that were relevant and captured a range of detransition experiences. Additionally, it is one of the largest studies of detransitioners to date. Limitations of the study include those associated with the use of anonymous surveys, cross-sectional design, targeted recruitment, and convenience samples, as described previously. The methods and limitations of this research study are similar to the methods and limitations of other research in this field of study (Turban et al. 2021; Vandenbussche 2021).

Although more research needs to be done, the findings from the detransition study support several of the findings from the parent-report study, including that GD began during or after puberty for some participants, social influence was relevant to how many people interpreted their experiences and concluded that they were transgender, social media sources encouraged people to believe that transitioning would be helpful to them, and participants felt pressured to transition by peers and online communities. The hypotheses to emerge from both studies are that psychosocial factors (such as trauma, mental health conditions, maladaptive coping mechanisms, internalised homophobia, and social influence) can cause or contribute to the development of GD in some individuals. Furthermore, there exists a population of individuals who lacked observable signs of GD before puberty and became gender dysphoric and transgender-identified during adolescence and young adulthood (during or after puberty). These hypotheses which are grounded in the developmental model of GD can be referred to as a psychosocial developmental pathway for GD, a psychosocial theory of GD, or ROGD theory (Churcher Clarke and Spiliadis 2019; D'Angelo et al. 2021; Zucker, Wood, et al. 2012).

Status of the ROGD hypotheses

The evidence to support the emerging theory of psychosocial factors as a developmental pathway to gender dysphoria is early but increasing in strength. The psychosocial theory of GD refers to individuals who lacked observable signs of gender dysphoria or gender incongruence before puberty and became gender dysphoric or transgender-identified as adolescents or young adults (during or after puberty) and proposes that psychosocial factors (such as social influence, maladaptive coping mechanisms, internalised homophobia, trauma, and mental health conditions) can cause or contribute to the development of GD and transgender identification in some individuals. This chapter has documented the development of this theory from the generation of hypotheses derived from parent reports of their children, through the acknowledgement of clinicians working with gender-dysphoric youth who have observed these findings in their own patients, through statements from detransitioners asserting that the research is consistent with their own experiences with GD, and to the published research of detransitioners providing first-person reports of their own experiences (Hutchinson et al. 2020; Littman 2018, 2021; Pique Resilience Project 2019; Zucker 2019).

Conclusion

Over the past 15 years, there have been monumental changes in the demographics of patients seeking care for GD, notable for a marked increase in adolescents seeking care, an even steeper increase for natal female teens, an inversion of the sex ratio in adolescent populations, and the emergence of a new presentation of GD, namely late-onset GD in natal females. Some of these changes might be explained by decreases in stigma, increases in the visibility of transgender people, and greater availability of information and services. However, other changes are better explained by the emergence of a psychosocial developmental pathway of GD. Emerging research suggests that psychosocial factors (social influence, social contagion, maladaptive coping mechanisms, trauma, psychological issues, internalised homophobia) may contribute to the development of GD and transgender identification in some individuals. The relevance of these psychosocial factors to the experiences of GD and transgender identification has been demonstrated by second-hand and first-hand accounts (Littman 2018, 2021). Future research is needed to better understand the developmental pathways of GD, the recent demographic changes, the trajectories of gender-dysphoric youth and the best approaches for evaluating and treating young people with GD.

References

Aitken, M., Steensma, T.D., Blanchard, R., VanderLaan, D.P., Wood, H., Fuentes, A., Spegg, C., Wasserman, L., Ames, M., Fitzsimmons, C.L. and Leef, J.H. (2015). Evidence for an altered sex ratio in clinic-referred adolescents with gender dysphoria. *Journal of Sexual Medicine*, *12*(3), pp.756–763.

American Psychiatric Association, 1980. *Diagnostic and statistical manual of mental disorders: DSM-III*. Washington, DC, American Psychiatric Association.

American Psychiatric Association, 1987. *Diagnostic and statistical manual of mental disorders: DSM-III-TR*. Washington, DC, American Psychiatric Association.

American Psychiatric Association, 1994. *Diagnostic and statistical manual of mental disorders: DSM-IV*. Washington, DC, American Psychiatric Association.

American Psychiatric Association, 2000. *Diagnostic and statistical manual of mental disorders: DSM-IV-TR*. Washington, DC, American Psychiatric Association.

American Psychiatric Association, 2013. *Diagnostic and statistical manual of mental disorders: DSM-5*. Arlington, VA, American Psychiatric Association.

Ashley, F., 2021. The misuse of gender dysphoria: Toward greater conceptual clarity in transgender health. *Perspectives on Psychological Science*, 16(6), pp.1159–1164.

Blanchard, R., 1985. Typology of male-to-female transsexualism. *Archives of Sexual Behavior*, 14(3), pp.247–261.

Blanchard, R., 1989. The classification and labeling of nonhomosexual gender dysphorias. *Archives of Sexual Behavior*, 18(4), pp.315–334.

Blanchard, R., Steiner, B.W., Clemmensen, L.H. and Dickey, R., 1989. Prediction of regrets in postoperative transsexuals. *The Canadian Journal of Psychiatry*, 34(1), pp.43–45.

Bonfatto, M. and Crasnow, E., 2018. Gender/ed identities: An overview of our current work as child psychotherapists in the Gender Identity Development Service. *Journal of Child Psychotherapy*, 44(1), pp.29–46.

Boyd, I., Hackett, T. and Bewley, S., 2022. Care of transgender patients: A general practice quality improvement approach. *Healthcare*, 10(1), p. 121.

Brik, T., Vrouenraets, L.J., de Vries, M.C. and Hannema, S.E., 2020. Trajectories of adolescents treated with gonadotropin-releasing hormone analogues for gender dysphoria. *Archives of Sexual Behavior*, 49(7), pp.2611–2618.

Butler, C. and Hutchinson, A., 2020. Debate: The pressing need for research and services for gender desisters/detransitioners. *Child and Adolescent Mental Health*, 25(1), pp.45–47.

Byne, W., Bradley, S.J., Coleman, E., Eyler, A.E., Green, R., Menvielle, E.J., Meyer-Bahlburg, H.F., Pleak, R.R. and Tompkins, D.A., 2012. Report of the American Psychiatric Association task force on treatment of gender identity disorder. *Archives of sexual behavior*, 41(4), pp.759–796.

Carmichael, P., Butler, G., Masic, U., Cole, T.J., De Stavola, B.L., Davidson, S., Skageberg, E.M., Khadr, S. and Viner, R.M., 2021. Short-term outcomes of pubertal suppression in a selected cohort of 12 to 15 year old young people with persistent gender dysphoria in the UK. *PLoS One*, 16(2), p.e0243894.

Chein, J., Albert, D., O'Brien, L., Uckert, K. and Steinberg, L., 2011. Peers increase adolescent risk taking by enhancing activity in the brain's reward circuitry. *Developmental Science*, 14(2), pp. F1–F10.

Churcher Clarke, A. and Spiliadis, A., 2019. 'Taking the lid off the box': The value of extended clinical assessment for adolescents presenting with gender identity difficulties. *Clinical Child Psychology and Psychiatry*, 24(2), pp.338–352.

D'Angelo, R., 2020. The complexity of childhood gender dysphoria. *Australasian Psychiatry*, 28(5), pp.530–532.

D'Angelo, R., Syrulnik, E., Ayad, S., Marchiano, L., Kenny, D.T. and Clarke, P., 2021. One size does not fit all: In support of psychotherapy for gender dysphoria. *Archives of Sexual Behavior*, 50(1), pp.7–16.

de Graaf, N.M., Giovanardi, G., Zitz, C. and Carmichael, P., 2018. Sex ratio in children and adolescents referred to the Gender Identity Development Service in the UK (2009–2016). *Archives of Sexual Behavior*, 47(5), pp.1301–1304.

de Vries, A.L., 2020. Challenges in timing puberty suppression for gender-nonconforming adolescents. *Pediatrics*, 146(4): e2020010611. doi:10.1542/peds.2020-010611

de Vries, A.L., McGuire, J.K., Steensma, T.D., Wagenaar, E.C., Doreleijers, T.A. and Cohen-Kettenis, P.T., 2014. Young adult psychological outcome after puberty suppression and gender reassignment. *Pediatrics*, 134(4), pp.696–704.

de Vries, A.L., Steensma, T.D., Doreleijers, T.A. and Cohen-Kettenis, P.T., 2011. Puberty suppression in adolescents with gender identity disorder: A prospective follow-up study. *The Journal of Sexual Medicine*, 8(8), pp.2276–2283.

Delemarre-Van De Waal, H.A. and Cohen-Kettenis, P.T., 2006. Clinical management of gender identity disorder in adolescents: a protocol on psychological and paediatric endocrinology aspects. *European Journal of Endocrinology*, 155(suppl. 1), pp.S131–S137.

Dhejne, C., Lichtenstein, P., Boman, M., Johansson, A.L., Långström, N. and Landén, M., 2011. Long-term follow-up of transsexual persons undergoing sex reassignment surgery: cohort study in Sweden. *PLoS One*, 6(2), p.e16885.

Dishion, T.J. and Tipsord, J.M., 2011. Peer contagion in child and adolescent social and emotional development. *Annual Review of Psychology*, 62, pp.189–214.

Ehrensaft, D., 2012. From gender identity disorder to gender identity creativity: True gender self child therapy. *Journal of Homosexuality*, 59(3), pp.337–356.

Flores, A.R., Herman, J., Gates, G.J. and Brown, T.N., 2016. *How many adults identify as transgender in the United States?* (Vol. 13). Los Angeles, CA: Williams Institute.

Guerra, M.P., Balaguer, M.G., Porras, M.G., Murillo, F.H., Izquierdo, E.S. and Ariño, C.M., 2020. Transexualidad: transiciones, detransiciones y arrepentimientos en España. *Endocrinología, Diabetes y Nutrición*, 67(9), pp.562–567.

Hall, R., Mitchell, L. and Sachdeva, J., 2021. Access to care and frequency of detransition among a cohort discharged by a UK national adult gender identity clinic: Retrospective case-note review. *BJPsych Open*, 7(6), p.e184. pp. 1–8. doi: 10.1192/bjo.2021.1022.

Harshbarger, J.L., Ahlers-Schmidt, C.R., Mayans, L., Mayans, D. and Hawkins, J.H., 2009. Pro-Anorexia websites: What a clinician should know. *International Journal of Eating Disorders*, 42(4), pp.367–370.

Hembree, W.C., Cohen-Kettenis, P.T., Gooren, L., Hannema, S.E., Meyer, W.J., Murad, M.H., Rosenthal, S.M., Safer, J.D., Tangpricha, V. and T'Sjoen, G.G., 2017. Endocrine treatment of gender-dysphoric/gender-incongruent persons: An endocrine society clinical practice guideline. *The Journal of Clinical Endocrinology & Metabolism*, 102(11), pp.3869–3903.

Hutchinson, A., Midgen, M. and Spiliadis, A., 2020. In support of research into rapid-onset gender dysphoria. *Archives of Sexual Behavior*, 49(1), pp.79–80.

Jacobsen, K., Devor, A. and Hodge, E., 2022. Who counts as trans? A critical discourse analysis of trans Tumblr posts. *Journal of Communication Inquiry*, 46(1), pp.60–81.

James, S., Herman, J., Rankin, S., Keisling, M., Mottet, L. and Anafi, M.A., 2016. *The report of the 2015 US transgender survey*. Washington, DC: Natl. Cent. Transgend. Equal.

Kaltiala-Heino, R., Sumia, M., Työläjärvi, M. and Lindberg, N., 2015. Two years of gender identity service for minors: overrepresentation of natal girls with severe problems in adolescent development. *Child and Adolescent Psychiatry and Mental Health*, 9(1), pp.1–9.

Korte, A., Goecker, D., Krude, H., Lehmkuhl, U., Grüters-Kieslich, A. and Beier, K.M., 2008. Gender identity disorders in childhood and adolescence: Currently debated concepts and treatment strategies. *Deutsches Ärzteblatt International*, 105(48), pp.834–841.

Littman, L., 2018. Parent reports of adolescents and young adults perceived to show signs of a rapid onset of gender dysphoria. *PLoS One*, 13(8), p.e0202330.

Littman, L., 2021. Individuals treated for gender dysphoria with medical and/or surgical transition who subsequently detransitioned: A survey of 100 detransitioners. *Archives of Sexual Behavior*, 50(8), pp.3353–3369.

Marchiano, L., 2017. Outbreak: on transgender teens and psychic epidemics. *Psychological Perspectives*, 60(3), pp.345–366.

Marchiano, L., 2020. *The ranks of gender detransitioners are growing. We need to understand why.* Quillette.

Murad, M.H., Elamin, M.B., Garcia, M.Z., Mullan, R.J., Murad, A., Erwin, P.J. and Montori, V.M., 2010. Hormonal therapy and sex reassignment: A systematic review and meta-analysis of quality of life and psychosocial outcomes. *Clinical Endocrinology*, 72(2), pp.214–231.

Olson, K.R., Durwood, L., DeMeules, M. and McLaughlin, K.A., 2016. Mental health of transgender children who are supported in their identities. *Pediatrics*, 137(3): e20153223.

Pique Resilience Project, 2019. URL https:// www.piqueresproject.com/

Prinstein, M.J., 2007. Moderators of peer contagion: A longitudinal examination of depression socialization between adolescents and their best friends. *Journal of Clinical Child and Adolescent Psychology*, 36(2), pp.159–170.

Rafferty, J., Yogman, M., Baum, R., Gambon, T.B., Lavin, A., Mattson, G., Wissow, L.S., Breuner, C., Alderman, E.M., Grubb, L.K. and Powers, M.E., 2018. Ensuring comprehensive care and support for transgender and gender-diverse children and adolescents. *Pediatrics*, 142(4): e20182162.

Ristori, J. and Steensma, T.D., 2016. Gender dysphoria in childhood. *International Review of Psychiatry*, 28(1), pp.13–20.

Schulz, S.L., 2018. The informed consent model of transgender care: An alternative to the diagnosis of gender dysphoria. *Journal of Humanistic Psychology*, 58(1), pp.72–92.

Singh, D., Bradley, S.J. and Zucker, K.J., 2021. A follow-up study of boys with gender identity disorder. *Frontiers in Psychiatry*, 12, p. 287.

Spiliadis, A., 2019. Towards a gender exploratory model: Slowing things down, opening things up and exploring identity development. *Metalogos Systemic Therapy Journal*, 35(1), pp.1–9.

Steensma, T.D., Biemond, R., de Boer, F. and Cohen-Kettenis, P.T., 2011. Desisting and persisting gender dysphoria after childhood: a qualitative follow-up study. *Clinical Child Psychology and Psychiatry*, 16(4), pp.499–516.

Steensma, T.D., Kreukels, B.P., de Vries, A.L. and Cohen-Kettenis, P.T., 2013. Gender identity development in adolescence. *Hormones and Behavior*, 64(2), pp.288–297.

Steinberg, L. and Monahan, K.C., 2007. Age differences in resistance to peer influence. *Developmental Psychology*, 43(6), p. 1531.

Temple Newhook, J., Pyne, J., Winters, K., Feder, S., Holmes, C., Tosh, J., Sinnott, M.L., Jamieson, A. and Pickett, S., 2018. A critical commentary on follow-up studies and "desistance" theories about transgender and gender-nonconforming children. *International Journal of Transgenderism*, 19(2), pp.212–224.

Turban, J.L., Loo, S.S., Almazan, A.N. and Keuroghlian, A.S., 2021. Factors leading to "detransition" among transgender and gender diverse people in the United States: A mixed-methods analysis. *LGBT health*, 8(4), pp.273–280.

Vandenbussche, E., 2022. Detransition-related needs and support: A cross-sectional online survey. *Journal of Homosexuality*, 69(9), pp.1602–1620.

Wagner, J., Sackett-Taylor, A.C., Hodax, J.K., Forcier, M. and Rafferty, J., 2019. Psychosocial overview of gender-affirmative care. *Journal of Pediatric and Adolescent Gynecology*, 32(6), pp.567–573.

Wallien, M.S. and Cohen-Kettenis, P.T., 2008. Psychosexual outcome of gender-dysphoric children. *Journal of the American Academy of Child & Adolescent Psychiatry*, 47(12), pp.1413–1423.

Wiepjes, C.M., Nota, N.M., de Blok, C.J., Klaver, M., de Vries, A.L., Wensing-Kruger, S.A., de Jongh, R.T., Bouman, M.B., Steensma, T.D., Cohen-Kettenis, P. and Gooren, L.J.,

2018. The Amsterdam cohort of gender dysphoria study (1972–2015): Trends in prevalence, treatment, and regrets. *The Journal of Sexual Medicine, 15*(4), pp.582–590.

Zucker, K.J., 2017. Epidemiology of gender dysphoria and transgender identity. *Sexual Health, 14*(5), pp.404–411.

Zucker, K.J., 2018. The myth of persistence: Response to "A critical commentary on follow-up studies and 'desistance'theories about transgender and gender non-conforming children" by Temple Newhook et al.(2018). *International Journal of Transgenderism, 19*(2), pp.231–245.

Zucker, K.J., 2019. Adolescents with gender dysphoria: Reflections on some contemporary clinical and research issues. *Archives of Sexual Behavior, 48*(7), pp.1983–1992.

Zucker, K.J., Bradley, S.J., Owen-Anderson, A., Kibblewhite, S.J., Wood, H., Singh, D. and Choi, K., 2012. Demographics, behavior problems, and psychosexual characteristics of adolescents with gender identity disorder or transvestic fetishism. *Journal of Sex & Marital Therapy, 38*(2), pp.151–189.

Zucker, K.J., Lawrence, A.A. and Kreukels, B.P., 2016. Gender dysphoria in adults. *Annual Review of Clinical Psychology, 12*(1), pp.217–247.

Zucker, K.J., Wood, H., Singh, D. and Bradley, S.J., 2012. A developmental, biopsychosocial model for the treatment of children with gender identity disorder. *Journal of Homosexuality, 59*(3), pp.369–397.

11

THE TECHNOLOGY OF PUBERTY SUPPRESSION

Michael Biggs

The theory and practice of transsexualism were institutionalised in the mid-twentieth century by men like Harry Benjamin and John Money, who helped males who wished to become women. Transgenderism, as it emerged in the 1990s, was created primarily by women and eventually recruited more young females than young males wanting to change sex. One of the progenitors of transgenderism was Judith Butler, the famous American academic theorist of gender. Her books articulated the negative axiom that gender bears no relation to sex and the positive axiom that gender is essential to the self (see Jones, this volume). Just as important, but less renowned, was a Dutch psychologist, Peggy Cohen-Kettenis. She was largely responsible for inventing a technology that promised to transform boys into women and girls into men. While the discursive theory of transgenderism was formulated at Berkeley, the endocrinological practice was assembled in Utrecht and Amsterdam. This chapter examines the origin of puberty suppression in the Netherlands in the 1990s, scrutinising the rationale for this intervention. It then traces the subsequent adoption of this Dutch protocol in the United States and Britain down to the 2010s. The chapter concludes by evaluating recent evidence for the outcomes of puberty suppression.

Gender dysphoria is used here to describe a persistent desire to escape one's natal sex. Medical terminology has changed over time, from 'gender identity disorder' and 'transsexualism' (both introduced in the *Diagnostic and Statistical Manual of Mental Disorders III*; American Psychiatric Association 1980) to 'gender dysphoria' (as renamed in *DSM-5*; American Psychiatric Association 2013) and 'gender incongruence' (as renamed in the *International Classification of Diseases–11*; World Health Organization 2019). In the nomenclature of transgender medicine, 'puberty blockers' refers to a class of drugs which stop the production of sex hormones: gonadotropin-releasing hormone agonists (GnRHa), alternatively known as luteinising hormone-releasing hormone (LHRH) agonists. (The literature sometimes refers to GnRH [or LHRH] analogues, which is a broader classification comprising antagonists as well as agonists.) Drugs in this class include triptorelin, which is used in the Netherlands and Britain, and leuprorelin (branded Lupron) in North America. GnRHa drugs are licensed to treat several medical conditions including precocious puberty in children, endometriosis and uterine fibroids in women, and advanced prostate cancer and sexual deviance in men. The drugs have never been licensed as a treatment for gender dysphoria. The justification comes by analogy with treatment for precocious puberty—when puberty commences before the age of 7 in girls or 9 in boys. But that treatment involves delaying a puberty that arrives abnormally early so that the child can undergo puberty at the normal age. Puberty suppression for gender dysphoria means stopping normal puberty in order to prepare the child for taking hormones of the opposite sex, typically at the age of 16. If GnRHa is started early enough, the child will barely experience puberty in their natal sex (on the importance of puberty, see Hilton and Wright, this volume). It is even possible for an adolescent who identifies as 'agender' to refuse the transition to cross-sex hormones, thus remaining in effect prepubescent for the rest of their life (Pang et al. 2020).

Only a tiny minority of those who identify as transgender have undergone early puberty suppression. The great majority who seek clinical treatment do so well after puberty. Even those who are referred to gender clinics early in adolescence often fail to obtain GnRHa due to lengthy waiting lists (in the United Kingdom) or high costs (in the United States). And those who do access GnRHa will often commence treatment towards the end of puberty (at the age of 15 for instance) and so will not undergo complete puberty suppression. Nevertheless, puberty blockers occupy a central place in the transgender imaginary. Cross-sex hormones and surgeries in adulthood have limited effects in transforming physical appearance, especially for males. Puberty blockers enable a fantasy of truly changing sex. That is why transgender youth celebrated in the media invariably have taken GnRHa from early puberty.

Creating the Dutch protocol

Cross-sex hormones and plastic surgery created the phenomenon of transsexualism in the mid-twentieth century (Hausman 1995). These novel physical interventions had their counterpart in the new theoretical constructs formulated by American psychologists and psychiatrists. It is telling that the first recorded use of the term *gender identity* was in the name of the Gender Identity Clinic at Johns Hopkins University, which pioneered physical treatments for intersex and transsexual patients. This name for the unit, previously known informally as the 'sex change clinic', was suggested by psychologist John Money (1994). Although gender identity was conceived as developing in infancy (e.g. Green 1968), physical treatment was confined to adults. It is worth quoting the Standards of Care formulated by the Harry Benjamin International Gender Dysphoria Association (HBIGDA), which had been created by clinicians and academics to professionalise the new field. 'Hormonal and surgical sex reassignment is extensive in its effects, is invasive to the integrity of the human body, has effects and consequences which are not, or are not readily, reversible' (HBIGDA 1985, 83). The standards did not specify a minimum age, and in practice, some clinicians were willing to give cross-sex hormones under the age of 18. Money advised a doctor to prescribe testosterone to a 15-year-old girl and even to consider mastectomy—but he was unusually reckless, and there is no evidence that his advice was followed (Gill-Peterson 2018, 163–64). Specialist clinics for children and adolescents with gender identity problems were founded in Toronto in 1975, in Utrecht in 1987, and in London in 1989. They provided counselling. Cross-sex hormones had to wait until the patient was referred to an adult clinic, at an age ranging from 16 to 18 (Bradley and Zucker 1990). Surgeries were never performed under the age of 18 (Petersen and Dickey 1995). Referrals to these clinics were rare. The Gender Identity Development Unit in London—the only one in the United Kingdom—over its first decade accepted an annual average of 14 patients (Di Ceglie 2018). In its first seven years, the Utrecht clinic averaged nine per year (Cohen-Kettenis 1994).

The age barrier was broken in the Netherlands. The innovator was Peggy Cohen-Kettenis, professor of psychology in the Department of Child and Adolescent Psychiatry at University Medical Centre Utrecht (Everaerd et al. 2014). She established herself in the field of gender medicine in the 1980s, presenting her research to the HBIGDA's international conferences and founding Europe's first clinic for children with gender dysphoria. She was closely connected to clinicians at VU Medical Centre Amsterdam (affiliated with the Free University), which housed the country's clinic for adult transsexuals.

Cohen-Kettenis believed that transsexuals would experience better outcomes if they started treatment before adulthood. By the mid-1990s, she was referring some patients aged 16 and 17 to the Amsterdam clinic for endocrinological treatment prior to cross-sex hormones (Cohen-Kettenis 1994). Males were given an antiandrogen, cyproterone acetate, which prevented erections and caused breast tissue to grow; females were given progestin to stop menstruation (Gooren and Delemarre-van de Waal 1996). Johanna, for example, 'fulfilled all necessary requirements for early treatment': she did not favour girly things (although neither did her sisters), she was fond of soccer, she never dated in school (hardly surprising given that she was evidently homosexual), and her parents discovered her wearing a tight T-shirt to conceal her breasts (Cohen-Kettenis et al. 1998, 124). Brought to the clinic at 17, she was prescribed progestin for four months and then testosterone. Within two years, Jaap (as Johanna had become) underwent a mastectomy, hysterectomy, and oophorectomy and obtained a new birth certificate. Evidence to support such early treatment came from the first 22 patients from Cohen-Kettenis's clinic, interviewed in their early 20s, no more than a year after surgery (Cohen-Kettenis and van Goozen 1997). They were compared to a larger group of transsexuals who had transitioned later in adulthood in previous decades (Kuiper and Cohen-Kettenis 1988). Her former patients showed better psychological functioning and 'more easily pass in the desired gender role' (Cohen-Kettenis and van Goozen 1997, 270). One problem with the comparison is that they had transitioned in a more tolerant era. Another is the fact that they were still young; most did not yet have a sexual partner. Moreover, they had not reached an age at which they might regret their inability to conceive children. (This group has not since been followed up.) Naturally her experiment was praised by Money (1998, xviii): he singled out her contribution to a conference in London as 'the bravest'.

Cohen-Kettenis had two collaborators at the Free University Amsterdam. One was Louis Gooren, an older endocrinologist who was installed as the world's first professor of transsexuality in 1989. His inaugural professorial lecture was addressed by Cohen-Kettenis and by Money, who flew over from Johns Hopkins University (Nederlands Tijdschrift voor Geneeskunde 1989). Like the pioneering generation who created transsexualism, Gooren saw gender dysphoria as an intersex condition: 'there is a contradiction between the genetic, gonadal and genital sex on the one hand, and the brain sex on the other', and therefore, 'we must provide them with reassignment treatment which meets their needs' (Gooren 1993, 238). The last of the triumvirate was a paediatric endocrinologist, Henriette Delemarre-van de Waal. She had expertise using the new GnRHa drugs—developed in the 1980s—to treat precocious puberty and other conditions (e.g. Schroor et al. 1995).

GnRHa was introduced as a treatment for gender dysphoria in two articles. Gooren and Delemarre-van der Waal (1996) proposed the 'Feasibility of Endocrine Interventions in Juvenile Transsexuals'. More influential was a case study of the first 'adolescent transsexual' treated with GnRHa (Cohen-Kettenis and van Goozen 1998). From the age of 5, FG 'had made it very clear that I was supposed to be a boy' (Bakker 2021, 131). It later transpired that FG was sexually attracted to women. FG's father, a very traditional Italian, disapproved of her masculinity, and serious conflict ensued. Extensive psychotherapy did not improve matters; FG even wrote a suicide note at the age of 12. When FG was 13, Delemarre-van der Waal prescribed triptorelin. The paediatric endocrinologist was not named in the original article, but her identity is clear from later sources (e.g. Delemarre-van de Waal 2014). FG is known as 'B' in the published literature. Three years later, around 1990, FG came to the Utrecht gender clinic, and Cohen-Kettenis was impressed by FG's 'boyish appearance' (Bakker 2021, 115). The clinic provided therapy and introduced FG to other adolescent girls who identified as transsexual. (Whether FG was introduced to any girls who identified as lesbian is not recorded.) Puberty suppression continued for five years until FG was 18, when testosterone commenced, followed by multiple surgeries: mastectomy, oophorectomy and hysterectomy, and metoidioplasty. Awaiting the last surgery, FG was 'happy with his life' and 'never felt any regrets'; the gender dysphoria was apparently cured (Cohen-Kettenis and van Goozen 1998, 247).

Puberty suppression for some years remained exceptional. By 2000, GnRHa had been administered to only seven children under the age of 16 (Cohen-Kettenis et al. 2000). A new treatment regime was codified at VU Medical Centre, where Cohen-Kettenis was appointed professor of medical psychology in 2002, moving with her clinic. This regime became known as the Dutch protocol; Ferring Pharmaceuticals, the manufacturer of triptorelin, provided financial support (Delemarre-van de Waal and Cohen-Kettenis 2006, S137). GnRHa could be administered to transsexuals as young as Tanner Stage Two—marked by the first growth of pubic hair and for girls by budding breasts and for boys by growing testicles—as long as they had reached the age of 12. The child would usually then begin 'to live permanently in the role of their desired sex' (Delemarre-van de Waal and Cohen-Kettenis 2006, S132). After some years of puberty suppression, the adolescent would start cross-sex hormones at the age of 16 and then surgeries at the age of 18. These were the key elements of the Dutch protocol adopted in other countries, albeit without the minimum age of 12—to which the Dutch did not strictly adhere anyway (de Vries 2010, 104). Less often adopted were the apparently strict eligibility criteria for puberty suppression. First, gender dysphoria should have begun early in childhood and worsened with the onset of puberty. Second, the patient should be psychologically stable and not suffer from other mental health problems. Third, the patient should have support from their family. The last criterion could be violated in practice. GnRHa was administered to a 14-year-old—who was institutionalised due to a physical handicap—against the parents' objections (Cohen-Kettenis and Pfäfflin 2003).

As the protocol was formalized, puberty suppression became routine rather than exceptional. Between 2000 and 2008, GnRHa was prescribed to 111 children, which is about one per month (de Vries et al. 2011). One of them was Valentijn de Hingh. After a teacher was disconcerted by the boy's passion for dolls, Cohen-Kettenis diagnosed de Hingh with gender dysphoria at the age of 5 (Bakker 2021). GnRHa was administered from the age of 12 in 2002. De Hingh's transition was celebrated in a television documentary broadcast in 2007.

The Dutch protocol scrutinised

The Dutch protocol comprised not just a drug (GnRHa) and a treatment regime (from 12 or Tanner Stage Two) but also two rhetorical devices. The first was the notion of reversibility. The initial article confidently declared GnRHa to be 'fully reversible; in other words, no lasting undesired effects are to be expected' (Gooren and Delemarre-van de Waal 1996, 72). The peculiar phrasing tacitly acknowledged the lack of actual evidence. Suppressing puberty for just one month would have a negligible effect on a child's development, of course. Yet the Dutch protocol entailed suppression for up to four years (from age 12 to 16), and for FG the duration was at least five years (from 13 to 18). It was simply incredible to claim that suppressing puberty for so many years would have no lasting effect if the child were to stop GnRHa and restart their natal sex hormones. Indeed, the final paragraph of Delemarre-van de Waal and Cohen-Kettenis's (2006, S137) manifesto admits as much: 'It is not clear yet how pubertal suppression will influence brain development'. The postulate of reversibility, however implausible, was crucial for circumventing the question of whether a child aged 12 could give consent to this endocrinological experiment.

Recall that the HBIGDA Standards of Care warned that cross-sex hormones 'are not, or are not readily, reversible'. By pronouncing GnRHa to be reversible, the Dutch clinicians created an imaginary boundary between one endocrinological intervention and another.

The second rhetorical device was the notion of puberty suppression as a diagnostic tool. FG's case study described GnRHa as an 'aid in diagnosis and treatment' (Cohen-Kettenis and van Goozen 1998). This echoed the prior conception of cross-sex hormones as 'both therapeutic and diagnostic in that the patient requesting such therapy either reports satisfaction or dissatisfaction regarding the results' (HBIGDA 1985, 85). GnRHa was posited to provide space for therapeutic exploration of gender identity without the pressure of the physical changes accompanying puberty (Delemarre-van de Waal and Cohen-Kettenis 2006). This claim was plausible, although it was also plausible that stopping normal sexual and intellectual development would impede such exploration. In the event, the Dutch clinicians found that the diagnostic test invariably turned up the same result: 'none of the [54] patients who were selected for pubertal suppression has decided to stop taking GnRHa' (Delemarre-van de Waal and Cohen-Kettenis 2006, S136). This might be explained by a rigorous selection process, as described by Dutch clinicians. An alternative explanation is that puberty suppression becomes a self-fulfilling prophecy. Subsequent experience in other countries confirms the fact that 96 percent or 98 percent of children who undergo puberty suppression continue to cross-sex hormones (Brik et al. 2020; Carmichael et al. 2021; Wiepjes et al. 2018). Does any other diagnostic test in medicine yield such singular results?

The fiction of diagnosis enabled the Dutch to escape a problem recognised in the earliest articles. 'Not all children with GID [gender-identity disorder] will turn out to be transsexuals after puberty', acknowledged Cohen-Kettenis and Gooren (1999, 319). 'Prospective studies of GID boys show that this phenomenon is more closely related to later homosexuality than to later transsexualism'. They cited four longitudinal studies of boys with gender dysphoria. The most famous was by Richard Green, who selected a group of 'sissy boys' to understand the psychology of 'pre-transsexuals'. To his surprise, after 15 years, two thirds of the 44 had become bisexual or homosexual men and only one was contemplating transsexuality (Green 1987). Given such studies, Cohen-Kettenis concluded that 'most GID children under 12 will not grow up to become transsexuals' (Cohen-Kettenis and van Goozen 1998, 246).

These findings were downplayed in their subsequent publications; the manifestos for the Dutch protocol did not mention homosexuality and did not cite any study of feminine boys (Cohen-Kettenis et al. 2008; Delemarre-van de Waal and Cohen-Kettenis 2006). The assertion that 'GID persisting into early puberty appears to be highly persistent' rested on slender evidence (Cohen-Kettenis et al. 2008, 1895). The only relevant cited source described adolescents who had been first assessed at ages ranging from 13 to 18, a range extending well beyond early puberty (Smith et al. 2001). This source did not support the hypothesis that the probability of gender dysphoria persisting to adulthood jumped suddenly on the cusp of age 12, from under 50 percent to virtually 100 percent. What is known is that most adolescents subjected to puberty suppression were homosexual. Of the first 70 adolescents referred to the Amsterdam clinic from 2000 to 2008 and given GnRHa, 62 were homosexual while only one was heterosexual (de Vries et al., 2011). The Dutch clinicians never questioned whether some of those homosexual adolescents might have developed naturally into butch lesbians or queeny gays, with their sexuality and fertility intact.

The crucial advantage of puberty suppression was creating 'individuals who more easily pass into the opposite gender role' (Delemarre-van de Waal and Cohen-Kettenis 2006, 155). The emphasis was on external appearance, as is revealed by an almost obsessive concern with height. Paediatric endocrinology's obsession with height has motivated the use of artificial oestrogen to accelerate puberty in girls judged as too tall (Cohen and Cosgrove 2009) and the use of GnRHa to delay puberty in girls judged as too short (Hayes 2016). The word *height* appears 23 times in Delemarre-van de Waal's (2014) review of puberty suppression. There is one cursory reference to 'loss of fertility'. The words *orgasm*, *libido*, and *sexuality* do not appear. This is curious because it was well known that men taking GnRHa for prostate cancer completely lose erotic interest (Marumo et al. 1999). This effect was exploited to treat men with sexual obsessions. Gooren himself cautiously advocated GnRHa as a treatment for paraphilias, though warning that the side effects 'may be very uncomfortable' (Gijs and Gooren 1996, 279). Curiously, the Dutch clinicians did not ask whether blocking the normal development of erotic desire would affect their patients' understanding of their own bodies and their interest in future romantic relationships.

One significant disadvantage of puberty suppression for males was not mentioned in the 2006 manifesto for the Dutch protocol, although it had been raised at a conference in the previous year (Gender Identity Research and Education Society [GIRES] 2005). Stopping sexual development meant the penis did not grow, and so 'the genital tissue available for vaginoplasty may be less than optimal' (Cohen-Kettenis et al. 2008, 1895). This made it more likely that the orifice would need to be lined with a portion of the patient's intestine rather than the inverted penis (van de Grift et al. 2020). This procedure is more invasive, requiring a second surgical site, and it entails a greater risk of complications such as rectal fistula. Surgical techniques have been refined so that the 'possible occurrence of intestinal discharge could be kept under control' (Bakker 2021, 141), but one quarter of the patients need further corrective surgeries (Bouman et al. 2016).

International adoption of the Dutch protocol

The Dutch protocol immediately attracted interest in other countries. Cohen-Kettenis and Gooren were already prominent in the field of transgender medicine, exemplified by their election to the board of directors of HBIGDA (the former served two 4-year terms from 1995 and 2003, while the latter served one term from 1999). Puberty suppression quickly entered HBIGDA's Standards of Care in the Sixth Version, approved in 2001. It closely followed the Dutch protocol but did not specify a minimum age. It was 'recommended that the adolescent experience the onset of puberty in his or her biologic sex, at least to Tanner Stage Two' while also allowing even earlier intervention on the recommendation of more than one psychiatrist (HBIGDA 2001, 10). Note that by then, the published evidence for the benefits of puberty suppression was a single case study of one patient—FG—at the age of 20.

The United States provides an example of adoption led by an enthusiast clinician: Norman Spack, a paediatric endocrinologist. He recalls 'salivating' at the prospect of treating patients with GnRHa (Hartocollis 2015; Spack 2008). In 2007, Spack co-founded the Gender Management Service at Boston Children's Hospital, which was the first dedicated clinic for transgender children in America. Its programme was based on the Dutch model; the hospital sent a psychologist to Amsterdam to be trained by Cohen-Kettenis (Tishelman et al. 2015). From the outset, the Boston clinic offered GnRHa at Tanner Stage Two or Three with no minimum age (Spack et al. 2012). The drug was not covered by health insurance and so patients paid an annual cost of $6,000–$12,000. Spack joined Cohen-Kettenis, Gooren, and Delemarre-van der Waal on the Endocrine Society's committee tasked with writing their first clinical guidelines for 'transsexual persons', which naturally recommended GnRHa for children at Tanner Stage Two or Three (Hembree et al. 2009). 'There was an attitudinal shift to be able to say that the Endocrine Society supports this', he later recalled (Ruttimann 2013, 19).

Puberty suppression was first advertised to an American audience in 2011 when Oprah Winfrey Television broadcast *I Am Jazz: A Family in Transition*. 'My heart and soul are female', declared Jazz Jennings. 'I just happen to have been born with male genitalia' (Jennings and Jennings 2016, 99; see Matthews, this volume, for further discussion of the case). Diagnosed with gender dysphoria at the age of 3, Jennings had already appeared on national television when 7 years old. The 2011 documentary focused on the threat of puberty as Jazz reached the age of 11. It showed the family consulting a paediatric endocrinologist, who confirmed that Tanner Stage Two had been reached. Jennings commenced puberty suppression some months later. Within a few years, there were 32 clinics for 'gender-nonconforming children and adolescents' which offered puberty blockers (Hsieh and Leininger 2014).

England provides an example of adoption driven by patients. The advantages of the Dutch approach were broadcast in a television documentary in 1996, watched by 3 million viewers (Morse 1996; Nataf 1999). Three transgender females from England—trapped in *The Wrong Body*, according to the title of the documentary—were taken to meet Gooren, Cohen-Kettenis, and their patients who had started cross-sex hormones at 16. The narrative was driven by the looming threat of puberty for the youngest, aged 13, Fredd Foley. It contrasted the compassion of the

Dutch clinicians with the complacency of the Gender Identity Development Unit in London, which refused to prescribe the desired drugs. At the end of the documentary, Foley's mother telephoned Gooren, who immediately agreed to provide a three-month prescription of triptorelin. 'If your child knows for sure he is transsexual', he said, 'I would not let puberty happen'. His willingness to prescribe drugs for a child in another country who he had met only briefly—and against the wishes of the child's own clinicians—suggests that the assessment process was less rigorous than was portrayed in the medical literature. As Cohen-Kettenis said in the documentary, 'it's very difficult to give exact criteria, in some cases you have the feeling that the adolescent has thought about it and knows pretty well what she or he is doing'.

Dissatisfaction at the cautious policy of the Gender Identity Development Unit—still headed by its founder, Domenico Di Ceglie—became increasingly vocal. Stephen Whittle, a seasoned transgender activist and law lecturer, argued that doctors who failed to provide GnRHa could be vulnerable to litigation (Downs and Whittle 2000). Sustained pressure came from the parents of children who identified as transgender, organised by GIRES and Mermaids. GIRES obtained funding from medical charities to organise an international symposium in London in 2005 to develop consensus guidelines for endocrinological intervention. Cohen-Kettenis and Delemarre-van der Waal extolled the virtues of the Dutch approach and found a receptive audience among the American clinicians, including Spack. Di Ceglie and the other local clinicians were evidently less impressed; a paediatric endocrinologist at Great Ormond Street Hospital observed sharply that 'current treatment is based upon theoretical or anecdotal considerations rather than evidence obtained from the outcomes of controlled research trials' (GIRES 2005). GIRES (2006) then warned that 'those who can in any way afford to do so have to consider taking their children to the USA'. The first was Susie Green, later the chief executive of Mermaids. In 2007, she took her son Jackie, aged 12, to Boston, to obtain GnRHa from Spack (Sloan 2011). A presentation at Mermaids (2007), presumably by Green, instructed parents in this medical tourism. Spack treated seven more British children over the next few years (Glass 2012).

The conflict between parents and clinicians climaxed in 2008, with two clashing conferences. The Royal Society of Medicine organised a meeting on adolescent gender dysphoria, which drew criticism for the lack of overseas speakers advocating for puberty blockers, even though it had invited Delemarre-van der Waal. The co-founder of GIRES, whose child transitioned in their late teens two decades earlier, used the new epithet 'transphobic' to describe the cautious clinicians. 'What we do know is what happens if you don't offer hormone blockers. You are stuck with unwanted secondary sex characteristics in the long term and in the short term these teenagers end up suicidal' (Groskop 2008). Green—the author of *Sissy Boys*, then a visiting professor at Imperial College—quickly organised a rival conference to demand puberty suppression (Green 2008). Speakers comprised the usual cast of clinicians, including Spack, and also patients and their parents, including two Dutch transgender adolescents. The demand for puberty suppression was becoming irresistible.

Di Ceglie was soon replaced as Director of the (renamed) Gender Identity Development Service (GIDS) by Polly Carmichael, a clinical psychologist. The GIDS in 2011 began to offer GnRHa from the age of 12, initially as part of an experimental study (Biggs 2019b, 2019c). Before any outcomes were published, Carmichael declared success: 'Now we've done the study and the results thus far have been positive we've decided to continue with it' (Manning and Adams 2014). She even appeared on BBC children's television to promote puberty suppression, in a documentary about a 13-year-old girl who wanted to be a boy, Leo. Carmichael reassured Leo about GnRHa: 'the good thing about it is, if you stop the injections, it's like pressing a start button and the body just carries on developing as it would if you hadn't taken the injection' (Niland 2014). England's National Health Service adopted a policy of offering GnRHa for adolescents at Tanner Stage Two, without age restriction (NHS England 2015).

Subsequent evidence

By the mid-2010s, then, the Dutch protocol was established as the standard for transgender medicine. Even sceptical clinicians could not resist the demand from patients, fuelled by increasing representations of transgender children in the media. The Dutch protocol was apparently vindicated when longitudinal data on the first cohort of 70 adolescents subjected to puberty suppression was published; the lead author was Cohen-Kettenis's student, Annelou de Vries (de Vries et al. 2011, 2014). Ultimate outcomes were measured at least one year after final surgery (vaginoplasty or mastectomy and hysterectomy with oophorectomy), at age 19–22. According to the authors, 'gender dysphoria had resolved, psychological functioning had steadily improved, and well-being was comparable to same-age peers' (de Vries et al. 2014, 696). When scrutinised, however, the evidence was less persuasive. The sample was quite small: the cohort began with 70 patients, but outcome measures were available for 32 to 55 patients, depending on the measure. The results omitted the outcomes for the eight patients who refused to participate in the follow-up or were ineligible for surgery and the one patient killed by necrotising fasciitis immediately after vaginoplasty. Unable to complete the post-surgery questionnaire, the dead patient counted for nothing. The authors withheld the fact that this death was caused by puberty suppression: having been prevented from developing normally, the patient's penis was too small for the normal vaginoplasty, and so surgery was attempted with a portion of the intestine, which became infected (Negenborn et al. 2017). A fatality rate exceeding 1 percent would surely halt any other experimental treatment on healthy teenagers. One inevitable limitation of the study was the measurement of results soon after surgery, which repeated the problem with the first study of adolescent transsexuals (Cohen-Kettenis and van Goozen 1997). No further follow-up of this cohort, now in their late 20s, has been published.

There is information on the very first patient, FG, who was followed up again at the age of 35. FG did not regret transitioning but scored high on the measure for depression. Owing to 'shame about his genital appearance and his feelings of inadequacy in sexual matters', he could not sustain a romantic relationship with a girlfriend (Cohen-Kettenis et al. 2011, 845). Ironically, a 'strong dislike of one's sexual anatomy' is one of the diagnostic criteria for gender dysphoria in children (according to *DSM*-5). But the clinicians were more interested in FG's height: although FG was much shorter than the average Dutch man, they also provided the Italian height distribution as a reference. Cohen-Kettenis concluded that 'the negative side effects are limited' (Cohen-Kettenis et al. 2011, 843). Delemarre-van der Waal's (2014, 194) summary was even more optimistic: 'He was functioning well psychologically, intellectually, and socially'. Now aged 48, FG has given two recent interviews. FG's situation seems to have improved, and he now has a girlfriend. He describes puberty suppression as 'life-saving' in his case (Bakker 2021, 132) but also recommends that children 'go through a significant assessment process' before intervention (Bazelon 2022). Another early Dutch patient, de Hingh, at the age of 31 now identifies as non-binary. Emphasising that 'diagnosis and treatment at a young age [5 years] were not wrong', de Hingh also observes that 'a diagnosis says you've got a problem that needs to be treated as well as possible. The medical process, with pills and protocols, takes over the normal process of identification formation' (Bakker 2021, 182–83).

As clinicians in other countries adopted the Dutch protocol, they did not collect any systematic data on outcomes. An exception was the GIDS in London. One article claimed to show a positive effect of puberty suppression after 12 months (Costa et al. 2015). In fact, the data showed that there was no significant difference between the group given GnRHa and counselling and the group given counselling only (Biggs 2019a). Full outcomes from the initial experiment—comprising 44 children aged 12 to 15—were withheld for years and presumably would have never appeared without my protracted campaign for disclosure (e.g. Health Research Authority 2019; Tominey and Walsh 2019; Biggs 2019d). The reluctance to publish became understandable when the article appeared: puberty suppression for two years produced no positive effects, contradicting Carmichael's (Carmichael et al. 2021) statements to the media. These results were significantly inferior to the Dutch results after puberty suppression and before cross-sex hormones (Biggs 2020). This comparison demonstrates that outcomes from the Netherlands cannot be extrapolated to other countries. Before treatment, adolescents referred to the Dutch clinic have fewer psychological problems and better peer relationships than those referred to the Belgian and Swiss clinics and especially to the GIDS (de Graaf et al. 2018).

Significantly more evidence has emerged on the side effects of puberty suppression. The fact that GnRHa could cause 'an insufficient formation of bone mass' was initially dismissed 'of no great concern' (Gooren and Delemarre-van de Waal 1996). Then it was recognised that patients could 'end with a decreased bone density, which is associated with a high risk of osteoporosis' (Delemarre-van de Waal and Cohen-Kettenis 2006, S134). According to my analysis of data from the GIDS experiment, one third of the adolescents who had taken GnRHa ended with bone density so low (two standard deviations below the norm for their sex and age) that they are at risk for osteoporosis (Biggs 2021). The hope was that bone density would improve following cross-sex hormones. A recent study, however, shows that some females taking testosterone do recover, but males taking oestrogen do not (Schagen et al. 2020). How many patients will eventually develop osteoporosis will not be known for some decades. A female who was given GnRHa from age 11 to 15 by the Karolinska University Hospital in Stockholm now suffers from severe osteoporosis, including continual skeletal pain (SVT 2022). This case—along with two others whose puberty suppression was terminated after concerns about bone density—led Sweden to curb the use of GnRHa.

The effects of puberty suppression on emotional and cognitive development are the hardest to ascertain but the most disturbing, because they affect the adolescent's ability to consent to cross-sex hormones and surgery. Evidence is now emerging from randomized control trials on non-human animals. GnRHa impairs spatial memory in sheep, and this effect remains after the treatment is stopped—in other words, puberty suppression is irreversible (Hough et al. 2017a, 2017b). Mice treated with GnRHa manifest significant differences: males develop a stronger preference for other males and an increased stress response; females exhibit increased anxiety and despair-like behaviour (Anacker et al. 2021). One wonders why Delemarre-van der Waal, whose research group worked with rats, did not undertake similar controlled experiments to test puberty suppression before choosing FG as her guinea pig.

Conclusion

The technology of puberty suppression has been more successful than Cohen-Kettenis could have imagined in the mid-1990s, becoming the international standard for treating gender dysphoria and attracting increasing numbers of patients. The GIDS, for example, from 2012 to 2020 administered GnRHa to 344 children under the age of 15. The total number of patients subjected to this experimental treatment, worldwide, must run to several thousand. What is striking is that the proponents of puberty suppression never reassessed the rationale for the intervention as the numbers multiplied. It is one thing to assert that in very rare cases of extreme gender dysphoria, the child is predestined to become transsexual—rare as in one per year in the Netherlands in the late 1990s. It is another to make this claim for numerous children—currently about two hundred a year in the Netherlands. A recent survey in one American school district found 7 percent of students identifying as 'gender diverse'; the authors urge that all receive 'access to gender affirming care', which in effect means giving GnRHa on request (Kidd et al. 2021, 3). Aside from increasing numbers, the logic of puberty suppression tends towards escalated intervention. The availability of GnRHa encourages parents to pretend their child is the opposite sex before puberty, which makes the onset of puberty more traumatic and thus endocrinological intervention more urgent. Logically enough, Delemarre-van der Waal

(2014) eventually advocated for GnRHa to be administered at the commencement of puberty, followed soon thereafter by cross-sex hormones.

The apparently inexorable rise of puberty suppression has recently been challenged. A handful of clinicians have publicly expressed doubts in the last few years (e.g. Levine et al. 2022; Malone et al. 2021), and they founded the Society for Evidence-Based Gender Medicine (I am on its advisory board). In England, Keira Bell—who took GnRHa at 16, followed by testosterone and then underwent mastectomy—won a surprising legal victory against the GIDS in 2020. The High Court ruled that consent to puberty suppression for a child under 16 was so problematic that it should require a court order. The judgment was overturned on appeal, but it spurred the National Health Service to commission a review of gender identity services for children and young people, led by Hilary Cass. The review is ongoing but has already underlined the lack of evidence for puberty suppression and prompted the closure of the GIDS (announced just as this chapter was submitted for publication). In the United States, Florida and several other states controlled by Republicans are attempting to prohibit endocrinological and surgical interventions for minors.

The ultimate outcome of such shifts in policy is uncertain. For one thing, many children and parents still seek puberty suppression. Unsatisfied demand provides an opportunity for profiteering. A company registered in Singapore and owned by a Welsh doctor will diagnose a 9-year-old with gender dysphoria over video and prescribe GnRHa on the same day (Biggs 2022). More generally, puberty suppression is still protected from scientific scrutiny by the prestige of transgenderism as a social and cultural movement; Butler's queer theory shores up Cohen-Kettenis's endocrinology (see Jones, this volume). Faith in gender among the professional and managerial classes is not shaken even by the tragic televised spectacle of Jazz Jennings—the inability to orgasm and the botched intestinal vaginoplasty which required multiple corrective surgeries, both consequences of early puberty suppression; and the depression which prevented Jennings from starting university. It is too soon to tell whether puberty suppression will go the way of lobotomy or whether it will be one step towards a transhumanist future of self-fabrication through biotechnology.

References

American Psychiatric Association. 1980. *Diagnostic and Statistical Manual of Mental Disorders: DSM-III*. Washington, D.C: American Psychiatric Association.

———. 2013. *Diagnostic and Statistical Manual of Mental Disorders: DSM-5*. Washington, D.C: American Psychiatric Association.

Anacker, Christoph, Ezra Sydnor, Briana K. Chen, Christina C. LaGamma, Josephine C. McGowan, Alessia Mastrodonato, Holly C. Hunsberger, et al. 2021. 'Behavioral and Neurobiological Effects of GnRH Agonist Treatment in Mice: Potential Implications for Puberty Suppression in Transgender Individuals'. *Neuropsychopharmacology* 46: 882–90. doi: 10.1038/s41386-020-00826-1.

Bakker, Alex. 2021. *The Dutch Approach: Fifty Years of Transgender Health Care at the VU Amsterdam Gender Clinic*. Amsterdam: Boom.

Bazelon, Emily. 2022. 'The Battle over Gender Therapy'. *New York Times*, 15 June. https://www.nytimes.com/2022/06/15/magazine/gender-therapy.html.
Biggs, Michael. 2019a. 'A Letter to the Editor Regarding the Original Article by Costa et al: Psychological Support, Puberty Suppression, and Psychosocial Functioning in Adolescents with Gender Dysphoria'. *Journal of Sexual Medicine* 16: 2043. doi: 10.1016/j.jsxm.2019.09.002.
———. 2019b. 'Britain's Experiment with Puberty Blockers'. In *Inventing Transgender Children and Young People*, edited by Michele Moore and Heather Brunskell-Evans, 40–55. Newcastle, UK: Cambridge Scholars Publishing.
———. 2019c. 'The Tavistock's Experiment with Puberty Blockers'. https://users.ox.ac.uk/~sfos0060/Biggs_ExperimentPubertyBlockers.pdf.
———. 2019d. 'Tavistock's Experimentation with Puberty Blockers: Scrutinizing the Evidence'. *Transgender Trend*. 5 March 2019. https://www.transgendertrend.com/tavistock-experiment-puberty-blockers/.
———. 2020. 'Gender Dysphoria and Psychological Functioning in Adolescents Treated with GnRHa: Comparing Dutch and English Prospective Studies'. *Archives of Sexual Behavior* 49: 2231–36. doi: 10.1007/s10508-020-01764-1.
———. 2021. 'Revisiting the Effect of GnRH Analogue Treatment on Bone Mineral Density in Young Adolescents with Gender Dysphoria'. *Journal of Pediatric Endocrinology and Metabolism* 34: 937–39. doi: 10.1515/jpem-2021-0180.
———. 2022. 'Why Are Health Talk and Oxford University Promoting GenderGP?' *The Critic*, 4 July. https://thecritic.co.uk/institutional-cover/.
Bouman, Mark-Bram, Wouter B. van der Sluis, Marlon E. Buncamper, Müjde Özer, Margriet G. Mullender, and Wilhelmus J. H. J. Meijerink. 2016. 'Primary Total Laparoscopic Sigmoid Vaginoplasty in Transgender Women with Penoscrotal Hypoplasia: A Prospective Cohort Study of Surgical Outcomes and Follow-up of 42 Patients'. *Plastic and Reconstructive Surgery* 138: 614e–623e. doi: 10.1097/PRS.0000000000002549.
Bradley, Susan J., and Kenneth J. Zucker. 1990. 'Gender Identity Disorder and Psychosexual Problems in Children and Adolescents'. *Canadian Journal of Psychiatry* 35: 477–86. doi: 10.1177/070674379003500603.
Brik, Tessa, Lieke J.J.J. Vrouenraets, Martine C. de Vries, and Sabine E. Hannema. 2020. 'Trajectories of Adolescents Treated with Gonadotropin-Releasing Hormone Analogues for Gender Dysphoria'. *Archives of Sexual Behavior* 49: 2611–18. doi: 10.1007/s10508-020-01660-8.
Carmichael, Polly, Gary Butler, Una Masic, Tim J. Cole, Bianca L. De Stavola, Sarah Davidson, Elin M. Skageberg, Sophie Khadr, and Russell Viner. 2021. 'Short-Term Outcomes of Pubertal Suppression in a Selected Cohort of 12 to 15 Year Old Young People with Persistent Gender Dysphoria in the UK'. *PLoS ONE* 16: e0243894. doi: 10.1371/journal.pone.0243894.
Cohen, Susan, and Christine Cosgrove. 2009. *Normal at Any Cost: Tall Girls, Short Boys, and the Medical Industry's Quest to Manipulate Height*. London: Penguin Publishing Group.
Cohen-Kettenis, Peggy T. 1994. 'Die Behandlung von Kindern und Jugendlichen mit Geschlechtsidentitätsstörungen an der Universität Utrecht'. *Zeitschrift für Sexualforschung* 7: 231–39.
Cohen-Kettenis, Peggy T., Henriette A. Delemarre-van de Waal, and Louis J.G. Gooren. 2008. 'The Treatment of Adolescent Transsexuals: Changing Insights'. *Journal of Sexual Medicine* 5: 1892–97. doi: 10.1111/j.1743–6109.2008.00870.x.
Cohen-Kettenis, P.T., C.M. Dillen, and L.J. Gooren. 2000. 'De behandeling van jonge transseksuelen in Nederland'. *Nederlands Tijdschrift voor Geneeskunde* 144: 698–702.

Cohen-Kettenis, P.T., and L.J.G. Gooren. 1999. 'Transsexualism: A Review of Etiology, Diagnosis and Treatment'. *Journal of Psychosomatic Research* 46: 315–33.

Cohen-Kettenis, Peggy T., and Friedemann Pfäfflin. 2003. *Transgenderism and Intersexuality in Childhood and Adolescence: Making Choices*. Thousand Oaks, CA: Sage.

Cohen-Kettenis, Peggy T., Sebastiaan E.E. Schagen, Thomas D. Steensma, Annelou L.C. de Vries, and Henriette A. Delemarre-van de Waal. 2011. 'Puberty Suppression in a Gender-Dysphoric Adolescent: A 22-Year Follow-Up'. *Archives of Sexual Behavior* 40: 843–47. doi: 10.1007/s10508-011-9758-9.

Cohen-Kettenis, P.T., and S.H.M. van Goozen. 1998. 'Pubertal Delay as an Aid in Diagnosis and Treatment of a Transsexual Adolescent'. *European Child and Adolescent Psychiatry* 7: 246–48. doi: 10.1007/s007870050073.

Cohen-Kettenis, Peggy T., and Stephanie H.M. van Goozen. 1997. 'Sex Reassignment of Adolescent Transsexuals: A Follow-up Study'. *Journal of the American Academy of Child and Adolescent Psychiatry* 36: 263–71. doi: 10.1097/00004583-199702000-00017.

Cohen-Kettenis, Peggy, Stephanie H. M. van Goozen, and Leo Cohen. 1998. 'Transsexualism during Adolescence'. In *A Stranger in My Own Body: Atypical Gender Identity Development and Mental Health*, edited by Domenico Di Ceglie and David Freedman, 118–25. London: Karnac Books.

Costa, Rosalia, Michael Dunsford, Elin Skagerberg, Victoria Holt, Polly Carmichael, and Marco Colizzi. 2015. 'Psychological Support, Puberty Suppression, and Psychosocial Functioning in Adolescents with Gender Dysphoria'. *Journal of Sexual Medicine* 12: 2206–14. doi: 10.1111/jsm.13034.

de Graaf, Nastasja M., Peggy T. Cohen-Kettenis, Polly Carmichael, Annelou L.C. de Vries, Karlien Dhondt, Jolien Laridaen, Dagmar Pauli, Juliane Ball, and Thomas D. Steensma. 2018. 'Psychological Functioning in Adolescents Referred to Specialist Gender Identity Clinics across Europe: A Clinical Comparison Study between Four Clinics'. *European Child and Adolescent Psychiatry* 27: 909–19. doi: 10.1007/s00787-017-1098-4.

de Vries, Annelou L.C. 2010. 'Gender Dysphoria in Adolescents: Mental Health and Treatment Evaluation'. PhD, Vrije Universiteit Amsterdam. https://research.vu.nl/en/publications/gender-dysphoria-in-adolescents-mental-health-and-treatment-evalu.

de Vries, Annelou L.C., Jennifer K. McGuire, Thomas D. Steensma, Eva C.F. Wagenaar, Theo A.H. Doreleijers, and Peggy T. Cohen-Kettenis. 2014. 'Young Adult Psychological Outcome after Puberty Suppression and Gender Reassignment'. *Pediatrics* 134: 696–704. doi: 10.1542/peds.2013-2958.

de Vries, Annelou L.C., Thomas D. Steensma, Theo A.H. Doreleijers, and Peggy T. Cohen-Kettenis. 2011. 'Puberty Suppression in Adolescents with Gender Identity Disorder: A Prospective Follow-up Study'. *Journal of Sexual Medicine* 8: 2276–83. doi: 10.1111/j.1743-6109.2010.01943.x.

Delemarre-van de Waal, Henriette A. 2014. 'Early Medical Intervention in Adolescents with Gender Dysphoria'. In *Gender Dysphoria and Disorders of Sex Development*, edited by Baudewijntje P.C. Kreukels, Thomas D. Steensma, and Annelou L.C. de Vries, 193–203. New York: Springer.

Delemarre-van de Waal, Henriette A., and Peggy T. Cohen-Kettenis. 2006. 'Clinical Management of Gender Identity Disorder in Adolescents: A Protocol on Psychological and Paediatric Endocrinology Aspects'. *European Journal of Endocrinology* 155 (suppl_1): S131–37. doi: 10.1530/eje.1.02231.

Di Ceglie, Domenico. 2018. 'The Use of Metaphors in Understanding Atypical Gender Identity Development and Its Psychosocial Impact'. *Journal of Child Psychotherapy* 44: 5–28. doi: 10.1080/0075417X.2018.1443151.

Downs, Catherine, and Stephen Whittle. 2000. 'Seeking a Gendered Adolescence: Legal and Ethical Problems of Puberty Suppression among Adolescents with Gender Dysphoria'. In *Of Innocence and Autonomy: Children, Sex and Human Rights*, edited by Eric A. Heinze, 195–208. Aldershot, UK: Ashgate.

Everaerd, Walter, Hanna Swaab, Louis Gooren, Jos Megens, and Mick van Trotsenburg. 2014. 'Preface'. In *Gender Dysphoria and Disorders of Sex Development: Progress in Care and Knowledge*, edited by Baudewijntje P.C. Kreukels, Thomas D. Steensma, and Annelou L.C. De Vries, vii–xxi. New York: Springer.

Gender Identity Research and Education Society. 2005. 'Consensus Report on Symposium in May 2005'. https://www.gires.org.uk/consensus-report-on-symposium-in-may-2005/.

———. 2006. 'Final Report to the Nuffield Foundation'. https://www.gires.org.uk/gires-final-report-to-the-nuffield-foundation/.

Gijs, Luk, and Louis Gooren. 1996. 'Hormonal and Psychopharmacological Interventions in the Treatment of Paraphilias: An Update'. *Journal of Sex Research* 33: 273–90. doi: 10.1080/00224499609551845.

Gill-Peterson, Julian. 2018. *Histories of the Transgender Child*. University of Minnesota Press.

Glass, Katie. 2012. 'A Boy's Own Story'. *Sunday Times*, 22 January. https://www.thetimes.co.uk/article/a-boys-own-story-2wpctfb6pxt.

Gooren, L.J.G. 1993. 'Closing Speech'. In *Transsexualism, Medicine and Law: Proceedings of the 23rd Colloquy on European Law*, 233–38. Strasbourg: Council of Europe Publishing.

Gooren, Louis, and Henriette Delemarre-van de Waal. 1996. 'The Feasibility of Endocrine Interventions in Juvenile Transsexuals'. *Journal of Psychology and Human Sexuality* 8: 69–74. doi: 10.1300/J056v08n04_05.

Green, Richard. 1968. 'Childhood Cross-Gender Identification'. *Journal of Nervous and Mental Disease* 147: 500–509. doi: 10.1097/00005053-196811000-00006.

———. 1987. *The Sissy Boy Syndrome: The Development of Homosexuality*. New Haven, CT: Yale University Press.

———. 2008. 'A Tale of Two Conferences'. *GT News*, Autumn.

Groskop, Viv. 2008. '"My Body Is Wrong"'. *Guardian*, 14 August. https://www.theguardian.com/society/2008/aug/14/children.youngpeople.

Harry Benjamin International Gender Dysphoria Association. 1985. 'Standards of Care: The Hormonal and Surgical Sex Reassignment of Gender Dysphoric Persons'. *Archives of Sexual Behavior* 14: 79–90. doi: 10.1007/BF01541354.

———. 2001. 'Standards of Care for Gender Identity Disorders, Sixth Version'. http://www.genderpsychology.org/transsexual/hbsoc_1990.html.

Hartocollis, Anemona. 2015. 'The New Girl in School: Transgender Surgery at 18'. *New York Times*, 17 June. https://www.nytimes.com/2015/06/17/nyregion/transgender-minors-gender-reassignment-surgery.html.

Hausman, Bernice L. 1995. *Changing Sex: Transsexualism, Technology and the Idea of Gender*. Durham, NC: Duke University Press.

Hayes, Peter. 2016. 'Early Puberty, Medicalisation and the Ideology of Normality'. *Women's Studies International Forum* 56: 9–18. doi: 10.1016/j.wsif.2016.01.003.

Health Research Authority. 2019. 'Investigation into the Study "Early Pubertal Suppression in a Carefully Selected Group of Adolescents with Gender Identity Disorders"'. 14 October 2019. https://www.hra.nhs.uk/about-us/governance/feedback-raising-concerns/investigation-study-early-pubertal-suppression-carefully-selected-group-adolescents-gender-identity-disorders/.

Hembree, Wylie C., Peggy Cohen-Kettenis, Henriette A. Delemarre-van de Waal, Louis J. Gooren, Walter J. Meyer, Norman P. Spack, Vin Tangpricha, and Victor M. Montori. 2009. 'Endocrine Treatment of Transsexual Persons: An Endocrine Society Clinical Practice Guideline'. *Journal of Clinical Endocrinology and Metabolism* 94: 3132–54. doi: 10.1210/jc.2009–0345.

Hough, D., M. Bellingham, I.R. Haraldsen, M. McLaughlin, J.E. Robinson, A.K. Solbakk, and N.P. Evans. 2017a. 'A Reduction in Long-Term Spatial Memory Persists after Discontinuation of Peripubertal GnRH Agonist Treatment in Sheep'. *Psychoneuroendocrinology* 77: 1–8. doi: 10.1016/j.psyneuen.2016.11.029.

Hough, D., M. Bellingham, I.R.H. Haraldsen, M. McLaughlin, M. Rennie, J.E. Robinson, A.K. Solbakk, and N.P. Evans. 2017b. 'Spatial Memory Is Impaired by Peripubertal GnRH Agonist Treatment and Testosterone Replacement in Sheep'. *Psychoneuroendocrinology* 75: 173–82. doi: 10.1016/j.psyneuen.2016.10.016.

Hsieh, Sam, and Jennifer Leininger. 2014. 'Resource List: Clinical Care Programs for Gender-Nonconforming Children and Adolescents'. *Pediatric Annals* 43: 238–44. doi: 10.3928/00904481–20140522–11.

Jennings, Jeanette, and Jazz Jennings. 2016. 'Trans Teen Shares Her Story'. *Pediatrics in Review* 37: 99–100. doi: 10.1542/pir.2016–002.

Kidd, Kacie Mk., Gina M. Sequeira, Claudia Douglas, Taylor Paglisotti, David J. Inwards-Breland, Elizabeth Miller, and Robert W.S. Coulter. 2021. 'Prevalence of Gender-Diverse Youth in an Urban School District'. *Pediatrics* 147: e2020049823. doi: 10.1542/peds.2020–049823.

Kuiper, Bram, and Peggy Cohen-Kettenis. 1988. 'Sex Reassignment Surgery: A Study of 141 Dutch Transsexuals'. *Archives of Sexual Behavior* 17: 439–57.

Levine, Stephen B., E. Abbruzzese, and Julia M. Mason. 2022. 'Reconsidering Informed Consent for Trans-Identified Children, Adolescents, and Young Adults'. *Journal of Sex and Marital Therapy*. doi: 10.1080/0092623X.2022.2046221.

Malone, William J., Paul W. Hruz, Julia W. Mason, and Stephen Beck. 2021. 'Letter to the Editor from William J. Malone et al: "Proper Care of Transgender and Gender-Diverse Persons in the Setting of Proposed Discrimination: A Policy Perspective"'. *Journal of Clinical Endocrinology and Metabolism* 106: e3287–88.

Manning, Sanchez, and Steven Adams. 2014. 'NHS to Give Sex Change Drugs to Nine-Year-Olds: Clinic Accused of "playing God" with Treatment That Stops Puberty'. *Mail on Sunday*, May 17.

Marumo, Ken, Shiro Baba, and Masaru Murai. 1999. 'Erectile Function and Nocturnal Penile Tumescence in Patients with Prostate Cancer Undergoing Luteinizing Hormone-releasing Hormone Agonist Therapy'. *International Journal of Urology* 6: 19–23. doi: 10.1046/j.1442–2042.1999.06128.x.

Mermaids. 2007. 'Obtaining Help from the Children's Hospital Boston'. In *Mermaids Annual Meeting*. http://www.gires.org.uk/wp-content/uploads/2014/08/mermaids-presentation.ppt.

Money, John. 1994. 'The Concept of Gender Identity Disorder in Childhood and Adolescence after 39 Years'. *Journal of Sex and Marital Therapy* 20: 163–77. doi: 10.1080/00926239408403428.

——. 1998. 'Foreword'. In *A Stranger in My Own Body: Atypical Gender Identity Development and Mental Health*, edited by Domenico Di Ceglie and David Freedman, xvii–xviii. London: Karnac Books.

Morse, Oliver, dir. 1996. 'The Wrong Body'. *The Decision*. Windfall Films, Channel 4.
Nataf, Zachary. 1999. 'Interview'. https://rainbowreeltokyo.com/99/English/interview/zacharynataf.html.
Nederlands Tijdschrift voor Geneeskunde. 1989. 'Transseksualiteit'. *Nederlands Tijdschrift voor Geneeskunde* 133: 1475.
Negenborn, Vera L., Wouter B. van der Sluis, Wilhelmus J.H.J. Meijerink, and Mark-Bram Bouman. 2017. 'Lethal Necrotizing Cellulitis Caused by ESBL-Producing E. Coli after Laparoscopic Intestinal Vaginoplasty'. *Journal of Pediatric and Adolescent Gynecology* 30: e19–e21. doi: 10.1016/j.jpag.2016.09.005.
NHS England. 2015. 'NHS Standard Contract for Gender Identity Development Service for Children and Adolescents'.
Niland, Phil, dir. 2014. 'I Am Leo'. *My Life*. CBBC.
Pang, Ken C., Lauren Notini, Rosalind McDougall, Lynn Gillam, Julian Savulescu, Dominic Wilkinson, Beth A. Clark, Johanna Olson-Kennedy, Michelle M. Telfer, and John D. Lantos. 2020. 'Long-Term Puberty Suppression for a Nonbinary Teenager'. *Pediatrics* 145: e20191606. doi: 10.1542/peds.2019-1606.
Petersen, Maxine E., and Robert Dickey. 1995. 'Surgical Sex Reassignment: A Comparative Survey of International Centers'. *Archives of Sexual Behavior* 24: 135–56. doi: 10.1007/BF01541578.
Ruttimann, Jacqueline. 2013. 'Blocking Puberty in Transgender Youth'. *Endocrine News*, January: 16–20.
Schagen, Sebastian E.E., Femke M. Wouters, Peggy T. Cohen-Kettenis, Louis J. Gooren, and Sabine E. Hannema. 2020. 'Bone Development in Transgender Adolescents Treated with GnRH Analogues and Subsequent Gender-Affirming Hormones'. *Journal of Clinical Endocrinology and Metabolism* 105: e4252–63. doi: 10.1210/clinem/dgaa604.
Schroor, E.J., M.M. Van Weissenbruch, and H.A. Delemarre-van de Waal. 1995. 'Long-Term GnRH-Agonist Treatment Does Not Postpone Central Development of the GnRH Pule Generator in Girls with Idiopathic Precocious Puberty.' *Journal of Clinical Endocrinology and Metabolism* 80: 1696–1701. doi: 10.1210/jcem.80.5.7745021.
Sloan, Jenna. 2011. 'I Had Sex Swap Op on My 16th Birthday'. *Sun*, 19 October. https://www.thesun.co.uk/fabulous/851138/i-had-sex-swap-op-on-my-16th-birthday/.
Smith, Yolanda L.S., Stephanie H.M. van Goozen, and Peggy T. Cohen-Kettenis. 2001. 'Adolescents with Gender Identity Disorder Who Were Accepted or Rejected for Sex Reassignment Surgery: A Prospective Follow-up Study'. *Journal of the American Academy of Child and Adolescent Psychiatry* 40: 472–81. doi: 10.1097/00004583-200104000-00017.
Spack, Norman. 2008. 'Foreword'. In *The Transgender Child: A Handbook for Families and Professionals*, by Stephanie A. Brill and Rachel Pepper, ix–xi. San Francisco, CA: Cleis Press.
Spack, N.P., L. Edwards-Leeper, H.A. Feldman, S. Leibowitz, F. Mandel, D.A. Diamond, and S.R. Vance. 2012. 'Children and Adolescents with Gender Identity Disorder Referred to a Pediatric Medical Center'. *Pediatrics* 129: 418–25. doi: 10.1542/peds.2011-0907.
SVT. 2022. 'Uppdrag granskning avslöjar: Flera barn har fått skador i transvården'. SVT Nyheter. 23 February. https://www.svt.se/nyheter/granskning/ug/uppdrag-granskning-avslojar-flera-barn-har-fatt-skador-i-transvarden.
Tishelman, Amy C., Randi Kaufman, Laura Edwards-Leeper, Francie H. Mandel, Daniel E. Shumer, and Norman P. Spack. 2015. 'Serving Transgender Youth: Challenges, Dilemmas, and Clinical Examples'. *Professional Psychology: Research and Practice* 46: 37–45. doi: 10.1037/a0037490.

Tominey, Camilla, and Joani Walsh. 2019. 'NHS Transgender Clinic Accused of Covering up Negative Impacts of Puberty Blockers on Children by Oxford Professor'. *Telegraph*, 7 March. https://www.telegraph.co.uk/news/2019/03/07/nhs-transgender-clinic-accused-covering-negative-impacts-puberty/.

van de Grift, Tim C., Zosha J. van Gelder, Margriet G. Mullender, Thomas D. Steensma, Annelou L.C. de Vries, and Mark-Bram Bouman. 2020. 'Timing of Puberty Suppression and Surgical Options for Transgender Youth'. *Pediatrics* 146: e20193653. doi: 10.1542/peds.2019–3653.

Wiepjes, Chantal M., Nienke M. Nota, Christel J.M. de Blok, Maartje Klaver, Annelou L.C. de Vries, S. Annelijn Wensing-Kruger, Renate T. de Jongh, et al. 2018. 'The Amsterdam Cohort of Gender Dysphoria Study (1972–2015): Trends in Prevalence, Treatment, and Regrets'. *Journal of Sexual Medicine* 15: 582–90. doi: 10.1016/j.jsxm.2018.01.016.

World Health Organization. 2019. *International Classification of Diseases, 11th Revision*. https://icd.who.int/

12
SCHOOLS, FEMINISM AND GENDER-IDENTITY THEORY

Shereen Benjamin

Feminists have long paid attention to the link between education and the liberation of girls and women. In the UK, prior to the second half of the 19th century, very few girls had access to schooling of any quality: working-class girls and boys had very few opportunities to attend school in England (although some working-class boys in Scotland had greater access to schooling), and middle-class and upper-class girls usually received education in traditional 'feminine accomplishments' only (Roach 1986). That began to change in the 1850s and 1860s when pioneering women educationists opened schools that aimed to give middle-class girls the kinds of intellectually challenging opportunities that were available to their brothers in the boys' high schools (Kamm 2014). This work was taken up by first-wave feminists in tandem with both the call for women's suffrage and for universal basic and then secondary education. Gradually, access to education for girls became more common and eventually universal, albeit along very different lines for children from different socio-economic backgrounds.

With girls' access to schooling more or less assured in the UK by the time second-wave feminism emerged in the 1960s, feminist educationists' attention turned to a number of questions relating to the significance of schooling for women's liberation. In essence, feminist teachers and researchers wanted to understand the ways in which schooling reproduces (intentionally or unintentionally) existing inequalities between the sexes, and they wanted to change school curricula (what is taught), pedagogy (how it is taught) and the school environment in order to produce better outcomes for girls. In the early days of second-wave feminism – the 1960s and 1970s – there were some clear disparities to address. In secondary schools, for example, girls were typically offered lessons in subjects such as cooking and dressmaking while boys were offered carpentry and metalwork. By the 1980s and 1990s, girls and boys were in principle offered the same curriculum choices, but the take-up of some

DOI: 10.4324/9781003286608-12

subjects remained traditionally gendered. Whilst the core concerns of many feminist educators today remain similar to those of the earlier second-wave feminists, the conceptual tools needed to understand the more subtle reproduction of gender through schooling have developed and evolved.

Education is an applied and multi-disciplinary discipline: sociologists, psychologists, philosophers and historians, as well as applied policy analysts and teachers themselves, have all contributed to its development as a distinct subject for study. A range of research methods is therefore used by educationists. Feminist education researchers have typically used quantitative methods to identify, measure and describe differences between the sexes in educational engagement and outcomes, and qualitative methods to understand how those differences are produced and experienced by pupils and teachers in schools. Gender and education evolved as a specialist field of study from the 1970s onwards and has always been an activist sub-discipline which sought to learn from and contribute to the project of women's and girls' liberation. The emergence of gender-identity theory has seen some feminist education researchers move away from the study of sex differences, focusing instead on children's and young people's 'gender creativity' and using methods such as linguistic deconstruction drawn from postmodernism and queer theory.

The first part of this chapter outlines what can be thought of as a current gender-critical take on enduring feminist concerns in education, although it is important to note that the term has emerged relatively recently, and most of the authors referenced in this chapter describe themselves simply as feminist rather than claiming the label gender-critical. The second part of the chapter looks at the emergence and subsequent popularisation of gender-identity theory and its implications for schools. The final part of the chapter compares the implications of the two framings (gender-critical and what I will refer to as 'trans-inclusive') for school curricula, for schools as institutions and for the provision of support to transgender-identifying and gender-non-conforming pupils in school. It argues that although approaches linked to gender-identity theory may appear to be radical and transformative, gender-critical feminist approaches are more likely to lead to social change and to fairer, more equal and more rewarding outcomes for both girls and boys.

A gender-critical framing: schools as places where children become gendered

Take a walk past any large primary school playground during playtime, and you are likely to see most of the central space dominated by boys playing physically active games, often football, and often in large groups. A small number of girls may be joining in, but they will be the exception rather than the rule. You are also likely to see small groups of girls walking and talking around the edges of the playground, sometimes practising dance routines, or playing with smaller playground equipment. Ask teachers about this gendered use of playground space, and chances are they will not have noticed, or if they have, they will regard it as a non-issue and simply the way things are.

Now have a look at sex-disaggregated data relating to end-of-school exam results. Education in the UK is devolved, meaning that the constituent nations of England, Northern Ireland, Scotland and Wales have their own distinct systems and collect their own data. Using the Scottish data as an example (but patterns are broadly similar in the other nations), we can see inequalities playing out in two main ways. The first is in subject choice. At Advanced Higher (the highest school-based qualification in Scotland), in 2020, girls were overrepresented in arts and humanities subjects such as English (73% of entries), art and design (86% of entries) and history (63% of entries). Girls were underrepresented in most of the STEM (science, technology, engineering and mathematics) subjects such as maths (40% of entries), physics (24% of entries) and music technology (34% of entries; Scottish Qualifications Authority, 2020). The second inequality is in attainment: girls outperform boys in most subjects, the widest gaps being evident in literacy-based subjects. This sex-based differential is commonly referred to as the 'gender attainment gap', and it has been widely publicised since the late 1990s, with much media commentary focused on boys' supposed underachievement (see, for instance, Epstein et al. 1998; Busby 2016; Ringrose & Epstein 2017). Whilst more attention is paid to boys' apparent disadvantage in the gender attainment gap, subject choice may be a better indicator of long-term material impact, since the STEM subjects, where boys predominate, continue to be associated with higher-status, more secure and better-paying jobs and careers.

Seen through a gender-critical lens, there is nothing natural or inevitable about any of this. The gender-critical educationist will look at a playground where the space is dominated by boys and will ask questions. Why are girls more likely to occupy the margins of the playground? What narratives about gender roles and expectations structure the apparent choices of girls and boys, and how do the local and specific narratives and practices in any particular school connect to wider, societal narratives and practices? Which girls, and which boys, are the exceptions to the rule, and why? What are the costs and benefits for girls and for boys of transgressing typical gendered expectations? And how might we go about changing things in order to achieve a more equal use of playground space?

Similarly, examination data provoke questions. Why are girls overrepresented in some subjects and underrepresented in others? How are the subject choices of girls and boys, respectively, shaped by gendered roles and expectations? How have some subjects come to be associated with one sex more than the other, and how might we change that?

Feminist educationists seek to explain and challenge these and other gendered patterns in schooling. Starting from the position that sex is dimorphic and immutable and that gender is external, socially located, hierarchical, and coercively imposed, schools can be understood as important locations in which children and young people learn to be gendered. Schools teach not only skills and content knowledge: they are also places where habits and dispositions are acquired and honed through what is sometimes called the 'hidden curriculum' (what schools teach through their cultural values and expectations; Assor and Gordon 1987; Eisner, 1994). Gender – defined as social roles and expectations – is a constituent part of children's social learning in schools. Seen this way, gender constrains both boys and girls, boxing them in by imposing socially constructed limitations to their aspirations and their sense of who they are and can be and holding in place an overall pattern of male dominance.

Although gender as conceived here is external and coercive, children are actors in the process of becoming gendered. Children and young people negotiate the gendered narratives and practices around them. For instance, in many primary school classrooms, there is a prevailing narrative that girls are helpful and sensible, manifested in practices such as girls being more likely to comply with teachers' instructions and more likely to perform tasks such as tidying up willingly and to a higher standard. Girls who accept this narrative and behave as their sex is expected to will receive approving feedback from both adults and peers: such feedback will confirm to them that their behaviour is appropriate and socially sanctioned, and the rewards may include high-status positions in friendship groups. Girls who resist the narrative and whose behaviour is considered 'silly' and 'unhelpful' may find themselves subtly sanctioned not just for classroom misbehaviour but for actions that fall outside of what is expected from a girl. Similarly, boys who position themselves as sensible and helpful may find, especially as they get older, that it is much harder for them to gain status in boys' peer groups where counter-authority behaviour is seen as more 'boyish'.

In negotiating their way around these narratives and practices, girls and boys gradually develop a sense of themselves as gendered, sometimes going with the grain and sometimes against it. This process of developing a gendered sense of self is ongoing and occurs in intersection with social class, race, physical appearance and other differences that may be significant at family, community, national and/or societal levels. Children are active in this process rather than the passive objects of socialisation. However, they are not the authors of the narratives and practices in which they are embedded, and their 'choices' are constrained and shaped in all sorts of ways.

Since the 1980s, feminist educators have studied girls' and boys' interactions in classrooms and playgrounds to understand how schools produce and reproduce gender. Many studies have considered the interplay of multiple axes of inequality, such as Hey (1997), who considered gender, sexuality and social class in schoolgirls' friendships; Benjamin's (2002) study of girls with 'special educational needs' in a mainstream school; Barnes's (2012) study of working-class boys' use of humour, and Eriksen (2018), who studied ethnic minority girls in a Norwegian upper secondary school. These and other studies try to understand how social inequalities, refracted through local communities and played out in school and classroom-level norms and values, shape children's experiences of schooling and the choices that, over time, become engrained as habits of mind and action.

In a recent example, Schriffin-Sands (2021) coined the term 'boysplaining' (derived from 'mansplaining') to describe behaviours she observed in primary school–aged boys 'whereby students belittle, condescend, ignore or shame their peers' and evident in boys 'dominating space and equipment, asserting knowledge, taking sole credit for collaborative work and interrupting, ignoring or shaming classmates' (664). She explains that boysplaining is repeated constantly, defended diligently, requires that boys position themselves in opposition to those against whom it is directed; and ultimately reinforces the subordination of girls. Crucially, the boys who were most likely to use boysplaining achieved the highest status in peer friendship groups, making boysplaining a highly attractive set of behaviours to boys and conferring rewards in terms of popularity. Not all boys engaged in boysplaining, and there were costs in terms of status and popularity for those who were unwilling or unable to do so: put simply, boys who refused or were unable to 'boysplain' were less popular and occupied places lower down the school's social pecking order. Moreover, the practice of boysplaining sustained a subordinate role for girls through repeated small slights and silencing, with concomitant costs of status and popularity for those girls who spoke back and refused to be silenced. Crucially, the ubiquity of the behaviour meant it was unseen and unnoticed, woven into the fabric of children's daily experience: it was unremarked, unremarkable and, therefore, unchallenged and seemingly inevitable.

Practices such as boysplaining can be understood as part of a school's 'gender order': the repeated social patterns through which children and young people acquire a sense of themselves as gendered. One of the consequences of a gender order that overall requires the subordination of girls through their relative silence and acquiescence is that the ubiquity and everydayness of small slights to girls enables an environment where more overt sexual harassment can become part of the fabric of 'how things are'. In 2021, following press and social media reports, the English schools' inspectorate Office for Standards in Education (OFSTED, 2021) carried out a rapid review of peer-on-peer sexual harassment. From a survey of about 900 young people, it found that an overwhelming majority of girls, and smaller but significant proportions of boys, had experienced harmful peer-on-peer sexual behaviours, both face-to-face and online. The prevailing gender order in a school also goes some way to explaining gendered subject choice: Francis et al. (2017) noted how STEM subjects, especially physics, were positioned as incompatible with 'girly' femininities in schooling. In that context, Girlguiding UK (2019) found that teenage girls felt they would be 'judged' for choosing to study maths and physics, believed that they may find themselves in classes of mainly boys where their efforts would be ridiculed, and experienced self-doubt about their ability to succeed in apparently male-dominated subjects.

A school's gender order therefore profoundly shapes what children learn and how they learn it: from the subjects that are considered desirable for boys and girls, respectively, to the friendship groupings that are so vital to children and young people. It is formed in the context of gender at a societal level but amenable to being nuanced at a local level. For gender-critical feminist educators, the task is to change a school's gender order so as to minimise the extent to which it constrains both girls and boys and address any practices that serve to hold male dominance in place. The final section of this chapter considers how that might be done.

A 'trans-inclusive' framing: schools as places where children assert their gender

'As more trans children find the confidence to make themselves known in our primary and secondary schools, school teachers and administrators look for guidance on how best to support trans pupils' (Horton 2020). This sentence, which appears in the introduction to an extensive literature review on the subject, illustrates the core belief of what I will call 'trans-inclusive' educators, namely that some children and young people can be considered innately transgender but that societal prejudice and ignorance has until recently rendered their existence invisible and misunderstood. It also correctly reflects that there has been an explosion of interest in the posited phenomenon of trans children and how they should best be supported in schools.

In this section, I use the term 'trans-inclusive' to describe educational principles and strategies derived from gender-identity theory: that is, the belief that physical sex is assigned at birth and is secondary to a child or young person's innate sense of maleness or femaleness when it comes to categorising that child as a girl, a boy or something else; that gender is a matter of personal identity and expression; and that schools are places where a child or young person's gender identity may reveal itself and, once asserted by a child or young person of any age, should be affirmed. The term *trans-inclusive* is widely used in guidance documents promoting gender-identity theory uncritically to schools and teachers (e.g. Brighton & Hove City Council 2021; Scottish Government 2021; Warwickshire Safeguarding n.d.). Its origins date back to the 1990s when the term 'inclusive education' was used to describe reforms to mainstream schools aimed at making them more welcoming and accessible to children with special educational needs and disabilities (Tomlinson 2017). The inclusive schools movement of the 1990s and 2000s was underscored by the social model of disability and thus by the view that it is the job of institutions to adapt in order to include disabled individuals rather than the task of individuals themselves to adapt to the demands of unwelcoming and inaccessible institutions (Oliver, 2013). Its scope in relation to schools gradually widened to encompass any group of children and young people who might be at risk of marginalisation, and the term *inclusion* is now widely applied in the context of sexual orientation and gender identity (e.g. Time for Inclusive Education 2021). The term *trans-positive* is also used in broadly similar ways in resources aimed at teachers (e.g. Labelle 2020; Proud Trust 2021), although it has a different history and has not traditionally been used widely by schools and teachers.

The reason I use *trans-inclusive* here is in part because many educators who are influenced by gender-identity theory use it themselves to describe their position. More important, however, the term is used to connote an affiliation with a movement for progressive social change and obscure the fact that the claims upon which it rests – including that sex is no longer politically relevant and has been superseded by gender identity and that children of any age can have a gender identity which must be regarded as their true self – are provisional and widely contested. The use of the term *trans-inclusive* is often highly political as its positive, progressive associations allow users to depict gender-critical perspectives by contrast as negative, exclusionary and, thereby, regressive. I use the term critically in this chapter to draw attention to its deployment as a rhetorical strategy and help readers understand and unpack what it means and how it is used.

The last ten years have seen an exponential rise in the number of children and young people whose distress around their gender is intense and persistent and who may be diagnosed with 'gender dysphoria' and, in a trans-inclusive framing, considered to be 'trans children'. Such children and young people may believe they are in the wrong body and express a desire to be, or the belief that they are of the opposite sex or no sex at all.

The number of under-18s referred to the UK's Gender Identity Development Service (GIDS) for (or with) diagnoses of gender dysphoria increased from 138 in 2010–11 to 2,748 in 2019–20 (GIDS 2021). Historically, most under-18s presenting with gender dysphoria have been pre-pubertal boys. For most of these boys, puberty has historically resolved their opposite-sex identification: drawing together three large-scale and a number of smaller-scale studies, Cantor (2016) found that between 60–90% 'desisted' by the end of puberty, with the differences reflecting variations in clinical protocols. The figures from GIDS show that the biggest increase in referrals is among adolescent girls amongst whom, until recently, gender dysphoria was unknown. In 2020–21 girls aged 13–16 accounted for 1,153 GIDS referrals, almost half of the total (GIDS, 2021). Schools and teachers report much greater increases in children and young people identifying as transgender but who are not referred to GIDS. Anecdotally, whereas it was extremely rare to find any transgender-identifying pupils in secondary schools in the UK until the last five years, it is now rare to find secondary schools where there are no pupils identifying as transgender or non-binary. It is hard to estimate the numbers in the UK as very little numerical data has been collected (see Sullivan et al., this volume).

Seen through a trans-inclusive lens, the single admissible explanation for this rise is the increased visibility and acceptance of transgenderism. There is a move away from understanding children as experiencing the psychological disorder of gender dysphoria, which trans-inclusive educators view as pathologising. Trans-inclusive educational researchers and scholars tend to draw on queer theory, and their work emphasises the importance of language in the construction of the self as a gendered being. Sinclair-Palm and Gilbert (2018) argue that '[g]ender is messy and difficult to narrate. . . . Gender vocabularies are always shifting and young people are its most creative authors'. Where gender-critical feminist scholars understand gender to be external and coercively imposed, trans-inclusive scholars understand it to be a process of individual discovery and a creative 'becoming'. And where gender-critical educationists seek to unravel how a school's gender order constrains opportunities for both girls and boys and reinforces male dominance, trans-inclusive educationists are interested in how 'cultural cisgenderism' (Kennedy, 2018:301) marginalises trans children and young people. Seen this way, the work of the progressive, trans-inclusive school is to bring about change based on 'paradigmatic and ontological reversals that dismantle the foundations that produce binary structures' (Sweet 2021). To put this in more down-to-earth language, schools are being encouraged to reject the dimorphic, embodied male–female division in its entirety. For trans-inclusive educationists, the key to ending sexism is to act as though biological sex is already redundant as a political category and cease to acknowledge the physical and social consequences of sexed bodies.

The language of queer theory seldom makes it into the toolkits and training courses for teachers that have proliferated in the last decade. But both queer theory and the more prosaic interpretations of gender identity aimed at teachers share the assumption that biological sex is no longer relevant and that gender and sex can be entirely separated. Where queer theory positions gender as a site of individual struggle and creativity, guidance for teachers tends to reduce it to 'gender identity', often portrayed as an essential component of the self, hard-wired in and possibly born into a wrongly-sexed body. In its non-statutory guidance for Scottish schools, the Scottish Government (2021) says:

> Not conforming to gender stereotypes is a healthy and normal part of growing up and should not lead to any assumptions being made that the child may be transgender, or lesbian, gay or bisexual. The distinction between 'gender non-conforming behaviour' and transgender young people is that transgender young people are likely to be 'persistent and insistent' that their gender identity does not align with the sex they were assigned at birth. (14–15)

Such statements, which are typical in guidance and training courses for teachers, suggest that there is a hard-and-fast difference between gender-non-conforming children and 'transgender children', yet the only proposed way to distinguish between them is the persistence and insistence of the child. What is being drawn on here is an idea of innate 'trans-ness': that a child who is persistent and insistent that they are of the opposite sex or of no sex at all is stating an empirical reality. It reflects one of the core beliefs of gender-identity theory, that an individual's gender identity is their 'true self' and supersedes sex as a way of categorising them as male, female or something else. For the trans-inclusive educator, when a child or young person asserts that they are of the opposite sex or no sex at all, they are stating an incontrovertible inner truth which should be affirmed by adults.

However, there is little credible empirical evidence for such a belief. It ignores the evidence, going back decades, that most pre-pubertal children who experience gender dysphoria will find it resolves during puberty (Cantor, 2016). It also disregards the possibility that the child's persistence and insistence may be socially produced and learned rather than innate. It is a belief with potentially profound implications and effects for schools, teachers and young people. As discussed in the final section of this chapter, when schools accept a trans-inclusive framing, they are urged to include its unproven claims (that sex is assigned at birth and gender identity is innate) as unassailable facts in their curricula, teaching children that it is possible to be born in the wrong body and encouraging the fantasy that it is possible to change sex. They are also encouraged to socially transition children of any age who request it (e.g. Portsmouth Education Partnership, 2018), potentially setting them on the path of unnecessary lifelong medical treatment (Singh, Bradley & Zucker 2021), and taking little account that social transition is 'an active intervention [which] may have significant effects on the child or young person in terms of their psychological functioning' (Cass Review 2022).

The trans-inclusive framing, then, although it may seem on the face of it politically progressive, has some distinctly regressive features. Its incorporation into school practices and policies via lobby groups such as Gendered Intelligence (2019), whose promotional material suggests its training courses have been widely taken up in schools and in teacher training, parallels the influence of lobby groups on a range of other public institutions, recently explored in the Nolan podcasts (BBC Sounds 2021) on the influence of Stonewall.

Gender and schools: two different ways forward

Earlier in the chapter, I suggested that schools are places where girls and boys become gendered through repeated patterns of interaction that constitute a school's 'gender order'. Such a view operates within a gender-critical frame that understands gender as external, socially-located and coercively imposed on individuals as a consequence of their sexed bodies and whose end result is the maintenance of male domination and the oppression of women. Schools are an important place in which girls as a group learn to subordinate their interests to those of boys as a group, although the actual practices through which this happens change over time and vary according to other societal structures and local contexts. It is in this change over time and interaction with local (including school- and community-level) contexts that gender-critical educators see the possibility for more equal outcomes. The aim of gender-critical educators is to disrupt the gender order, seeking as their end goal the dismantling of the boxes that constrain both boys and girls – and, in the interim, the expansion of possibilities within those boxes. This project is a continuation of the successful work of first- and second-wave feminists to secure access to education for girls on the same terms as boys, building on the successes that have seen girls' levels of achievement in all subjects rise over the decades.

A trans-inclusive framing, however, sees gender as an individual attribute and sex either as irrelevant or, at any rate, as subsidiary to an individual's gender identity. Within this frame, schools are seen as places that historically have made it difficult for those children whose gender identity is supposedly misaligned with their sex to be their true selves. The task for schools becomes to support children and young people in coming to a realisation of their 'true' gender identity. In common with gender-critical feminism there is a realisation that socially-constructed gender norms can box children in and constrain their opportunities, but the end goal within a trans-inclusive framing is more about enabling some children and young people to swap from the box labelled 'girl' to the box labelled 'boy' and vice versa and construct alternative non-binary box(es) for a minority rather than dismantling the boxes completely. As I discuss later, this is a less radical endeavour than that of gender-critical feminism, although it is usually presented and often perceived as politically cutting-edge.

Schools have to recognise the reality of children's and young people's experiences and help them understand their social worlds. Given the salience of gender, the permeation of gender-identity theory in children's and young people's popular culture and peer cultures, and the rise in numbers of children and young people asserting a transgender identity, schools and teachers cannot remain silent on the issues. However, the two alternative framings have very different implications for work in schools, including in

- the explicit curriculum – how schools and teachers explain issues around gender.
- the 'hidden' or implicit curriculum – how sex and gender operate in a school's unwritten rules, values, normative patterns of behaviour and relationships (a school's gender order).
- pastoral care – how schools support children and young people who are gender-non-conforming and transgender-identifying and how policies ensure safeguarding for all pupils.

These implications are examined in turn in the remainder of this chapter.

The explicit curriculum: teaching children and young people about sex and gender

Gender-critical feminist educators seek to teach children and young people to recognise gender as a constituent force in their lives: to notice when, as a consequence of their sex, they are expected to behave in particular ways and acquire particular tastes and habits, help them question how these expectations constrain them as individuals and hold in place structures of male dominance, and increase each individual's 'room for manoeuvre' through their growing understanding of the mutability of gendered norms.

One popular and effective way to equip children with the skills and knowledge to uncover and understand how gender operates in their lives is through critical literacy. Critical literacy is an approach to texts (including not only books but also magazines, computer games, TV adverts, artefacts and so on) in which readers are encouraged to read between and beyond the lines, asking questions about how the text was constructed, whose interests it serves, how gender (and class, race, nationality, disability, *etc*) are presented in the text, whose voices are silent or absent, and, crucially, whether the text tries to persuade the reader to take a particular view or action (Pratt & Foley 2020). So teachers might, for instance, explore with their classes adverts for toys or clothes targeted at children, aiming to help children develop the skills and knowledge to decode the many implicit messages (such as pink = a girl's toy, associated with being pretty and compliant) with which their lives are saturated. Or they might discuss with children the popular fairy-tale format in which a prince rescues a princess and they get married, sometimes using stories in which the gender roles have been inverted as a stimulus (Davies 2003).

What used to be called 'sex education' (now variously known as relationships, sexual health and parenthood education in Scotland, relationships and sexuality education in Wales and relationships and sex education in England) is another key site for explicit curriculum coverage relating to sex and gender. A gender-critical approach to the subject presents the scientifically verifiable reality of biological sex and reproduction as core factual information. It allows space for discussion of themes such as boundaries, consent, safety, bodily integrity and the right to privacy as age-appropriate and with regard to how the experiences of girls and boys are likely to differ: for older pupils, the coverage of harms to girls is important. A gender-critical sex education curriculum includes a positive discussion of healthy same-sex relationships, which for younger children is likely to mean discussion of different kinds of families including those with same-sex parents. Given the likelihood that children and young people will encounter the belief in innate gender identity online and in popular culture, the view that everyone has a gender identity needs to be taught to children and young people, but as a contested belief, and its implications explored. Examples of how a gender-critical sex education curriculum could be constructed are available in the guides available from Transgender Trend (2021). It seems to be the case, however, that with the dominance of LGBT+ advocacy groups in education in recent years, gender-critical sex education curricula have not been widely developed or publicised.

Other actions taken by educators who seek to challenge sex stereotypes within the explicit curriculum can include paying attention to role models, presenting children with images of men and women in gender-atypical roles, inviting adults who do gender-atypical jobs into school to talk about their work (e.g. women firefighters and men in caring jobs) and setting up mentoring schemes for secondary school students to get to know such adults. There may be one-off events and/or ongoing interventions to encourage girls and boys to engage with subjects commonly associated with the opposite sex. These can include 'girls into engineering' days run in conjunction with local employers or universities and colleges and 'boys' reading retreats' during which boys may be taken off-site to engage in sustained reading activities. At the point of making subject choices, young people may be specifically encouraged to consider gender-atypical options and careers.

A trans-inclusive curriculum takes a different approach. Here, an important part of the job is to teach young people that they have an inner sense of maleness or femaleness or something else, that only they know whether they are a boy or a girl or neither, that they are on a complex journey of gender self-discovery and that their sex as 'assigned at birth' may be different and separate from their real self (Miller,

Mayo & Lugg, 2018). The other, complementary, perspective to be taught as truth is that all individuals can decide whether to be a man or woman or something else and that to question someone else's gender identity is to express bigotry akin to sexism, racism or homophobia.

In its guidance, the Scottish Government (2021) recommends a number of books for use in primary schools. Among them is the picture book *I Am Jazz* (Herthel & Jennings, 2014). Based on the real-life experiences of Jazz Jennings, who was transitioned at a young age, and aimed at children under 8, *I Am Jazz* tells children, 'I have a girl brain but a boy body. This is called transgender. I was born this way!' Jazz, in the role of narrator, explains: 'As I got a little older, I hardly ever played with trucks or tools or superheroes. Only princesses and mermaid costumes' (n.p.; see also Matthews, this volume). The message is clear: despite having a male body (or, to use the language recommended in the Scottish Government's guidance, despite being assigned male at birth) Jazz is really a girl and knew it from a pre-verbal age. In another picture book recommended by the Scottish Government for primary schools, *Introducing Teddy* (Walton 2016), Thomas the Teddy takes a deep breath and says to his owner and friend, 'I need to be myself, Errol. In my heart I've always known that I'm a girl teddy, not a boy teddy. I wish my name was Tilly, not Thomas'. Again, the message is that an individual's gender identity is an essential truth about them, their real self, wired in from birth and knowable only to that individual.

Both *I Am Jazz* and *Introducing Teddy* depict unquestioning acceptance of a person's declared gendered identity as the only proper response. In *I Am Jazz*, the initial confusion of Jazz's family transforms to unconditional affirmation after a meeting with a doctor. 'That night at bedtime, my parents both hugged me and said, "We understand now. Be who you are. We love you no matter what"' (n.p.). At the end of the book, an older Jazz says,

> Even today there are kids who tease me, or call me by a boy name, or ignore me altogether. This makes me feel crummy. Then I remember that the kids who get to know me usually want to be my friend. They say I'm one of the nicest girls at school. (n.p.)

Not accepting Jazz as a girl, then, is associated with unkindness and rudeness, and is an act of needless cruelty. This is an especially powerful message to give to girls who are more susceptible to being shamed for not being kind or caring. When Thomas the Teddy becomes Tilly, her new name and 'girl' status are unconditionally accepted by both Errol and his friend Ava. Errol declares, 'I don't care whether you are a girl teddy or a boy teddy. What matters is that you are my friend'. Errol's human friend Ava simply responds, 'What a great name. . . . Let's go and play, Tilly' (n.p.). Part of this messaging is that you can be friends with someone whether they are a boy or a girl: something gender-critical feminists would support. But the messaging is contradictory. On one hand, it does not matter whether someone is a girl or a boy; what matters is the person inside. On the other hand, the person inside, it seems, is inherently gendered; their gender is 'who they are' and unconditional affirmation of that is important. This is a confusing message for young children (and everyone else). What makes you a girl or a boy, beyond a deep-seated feeling that only you can know, is not explained, and yet children are told it must be unconditionally accepted.

One set of problems with teaching gender identity beliefs as though they are unassailable truths arises from the associated misconceptions and confusion. Telling children that sex is assigned at birth rather than determined at conception and observed at or before birth is scientifically inaccurate; encouraging the fantasy that it is possible to change sex is potentially damaging (Littman, this volume). The other set of problems with teaching gender-identity beliefs – or any set of beliefs – as though they are unassailable truths is that doing so models to children and young people that there are some belief systems and ideologies that should be regarded as unquestionable. This contradicts the fundamental pedagogical value of teaching critical thinking rather than teaching children and young people what to think.

At present, we do not know the extent to which either gender-critical or trans-inclusive approaches are embedded in school curricula. It is the case that little guidance supporting gender-critical approaches exists, whilst trans-inclusive approaches are promoted via guidance from a range of statutory- and voluntary-sector organisations, including those referred to in this chapter, that, in addition to providing materials and resources, are also involved in training school staff (For Women Scotland 2020). Gender-identity theory is a constituent part of the Stonewall School and College Champions Scheme, which promotes trans-inclusive curricula to schools and encourages schools to embed them in policy and practice, measuring how well a school does so by awarding bronze, silver and gold status (Stonewall, 2017). Again, the extent of the influence of these materials, training and accreditation programmes on school curricula and policies has yet to be established, but their proliferation suggests it is significant.

The implicit curriculum: changing a school's gender order

Both gender-critical feminist and trans-inclusive educators are interested in addressing the gender order in schools. There are points of commonality, with both groups problematising stereotypical gendered expectations and values. Both groups of educators, therefore, pay attention to overtly gendered practices, such as posters and resources around the school, gendered routines (such as boys and girls lining up in separate lines) and language.

For gender-critical feminists, challenging how gender operates in school is a fundamental and ongoing challenge, encompassing just about every area of a school's work and penetrating into the heart of unseen and unspoken practices. Earlier in the chapter, I described the practice of 'boysplaining' in a primary school, suggesting that its everydayness meant that it had become woven into the fabric of the school, with consequences for both boys and girls. Addressing such practices (which are likely to take local, institutional forms in relation to broader social conditions) implies as a first step making everyone aware of them and then involving everyone – staff, children, parents and others – in tackling them. Sometimes this can be relatively straightforward. When, for instance, a teacher realises that more boys than girls are speaking up in class discussions, children and young people themselves can be enlisted in ensuring a fairer representation by keeping checks themselves, using tally charts or something similar. Other practices may be more deeply ingrained, and children and young people may be very deeply invested in them. For instance, being a gentle, studious boy is typically so against the grain of high-status masculinities (and more especially for working-class boys) that establishing a school gender order in which being gentle and studious confers status for a boy is likely to require very serious engagement with all members of a school community, and even then, the extent to which it can be achieved may be limited (Benjamin 2001, 2010). There are some examples of schools having measures of success by harnessing parent and community groups to provide an environment that rewards girls for being assertive and physically active and boys for being quiet and studious. But without sensitive exploration of the costs and consequences, for girls and boys, of different modes of femininity and masculinity, and determined efforts to make counter-typical behaviour and aspirations not just possible but also desirable, long-lasting changes to the gender order are unlikely.

For trans-inclusive educators, the changes needed to a school's gender order are simpler and more superficial. Here the impetus for addressing a school's implicit curriculum is associated with simply not assuming that any individual is 'the gender that corresponds with their sex assigned at birth'. There is no need to try to transform the expectations of girls and boys, respectively, when an apparent option is for individuals to identify as another gender, leaving the prevailing expectations in place. The hard work of uncovering and challenging deeply embedded practices that may have endured stubbornly over time is made unnecessary. This is one of the reasons why, despite being promoted as radical and transformative, trans-inclusive approaches to schooling contain an innate conservativism. Instead of seeking deep, fundamental and lasting change to a school's gender order and challenging the practices that box in both girls and boys, the onus is on making it possible for a minority of individuals to move from one gender 'box' to another.

Responding to gender-non-conforming and transgender-identifying children and young people

Again, there is a common starting point: both gender-critical and trans-inclusive educators hold that any child or young person experiencing distress and/or confusion around gender issues should be listened to, taken seriously, and treated with compassion and respect.

As discussed earlier, for gender-critical feminists, gender is a social structure requiring habits of mind and behaviour that in general terms privilege the interests of men and boys over those of women and girls and constrain people of both sexes. Seen this way, it is unsurprising that some girls and boys behave in ways that do not conform to gender-stereotypical expectations since there is nothing natural or inevitable about those stereotypes. However, whereas feminists may see gender non-conformity as something to be celebrated, in our patriarchal world, it can be seen as pathological, and the result can be highly distressing for some individuals. Learning to negotiate gendered expectations, and finding a way to exist within the boxes made available by the prevailing gender order, is problematic and painful for some children and young people: assertive, physically-active girls who are disinterested in their appearance; gentle, studious, timid boys; and teenage gay and lesbian young people may be among those who come to perceive themselves as in some way odd or out of line.

One of the axioms of inclusive education (the movement to make schooling universally accessible) is that when an individual child or young person experiences difficulty fitting into an institution, it is the institution that should change to accommodate them (Shuelka 2018). As already mentioned, this is sometimes called a 'social model' response, which locates difficulties as institutional deficits requiring institutional change, rather than seeing the individual as a person with a defect that needs to be 'fixed'. A social model response to a child or young person experiencing distress around gender thus involves addressing the school's gender order, as discussed in the previous section, and changing curricula and school cultures to make the school an environment in which gender-non-conforming children and young people can flourish.

Gender-critical feminists do not accept that transgender-identifying children and young people are innately 'transgender' and speaking an empirical, incontrovertible truth. At the time of writing, far too little is known about the reasons for the sharp increase in transgender-identifying children, in particular girls (Cass Review 2022). It is at least plausible that faced with the difficulties of being an adolescent girl – which include navigating expectations of being hard-working, physically attractive, subordinate to boys and so on, while also dealing with face-to-face and online sexist harassment and often exposure to online porn, alongside experiencing the body discomfort that often accompanies female puberty – some girls, when apparently offered an alternative, can come to believe they are 'really' a boy or non-binary. For girls who are finding it difficult to find their social 'tribe' and gain a sense of status, security and belonging in female friendship groups, the idea that all their difficulties are due to being born in the wrong body, and the promise that their life will be transformed for the better if they transition, is desperately seductive. Littman (2019) and others have suggested that social media and peer groups are playing a part in this unprecedented rise in transgender-identifying adolescent girls, a phenomenon Littman has called 'rapid-onset gender dysphoria' in recognition that it often manifests suddenly, and often in conjunction with others in the peer group and/or online. Given how little is known about this group, given the wider context of a sharp rise in mental health symptoms among young people, especially girls (Patalay &

Fitzsimons 2017), and given earlier findings that puberty resolves gender dysphoria in most prepubescent children, gender-critical feminists continue to advocate for supporting the child or young person in school and doing everything possible to build a school culture that supports gender non-conformity.

Trans-inclusive educators, however, are more likely to argue that children who assert a transgender identity are speaking an empirical truth and that it would be cruel to do anything other than unconditionally affirm that a child is of the gender they believe themselves to be. This is known as the 'affirmative' response. In its extensive advice on 'Coming out', the Scottish Government (2021) advises teachers to take a range of steps if requested by a young person, including changing their name and pronouns in general use and in school records, and making 'gender neutral' (mixed-sex) toilet facilities available to them. This is social transitioning, and there are three significant problems with it. First, if a child has socially transitioned and been accepted by peers and teachers as the opposite sex (especially pre-puberty, when 'passing' may be more straightforward), there is evidence that it is more difficult for their gender dysphoria to resolve when they reach adolescence as it would have done for most, raising the possibility that they may unnecessarily be put on the path to lifelong medical treatment (Singh, Bradley & Zucker 2021). As the Cass Review interim report (2022) noted, 'better information is needed about outcomes' of social transition, and it should not be seen as a straightforward or neutral act. Second, toilets and changing facilities increasingly becoming *de facto* mixed sex has implications for all pupils, especially girls in secondary schools, where single-sex facilities are vital for safety and privacy. Third, the underlying message to all children and young people is that their unrealisable fantasies of being of the opposite sex can be made to come true and that the answer to a restrictive gender order is to make an 'escape route' available to the individuals for whom it is most restrictive, rather than challenging that order for everyone.

Much of the guidance tells teachers they should only disclose a child or young person's 'coming out' as transgender with the child's permission. Brighton and Hove City Council (2021) for example, recommends that when contacting families, "respecting a trans or gender exploring child's confidentiality may very occasionally require staff to use their legal name and the pronoun corresponding to their sex registered at birth" (16). There is a clear safeguarding red flag here, with teachers arguably being advised to collude with children in keeping significant secrets from their parents and putting a child's friends and teachers, as well as the child themselves, in a compromised position if they live 'as a boy' in school and 'as a girl' outside school or vice versa. We do not, at present, know how widely this advice is being taken up in schools. The pressure group Safe Schools Alliance (2021) reports being contacted by parents concerned about their children being transitioned in schools without their knowledge, but robust data on schools incorporating such advice into policy and practice does not yet exist. Anecdotally, the prevalence of socially-transitioned children in schools has gone from almost non-existent to widespread, although it seems likely that in the majority of cases social transition happens with parents' knowledge.

Conclusion

The feminist project of addressing sexism and sex inequalities through education is incomplete. Huge strides have been made since the pioneering first-wave feminists of the mid-1800s set up the first academic schools for girls, and second-wave feminists fought for equality in the curriculum. Yet typically the gender order in schools still constrains girls' and boys' experiences and options: girls disproportionately learn to excel in the arts and humanities, take up less physical and 'air' space than boys and subordinate their interests to those of boys, while boys disproportionately learn to excel in the physical sciences and practical subjects, dominate physical and 'air' space and assert their interests through boisterous and non-compliant behaviour. Most educators intuitively know this to be the case, even as its ubiquity means it goes too often unnoticed and unremarked.

Trans-inclusive approaches to education, as advocated in the guidance, toolkits and training widely available to schools, seem to offer a radical way forward. Reconfiguring gender as a matter of individual identity and expression offers a few individuals – those who, for whatever reason, do not or cannot conform to societal gendered expectations – the opportunity to escape from one gendered box into another. The creation of non-binary boxes seems to offer additional possibilities for individual self-actualisation. But offering escape routes to individuals does not require schools, or society, to radically change the gender order. It also brings some regressive practices in its wake, including teaching scientifically unverifiable beliefs as established and unassailable truths and encouraging children to fantasise that they can change sex, which could have very serious medical and psychological implications.

A gender-critical feminist framing of education, as discussed in this chapter, foregrounds structural, institutional change. In framing sex as dimorphic and immutable and gender as external, hierarchical and coercively imposed, gender-critical feminism requires schools and teachers to work at identifying and challenging the prevailing gender order in their schools, so as to address the ways in which girls' and boys' opportunities become constrained, and the subordination of girls is reinforced. For educators who wish to work towards a more inclusive and more equal future, gender-critical approaches offer a difficult and, at the moment unpopular, way forward. But that is nothing new for feminist educators. The feminist project in schools has always been hard, but the rewards have been and will continue to be hugely significant for generations of girls – and boys.

References

Assor, A. & Gordon, D. (1987) 'The Implicit Learning Theory of Hidden-Curriculum Research'. *Journal of Curriculum Studies* 19/4 329–339.

Barnes, C. (2012) 'It's No Laughing Matter . . . Boys' Humour and the Performance of Defensive Masculinities in the Classroom'. *Journal of Gender Studies* 21/3 239–251.

BBC Sounds (2021) Nolan Investigates. (Podcast series, first broadcast 13/10/2021). https://www.bbc.co.uk/sounds/brand/p09yjmph Date of access 19/11/2021.

Benjamin, S. (2001) 'Challenging Masculinities: Disability and Achievement in Testing Times'. *Gender and Education* 13/1 39–55.

Benjamin, S. (2002) *The Micropolitics of Inclusive Education: An Ethnography*. Milton Keynes, UK: Open University Press.

Benjamin, S. (2010) 'Gender and Schooling'. In *Gender and Child Welfare in Society*, edited by Brid Featherstone, Carol-Ann Hooper, Jonathan Scourfield and Julie Taylor, 95–120. Hoboken, NJ: Wiley.

Brighton & Hove City Council (2021) Trans Inclusion: Schools Toolkit. https://mermaidsuk.org.uk/wp-content/uploads/2019/12/BHCC_Trans-Inclusion-Schools-Toolkit-_Version4_Sept21.pdf Date of access 16/11/2021.

Busby, E. (2016) GCSE Results: Gender Gap Widens as Girls Pull Further Ahead. Times Educational Supplement 25/08/2016 https://www.tes.com/news/gcse-results-gender-gap-widens-girls-pull-further-ahead Date of access 30/08/2021.

Cantor, J. (2016) 'Do Trans- Kids Stay Trans- When They Grow Up?' *Sexology Today* http://www.sexologytoday.org/2016/01/do-trans-kids-stay-trans-when-they-grow_99.html Date of access 28/07/2021.

Cass Review (2022) *Independent Review of Gender Identity Services for Children and Young People: Interim Report*. Available at https://cass.independent-review.uk Date of access 25/07/2022.

Coyne, S. N., Linder, J. R., Rasmussen, E. E., Nelson, D. A. & Collier K. M. (2014) 'It's a Bird! It's a Plane! It's a Gender Stereotype! Longitudinal Associations between Superhero Viewing and Gender Stereotyped Play'. *Sex Roles* 70 416–430.

Davies, B. (2003) *Frogs and Snails and Feminist Tales*. New York: Hampton Press.

Eisner, E. (1994) *The Educational Imagination: On the Design and Evaluation of School Programmes*. New York: Macmillan.

Epstein, D., Elwood, J., Hey, V., & Maw, J. (Eds.) (1998) *Failing Boys? Issues in Gender and Achievement*. Milton Keynes: Open University Press.

Eriksen, I. M. (2018) 'Tough Femininities: Ethnic Minority Girls' Aggressive School Opposition'. *British Journal of Sociology of Education* 40/8 1090–1104.

For Women Scotland (2020) George Watson's College – Staff Transgender Training. https://forwomen.scot/13/12/2020/george-watsons-college-staff-transgender-training/ Date of access 20/11/2021.

Francis, B., Archer, L., Moote, J., De Witt, J. & Yeomans, L. (2017) 'Femininity, Science and the Denigration of the "Girly Girl"'. *British Journal of Sociology of Education* 38/3 1097–1110.

GIDS (2021) Referrals to GIDS 2011–2021. https://gids.nhs.uk/number-referrals Date of access 28/07/2021.

Girlguiding UK (2019) *Girls' Attitudes Survey*. https://www.girlguiding.org.uk/globalassets/docs-and-resources/research-and-campaigns/girls-attitudes-survey-2019.pdf Date of access 29/07/2021.

Gendered Intelligence (2019) *Achieving Trans Inclusion and Valuing Gender Diversity in Educational Settings*. http://genderedintelligence.co.uk/static/images/2019/08/27/14-50-47-GI_Education_booklet_%20Apr19.pdf? Date of access 22/11/2021.

Herthel, J. & Jennings, J. (2014) *I Am Jazz*. New York: Penguin

Hey, V. (1997) *The Company She Keeps: An ethnography of girls' friendships*. Milton Keynes, UK: Open University Press.

Horton, C. (2020) 'Thriving or Surviving? Raising our ambition for trans children in primary and secondary schools'. *Frontiers in Sociology* https://www.frontiersin.org/articles/10.3389/fsoc.2020.00067/full Date of access 02/11/2021.

Kamm, J. (2014) *How Different from Us: A Biography of Miss Buss and Miss Beale*. London: Routledge.

Kennedy, N. (2018) 'Prisoners of Lexicon: Cultural Cisgenderism and Transgender Children'. In *Normed Children: Effects of Gender and Sex Related Normativity on Childhood and Adolescence* edited by Erik Schneider and Christel Baltes-Lohr, 297–312. Bielefeld, Germany: Transcript Verlag. https://library.oapen.org/bitstream/handle/20.500.12657/37406/9783839430200.pdf?sequence=1#page=298 Date of access 03/11/2021.

Labelle, S. (2020) *My Dad Thinks I'm a Boy?! A Trans-Positive Children's Book*. London: Jessica Kingsley.

Littman, L. (2019) 'Parent Reports of Adolescents and Young Adults Perceived to Show Signs of a Rapid Onset Gender Dysphoria' (revised version). *PLoS One* 14/3 e0214157 https://journals.plos.org/plosone/article?id=10.1371/journal.pone.0214157 Date of access 28/07/2021.

Miller, sj., Mayo, C. & Lugg, C.A. (2018) 'Sex and Gender in Transition in US Schools: Ways Forward'. *Sexuality, Society and Learning* 18/4 345–359.

OFSTED (The Office for Standards in Education) (2021) Review of Sexual Abuse in Schools and Colleges. https://www.gov.uk/government/publications/review-of-sexual-abuse-in-schools-and-colleges/review-of-sexual-abuse-in-schools-and-colleges#what-did-we-find-out-about-the-scale-and-nature-of-sexual-abuse-in-schools Date of access 30/07/2021.

Oliver, M. (2013) 'The Social Model of Disability: 30 years on'. *Disability and Society* 28/7 1024–1026.

Patalay, P. & Fitzsimons, E. (2017) *Mental Ill-Health Among Children of the New Century: Trends across Childhood with a Focus on Age 14*. London: Centre for Longitudinal Studies.

Portsmouth Education Partnership (2018) Portsmouth Trans Inclusion Guidance for Schools and Colleges. https://www.portsmoutheducationpartnership.co.uk/wp-content/uploads/2018/04/1.157-Trans-Inclusion-Guidance-for-Schools-and-Colleges-PROOF-5.pdf Date of access 21/11/2021.

Pratt, L. & Foley, Y. (2020) 'Using Critical Literacy to 'Do' Identity and Gender'. In *Social Justice Re-Examined: Dilemmas and Solutions for the Classroom Teacher*, edited by Rowena Arshad, Terry Wrigley and Lynne Pratt, 72–91. London: UCL-IoE Press.

Proud Trust (2021) Trans Positive Education for Primary Schools pack. https://www.theproudtrust.org/product/trans-positive-education-for-primary-schools-pack-upper-ks2/ Date of access 19/11/2021.

Ringrose, J. & Epstein, D. (2017) Postfeminist Educational Media Panics, Girl Power and the Problem/Promise of 'Successful Girls'.' In *A Companion to Research in Teacher Education*, edited by Michael A. Peters, Bronwen Cowie, and Ian Menter, 385–399. Singapore: Springer Singapore.

Roach, J. (1986) 'Boys and Girls at School 1800–1870'. *History of Education* 15/3 147–159.

Safe Schools Alliance UK (2021) Advice on Social Transitioning of Trans-Identified Children. https://safeschoolsallianceuk.net/2021/08/22/advice-for-parents-on-social-transitioning-by-schools/ Date of access: 20/11/2021.

Schriffin-Sands (2021) 'He Said He Said: Boysplaining in a Primary Classroom'. *Gender and Education* 33/6 661–675.

Scottish Government (2021) Supporting Transgender Young People in Schools: Guidance for Scottish Schools. The Scottish Government. https://www.gov.scot/publications/supporting-transgender-young-people-schools-guidance-scottish-schools/pages/2/ Date of access 09/11/2021.

Scottish Qualifications Authority (2020) *Annual Statistical Report 2020.* https://www.sqa.org.uk/sqa/64717.html Date of access 31/07/2021.

Shuelka, M. J. (2018) 'Implementing Inclusive Education. UK Aid, K4D'. https://assets.publishing.service.gov.uk/media/5c6eb77340f0b647b214c599/374_Implementing_Inclusive_Education.pdf Date of access 28/07/21.

Sinclair-Palm, J. & Gilbert, J. (2018) 'Naming New Realities: Supporting Trans Youth in Education'. *Sexuality, Society and Learning* 18/4 321–327.

Singh, D., Bradley, S. J. and Zucker, K. J. (2021) 'A Follow-Up Study of Boys with Gender Identity Disorder'. *Frontiers in Psychiatry.* https://doi.org/10.3389/fpsyt.2021.632784.

Stonewall (2017) School and College Champion Membership. https://www.stonewall.org.uk/stonewall-school-college-champion-membership Date of access 16/11/2021.

Sweet, J. (2021) '"Jack Was Just Jack": Performance Ethnography of One Trans Student's Secondary School Experiences'. *Gender and Education* 34/5 593–608.

Time for Inclusive Education (2021) Tackling Prejudice with an Inclusive Approach. https://www.tie.scot Date of access 21/11/2021.

Tomlinson, S. (2017) *A Sociology of Special and Inclusive Education: Exploring the Manufacture of Inability.* London: Routledge.

Transgender Trend (2021) Inclusive Relationships and Sex Education in Schools. https://www.transgendertrend.com/product/inclusive-relationships-and-sex-education-in-schools-rse/ Date of access 29/07/2021.

Walkerdine, V. (1989) 'Femininity as Performance'. *Oxford Review of Education* 15/3 267–279.

Walton, J. (2016) *Introducing Teddy: A gentle story about gender and Friendship.* New York: Bloomsbury.

Warwickshire Safeguarding (n.d.) Trans Inclusion Toolkit for Schools. https://www.safeguardingwarwickshire.co.uk/images/downloads/ESS-PB/PoliciesandProcedures/Trans-Toolkit-for-schools-2017.pdf Date of access 22/11/2021.

13

THE CHILDREN WHO WOULDN'T GROW UP

Gender in Children's Literature Over Fifty Years

Susan Matthews

Children's literature—written by adults, bought by adults and often read by adults to children—tells us about the dreams and desires of adult culture (Rose 1993, 1) This chapter uses representative books for children published in the United States of America (US) and Britain over the last fifty years to trace changing cultural beliefs about gender and about childhood. The work of cultural history is to unpick contemporary myths, excavating earlier and different models of human culture. Since the cultural historian Philip Ariès wrote *Centuries of Childhood* in 1960 (Ariès, 1996), historians have explored the ways that childhood has changed over time. The long white dresses worn by infants of both sexes before the First World War represented their life stage (babyhood) rather than their sex (Paoletti 2012, 29). The shift for boys from skirts to trousers, known as 'breeching', symbolised the transition to masculinity and the end of the close relationship with the mother. As the century progressed, the transition to a gendered world occurred at ever-earlier ages, and with the arrival of prenatal ultrasound and amniocentesis, gendering could for the first time occur before birth (Paoletti 2012, 127). A favourite illustration of changing cultural codes is the rise of pink and blue as gender signifiers: according to clothing historian Jo Paoletti (2012) this coding 'was not dominant until the 1950s in most parts of the United States and not universal until a generation later' (89).

The first half of my chapter looks at representations of feminine or gender-nonconforming boys in books from the 1970s until about 2008. In books influenced by second-wave feminism, gender rules are seen as culturally constructed and subject to change. The rules of femininity are assumed to be as constricting for girls as the rules of masculinity for boys. These books often challenge the century-long progress towards greater gender codification. As white dresses for babies were replaced by clothes marked by gender, manifestations of femininity in boys became a subject of

DOI: 10.4324/9781003286608-13

concern at increasingly earlier ages. Various explanations for this anxiety have been offered, from the crises of masculinity created by economic hardship in the 1930s to the increased visibility of homosexuality and transsexuality in the 1960s and 1970s (Bryant 2006, 25).

From around 2008, a new version of gender begins to appear, often alongside second-wave feminist ideas, in stories about a child whose gender identity lies 'deep down where the music plays' (Meadow 2011, 740). Most academic accounts of gender in children's literature welcome this new story as a mark of progress, of the gradual breaking down of prejudice (Malcom and Sheehan 2014; Herzog 2009). This chapter tells a more complex story. Rather than a belated recognition of transgender children as a category which always existed, gender-identity books, I argue, reinterpret gender nonconformity as cross-gender conformity (i.e., that if a child likes activities or roles considered 'feminine', they must be female) and obscure signals of emergent same-sex attraction. As second-wave feminist understandings of gender are displaced by a newer gender-identity model, academic critics return to earlier children's books, producing new readings that work to align older fiction with a new, and inherently incompatible, theory (Butler 2009; Butler 2020). Finally, *Histories of the Transgender Child* (Gill Peterson 2018) argues that the transgender child always existed. Children's literature and academic criticism of children's books shape cultural assumptions about childhood and gender, creating myths from history. My chapter offers a revisionary history in place of a currently powerful myth.

I argue that the 'Dutch protocol', which allowed the signs of puberty to be chemically arrested in children who displayed discomfort with social gender conventions (Biggs, this volume), made possible a new model of gender and childhood. 'All children, except one, grow up' is the famous opening line of J.M. Barrie's (1904) *Peter Pan*, but new techniques for blocking puberty meant that James Barrie's fantasy became a medical possibility. In this new world, it became important to discover 'gender identity' in ever younger children. Books for children as young as 3 or 4 explained the concept of innate gender. And as the number of teenagers with gender dysphoria rose (Littman, this volume), books for children cast the figure of the trans teenager in a glamorous light. The fascination with the gender-bending figure of the 'boy in a dress' was recast as the trans child who knows their own gender even before they can speak. These new assumptions run the danger of misreading sexual orientation as gender identity and reimposing outmoded gender stereotypes.

Gender as a social construction in the twentieth century

In 1972, Ann Oakley (2005) explained that '"[s]ex" is a biological term; "gender" is a psychological and cultural one' (7). Oakley's understanding of gender draws on two distinct intellectual traditions: anthropologists such as Margaret Mead had shown how temperament and personality is shaped by culture, while psychologist John Money and psychoanalyst Robert Stoller sought to understand how individuals born with intersex conditions in which sex was ambiguous at birth understood their psychological sex. The new terms, 'gender role' and 'gender expression', were introduced by psychiatrist John Money in 1955 with the addition of 'gender identity' by psychoanalyst Robert Stoller in 1964 (Di Ceglie 2018, 4).

At first, 'gender identity' proved a useful concept to second-wave feminists. Ann Oakley (2005, 8) cites Stoller's 1968 book *Sex and Gender*; Kate Millett's ([1969] 1997) *Sexual Politics* takes from Stoller the idea that 'core gender identity' is established by the age of eighteen months' (29) and from Money the proposition that the rules of gender are imprinted 'with the establishment of a native language' (31). Gender identity, Millett writes, is shaped by culture during childhood:

> Implicit in all the gender identity development which takes place through childhood is the sum total of the parents', the peers', and the culture's notions of what is appropriate to each gender by way of temperament, character, interests, status, worth, gesture, and expression. Every moment of the child's life is a clue to how he or she must think and behave to attain or satisfy the demands which gender places upon one. (31)

In *Woman Hating*, the radical feminist Andrea Dworkin (1974) quotes Money in support of her argument that androgyny offers an escape from gender stereotypes (182). The debate was between 'nature' and 'nurture': Did children come into the world already gendered, with their personalities and intelligence fixed, or could the way they were raised and educated free them from the limitations and stereotypes associated with their sex? Money and Stoller lent biomedical support to the feminist view that gender differences are culturally constructed (Cortez et al. 2019).

The fact that John Money and Robert Stoller encouraged conformity to sex stereotypes while the feminists were challenging those very stereotypes seemed at the time unimportant. Money's most famous case seemed to show the power of nurture to determine a child's gender: in the 'John/Joan' case, a baby boy who had lost his penis in an accident during circumcision was raised as a girl. Money reports that the mother

> made a special effort at keeping her girl in dresses, almost exclusively, changing any item of clothes into something that was clearly feminine. "I even made all her nightwear into granny gowns and she wears bracelets and hair ribbons." The effects of emphasizing feminine clothing became clearly noticeable in the girl's attitude towards clothes and hairdo another year later, when she was observed to have a clear preference for dresses over slacks and to take a pride in her long hair.
> *(Money and Ehrhardt 1973, 119)*

Money's belief that putting a child in a dress would create a female gender identity depended on the convention, cemented over the first half of the twentieth century, that dresses are the clothes of girls. Kate Millett mentions similar experiments, noting that

> [i]n cases of genital malformation and consequent erroneous gender assignment at birth, studied at the California Gender Identity Center, the discovery was made that it is easier to change the sex of an adolescent male, whose biological identity turns out to be contrary to his gender assignment and conditioning – through surgery – than to undo the educational consequences of years, which have succeeded in making the subject temperamentally feminine in gesture, sense of self, personality and interests.
>
> *(Millett [1969] 1997, 30)*

Gender identity (internalised by rearing) appeared to be more important than bodily sex.

The new concept of gender-identity disorder of childhood, introduced in the third edition of the US *Diagnostic and Statistical Manual of Mental Disorders* (*DSM*) in 1980 (Bryant 2006, 31) developed from concern about feminine boys, known at the time as 'sissies'. Robert Stoller attributed what he called 'childhood transsexualism' to excessive closeness with the mother (Bryant 2006, 26). Richard Green (who had studied with John Money) led the Feminine Boy Study at the University of California Los Angeles from 1972 to 1987, which followed the development of 66 boys and their families. These were boys who

> differed from many other boys also called 'sissy.' Our boys would have preferred being girls. They liked to dress in girls' or women's clothes. They preferred Barbie dolls to trucks. Their playmates were girls. When they played 'mommydaddy' games, they were mommy.
>
> *(Green 1987)*

Green takes for granted the gendered meanings of clothes and toys which, since the invention of the Barbie doll in 1959, had become more clearly gendered. The results were published in 1987 as *The Sissy Boy Syndrome: The Development of Homosexuality*. Like Stoller, Green had expected that the boys would develop as transsexuals. But only one became a transsexual whereas three quarters of the boys grew up to be homosexual or bisexual. Gender choices in childhood, it seemed, were indicative of adult sexual orientation.

The first gender identity clinic for children opened in the Netherlands in 1987, followed by the British clinic for children (later known as the GIDS or Gender Identity Development Service) in 1989. But some critics (Sedgwick 1991; Bem 1993) saw the new disorder as an attempt to pathologise the early indications of homosexuality because the childhood diagnosis appeared soon after adult homosexuality had been removed from the *DSM* in 1973. Feminist ideas also challenged the new disorder: psychiatrists such as Anne Chappell rejected the idea that gender non-conformity is a disorder and argued that androgyny contributes to mental health in both sexes (Bryant 2006, 32). Post-war welfare states offered widening economic and social opportunities for girls and a strong feminist movement developed in western countries. In the US, Betty Friedan's ([1963] 2010) *The Feminine Mystique* criticised the attempt to persuade women that fulfilment could only be found in housekeeping and child-rearing. In the early 1970s, a movement to raise children free of gender stereotypes gained force (Todd, this volume).

In the US, picture books sought to reassure parents that feminine traits in boys are not pathological. In *William's Doll* (Zolotow and Du Bois, 1972) for ages 4 to 8, a boy is called 'Sissy, sissy, sissy!' by the boy next door (11). But while William's desire for a doll is portrayed as acceptable, the book reassures the reader that he will not grow up to be gay. The book belongs to the feminist project of encouraging fathers to share the burden of childcare. William doesn't want a Barbie. He wants an ungendered baby:

> It would have blue eyes
> and curly eyelashes
> and a long white dress
> and a bonnet
> and when the eyes closed
> they would make a little click (12)

His grandmother gets him a doll 'so that he can practice being a father' (26). A song based on *William's Doll* featured in a 1974 US TV series designed to counter gender stereotyping called *Free to Be . . . You and Me* (Nel 2015, 283). In the opening sequence, children ride off a traditional merry-go-round in Central Park New York to emerge in a golden Western landscape. The theme song by the New Seekers tells of an escape from gender stereotypes:

> In a land where the river runs free
> In a land through the green country
> In a land to a shining sea
> And you and me are free to be you and me

This is a new version of the myth of the US as a 'land of the free' and the phrase 'to a shining sea' echoes patriotic songs. The idea that the West Coast offers new forms of gender freedom persists into the twenty-first century as a new model of gender emerges.

Returning from California in the 1980s, the English writer Anne Fine was shocked by what she saw as outmoded gender stereotypes in British schools. In California, 'the schools had a rule to treat girls and boys the same, and make sure the workbooks they used weren't old-fashioned and "sexist". (If anyone ignored the rule, parents were quick to complain.)' ('About Bill's New Frock' n.d.). In Britain, her children reported 'often the boys did one thing, but the girls did another' ('About Bill's New Frock' n.d.). Fine's 1989 book for 7- to 9-year-olds, *Bill's New Frock,* aimed to change the ways in which teachers treated boys and girls (Fine and Beech, 2017). In the story, simply putting on a flouncy pink frock subjects Bill to gendered expectations: to be compliant, write neatly, and hang out with the girls at break time. When Bill and another boy are caught fighting and set to write lines, the boys 'looked for all the world like a pair of scowling and bad-tempered twins' (Fine and Beech 2017, 78). Yet their behaviour is interpreted according to gendered conventions:

> every now and again, someone would tiptoe past and whisper in Rohan's ear:
> 'You look so angry.'
> But in Bill's they whispered:
> 'You look so *upset*.' (78, emphasis in original)

Anne Fine selects this as an example of sexism in the 'Q & A' that follows the text in the 2017 edition. The book has been used in primary schools in the UK to initiate discussion of gender stereotypes and praised as 'exemplary in its humorous approach to these issues' (Francis et al. 2002, 27). This is not a book about a feminine boy but a book about the effects of socially imposed femininity.

David Walliams's 2008 *The Boy in the Dress* (for 9 to 12 years) shares the second-wave assumption that biological sex is fixed while the cultural rules of gender can change. Fine portrays Talilah's red salwar kameez as a garment that allows free movement for girls, Walliams shows how Dennis's Sikh friend Darwesh breaks British conventions of clothing. But in neither book do clothes magically change the identity of the wearer: putting on a dress does not turn a boy into a girl nor does trying on Darvesh's patka turn Dennis into a Sikh: '"On you it's just a hat. It's just dressing up, innit?"' Darwesh decides (Walliams 2008, 93). When Dennis, wearing a dress, pretends to be a French exchange student, he is found out because he can't speak French. A similar assumption guides psychiatrist Domenico di Ceglie (2009; who founded England's gender clinic for children in 1989) when he warns a child who wants to pass as the opposite sex:

> it's a bit similar to an English boy, born in England, brought up in England, about fifteen, sixteen, who emigrates to France and then goes around and says to everybody that I'm French. That I want to be considered French. While his accent will show that he is not French. (63)

In these stories from the last decades of the twentieth century and the first decade of the twenty-first, identity is a negotiation between an individual's sense of themselves and society's meanings.

But David Walliams attaches an importance to a psychological explanation of gender which is not present in Fine's story. Dennis's desire to cross-dress is explained by the loss of his mother, who had left the home and an unhappy marriage. His father had burned every photograph of her – except one which Dennis salvaged from the fire:

> It showed a joyful scene: a younger John and Dennis with Mum at the beach, Mum wearing a lovely yellow dress with flowers on it. Dennis loved that dress; it was full of colour and life, and soft to the touch. (14)

The house rules are 'No talking about Mum', 'no crying', and 'no hugging' (17) This is a home which actively represses behaviour coded as feminine.

In contrast to Fine's feminist fable, Walliams's story represents gender as a series of choices which express inner meanings. Dresses are objects of fascination to Dennis. He loves 'having Lisa fuss over him, applying make-up to his face, squeezing his feet into matching silver high-heeled shoes, and styling the wig, had been so much fun he didn't complain' (115). In this, he is not alone: Mr Hawtrey, the headteacher who polices gender non-conformity, turns out to be a secret cross-dresser. The shopkeeper Raj cross-dresses in his wife's sari. But Dennis is also established as masculine by his key role in the school football match when the whole team turns up in girls' clothes and wins. This is a book about transvestism rather than gender identity, and its message proved to have a wide cultural acceptance. By 2014, when *The Boy in a Dress* was adapted as a comedy drama for BBC TV, it had sold more than half a million copies (Groves, 2014). In 2019, the Royal Shakespeare Company commissioned a stage version.

Whereas Ann Fine presents gender in terms derived from second-wave feminism as a form of social imposition which can constrain individual identity, David Walliams offers a new version of gender as individual choice. As early as 1986, Judith Butler wrote that gender is not 'passively determined, constructed by a personified system of patriarchy or phallogocentric language which precedes and determines the subject itself' but an active, 'voluntaristic' choice (36). This model presented a quandary for Butler because she also believed that children cannot escape the cultural construction of gender. A large body of work in the late 1970s showed that adults engage in more physical play with babies they believe to be boys and talk more to babies they believe to be girls (Paoletti 2012, 13). Cultural historian Jo Paoletti (2012) points out that '[t]he mid 1980s witnessed the introduction of "his and hers" disposable diapers, headbands for bald girl babies (serving no function other than as a gender marker), and the disappearance of most unisex baby clothing' (16). Judith Butler's model of gender as performance derives from a moment at which infancy was gendered more strongly than ever before. In place of androgyny, cross-dressing became a new image of freedom, and in 1992, transvestism and transsexualism were subsumed by a new umbrella term: 'transgender' (Feinberg 1992; see Jones, this volume).

Gender identity in the twenty-first century

In 2008, the same year that *The Boy in a Dress* appeared in the UK, the first gender-identity picture book was published in the US. The cataloguing instruction for Marcus Ewert's *10,000 Dresses* is '1. Identity – Fiction. 2. Transgender people – Fiction'. In this picture book for 5- to 8-year-olds, Bailey is called 'she' from the start: we only discover that Bailey is a boy when his mother tells him that he can't have a dress: "Bailey, what are you talking about: You're a boy" (Ewert and Ray 2008, 9). The narrator's choice of pronoun asserts that identity rather than biology is true. Children's books published in the 1970s accepted boyish femininity and Walliams's 2008 book accepts that a boy can wear a dress in play. But the new gender-identity model cannot allow gender nonconformity: a boy who wears a dress must be normalised as a girl. Bailey is a perfect representation of the Romantic child. He speaks in lines which are centred on the page like poetry. "Mom, I dreamt about a dress," he says like a child from Blake's *Songs of Innocence*. In Bailey's dreams, dresses are part of nature, not culture:

> That night, Bailey walked right past the crystal dress,
> and went to the second stair.
> there was a dress made of lilies and roses! When
> she slipped it on, she saw that the sleeves
> were made of honeysuckles!
> Bailey picked a few of the blossoms,
> to taste the little drops of honey.
> With all her heart, Bailey loved the dress made of
> lilies and roses, with honeysuckle sleeves. (11)

The lexicon derives via Blake from the Bible: lilies and roses, a promised land where honeysuckle blossom turns into drops of honey. Like the child in Wordsworth's 'Ode: Intimations of Immortality', Bailey comes into the world trailing clouds of glory. His infinite imagination can 'dream up 10,000' dresses. He makes dresses 'covered with mirrors of all shapes and sizes' which "'show us OURSELVES.'" Feeling rather than reason makes sense of the world in this book: "'But . . . I don't feel like a boy,' Bailey said' (9). Anthropologist Sahar Sadjadi (2019) noticed a 'merging of science, magic and religion in explaining children's gender transition' (104). In this model, according to Sadjadi, 'The self, if true to itself, is . . . perceived as inherently good and trustworthy. Tautological phrases such as "be yourself," a common piece of adult advice given to children, capture this culturally commonsensical belief and mistrust of external forces' (113). This version of childhood can be traced back to the eighteenth-century thinker Jean-Jacques Rousseau who believed that we come into the world as our true selves. His *Emile, Or Treatise on Education* ([1762] 1979) announces that '[e]verything is good as it leaves the hands of the Author of things; everything degenerates in the hands of man' (37). The twenty-first-century transgender child, likewise, is the child whose gender identity is felt 'deep down where the music plays' (Meadow 2011), whose true self is innocent of the social world.

The fullest application of gender identity to childhood is found in the work of Californian psychologist Diane Ehrensaft, who announced in 2011 that gender feelings are 'rooted in complex biological factors that exist at birth' (533). Ehrensaft draws on an idea of the 'authentic self' which she finds in writing by the English paediatrician and psychoanalyst Donald Winnicott (1896–1971):

> In his concepts of human development, Winnicott identified the true self as the authentic core of one's personality, from which spontaneous action and a

sense of realness come. He proposed that the original kernel of the true self is evident at birth.

(Ehrensaft 2011, 533)

In Winnicott's ([1960] 1965) thinking, the development of the 'true self' depends on the capacity of the 'good enough mother' to display 'devotion' ([148). Winnicott was writing after the Second World War in the early years of the British National Health Service. As Sally Alexander (2012) explains, 'Winnicott's vision is social – the maternal environment, the two-body relation inaugurates subjectivity; the space between them both instils what he calls the "maturational process," and forms the basis of creative life and culture' (151). Ehrensaft repurposes Winnicott's ideas to fit an individualist culture with an exclusive focus on gender. The 'authentic self' is now within, ready formed at birth. The work of the parent is to decode the child's 'gender signals': a baby boy who undoes his sleepsuit may be trying to turn the garment into a dress. Such a claim depends on the assumption that only baby girls wear dresses – something that would have made no sense to earlier generations. It also reflects the move to impose gender on ever younger babies. As ultrasound and prenatal testing became routine in the 1990s, biological sex could not only be identified before birth but announced in a choice of pink or blue cake (Schiller 2019). Parents were encouraged to buy newborn baby clothes which marked gender: in the mid-1980s in the US 'headbands and baby barrettes appeared in the stores, and Luvs introduced pink and blue disposable diapers' (Paoletti 2012, 114). Although gender-identity ideology claims to manifest a form of gender freedom it can also be seen as a response to the gendering of early childhood: 2008 saw not only the first gender-identity picture book but also the first 'gender-reveal party'.

From 2008 onwards, trans children increasingly appear in children's books (Butler 2020, 15; Bartholomaeus and Riggs 2019, 137). Kate Millett borrowed from John Money the idea that gender is 'first established "with the establishment of a native language"' (Millett [1969] 1997, 31). To remap our understanding of gender, activists had to change grammar. A new movement insists that pronouns reflect gender identity rather than biological sex. The reasons for this cultural shift are complex (Stock 2021; Joyce 2021; Jones, this volume). Here I want to focus on two moments: one is the fall from grace of John Money. The experimental transition of one of a pair of identical twin boys (the 'John/Joan' case) which began in 1967 had already begun to fail as 'Brenda' reached adolescence, refused to take female hormones and chose to retransition to male. But Money continued to publish articles claiming that the transition was a success. The story might have remained a minor academic scandal, but in 1998, it was the subject of an article in *Rolling Stone* (Colapinto 1998) and, in 2000, a popular book, *As Nature Made Him: The Boy Who Was Raised as a Girl* (Colapinto [2000] 2006). The same year, a BBC documentary '*The Boy Who Was Turned into a Girl*' opened with the words: 'For many years science has believed it could turn a boy into a girl. Not just make a boy look like a girl but make him think like a girl, feel like a girl, be a girl, to turn a boy's brain into a girl's brain'. The popular conclusion was not just that Money was an unethical doctor but also that feminists were wrong: gender identity was part of nature, and a 'non-sexist' upbringing could not modify the expression of masculinity or femininity. Out of this cultural turn, a revised belief in gender identity as an innate and unmodifiable aspect of the self was born.

These years also saw the spread of puberty blockers (Biggs, this volume), an experimental repurposing of an existing therapy which would be fundamental to the invention of the transgender child. In 2006 a team from the Netherlands published a paper which described the use of GNRH agonists on a group of children with long-standing gender dysphoria and offered a detailed recipe by which clinicians could reproduce this treatment (Delemarre-van de Waal and Cohen-Kettenis, 2006). Inspired by the 'Dutch protocol', endocrinologist Norman Spack opened the first US gender clinic for children in Boston in 2007. From there the number of children's gender clinics, the number of referrals to gender clinics, and the spread of gender identity ideology developed fast in the US and worldwide. Bernice Hausman has argued that the concept of 'gender identity' can be understood as a response to new medical technologies: the isolation of hormones and the development of plastic surgery from the 1930s onwards (Hausman 1995, 7). Following Hausman's logic, it could be argued that the dissemination of the Dutch protocol in 2006 allowed the creation of the transgender child who appears from that year onwards in journalism and TV.

As gender-identity ideology spread, the link between childhood gender non-conformity and later same-sex attraction, established by Richard Green in the 1970s and 1980s, was forgotten. In 1998 in Washington D.C., a mother, Catherine Tuerk (2011), founded a support group for parents who believed that 'expression of feminine interests was part of the normal childhood development of many gay men' (768). But in 2006, Tuerk noticed a new 'trend' as more parents 'felt their sons were transsexual girls rather than gay boys' (768). Tuerk thought this reflected 'the intense interest in stories in the media of children beginning gender transition at early ages' (768). One such story in *Village Voice* described a feminine boy named (pseudonymously) Nicole (Reischel, 2006). 'Nicole' was then aged 5, and the family had just contacted Mark Angelo Cummings, a female-to-male transsexual who was on television promoting his memoir, *The Mirror Makes No Sense*. According to Reischel (2006), Cummings decided that Nicole 'should become a poster child for childhood transsexuality' (12). The following year, under the name Jazz Jennings, the 6-year-old appeared on Barbara Walters's television show *20/20* 'My Secret Self, 2'. A picture book called *I Am Jazz* appeared in 2014 and a reality show with the same name in 2015. The book begins: 'For as long as I can remember, my favorite color has been pink' (Herthel, Jennings and McNicholas, 2014, 2). Jazz explains: 'I have a girl brain but a boy body. This is called transgender. I was born this way!' (8) Gender is now innate and fixed rather than culturally constructed. Jazz behaves just like the 'sissy boys' described by Richard Green in 1987, but the likelihood that he might grow up to be homosexual has been forgotten – even though the 1987 finding that childhood gender non-conformity is associated with an adult homosexual outcome has been replicated in a series of studies (Rieger et al. 2008; Li et al. 2017).

As gender-identity beliefs became culturally entrenched, academic literary critics set about rereading feminist children's literature to fit the new ideology. Children's literature expert Charles (later Catherine) Butler applies gender-identity theory to *Bill's New Frock*, noting that 'the narrative refers to Bill by male pronouns throughout, *even though both he and other characters acknowledge that he is a girl*' (Butler 2009, 11, my emphasis). Armed with the concept of gender identity, Butler reads Fine's feminist fable as a flawed psychological text. Missing the point of Fine's story, he argues that because Bill is treated as a girl in the novel, the narrative should call him a girl. He criticises Fine for rendering 'the experience of being female as more or less uniformly disempowering, unpleasant, and (as far as a boy is concerned) humiliating' (Butler 2009, 11). This is a misreading: the girls in the story show agency, conspiring to rig success for a disabled boy in the class sports. Bill has a terrible day because (unlike the actual girls) he conforms to gender stereotypes: the 'other girls' turn up in an assortment of clothes: Flora wears trousers and a blue blouse, Kirsty jeans and a shirt. Bill's day as a girl also introduces him to the pleasures of female culture: forced to read *Bunty*, he discovers that girls' comics are full of mischief. Butler is correct that 'Bill is effectively policed into femininity from without – . . . – rather than being driven by any subjective identification as female' (Butler, 2009, 16). But that is because Bill does not identify as female. Neither do the girls: they are simply female. Butler prefers Louis Sachar's 2010 *Marvin Redpost: Is He a Girl?* because (in Butler's words) it describes a boy who 'daydreams about having long hair, imagining the feel of it falling over his face', who 'finds that the voice in his own head is "a girl's voice"' (Butler 2009, 14). This recalls Julia Serano's 2007 *Whipping Girl: A Transsexual Woman on Sexism and the Scapegoating of Femininity* which defines femininity in terms of gender stereotypes (in this case the pink dress, the loss of agency and the denigration of female imagination). To illustrate what he sees as the limitations of second-wave feminism, Charles Butler (2009) quotes from Susan Griffin's 1970s' poem 'An Answer to a Man's Question, "What Can I Do About Women's Liberation?"' which tells a male interlocutor to 'Wear a dress':

> Borrow a child and stay in the house all day with the child,
> or go to the public park with the child, and take the child
> to the welfare office and cry and say your man left you and
> be humble and wear your dress and your smile, and don't talk
> back, keep your dress on, cook more nice dinners, stay
> away from Telegraph Avenue, *and still, you won't know the
> half of it, not in a million years.* (6, Butler's emphasis)

This is a failure of humanism, Butler suggests, because it denies the ability of men to fully comprehend the female experience. But his own reading tends to corroborate Griffin's point because he notices the dress but ignores the child (mentioned four times in the first two lines). From a feminist perspective, it is the work of caring for children – not the gendered clothing associated with this work – which limits women's lives.

As Charles Butler's work shows, gender-identity theory is incompatible with second-wave feminism. It also denies the link between gender nonconformity and later same-sex attraction. In doing so, it reverses progress achieved since the AIDS crisis of the 1980s and the backlash against tolerance of homosexuality. In the UK, Section 28 of the Local Government Act passed in 1988 prohibited 'the teaching of the acceptability of homosexuality as a pretended family relationship' in councils and schools. After the repeal of Section 28 in 2000 (England and Wales) and 2003 (Scotland), there were new attempts to encourage positive representations of homosexuality in education. The 'No Outsiders' project – funded by one of the UK's major research funding bodies, the Economic and Social Research Council, in 2006 – aimed to challenge the exclusive representation of heterosexual relationships in schools (Atkinson 2009). But by 2016 the emphasis shifted from sexual orientation to gender identity on the grounds that children no longer need to be taught that 'gay and lesbian men and women exist' (Moffat 2016, 2). In 2015, Stonewall added T to LGB and the politicising of transgender identities moved stage centre in the UK (Jones, this volume; Freedman and Auchmuty, this volume).

The shift from sexual orientation to gender identity can be seen in a 2015 novel aimed at teenage readers: Lisa Williamson's (2015) *The Art of Being Normal* is dedicated to '[t]he magnificent Gender Identity Development Service team at [t]he Tavistock Centre, past and present' (357). Williamson worked as an administrator at the Tavistock from 2010 onwards, and her book reveals some of the issues which have subsequently damaged the reputation of the Gender Identity Development Service, including a failure to provide adequate accounts of the medical effects of puberty blockers and the failure to explore sexual orientation (Biggs, this volume). *The Art of Being Normal* tells a story about the awakening of adolescent sexuality. Two young people who attend the same school narrate the story in alternating first-person sections: 14-year-old David identifies as a girl called Melissa but has not come out to his middle-class parents, and 15-year-old Leo is a natal girl who identifies as a boy and comes from a troubled working-class home. Leo is on puberty blockers and attends school in 'stealth' (no one knows that Leo was born female). Both are same-sex-attracted. David tells us:

> I have loved Zachary Olsen ever since we shared the same paddling pool, aged four. The fact I was once in such close proximity to his semi-naked body is sometimes too much to bear (33).

Leo longs to take his friendship with Alicia a step further:

> All I can think about is kissing Alicia and my hands on her bare back and how this is the best moment of my life bar none. And she's making all these *mmmmmm* noises and then she's kissing my neck and breathing, 'Oh Leo,' and my God, I'm so turned on it's unreal'. (154)

But the narrative rejects the possibility that David might be gay, or Leo a lesbian. Leo's story also presents an unrealistic picture of puberty blockers. GnRH agonists are used to halt the progress of puberty in transgender children and mask sexual feelings. These drugs are used off-licence with children but are licensed to suppress sexual fantasy and urges in adult sex offenders 'with the highest risk of sexual recidivism' (Sauter et al. 2021). Despite this, Leo is presented as hyper-masculine: highly sexed, impulsive, physical, good at maths, taciturn, just as David is presented as hyper-feminine: interested in clothes, empathetic, bad at maths, cautious.

The Art of Being Normal (Williamson, 2015) reveals the widespread view at the time that transgender children are the new frontier for social liberation. On the cover, children's author Philip Pullman describes it as '[a] life-changing and life-saving book', gesturing towards the widely held belief that the medical transition of children with gender dysphoria reduces suicidality. Inside, the book contains an endorsement from Amnesty International which states that '[s]exuality and gender identity are often confused'. But Williamson's (2015) book could equally be viewed as both homophobic and medically illiterate. The novel casts same-sex attraction as transgenderism and presents puberty blockers as the route to hot adolescent sex. As is characteristic of gender-identity literature, Williamson relies uncritically on gender (and class) stereotypes to portray David's femininity and Leo's masculinity.

Perhaps the clearest demonstration of the hegemony of gender-identity ideology at the end of the second decade of the twenty-first century is provided by the critical response to Jessica Love's 2018 picture book *Julian Is a Mermaid* (published as *Julián Is a Mermaid* in the US; Love, 2019). This beautifully illustrated picture book tells the story of a 'boy named Julian' who loves swimming and mermaids. The book makes no explicit statement about gender identity and uses natal pronouns. Yet it offers a series of clues which allow the reader to interpret Julian as transgender: 'A children's picture book about a trans mermaid called Julian has won the prestigious Klaus Flugge prize' was the *Pink News* headline in September 2019. It is the assumption that Julian is transgender that allows the description of the book as 'groundbreaking' even while it reprises the familiar trope of the boy in the dress.

Jessica Love has no need to spell out gender identity in order to present Julian as a transgender child. Instead, she depends on mobilizing culturally potent symbols associated with transgender children. Love's original plan was to represent a child's fascination with drag queens but after visiting chat rooms for parents of trans children she found that mermaids 'have become symbolic to transgender people' (Flood 2019). The association stretches back to 1994 when a new support group for parents of children attending the GIDS service chose the name Mermaids because 'male to female children quite often expressed a fascination' with these fabled creatures (Griffiths 2018, 90). *I Am Jazz* includes a page of mermaids with the words: 'Most of all, I love mermaids. Sometimes I wear a mermaid tail in the pool!' As a symbol for the transgender child, the mermaid announces that gender identity has nothing to do with sexual orientation: 'they are depicted as nothing below their waist but a tail' (Flood 2019). It reconceives femininity in terms of Disney's 1989 *The Little Mermaid* to create an image of childhood that is heterosexual, gender-conforming and sexless – an apt image for the puberty-blocked child.

The success of *Julian Is a Mermaid* (fully justified by the illustrations) owes something to an adult reading of the story. Where a child might view the scene in which Julian turns a curtain into a mermaid costume as imaginative play, an adult might also detect a reference to the moment in *Whipping Girl* when Serano ([2007] 2016), coming back from school, 'found myself inexplicably compelled to remove a set of white, lacy curtains from the window and wrap them around my body like a dress' (79). According to Serano, this is a gender-identity signal, a sign of 'subconscious sex'. A child reader of Love's story might assume that the women dressed as mermaids on the subway are women dressed as mermaids. The adult reader may realise that the mermaids in the story are transvestites (like Disney's figure of Ursula, based on the drag artist Divine). In a culture fascinated by the figure of the transgender child, Julian's future is already foreclosed. We expect that he will be transitioned before puberty.

One reason why the shift from second-wave feminism to gender-identity ideology in children's books has gone unremarked is that many gender-identity texts start from or incorporate a second-wave feminist explanation of gender. But they pivot into an explanation which is incompatible with the earlier model. And that's because gender-identity ideology emerges from some strands in second-wave feminism: having separated sex and gender, some – following Judith Butler – went on to throw away sex, leaving the culturally constructed 'gender' as the sole referent. Take for instance *Are You a Boy or Are You a Girl?* (Savage and Fisher 2017), a picture book for ages three and over. A child called Tiny encounters and challenges stereotypes: 'My sister is a cowboy', 'When we get home, Dad is back from work and is cooking dinner'. The feminist critique of sex role stereotypes has become common sense in this kind of literature – in theory if not in the playground. What marks this book out as 2017 is that Tiny is repeatedly asked, 'Are you a boy or are you a girl?' This question belongs to playground gender policing, aimed at children and young people perceived to be gay. It is also the title of a 1965 song by the American band The Barbarians, which gave voice to new possibilities of androgynous clothes and haircuts for young people. But the 2017 children's book ends with links to groups which support medical gender transition: GIRES (the Gender Identity Research and Education Society), Mermaids (a support group for children and teenagers with gender identity issues) and My Genderation (a film project run by young trans people; Davies-Arai and Matthews, 2019, 206). The conclusion, unstated but unavoidable, is that gender fluidity leads to the clinic.

Conclusion

This chapter has argued that the 'transgender child' is an invention of the twenty-first century, born out of a new understanding of childhood and made possible by technological innovation. This new figure appears in 2008 in books written by adults for children. In 2014, *Transgender Studies Quarterly* described the transgender child as a 'relatively new social form' and found 'no references to transgender children prior to the mid-1990s' (Meadow, 2014, 57). But just as critics like Catherine Butler reread texts by second-wave authors through a gender identity lens, so historians have searched hospital archives for evidence to fit twenty-first-century categories. Historian Jules Gill Peterson (2018) explains that the choice of the term 'Trans' is political: 'While it is technically anachronistic to name a child in 1930 "trans," I do so precisely to make an intervention' (2018, 8). Bernice Hausman (1995) claimed that 'as a myth, gender depends upon a history that is erased in the process of signification and a meaning that is naturalised in the moment of its elaboration' (190). This isn't the first time that children's literature has been mobilised to provide support for medical intervention: in 1929, James Barrie gifted the copyright to *Peter Pan, or the Boy Who Wouldn't Grow Up* to support the work of Great Ormond Street children's hospital (Rose 1993, 1). Following stage conventions of the time, Peter Pan has been played by a female actress from the first stage production in 1904. In the theatre, it is the belief in fairies voiced by the audience that saves the life of Tinkerbell. As gender-identity theory comes to dominate children's literature, the history of childhood is rewritten and the possibilities envisioned by second-wave feminists forgotten. In its place, medical intervention for gender non-conformity becomes a part of childhood fantasy.

References

'About Bill's New Frock'. n.d. https://www.annefine.co.uk/books/billsnew.php. Accessed 03.12.2021.

Alexander, Sally. 2012. 'Primary Maternal Preoccupation: D.W. Winnicott and Social Democracy in Mid Twentieth Century Britain'. In *History and Psyche: Culture, Psychoanalysis and the Past*, edited by Sally Alexander and Barbara Taylor, pp. 149–172. New York: Palgrave Macmillan.

Ariès, Philippe. 1996. *Centuries of Childhood*, with a new introduction by Adam Phillips. London: Pimlico.

Atkinson, Elizabeth. 2009. 'No Outsiders: Researching Approaches to Sexualities Equality in Primary Schools: Full Research Report ESRC End of Award Report'. Economic and Social Research Council.

Barrie, James M. 2004. *Peter Pan*. New York: Penguin Books.

Bartholomaeus, Clare and Damien W. Riggs. 2019. '"Girl Brain . . . Boy Body": Representations of Trans Characters in Children's Picture Books'. In *The Emergence of Trans: Cultures, Politics and Everyday Lives*, edited by Ruth Pearce, Igi Moon, Kat Gupta, and Deborah Lynn Steinberg, pp. 135–149. London: Routledge.

Bem, Sandra Lipsitz. 1993. *The Lenses of Gender: Transforming the Debate on Sexual Inequality*. New Haven, CT: Yale University Press.

Bryant, Karl. 2006. 'Making Gender Identity Disorder of Childhood: Historical Lessons for Contemporary Debates'. *Sexuality Research and Social Policy* 3(3): pp. 23–39. https://doi.org/10.1525/srsp.2006.3.3.23.

Butler, Catherine. 2020. 'Portraying Trans People in Children's and Young Adult Literature: Problems and Challenges'. *Journal of Literary Education* 3: p. 10. https://doi.org/10.7203/JLE.3.15992.

Butler, Charles. 2009. 'Experimental Girls: Feminist and Transgender Discourses in *Bill's New Frock* and *Marvin Redpost: Is He a Girl?*' *Children's Literature Association Quarterly*: pp. 3–20. https://doi.org/10.1353/chq.0.1889

Butler, Judith. 1986. 'Sex and Gender in Simone de Beauvoir's Second Sex'. *Yale French Studies* 72: pp. 35–49. https://doi.org/10.2307/2930225.

Colapinto, John. 1998. 'The True Story of John/Joan'. *Rolling Stone*, 11 December, pp. 54–97.

Colapinto, John. (2000) 2006. *As Nature Made Him: The Boy Who Was Raised as a Girl*. 1st Harper Perennial edition. New York: Harper Perennial.

Cortez, Marina, Gaudenzi, Paula, and Ivia Maksud. 2019. 'Gender: Pathways and Dialogues between Feminist and Biomedical Studies from the 1950s to 1970s'. *Physis: Revista de Saude Coletiva* 29(1). https://doi.org/10.1590/s0103-73312019290103

Davies-Arai, Stephanie and Matthews, Susan. 2019. 'Queering the Curriculum: Creating Gendered Subjectivity in Resources for Schools'. In *Inventing Transgender Children and Young People*, edited by Michele Moore and Heather Brunskell-Evans, pp. 199–217. Newcastle, UK: Cambridge Scholars Publishing.

Delemarre-van de Waal, Henrietta A. and Cohen-Kettenis, Peggy T. 2006. 'Clinical Management of Gender Identity Disorder in Adolescents: A Protocol on Psychological and Paediatric Endocrinology Aspects'. *European Journal of Endocrinology* 155(suppl. 1): pp. S131–S137. https://doi.org/10.1530/eje.1.02231.

Di Ceglie, Domenico. 2009. 'Between Scylla and Charybdis: Exploring Atypical Gender Identity Development in Children and Adolescents'. In *Transvestism, Transsexualism in the Psychoanalytic Dimension*, edited by G. Ambrosio, pp. 55–71. London: Routledge. doi:10.4324/9780429484261-3.

Del Giudice, Marco. 2012. 'The Twentieth Century Reversal of Pink-Blue Gender Coding: A Scientific Urban Legend?' *Archives of Sexual Behavior* 41: pp. 1321–1323.

Di Ceglie, Domenico. 2018. 'The Use of Metaphors in Understanding Atypical Gender Identity Development and Its Psychosocial Impact'. *Journal of Child Psychotherapy* 44: pp. 1–24. https://doi.org/10.1080/0075417X.2018.1443151.

Dworkin, Andrea. 1974. *Woman Hating*. New York: Penguin.

Ehrensaft, Diane. 2011. 'Boys Will Be Girls, Girls Will Be Boys: Children Affect Parents as Parents Affect Children in Gender Nonconformity'. *Psychoanalytic Psychology* 28(4): pp. 528–548. https://doi.org/10.1037/a0023828

Ewert, Marcus and Ray, Rex 2008. *10,000 dresses*. 1st ed. New York: Seven Stories Press.

Feinberg, Leslie. 1992. *Transgender Liberation: an idea whose time has come*. New York: World View Forum.

Fine, Anne and Beech, Mark. 2017. *Bill's New Frock*. London: HarperCollins Children's Books.

Flood, Alison. 2019. '"I Am Proven Joyously Wrong": Picture Book about Trans Child Wins Major Prize amid Moral Panic'. *The Guardian*, 11 September.

Friedan, Betty. (1963) 2010. *The Feminine Mystique*. London: Penguin.

Francis, Becky, Skelton, Christine and Archer, Louise. 2002. 'A systematic review of classroom strategies for reducing stereotypical gender constructions among girls and boys in mixed-sex UK primary schools (EPPI-Centre Review, version 1.1*)'. In: Research Evidence in Education Library. London: EPPI-Centre, Social Science Research Unit, Institute of Education.

https://eppi.ioe.ac.uk

Gill-Peterson, Jules. 2018. *Histories of the Transgender Child*. Minneapolis: University of Minnesota Press.

Green, Richard. 1987. *The Sissy Boy Syndrome: The Development of Homosexuality*. New Haven, CT: Yale University Press.

Griffiths, Margaret. 2018. 'Where Do the Mermaids Stand?' In *Trans Britain: Our Journey from the Shadows*, edited by Christine Burns, pp. 82–91. London: Unbound.

Groves, Nancy. 2014. 'David Walliams and Quentin Blake: How We Made *The Boy in the Dress*'. *The Guardian*, 7 July.

Hausman, Bernice. L. 1995. *Changing Sex: Transsexuality, Technology and the Idea of Gender*. Durham, NC: Duke University Press.

Herthel, J., Jennings, J. and McNicholas, S. 2014. *I Am Jazz!* New York: Dial Books.

Herzog, Ricky. 2009. 'Sissies, Dolls, And Dancing: Children's Literature and Gender Deviance in the Seventies". *The Lion and the Unicorn* 33(1): pp. 60–76. https://doi.org/10.1353/uni.0.0444.

Joyce, Helen. 2021. *Trans: When Ideology Meets Reality*. London: One World.

Li, Gu, Kung, Karson T.F. and Hines, Melissa. 2016. 'Childhood Gender-Typed Behavior and Adolescent Sexual Orientation: A Longitudinal Population-Based Study'. *Developmental Psychology* 53: pp. 764–777.

Love, Jessica. 2019. *Julian Is a Mermaid*. London: Walker Books.

Malcom, Nancy L. and Sheahan, Nicole. 'From *William's Doll* to *Jacob's New Dress*: The Depiction of Gender Non-Conforming Boys in Children's Picture Books From 1972 to 2014'. *Journal of Homosexuality* 66(7): pp. 914–936. https://doi.org/10.1080/00918369.2018.1484635

Meadow, Tey. 2011. '"Deep Down Where the Music Plays": How Parents Account for Childhood Gender Variance'. *Sexualities* 14(6): pp. 725–747. https://doi.org/10.1177/1363460711420463.

Meadow, Tey. 2014. 'Child'. *TSQ: Transgender Studies Quarterly* 1(1–2): pp. 57–59. https://doi.org/10.1215/23289252-2399596.

Millett, Kate. (1969) 1997. *Sexual Politics*. London: Virago Press.

Moffat, Andrew. 2016. *No Outsiders in our School: Teaching the Equality Act in Primary Schools*. London: Speechmark.

Money, John and Ehrhardt, Anke A. 1973. *Man and Woman, Boy and Girl: Gender Identity from Conception to Maturity*. Northvale, NJ: Jason Aronson Inc.

Nel, Philip. 2015. 'When Will the Children Be Free?: Looking Back on "Free to Be . . . You and Me"'. *Women's Studies Quarterly* 43(1/2): pp. 282–286.

Oakley, Ann. 2005. *The Ann Oakley Reader: Gender, Women, and Social Science*. Bristol, UK: Policy Press.

Paoletti, Jo B. 1987. 'Clothing and Gender in America: Children's Fashions, 1890–1920'. *Signs: Journal of Women in Culture and Society* 13(1): pp. 136–143.

Paoletti, Jo B. 2012. *Pink and Blue: Telling the Boys from the Girls in America*. Bloomington and Indianapolis: Indiana University Press.

Rieger, Gerulf et al. 2008. 'Sexual Orientation and Childhood Gender Nonconformity: Evidence from Home Videos'. *Developmental Psychology* 44(1): pp. 46–58. https://doi.org/10.1037/0012-1649.44.1.46

Reischel, Julia. 2006. 'See Tom Be Jane'. *Village Voice*, 30 May. https://www.villagevoice.com/2006/05/30/see-tom-be-jane/.

Rose, Jacqueline. 1993. *The Case of Peter Pan, or, The impossibility of Children's Fiction*. Philadelphia: University of Pennsylvania Press.

Rousseau, Jean-Jacques. (1762) 1979. *Emile: or, On Education*. Translated by Allan Bloom. New York: Basic Books.

Sachar, Louis. [2004] 2010. *Marvin Redpost: Is He a Girl?* London: Bloomsbury.

Sadjadi, Sahar. 2019. 'Deep in the Brain: Identity and Authenticity in Pediatric Gender Transition'. *Cultural Anthropology* 34(1): pp. 103–129. https://doi.org/10.14506/ca34.1.10.

Sauter, Julia et al. 2021. 'Testosterone-Lowering Medication and Its Association with Recidivism Risk in Individuals Convicted of Sexual Offenses'. *Sexual Abuse* 33(4): pp. 475–500. https://doi.org/10.1177/1079063220910723.

Savage, Sarah and Fisher, Fox. 2017. *Are You a Boy or Are You a Girl?* London: Philadelphia: Jessica Kingsley Publishers.

Schiller, Rebecca. 2019. 'Why the mother who started gender reveal parties regrets them'. *The Guardian*, 28 October 2019. https://www.theguardian.com/lifeandstyle/2019/oct/20/why-the-mother-who-started-gender-reveal-parties-regrets-them

Sedgwick, Eve Kosofsky. 1991. 'How to Bring Your Kids Up Gay: The War on Effeminate Boys'. In *Curiouser: On the Queerness of Children*, edited by Steven Bruhm and Natasha Hurley, pp. 139–149. Minneapolis: University of Minneapolis Press.

Serano, Julia. (2007) 2016. *Whipping Girl: A Transsexual Woman on Sexism and the Scapegoating of Femininity*. Berkeley, CA: Seal Press.

Tuerk, Catherine. 2011. 'Considerations for Affirming Gender Nonconforming Boys and Their Families: New Approaches, New Challenges'. *Child and Adolescent Psychiatric Clinics of North America* 20(4): pp. 767–777. https://doi.org/10.1016/j.chc.2011.07.005.

Walliams, David. (2008) 2013. *The Boy in the Dress*. Illustrated by Quentin Blake. London: HarperCollins Children's Books.

Williamson, Lisa 2015. *The Art of Being Normal*. Oxford: David Fickling Books.

Winnicott, Donald W. (1960) 1965. 'Ego Distortion in Terms of True and False Self'. In *The Maturational Processes and the Facilitating Environment: Studies in the Theory of Emotional Development*, pp 140–152. New York: International Universities Press, Inc.

Zolotow, Charlotte and Du Bois, William. P. 1972. *William's Doll*. New York: HarperCollins Publishers.

14
SEX, GENDER IDENTITY AND SPORT

Cathy Devine

> Sport . . . is the paragon of body-subject. Patriarchal culture, on the other hand, has defined women as other or object, more specifically body-object. What follows for women and sport is that a culture that defines sport as body-subject and woman as body-object forces an incompatibility between women and sport.
> —Hall (1990, 235)

Most sports are sex-affected which means the sex-linked advantage enjoyed by males as a result of androgenisation, primarily at puberty, necessitates dedicated female categories. This is a prerequisite for equal sporting opportunities for girls and women. Human sexual dimorphism gifts males a sport-dependent 10–30 percent puberty-related advantage in most sports (Hilton and Lundberg 2021). As a consequence, the ideological and theoretical project to overwrite sex with gender identity impacts disproportionately on girls and women, who are already significantly under-represented, particularly in competitive sport.

This asymmetrical impact is illustrated by the evidence that transmen, who are uncompetitive against males, generally remain in female categories in order to retain a competitive career. In contrast, transwomen, if eligibility criteria permit, invariably transition into female categories where retained puberty-related male advantage gifts them significant performance advantages as a result of their sex. This means girls and women are losing out on rankings, selection, qualification (for heats and finals in local, regional, national, international and Olympic events), podium places, medals, prize money and career opportunities in sport. Furthermore, women's records set by transwomen may be impossible for female athletes to reach.

This chapter analyses the significant impact of gender-identity theory, first, on sport scholarship and, second, on sport policy. The study of sport spans the academic disciplines. This chapter adopts a multidisciplinary approach drawing primarily on feminist political philosophy, human rights and the sociology of sport whilst also being informed by the biological sciences and the reality of the biological differences between the two sexes. Given the views of female athletes are often missing in this policy arena, I include some of my own data, which present invaluable testimony from female Olympians. The philosophers whose work I use are second-wave materialist feminists. They understand that biological sex differences, and economic and political life, do not owe their existence to ideology, although they are influenced by it (Todd, this volume). The feminist political philosophy of Pateman (1988), Lister (2003) and Fraser (2008) offers a conceptual context in which to assess the extent to which girls and women have equal rights in sport.

Historical Exclusion

Pateman's (1988) classic text *The Sexual Contract* argues that historically, the very legitimacy of civil government has been based on the gendered construction of a hierarchical difference between the sexes. As she puts it, 'the contract establishes men's political right over women' (2). Therefore, women do not have 'property in the person', bodily autonomy or self-determination. Lister (2003) argues that universality masks androcentric citizenship so that 'behind the cloak of gender-neutrality . . . [there is] a definitely male citizen, and it is his interests and concerns that have traditionally dictated the agenda' (4). Furthermore, citizenship or even personhood involves both *status* as membership of a community and *practice* as political participation or 'voice' (Lister 2003). Finally, Fraser's (2008) concept of justice necessitates interrogation of the mapping of political space. She argues that 'all those affected by a given social structure or institution have moral standing as subjects of justice in relation to it' (24). Fraser's justice requires recoupling the inextricably linked components of cultural recognition, political representation and economic redistribution. This chapter assesses whether women and girls have equal rights and full inclusion in sport by evaluating how far they enjoy bodily autonomy, voice, recognition, representation and redistribution.

Construction of Difference between the Sexes

Historically, sport has been an important space for the ideological project to naturalise, reinforce and reproduce socio-culturally constructed differences between the sexes, mediated through class and race. Sport has long been considered the natural preserve of males, constructing them as active body-subjects and essentialising hegemonic masculinity (leadership, aggression, competition, physical *and therefore* moral superiority) as an inherent property of maleness (Birrell 2000; Bryson 1987). In contrast, girls and women have been constructed as passive body-objects, and the naturalisation, reinforcement and reproduction of hegemonic femininities (followers, carers, cooperators, nurturers, decorative, physical *and therefore* moral inferiority) are considered incompatible with sport.

Bodily Autonomy and Self-Determination

The extent to which girls and women have been denied bodily autonomy, self-determination and recognition as athletes and sports participants has been mapped by second-wave feminist sport scholars (Bryson 1987; Hall 2016; Hargreaves 1994). The early 20th-century zeitgeist was exemplified by Baron Pierre de Coubertin (1912), founder of the modern Olympic movement who believed, 'this feminine semi-Olympiad is impractical, uninteresting, ungainly, and . . . improper. It is not in keeping with my concept of the Olympic Games . . . the solemn and periodic exaltation of male athleticism . . . with the applause of women as a reward' (713). This aligned with the views of well-known gynaecologist Sellheim, (1931, cited in Drinkwater 2000, 11), who maintained 'femininity and masculine build are contradictions. . . . Too frequent exercise, as practised by males, will lead to masculinisation. . . . The female abdominal organs wither and the artificially created virago is complete'.

Feminist sport scholars uncovered the underpinning relationships of power between the sexes, as female sporting pioneers struggled for recognition, inclusion and female categories. Endurance sports were considered particularly unsuited to women, and Drinkwater (2000) outlines two legendary attempts to run the male-only Boston Marathon, by Roberta Gibb in 1966 – without a start number – and Katherine Switzer in 1967. Switzer entered formally by initialling her first names and a race official was so incensed to see a woman racing, he attempted to remove her by force. Not until 1972 were women formally admitted to the Boston Marathon, whereas at the Olympics, the marathon for women was not introduced until 1984.

Androcentric Citizenship

In the face of women's exclusion from male governance structures, women set up their own. However, as women's sport gained recognition, men's governing bodies stepped in to administer it. As Hargreaves (1994) documents, the Fédération Sportive Féminine Internationale (FSFI) organised an alternative Olympics in Paris, Gothenburg, Prague and London, in 1922, 1926, 1930 and 1934, respectively. But only when the all-male International Amateur Athletic Federation which became the International Association of Athletics Federations (IAAF) agreed to take control was women's athletics considered for the Olympics and 'the lure of the Olympics . . . was now the bait for women to surrender control to the IAAF, in exchange for a recommendation that female athletic events be put on the next Olympic programme' (213). However,

> the FSFI made a fundamental compromise. It was a decision surrounded by controversy, and in protest at the limited number of events, British women athletes,

strongly supported by their male colleagues, boycotted the new track and field programme for women at the 1928 Amsterdam Olympic Games. (213, 214)

Similarly, between 1985 and 2000 UK Sports Councils were instrumental in driving what became 'takeovers', whereby female administrators were forced to 'cede governance of their sports to male-run bodies whose priority and focus remained men's sport' (Nicholson 2022, 51). This paralleled equivalent international mergers which effectively sacrificed female autonomy and substituted male control. Lapchick et al. (2016) reveal the significant degree to which international sport remains androcentric since in 2016 'women held 117 (14.5 percent) of the 805 leadership positions for International Federations (IFs)' (7) and 14 IFs including FIFA, IAAF, World Rugby and the International Swimming Federation (10) had executive committees which included no women.

It is against this backdrop that the claims of gender-identity theorists, activists and transgender interest organisations manifest in sport. This is primarily in sports which are significantly sex-affected and remain heavily male-dominated. Figure 14.1 shows the sex gap in sports participation where competition is integral to the activity.

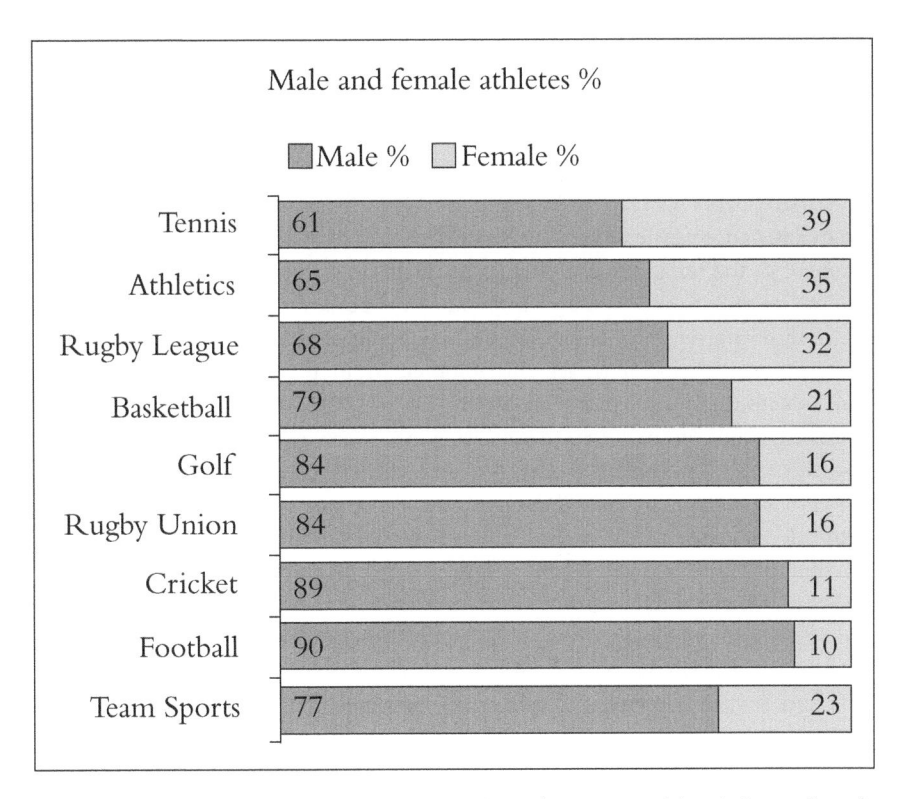

Male and female athletes %

■ Male % □ Female %

Sport	Male %	Female %
Tennis	61	39
Athletics	65	35
Rugby League	68	32
Basketball	79	21
Golf	84	16
Rugby Union	84	16
Cricket	89	11
Football	90	10
Team Sports	77	23

FIGURE 14.1 The sex gap in sports participation where competition is integral to the activity. (Data: Devine 2021b, visuals: Emma Hilton)

In essence, gender-identity theorists and activists argue, campaign and lobby for eligibility criteria for single-sex sport categories based on internal subjective gender identities rather than the material reality of sex, even in sex-affected sports.

Theoretical Debates

Sex and Gender

Biological scientists understand humans as sexually dimorphic and occasionally use *gender* as a synonym for *sex* but more usually refer accurately to sex (Bhargava et al. 2021; Heidari et al. 2016). The very small numbers of people with disorders/variations of sexual development (DSDs/VSDs) do not represent additional sexes and are usually easily classified as female or male (Hilton and Wright, this volume). As a consequence of sexual dimorphism, most sports are sex-affected, given clear performance-related male advantages as a result of androgenisation. Sex-affected sports are played in single-sex categories for the very purpose of including girls and women. Until the 1980s there was a narrowing of the performance gap as girls and women campaigned for progressive inclusion. However, '[a] stabilization of the gender [sex] gap in world records is observed after 1983' (Thibault et al 2010, 214), and consequently, 'the gap may be set' (221).

Feminist sport scholars have detailed how sport is inextricably linked to the ideological project to construct females as feminine: subordinate, emotional, gentle and passive and males as masculine: superior, rational, aggressive and active (Birrell 2000; Bryson 1987; Hall 1990; Hargreaves 1994). These stereotypes are essential to the maintenance of hierarchical, androcentric, patriarchal sport and damage the attainment of the broad physical literacy (Whitehead 2010), personhood and human flourishing of both sexes. Materialist feminists reject sex stereotypes but not human sexual dimorphism or an embodied understanding of gender as part of 'becoming' and written-in-the-body (Jones, this volume). Arguing otherwise reprises the substance dualism of minds and bodies.

Iris Marion Young's (1980) definitive essay 'Throwing Like a Girl' draws on de Beauvoir to explore 'woman's bodily existence'. It details ways in which gendered movement practices are *embodied* as an integral part of becoming a woman. Young acknowledges the 'real physical differences between men and woman in the kind and limit of their physical strength' and that 'any lived body exists as a material thing as well as a transcending subject' (142). It is therefore disappointing that 'throwing like a girl' is still used pejoratively, and/or that Young's work is appropriated to claim *all* differences between the sexes are the result of gendered practices, rather than biological sex. In actuality, as I have argued 'throwing like a girl',

> captures both the innate morphology, anatomy, physiology and biomechanics of females . . ., *and also at the same time*, the sociocultural-historical embodiment of gender. This occurs by way of the *interaction* of this underlying biology

with being-female-in-the-androcentric-world and becoming-woman-in-the-androcentric-world.

(Devine 2021b)

Gender Identity and Sex

Transgender rights activists and organisations have lobbied for the inclusion of natal males who identify as women in female sport. In response, biological scientists have attempted to devise scientific protocols which mitigate or eliminate male performance advantage via testosterone suppression. Often, mitigation rather than elimination has been considered a 'tolerable unfairness' or 'meaningful' competition by scientists and policymakers, if not by female athletes. However, two scientific reviews conclude that a significant male advantage remains. Harper (a transwoman) et al. (2021) explain 'strength may be well preserved in transwomen during the first three years of hormone therapy' (865), and Hilton and Lundberg (2021), that 'muscular advantage enjoyed by transgender women is only minimally reduced when testosterone is suppressed' (199). In contrast, transmen who have medically transitioned post-puberty are disadvantaged in male categories, since testosterone supplementation cannot reverse puberty.

Meanwhile, sport sociologists and philosophers have abandoned, or even reversed, the attempt by feminist scholars to liberate both females and males from gendered expectations in sport (Jones, this volume). This plays out in sports scholarship and sport policy in four linked stages.

Denying Human Sexual Dimorphism

Gender-identity theorists, usually with no biological science background, attempt to unsettle biological as well as socio-cultural differences between females and males in four ways: first, by conflating sex and gender; second, by conceptualising sex as a spectrum; third, by reversing sex and gender; finally and fourth, by claiming that because some females outperform some males due to the overlap in sport performance between the sexes, single-sex categories constitute 'coercive sex segregation'. *Sex* becomes socio-culturally constructed and coercively 'assigned at birth' whereas *gender identities* are innate and immutable (Jones, this volume). Single-sex categories in sex-affected sports are not biological categories recognising the material reality of sex but rather oppressive, patriarchal, ideological constructions. In this way, gender-identity theorists believe single-sex sport, rather than gender stereotypes, reproduces power differentials between, first, women and men (social categories now floating free of biological sex; Stock, this volume) and, second, so-called cisgender and transgender athletes.

The Canadian transgender academic Travers exemplifies this discourse by routinely conflating sex and gender. Travers (2008) claims sport has a 'powerful role in normalizing and legitimating the ideology of the two-*sex* system' (80, emphasis added) 'thereby institutionalizing and reinforcing *gender* inequality, homophobia and transphobia' (81, emphasis added). In consequence, 'this two-sex system is ideological rather than natural' (82). McDonagh and Pappano (2009), concur, arguing that '[a]thletics should be *gender*-neutral, a human activity and not a pumped-up, artificial rendition of men's strength and woman's weakness' (3, emphasis added). They reframe single-sex categories as 'coercive *sex* segregation' (6, emphasis added). As Jones argues (this volume), gender-identity ideology argues that sex is constructed in the interests of the powerful. Sport is understood as an important site for this construction.

McDonagh and Pappano (2009) are sex denialists rather than gender-identity theorists. Their influential text 'Playing with the Boys: Why Separate Is Not Equal in Sports', routinely conflates sex with gender:

Dividing sports by *sex* – segregating organised athletics based on *gender* – doesn't reliably reflect actual physical differences between males and females at all. Rather, it reflects antiquated social patterns and false beliefs. (x, emphasis added)

McDonagh and Pappano's admirable project is to assert the equal personhood of girls and women. However, they see no way to do so without denying the material reality of sexed bodies. They rightly explain, 'The assumption that women are physically different from men translates into the assumption that women are physically inferior to men' (x) but then proceed, stating, 'If women cannot compete fairly on the field, they cannot compete fairly off it either' (6). By fairness and equality here, they mean individual women 'competing up' in male categories.

This means that females are only considered physically active, powerful and strong to the extent that they match the androcentric male default rather than in their own right. Sex denialists and gender-identity theorists concur on this. Their approach measures female bodies against the male ideal, and the only route to equal personhood they offer is to deny the sport-relevant biological differences between the sexes.

Fairness and equality for sex denialists and gender-identity theorists mean one of three things: self-identification according to 'gender identity', or categories based on skill and talent rather than sex misunderstanding both human sexual dimorphism and statistical significance, and/or the eventual elimination of single-sex categories altogether once females have transcended their socio-culturally constructed 'physical inferiority' (Anderson and Travers 2017; Gleaves and Lehrbach 2016; McDonagh and Pappano 2009). Important to gender identity theory is the belief that heteronormative patriarchy has held back girls' and women's progress in sport (true) *and that therefore*, once girls and women are liberated from patriarchal oppression, regardless of the material reality of human sexual dimorphism, *'gender neutral' sport categories represent true equality in sport* (false).

For materialist feminists, females are not 'physically inferior' either. Their sex-linked physical capabilities differ significantly from those of males, because female sexed bodies have the biological capacity for conception, gestation, childbirth and lactation, but this does not equate with inferiority. And, crucially, female sexed bodies do not exclude females from full personhood.

Conflating Transgender Athletes and Athletes with DSDs

The claim by gender-identity theorists that sex is a spectrum is legitimised via a conflation of transgender athletes and athletes with DSDs. However, most transgender athletes do not have DSDs, and most athletes with DSDs are not transgender. DSDs are disorders/differences of female or male sexual development rather than additional sexes, and over 99.98 percent of people, including those with DSDs, are unproblematically classified at birth as female or male (Hilton and Wright, this volume). The instrumentalisation of DSD athletes to unsettle the sex binary supports the claim for transgender inclusion in opposite-sex categories.

This argument also fuels the contention that human sexual dimorphism and binary sex categories are an imposition of whiteness and colonialism (see Jones, this volume). In this vein, Anderson and Travers (2017) believe that '[a]ssumptions of unfair male advantage . . . lean heavily on a Western image of white, middle- and upper-class female frailty' (3). These beliefs lack evidence. They often rely on the testimony of athletes from the global south with XY DSD conditions involving androgenisation at puberty (Human Rights Watch [HRW] 2020). These athletes may be legally female having been assigned female at birth (sex is *observable* at birth in the vast majority of cases, but in the case of people with certain DSDs, it is *assigned*), but the Court of Arbitration for Sport (CAS, 2019a) describes how different these athletes are from natal females without these conditions:

> Individuals with 5-ARD have what is commonly identified as the male chromosomal sex (XY and not XX), male gonads (testes not ovaries) and levels of circulating testosterone in the male range (7.7–29.4 nmol/L), which are significantly higher than the female range (0.06–1.68 nmol/L). (131)

Tellingly, the testimony of black female athletes from the global South *without* these developmental conditions is never sought.

Routine sex verification procedures for elite female athletes initially introduced to detect males masquerading as female, and DSD athletes with significant androgenisation at puberty, have now been discontinued. Instead, 'relevant athletes' and national federations are required to advise governing bodies of their status (IAAF 2019). The argument that the now minimally invasive sex testing would contravene the human rights of female athletes (HRW 2020), is not supported by female athletes since

> all female athletes at the Atlanta Games were offered a questionnaire . . . asking whether in their view testing of females should be continued in future

240 Cathy Devine

> Olympics. . . . Of the 928 athletes who responded, 82 percent felt that testing should be continued and 94 percent indicated that they were not made anxious by the procedure.
>
> *(Elsas et al. 2000, 252)*

The reality of human sexual dimorphism is readily apparent in sport, and the assumption it relates to whiteness and colonialism is easily refuted, given the biological reality of the performance gap between female (black and white) and male (black and white) athletes. Table 14.1 gives the 2020 Tokyo Olympics 400m results. The female finalists were all black and five were from the global South. All would be beaten by male athletes in mixed-sex categories. Indeed, the iconic Shaunae Miller-Uibo, the fastest 400m female runner in the world in 2021, has a time beaten by 2047 ranked male runners in 2021 alone (World Athletics 2022).

Furthermore, athletes with XY DSDs and significant androgenisation are over-represented in elite sport (CAS 2019a) and took all three podium places in the 2016 Rio Olympic 800m (Snider-McGrath 2021). However, in 2019, World Athletics required 'athletes with "46 XY DSD"', who 'experience a "material androgenizing effect"', to lower testosterone to below 5nmol/l in 'restricted events' (the 400m, 800m and mile; CAS 2019b). This delayed an inevitable extension of the restriction to all events with a still lower ceiling of 2.5nmols/L in 2023. At the 2022 World Athletics Championships, Aminatou Seyni and Beatrice Masilingi, both athletes with XY DSDs, chose not to compete in their favourite 400m, a restricted event at the time requiring the 5nmols/L testosterone ceiling, and competed instead in the 200m. Both qualified for the semi-finals ahead of two Olympians, Shelly-Ann

TABLE 14.1 Tokyo Olympics: 400m Results (BBC, 2021a, 2021b)

Rank	Female Athlete	Time (s)	Country	Male Athlete	Time (s)	Country
1	Shaunae MILLER-UIBO	48.36	Bahamas	Steven GARDINER	43.85	Bahamas
2	Marileidy PAULINO	49.20	Dominican Republic	Anthony Jose ZAMBRANO	44.08	Colombia
3	Allyson FELIX	49.46	USA	Kirani JAMES	44.19	Grenada
4	Stephenie Ann MCPHERSON	49.61	Jamaica	Michael CHERRY	44.21	USA
5	Candice MCLEOD	49.87	Jamaica	Michael NORMAN	44.31	USA
6	Jodie WILLIAMS	49.97	Great Britain	Christopher TAYLOR	44.79	Jamaica
7	Quanera HAYES	50.88	USA	Isaac MAKWALA	44.94	Botswana
8	Roxana GOMEZ	DNF	Cuba	Liemarvin BONEVACIA	45.07	Netherlands

Fraser-Pryce, and Elaine Thompson-Herah, the 200m Olympic Champion (Ingle 2022), and Seyni just missed out on a podium place.

If single-sex sport was replaced by mixed-sex categories, there would be no female athletes in elite athletics. Furthermore, including either transwomen athletes or athletes with XY DSDs with androgenisation at puberty in female categories, affects both white and black athletes who are not transwomen and do not have these DSD conditions. Black female athletes, including those from the global South, are well represented in elite athletics and depend on female categories which exclude male advantage for their success. Indeed, Miller-Uibo has questioned why the 2019 World Athletics restrictions applied to 'just a few events and not straight across the board' (Ingle 2021a).

Without single-sex categories, the iconic sportswomen of their generations: Simone Biles, Shelly-Ann Fraser-Pryce, Althea Gibson, Sifan Hassan, Shaunae Miller-Uibo, Serena and Venus Williams would be erased from podiums, record books and television screens. Alternatively, if transwomen athletes, and/or XY DSD athletes with androgenisation at puberty, remain eligible for female categories this displaces biologically female athletes down the rankings, and from selection, qualification, podium places, medals, prize money and career opportunities in sport.

Balancing Values Instead of Balancing Rights

In sex-affected sports, female categories are designed to equally distribute the socio-cultural goods of sport to females as well as males. However, eligibility deliberations often attempt to 'balance' incommensurate values (inclusion, fairness, safety) rather than commensurate rights (of females and males). This involves technical attempts to 'balance' or 'rank' inclusion, fairness and safety, posited as being in tension. However, equal opportunities for girls and women, and therefore female inclusion, necessitate female-only sport categories and balancing values sets up a false opposition.

Attempts to frame inclusion as the inclusion of athletes with male advantage in female categories is another conceptual reversal. Inclusion narratives often apply asymmetrically to the inclusion of transwomen (biological males) in female categories, rather than female inclusion in sport. They conceal underpinning rights conflicts between the sexes. Including transwomen in female categories means they have two categories in which to participate (male and female), and females lose the one category designed to include them by excluding male advantage. For materialist feminists, this is an inclusion of the already included (males) in categories designed for the otherwise biologically excluded (females) and constitutes *unequal* opportunities on the basis of sex.

This sleight of hand is evident in both the 2021 International Olympic Committee (IOC) and the 2016 Canadian Centre for Ethics in Sport (CCES) transgender inclusion guidelines, which adopt a so-called (transgender) inclusion narrative. The CCES (2016) outlines '[t]he *inclusion-first philosophy* continues to apply when developing policy at the high-performance level' (17) so that 'trans athletes should be able to participate in the gender with which they identify, regardless of whether or not they have undergone hormone therapy'. (19) Some of the CCES reasoning is extraordinarily science-free, since for the CCES, 'transfemales are not males who became females. Rather these are people who have always been psychologically female but whose anatomy and physiology, *for reasons as yet unexplained,* have manifested as male' (20, emphasis added). Furthermore, '[w]hile we can observe that participants in men's sport, on average, out-perform participants in women's sport, current science *is unable to isolate why this is the case*' (20 emphasis added) Tellingly, both sets of guidelines advocate inclusion in opposite sex categories by way of gender identity primarily for transwomen, referred to by the CCES as 'transfemales' or 'trans women' – in other words, biological males. Even gender-identity theorists know that transmen (females) will be disadvantaged in male categories (20).

Sport and/or Gender Identity as a Human Right

Increasingly gender-identity theorists argue that recognition of gender identities in sport is a human right. This neatly sidesteps scientifically informed policy development altogether. Gleaves and Lehrman (2016) argue that the 'rationale for inclusion of transgender and intersex athletes must move beyond the idea of fairness' (323) to be 'unaffected by contingent appeals to science' (314). They ignore completely the rights claims of female athletes and advocate for transwomen and athletes with XY DSDs and significant androgenisation at puberty to be included in female categories. This represents a continuity with androcentric sports citizenship, since females are not recognised equally as athletes, decision-makers or stakeholders, and the focus is on the inclusion of biological males in female categories that were designed to exclude male advantage.

Notwithstanding the IOC assertion that 'sport is a human right', neither sport nor gender identity is recognised as a human right by the definitive International Bill of Human Rights (United Nations [UN] 1967). In contrast, rights on the basis of sex are referred to multiple times. Furthermore, the Convention on the Elimination of All Forms of Discrimination against Women (CEDAW; UN 1979) specifically addresses the human rights of women, referring to rights and freedoms 'without distinction of any kind, including distinction based on sex'. Article 13 requires states parties to 'take all appropriate measures to eliminate discrimination against women . . . to ensure, on a basis of equality of men and women, the same rights, in particular. . . . The right to participate in . . . sports'.

In contrast, 'gender reassignment' or 'gender identity' is incorporated into the legislation of some countries (e.g., Britain and Canada) as a protected characteristic, with, usually, recognition of the rights conflicts that may arise between people with different protected characteristics. This requires a consideration of the rights of female participants with the protected characteristic of 'sex' to equal opportunities in sport (as compared with male participants) and transgender athletes with the protected characteristic of 'gender reassignment' or 'gender identity' to equal opportunities in sport (as compared with athletes with different/no gender reassignment or gender identity) before introducing eligibility criteria for inclusion in opposite *sex* categories by way of *gender reassignment or identity*. It may well be that just as transmen generally compete in female categories without discrimination or harassment as a result of their gender identity, male sport should address discrimination and harassment against gender-non-conforming males participating in male categories and adopt strong anti-bullying policies.

Sport Policy, Sex and Gender Identity

Sport policy is a component of social policy and must work for girls and women as well as those with transgender identities. Robust policy processes which recognise competing rights can usefully be based on Fraser's 2008 principles of justice to address:

1. Recognition: of female people with sexed bodies, and of transgender people with a range of gender identities.
2. Representation: of female and transgender participants and athletes.
3. (Re)distribution: of participation and competition opportunities and resources, to female (from male) and transgender (from same-sex non-transgender) athletes, if either demographic is under-represented or under-resourced.

Recognition

Democratic governments are accountable to the electorate and girls' and women's rights as a sex, including in sport, often legally protected (Auchmuty and Freedman, this volume). However, governments increasingly 'contract out' sport policy development to unaccountable organisations, including national governing bodies of sport (NGBs), single-interest lobbying organisations and equality, diversity and inclusion 'specialists'. As Murray and Blackburn (2019) explain, this can result in 'losing sight of women's rights' leaving androcentric sport institutions intact. The UK 2013 'Transgender Inclusion Guidelines' (now superseded), involved consultation with five transgender interest groups but none representing female athletes (Devine, 2021b). Similarly, the CCES 2016 guidance solicited 'a formal survey of sport organizations and individuals known by the CCES to have an interest in the issue', but consultation with just two female athletes (5). CCES guidance conflates sex and gender throughout and claims 'notions of "male" and "female" are complex social constructs largely made up of two separate continuums that are often confused—that of sex and gender' (11).

Global sport governance is the domain of IFs and the IOC, and the accountability of these organisations is notoriously weak (Gauthier 2017). In this context, opportunities for global policy capture, prioritising transgender inclusion at the expense of women's rights, are widespread. At most, lip service is paid to human rights, by 'contracting out' responsibility to unaccountable neoliberal global organisations heavily funded by global capital. These include the US-based Shift (2022), self-branded 'the leading center of expertise on the UN Guiding Principles on Business and Human Rights', and the Centre for Sport and Human Rights (CSHR, 2022) conceived as 'a human rights organisation for the world of sport'. Both prioritise transgender inclusion and gender identity, in contrast with the International Bill of Human Rights which refers throughout to sex. Nevertheless,

> [f]rom 2019 to 2021, Shift supported the IOC in its process to update its position on eligibility criteria for gender-based [sic] competitive sport. Shift's role included: the design and facilitation of internal and external stakeholder consultations, including with affected athletes; expert guidance on the rights of transgender and intersex people; and support in developing the Framework on Fairness, Inclusion and Non-Discrimination on the Basis of Gender Identity and Sex Variations, which was ADOPTED in November 2021.
>
> *(Shift 2022)*

The IOC (2004, 2015, 2021) guidelines have progressively removed requirements for a medical or surgical transition of transwomen and shape the transgender policies of IFs. The current 2021 IOC Framework, whilst purporting to centre inclusion, human rights, fairness, robust evidence and athlete consultation, outlines there should be '*no presumption of advantage*' for transgender athletes (presumably transwomen) 'until evidence determines otherwise' (emphasis added). This should be data from high-performance transgender athletes on a sport-by-sport basis. In other words, the *presumption* of the well-evidenced male performance advantage (Harper et al. 2021; Hilton and Lundberg 2021) is reversed. IOC policy capture is further revealed in the startlingly transformed views of the IOC Medical and Scientific Director. In 2003, whilst at the British Olympic Association, Dr Richard Budgett wrote, '[t]he effect of allowing male transsexuals to compete as women would be to make competition unfair and potentially dangerous in some sports and would undermine women's sports' (Ingle 2021b). However, the 2021 IOC framework, presided over by Dr Budgett, now adopts the 'no presumption of advantage' position.

Asymmetrical recognition, inclusion, and rights narratives prioritising primarily male transgender identities are contrary to the International Bill of Human Rights. They elevate the rights of male transgender athletes (transwomen) over the rights of female athletes. Gender identity over-writes sex, and the unfair inclusion of transwomen in female categories in sex-affected sports has more political traction than equal opportunities for females. This new hierarchy of rights represents a continuity with androcentric sport governance, where the rights of females have always been secondary.

In the absence of IOC leadership, IFs and NGBs have developed a range of transgender inclusion strategies. Many still retain the legacy 2015 IOC scientific 'fix' of including transwomen in female categories based on testosterone suppression.

In 2015, the IOC specified a 10nmols/L ceiling for 1 year, but several IFs, including World Athletics in 2019 moved initially to 5nmols/L, and in 2022 the Union Cycliste Internationale (UCI) and World Triathlon reduced this further to 2.5nmols/L for 2 years. These policies disregard the clear scientific consensus that testosterone suppression minimally affects male advantage. In these sports, although transmen are eligible for male categories, sometimes following a risk assessment (of risk to the transman rather than the males), in reality, transmen and female non-binary athletes often delay medical transition and remain in female categories, given testosterone supplementation does not undo female competitive disadvantage.

During 2022, the increasing success of transwomen in female sport motivated a number of IFs, including FINA and the UCI, to reconsider their policies. The transgender swimmer Lia Thomas shot up the National Collegiate Athletics Association (NCAA) rankings following transitioning from male to female categories by 547, 61 and 13 places in the 200-, 500-, and 1650-yard events, respectively, between the 2018/19 and 2021/22 seasons (Senefeld et al. 2021). Thomas achieved number one rankings in female categories in both 200- and 500-yard events with times that threatened records of the iconic Missy Franklin and Katie Ledecky. In March 2022, Thomas won NCAA gold in the *women's* 500-yard freestyle ahead of Olympic medallists Emma Weyant, Erica Sullivan and Brooke Forde. Tellingly, at the same event, transman Iszac Henig (biologically female) placed joint fifth in the women's 100m freestyle. Henig explained: 'Coming out as a trans guy put me in a weird position. I could start hormones to align more with myself, or wait, transition socially, and keep competing on a women's swim team. I decided on the latter' (Cohen 2022). There has been widespread dissatisfaction amongst female swimmers, and triple Olympic gold medallist Nancy Hogshead-Makar coordinated two petitions signed by

> [o]ver 5446 athletes, parents, coaches and sports officials . . . including almost 300 Olympians and Paralympians' asking 'that legislative bodies and sports organizations ensure that females receive equal opportunities to participate in competitive sports, in the same fair and safe competitive environment as afforded to male athletes.
>
> *(Swimming World 2022)*

In the UK, transwoman Emily Bridges won bronze in the men's Team Pursuit and gold in the men's point race at the British Universities and Colleges Sport (BUCS) Championships in February 2022 but was listed in the women's category at the National Omnium Championships 2 months later. Bridges might have lined up against Dame Laura Kenny, Britain's joint most decorated female Olympian. But, amidst rumours of a boycott by British female riders and a Union Cycliste Feminine (UCF) letter to the UCI (2022), the UCI ruled Bridges ineligible. The UCF letter was signed by over 650 female cyclists and numerous Olympic medallists and Olympians, including Sara Symington, head of British Cycling's Olympic and Paralympic programme. In April, the UCI ruled Bridges ineligible for competition in female categories while still registered with British Cycling as a male and, in July, lowered the testosterone ceiling to 2.5nmols/L for 2 years (Thewlis, 2022).

Increasingly, both IFs and NGBs recognise the right of female participants to equal opportunities with males, rather than attempt to 'balance' values. First, World Rugby, then FINA and the International Rugby League, and now World Athletics just announced that they are offering female categories based on biological sex regardless of gender identity, and FINA is exploring additional categories options. World Rugby (2020a) states clearly that '[t]ransgender women who . . . have experienced the biological effects of testosterone during puberty and adolescence cannot currently play women's rugby'. Furthermore, NGBs, including USA Powerlifting (commendably in 2019 but then contested in 2023), the British Triathlon (2022a), the Rugby Football Union (2022) and the Rugby Football League (2022), all offer equal competitive opportunities to females via dedicated female categories. The Sports Council Equality Group (SCEG, 2021) Guidelines set the agenda in the UK and outline that 'fairness cannot be reconciled with self-identification into the female category in gender-affected sport' (7).

The FINA Policy (2022a) is ground-breaking in recognising the human rights of females to equality with males. FINA sets out three foundational human rights principles which have often been completely disregarded in transgender inclusion policies. First, no hierarchy of human rights, outlining that 'FINA is committed to providing safe, fair, inclusive, and non-discriminatory opportunities for all Aquatics athletes'; second, that inclusion is upheld via categories, which include participants who would be excluded in their absence explaining, '[w]ithout eligibility standards based on biological sex or sex-linked traits, we are very unlikely to see biological females in finals, on podiums, or in championship positions' and, crucially, that 'FINA's effort not to discriminate against female athletes and thus to ensure a sex-based women's category itself has exclusionary effects'; and, thirdly, equality of opportunity and non-discrimination on the basis of sex, setting out a commitment to, 'ensuring equal opportunity for both male and female athletes to participate and succeed in the sport, including through the equal representation in its programs and competitions of athletes of both biological sexes'.

FINA modelled a robust policy process (as did World Rugby) developed by a Working Group consisting of an Athlete Group, Science and Medicine Group, and Legal and Human Rights Group. Importantly, the Athlete Group 'was comprised of current and retired Aquatics athletes and coaches (including transgender athletes and coaches)' (FINA, 2022a 2), and the Legal and Human Rights Group 'was comprised of legal experts in *sex discrimination*, human rights, and international sports law, including the jurisprudence of the Court of Arbitration for Sport (CAS)' (3, emphasis added).

Representation

Whilst formal women's, human rights, and sport organisations funded by governments and global capital have almost unanimously reproduced and reinforced gender identity ideology (the IOC, Shift, the CSHR, HRW, the Women's Sports Foundation [WSF], Canadian Women and Sport [CWS], CCES), resistance to the erosion of female sport categories has come primarily from female athletes and grassroots women's organisations. These include Fair Play for Women (UK), Sex Matters (UK), Women's Sports Policy Working Group (WSPWG; US), Champion Women (US), Save Women's Sports (US, New Zealand, Spain) and the International Consortium on Female Sport.

In 2019, I asked 19 female Olympians for their views on the 2015 IOC Transgender guidelines (Devine 2021a). They thought both female and transgender athletes should be fairly included in elite sport but unanimously agreed that the scientific evidence shows transwomen have a competitive advantage. One athlete explained: 'I agree in principle that transgender athletes need support and protection to compete without discrimination, but this cannot be at the expense of female athletes' (344–345), and another commented, 'It is not right that females are disadvantaged by an altruistic desire to include transgender athletes under an unfair policy' (348).

Of extreme concern was that the majority felt that they could not discuss this issue without being labelled transphobic. One Olympian disclosed,

> In my role with a sporting organisation I have been advised to be careful about what I say on the matter. . . . Athletes are wary. I have been abused on social media for commenting on this issue. The abuse is generally vitriolic and aggressive.
> (Devine 2021a 351)

Another advised that 'consultation anonymously will be only way to get current (active sport career) females to speak up' (353).

This reveals the extent to which the inclusion and rights claims of males who identify as transgender (transwomen) have been prioritised by the IOC over and above those of females. One Olympian explained that '[n]ew guidelines do not level the playing field or protect equal opportunities for female athletes. . . . Our human rights to equal opportunities [are] not being protected' (Devine 2021a, 358). Another simply asked, 'Why don't women matter? . . . [T]o try and say this wouldn't disadvantage women in sport is a lie' (352). Given that they did not accept the inclusion of transwomen in female categories with no male advantage mitigation, the 2021 IOC guidelines outlining 'no presumption of advantage' are presumably totally unacceptable to them.

These findings are corroborated by a growing number of athlete consultations. World Rugby's elite female survey (World Rugby 2020b) found only a minority supported introducing the 2015 IOC guidelines (Women's Sevens World Series: 17 of 86, 20 percent; Women's Six Nations: 7 of 65, 11 percent; and other elite players: 10 of 29, 34 percent). FINA (2022b) found 84 percent of those surveyed thought eligibility for women's events should be based solely on birth sex, British Triathlon (2022b) found over 80 percent of 3167 members favoured a dedicated female category and Rugby Football Union (2022) received 11 000 responses but have not released a response breakdown. Furthermore, the SCEG (2021) consultation provided extensive qualitative evidence.

The British Olympic silver medallist swimmer Sharron Davies coordinated a letter to the IOC from 60 Olympians opposed to the 2015 IOC Guidelines (Davies 2022), and the WSPWG (2022) opposes 'the effort to disadvantage females by forcing them to compete against some trans athletes with male sex-linked physical advantages' whilst advocating for a third way. The WSPWG includes three female Olympians, including Martina Navratilova, supported by eight additional Olympians and three transgender athletes, including elite transwoman tennis player Renee Richards. Almost all elite female athletes who have commented publicly support the retention of female categories in elite sport. These include Olympians Paula Radcliffe and Mara Yamauchi, the UK's first- and third-fastest female marathon runners; Olympic silver medallist cyclist Alison Sydor; Olympic silver medallist swimmer Sharron Davies; tennis superstars Martina Navratilova and Chris Evert; triple Olympic gold medallist swimmer Nancy Hogshead-Makar and many more. It appears that the global sport governance infrastructure, including formal women's and human rights organisations, such as the WSF, CWS, CSHR and Shift, does not represent the female athletes whose rights they purport to uphold.

Opposition to the inclusion of transwomen in female categories has also come from a number of trans athletes including the Olympic decathlete Caitlyn (formally Bruce) Jenner, and Renee Richards (Devine 2021a).

Redistribution

The rights conflict between female inclusion via same-sex categories, and transwoman inclusion via opposite-sex categories, has usually centred elite sport and involved either male-advantage mitigation in opposite-sex categories or same-sex rather than gender-identity categories. However, in participation settings, notwithstanding the International Bill of Human Rights and national equality legislation in relation to women's rights, many sports adopt gender-identity eligibility criteria for inclusion in opposite-sex categories (see LTA 2019), with some notable exceptions, including British Triathlon. Consequently, I investigated the impact of eligibility criteria permitting participation in opposite-sex categories by way of gender identity (Devine 2021b).

In Britain, sport policy must comply with the Equality Act (HM Government) and Section 195 enshrines the right to single-sex categories in sports, 'in which the physical strength, stamina or physique of average persons of one *sex* would put them at a disadvantage compared to average persons of the other *sex*' (emphasis added). I calculated gender-identity eligibility criteria could increase, possibly 100-fold in some sports, biological and legal males, mostly without medical transition, in female sport (Figures 14.2 and 14.3). This is because most competitive team sports are heavily male-dominated (Figure 14.1), most people identifying as transgender are males, and a large majority of transgender people undertake no medical transition (Collin et al. 2016). For competitive sports, the percentage of transwomen footballers in female categories could be up to 10.5 percent (24 690), whereas the percentage of transmen footballers in male categories would only be 0.1 percent (1 404). Similarly, the percentage of transwomen cricketers in female categories could be up to 9.8 percent (3 481), whereas the percentage of transmen cricketers in male categories would be only 0.1 percent (212).

Transwomen in the female category
Potential transwoman frequency ■ Female %

Sport	Potential transwoman frequency	Female %
Tennis	1 in 48	97.9
Athletics	1 in 40	97.5
Rugby League	1 in 37	97.3
Basketball	1 in 20	95.1
Golf	1 in 15	93.5
Rugby Union	1 in 15	93.5
Cricket	1 in 10	90.2
Football	1 in 10	89.5
Team Sports	1 in 23	95.6

Transmen in the male category
Potential transman frequency ■ Male %

Sport	Potential transman frequency	Male %
Tennis	1 in 250	99.6
Athletics	1 in 250	99.6
Rugby League	1 in 333	99.7
Basketball	1 in 500	99.8
Golf	1 in 1000	99.9
Rugby Union	1 in 1000	99.9
Cricket	1 in 1000	99.9
Football	1 in 1000	99.9
Team Sports	1 in 500	99.8

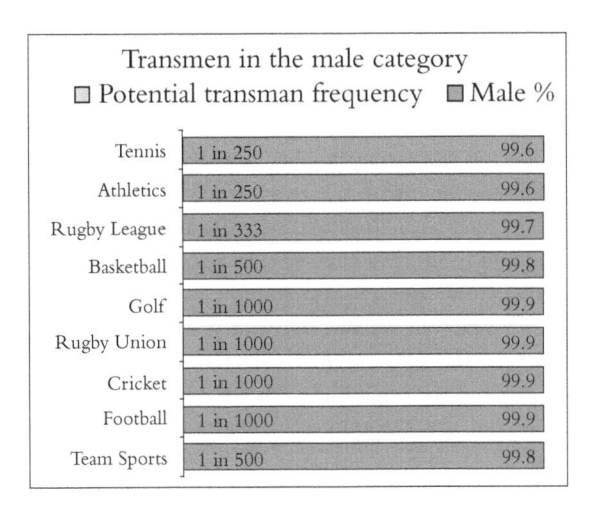

FIGURES 14.2 AND 14.3 The impact on single-sex categories of gender-identity eligibility (data: Devine 2021a, visuals: Emma Hilton).

Gender identity, rather than biological sex, eligibility criteria disproportionately and asymmetrically affect the proportionate and lawful means of including females in sport, via female categories, in sex-affected sports. These policies, even at participation levels, may therefore indirectly and unlawfully discriminate against females, and contravene the Equality Act. Furthermore, British Sports Council should ensure compliance with the SCEG guidance and the Public Sector Equality Duty outlined in the act regarding the investment of public money in NGBs.

Meaningful equality impact assessments of gender-identity eligibility criteria are notable by their absence. However, the WSPWG (2021), researched the impacts on female athletes of two athletes who transitioned from male to female teams between 2017–2020 explaining that

> [t]hey immediately dominated their events at their conference, state, and regional competitions, even though their performances would have been insufficient to qualify them for post-season play had they competed in the boys' divisions. (27)

The WSPWG details 93 instances in which a female was denied an individual or relay championship, 17 in which a female was denied an All-New England honour, 11 in which a female lost a meet record, 39 in which a female was denied the opportunity to advance to the finals and 52 in which a female was denied the opportunity to advance to a championship meet. Furthermore, these two athletes denied 23 females a Connecticut State Open team championship and significantly improved their rankings following transition from male to female categories (WSPWG 2021, 28–29). (See Figures 14.4 and 14.5.)

In elite sport, the 2021 Tokyo Olympics saw the first openly transgender athlete, Laurel Hubbard, compete in an opposite-sex category in the women's superheavyweight 87+kg. At 43, Hubbard was nearly twice the average age of other qualifiers. Hubbard's inclusion excluded, initially, 21-year-old Kuinini 'Nini' Manumua, awarded a wild-card place following a public outcry, and ultimately 18-year-old Roviel Detenamo (Ingle 2021c). Furthermore, Hubbard lifts in the male range for age and is another transwoman athlete benefitting from a ranking boost following transition, in this case straight into an Olympic final, beyond the reach of any 43-year-old female. Furthermore, the operative word here is 'openly', given that 42-year-old Stephanie Barrett, similarly much older than the average age of the rest of the qualifiers who were mostly in their 20s, is also a transwoman athlete and was the only Canadian competitor in women's archery (*The Economist* 2021).

Notwithstanding widespread opposition to gender-identity eligibility criteria for opposite-sex categories, there is overwhelming support for transgender inclusion in categories that do not relegate the rights of female athletes to second place

T MILLER - SPRINTS
55 meters indoors and 100 meters outdoors

GRADE	Hormone status*	Event	Connecticut Boys' State Rankings	Connecticut Girls' State Rankings
9th	not on gender affirming hormones	Indoor-55m	662nd	32nd
		Outdoor-100m	326th	2th
10th	not on gender affirming hormones	Indoor-55m	377th	5th
		Outdoor-100m	181st	1st
11th	not on gender affirming hormones	Indoor-55m	118th	1st
		Outdoor-100m	165th	1st
12th	on gender affirming hormones	Indoor-55m	335th	3rd
		Outdoor-100m	-/-	-/-

A YEARWOOD - SPRINTS
55 meters indoors and 100 meters outdoors

GRADE	Hormone Status*	Event	Connecticut Boys' State Rankings	Connectcut Girls' State Rankings
9th	not on gender affirming hormones	Indoor-55m	-/-	-/-
		Outdoor-100m	422nd	4th
10th	on gender affirming hormones	Indoor-55m	392nd	5th
		Outdoor-100m	470th	3rd
11th	on gender affirming hormones	Indoor-55m	194th	2nd
		Outdoor-100m	449th	5th
12th	on gender affirming hormones	Indoor-55m	170th	1st
		Outdoor-100m	-/-	-/-

FIGURES 14.4 AND 14.5 Ranking boosts of transitioning from male to female categories (WSPWG 2021, 29)

(Devine 2021a; FINA 2022a; Sailors 2020; SCEG 2021; WSPWG 2022). A range of alternative inclusion options have been suggested:

1. Retain single-sex categories in sex-affected sports

Athletes compete according to sex regardless of gender identities. This benefits all females, including transmen and female non-binary athletes who would be uncompetitive in male or open categories. At present, they choose between medical transition and a competitive career. Transman swimmer Iszac Henig, Olympian non-binary soccer player Quinn and skateboarder Alana Smith all compete in female categories. Transmen and non-binary female athletes depend on female categories for qualification into elite sport events, given they are unlikely to qualify into mixed-sex, open or male categories. Nevertheless, Quinn, a female athlete competing in female categories, benefits from a boosted media profile as a result of a non-binary status, with associated accolades for being the first transgender or non-binary athlete to win an Olympic gold.

Similarly, in common with Olympic decathlete Caitlyn Jenner, slalom canoeist Sandra Forgues and Tour de France cyclist Phillipa York, transwomen could delay medical transition and compete in male categories. Clearly acknowledging male advantage, Phillipa York explains, 'If I had the information . . . back then . . . I would have chosen to transition and not become a cyclist' (Hind 2017). However, the transition from male to female categories results in significant ranking boosts due to male advantage. This exemplifies the sex discrimination against female athletes inherent in gender-identity eligibility for opposite-sex categories. It disproportionately boosts the rankings of transwomen (males) whilst undermining those of all females (transmen, non-binary, those who identify as neither). Furthermore, given most people who identify as transgender do not medically transition (Collin et al. 2016), retaining single sex categories would be maximally inclusive of all transgender athletes.

This option would require a shift in focus from opening up the female category to reforming male sport. Welcoming all males, including those attempting a flight from 'toxic masculinity', means addressing hegemonic masculinities and heteronormativity in androcentric sport. This socio-cultural solution is unproblematic in American Samoa, where Jaiyah Saelua became the first openly transgender woman and fa'afafine to compete in a FIFA World Cup–qualifying match in the *male* category. Saelua explains, 'It's very common, actually, for fa'afafine to play sports. . . . Sāmoan society has no limits on what fa'afafine can pursue in life'. *Fa'afafine* is an umbrella term in Sāmoa 'for people who identify as a gay man, a trans woman, or as nonbinary but with female characteristics' (Faatau'uu-Satiu 2020).

2. Additional categories for transgender athletes

These would involve separate categories for transmen and transwomen and be further sub-divided for those with and without medical transition. However, athletes without medical transition could also choose same-sex categories. In common with Paralympic categories, additional categories may be relatively small but could grow transgender sport, given that the prevalence data indicate increasing numbers identifying as transgender.

3. Parallel categories

The WSPWG (2021) has suggested 'accommodations that might be adopted . . . might include handicapping, multiple leagues, events, and/or podiums' in opposite-sex categories (10). This solution would also work in same-sex categories which could include transwomen in male categories and transmen not taking testosterone in female categories, with parallel results, prizes and podiums.

4. Female and open category combination

This involves the recategorisation of male categories not already designated as open, as open categories, with retention of dedicated female categories.

This is not unproblematic given medically and surgically transitioned transmen and transwomen, plus transmen without medical transition and female non-binary athletes, would be uncompetitive in open categories. It may therefore be an interim solution whilst sport governance explores the potential of additional categories. The World Swimming Coaches Association (2022) recognises that '[t]here is an argument that the Trans Males [biological women] have been completely lost in this debate because they are uncompetitive in our current structure' and also that '[w]ith an Open division, Trans females [biological males] swimming against biological males may not even make the required time standards to be able to enter certain events/meets'. The WSCA concludes '[a]n Open competition takes care of the issue we face, but we also have to ask if it takes care of the athletes holistically' and therefore recommends additional transgender categories.

The 'open' branding is also a misnomer given, for example, wheelchair marathon athletes, and possibly given ongoing disputes, runners using blades, may not be eligible to 'compete down' into equivalent able-bodied categories.

Furthermore, this category combination may be a compromise for female athletes who have fought long and hard against the asymmetry of branding categories 'sport' and 'women's sport'. The Olympians in my study (Devine 2021a) marginally preferred additional categories to the open/female category combination.

5. Additional versions (universal admission).

This option is suggested by the SCEG (2021), which explains that 'NGBs and SGBs are encouraged to develop a model of their sport in which participation is not dependent on a competitor's sex or gender, and the classification based on the sex binary is withdrawn for this competition' (14).

Conclusion

Materialist feminists and gender-critical sport scholars represent a continuity with second-wave feminist sociologists and philosophers of sport. They critique gendered expectations in sport as part of a feminine/masculine gender order which naturalises male superiority and female inferiority, thus reinforcing a hierarchy of power between the sexes. In contrast, gender-identity theorists celebrate and essentialise gender identity whilst problematising human sexual dimorphism as socially constructed and a product of racist colonial patriarchy.

Almost a century since the disintegration of the FSFI and 30 years since the takeover of women's NGBs in England, refocussing on egalitarian, transparent, accountable and democratic decision-making in sport, is long overdue. Androcentric technocratic and authoritarian approaches to categorical disputes do nothing to dismantle and replace hierarchical power relations between the sexes. Indeed, they may reinforce the political and moral authority of already included male experts (neither female nor transgender) at the expense of self-determination and bodily autonomy for both female and transgender athletes. The exclusion of female athletes from decision-making regarding their own categories contravenes Lister's principles of 'status' as members of sports communities and 'practice' as decision-makers within them. Female and transgender athlete rights in sport, as in other areas of public policy, necessitate policy development according to Fraser's (2008) 'all-affected principle'.

Egalitarian sport policy should involve evidence-based democratic decision-making. Unaccountable organisations claiming to speak on behalf of female athletes or human rights advocate for eligibility into female categories by way of gender identity rather than sex. This policy capture is diametrically opposed to the evidence we have regarding female athletes' views. The evidence is clear. First, there is no protocol to remove male advantage in transwomen. Second, female athletes do not consent to the inclusion of transwomen in female categories. Consequently, female categories should be retained for female athletes/participants only.

Transgender athletes/participants also have a right to self-determination and inclusion in decision-making as to appropriate category solutions. This responsibility should not be ceded to one or two transgender advocates who, or transgender interest organisations which, may not be representative of the transgender population. In particular, the views of transmen have been marginalised. Inclusion solutions must, however, exclude female categories in sex-affected sports for both transwomen, and transmen taking testosterone, for reasons of fairness and safety, and because female athletes do not consent.

Finally, materialist feminists and gender-critical sport scholars, together with governing bodies of sport which recognise the equal rights claims of female athletes, agree dedicated female categories are essential for the equal opportunities and inclusion of girls and women in sport. Including transwomen in female categories by way of gender identity rather than sex is a 'solution' that does not work for females.

References

Anderson, Eric, and Ann Travers. 2017. *Transgender athletes in competitive sport*. London: Routledge.

BBC. 2021a. Tokyo Olympics: Athletics - Women's 400m results: https://www.bbc.co.uk/sport/olympics/58065822

BBC. 2021b. Tokyo Olympics: Athletics - Men's 400m results: https://www.bbc.co.uk/sport/olympics/58022286

Bhargava, Aditi, Arthur Arnold, Debra Bangasser, et al. 2021. 'Considering Sex as a Biological Variable in Basic and Clinical Studies: An Endocrine Society Scientific Statement', *Endocrine Reviews 42 (3)*: pp. 219–258.

Birrell, Susan. 2000. 'Feminist Theories for Sport'. In *Handbook of Sport Studies*, edited by Jay Coakley and Eric Dunning, pp. 61–76. London: Sage.

British Triathlon. 2022a. 'Statement from British Triathlon Federation'. https://www.britishtriathlon.org/news/statement-from-british-triathlon-federation_17073

British Triathlon. 2022b. 'Transgender Policy Consultation Process 2022'. https://www.britishtriathlon.org/britain/documents/about/edi/transgender-policy-consultation-process-2022.pdf

Bryson, Lois. 1987. 'Sport and the Maintenance of Masculine Hegemony'. *Women's Studies International Forum 19 (4:)* pp. 349–360.

Canadian Centre for Ethics in Sport. 2016. 'Creating Inclusive Environments for Trans Participants in Canadian Sport'. https://cces.ca/sites/default/files/content/docs/pdf/cces-transinclusionpolicyguidance-e.pdf

Centre for Sport and Human Rights. 2022. About us. https://sporthumanrights.org/about-us/

Cohen, Shawn. 2022. 'Trans UPenn Swimmer Lia Thomas Is CRUSHED Twice in Ivy League Women's Swim Meet by Yale Competitor Iszac Henig, Who Is Transitioning from Female to Male'. *Daily Mail*, January 8. https://www.dailymail.co.uk/news/article-10382019/Trans-UPenn-swimmer-Lia-Thomas-wins-200m-freestyle-race-two-seconds.html

Collin, Lindsay, Sari Reisner, Vin Tangpricha, and Michael Goodman. 2016. 'Prevalence of Transgender Depends on the "Case" Definition: A Systematic Review'. *The Journal of Sexual Medicine 13 (4):* pp. 613–626.

Court of Arbitration for Sport. 2019a. 'CAS 2018/0/5794 Mokgadi Caster Semenya v. International Association of Athletics Federations'. https://www.tas-cas.org/fileadmin/user_upload/CAS_Award_-_redacted_-_Semenya_ASA_IAAF.pdf

Court of Arbitration for Sport. 2019b. 'Cas Arbitration: Caster Semenya, Athletics South Africa (ASA) and International Association of Athletics Federations (IAAF): Decision'. https://www.tas-cas.org/fileadmin/user_upload/Media_Release_Semenya_ASA_IAAF_decision.pdf

Davies, Sharron. 2022. Tweet: https://twitter.com/sharrond62/status/1482792047832616963?s=20

de Coubertin, Pierre. 1912. 'The Women at the Olympic Games'. In *Olympism: Selected Writings/Pierre De Coubertin. 2000*, edited by IOC, pp. 711–713. Lausanne: IOC.

Devine, Cathy. 2021a. 'Female Olympians' Voices: Female Sport Categories and IOC Transgender Guidelines'. *International Review for the Sociology of Sport 57 (3):* pp. 335–361.

Devine, Cathy. 2021b. 'Female Sports Participation, Gender Identity and the British 2010 Equality Act'. *Sport, Ethics and Philosophy*. Advanced online publication. https://doi.org/10.1080/17511321.2021.1993982

Drinkwater, Barbara. (ed.) 2000. *Women in Sport*. Oxford: Blackwell Science.

The Economist. 2021. 'Why Are Transgender Olympians Proving So Controversial?' July 16. https://www.economist.com/the-economist-explains/2021/07/16/why-are-transgender-olympians-proving-so-controversial

Elsas, Louis, Arne Ljungqvist, Malcolm Ferguson-Smith, et al. 2000. 'Gender verification of female athletes'. *Genetics in Medicine 2:* pp. 249–254.

Faatau'uu-Satiu, Gabriel. 2020. 'Football's First Fa'afafine: Trans Rights Trailblazer Jaiyah Saelua on Stardom and Sisterhood'. The Guardian, August 1. https://www.theguardian.com/world/2020/aug/01/footballs-first-faafafine-trans-rights-trailblazer-jaiyah-saelua-on-stardom-and-sisterhood

FINA. 2022a. Policy on Eligibility for the Men's and Women's Competition Categories. https://resources.fina.org/fina/document/2022/06/19/525de003-51f4-47d3-8d5a-716dac5f77c7/FINA-INCLUSION-POLICY-AND-APPENDICES-FINAL-.pdf

FINA. 2022b. Extraordinary General Congress| 19th FINA World Championships | Budapest https://www.youtube.com/watch?v=tiujU5nUq6A

Fraser, Nancy. 2008. *Scales of Justice*. Cambridge, UK: Polity Press.

Gleaves, John, and Tim Lehrbach. 2016. 'Beyond Fairness: The Ethics of Inclusion for Transgender and Intersex Athletes'. *Journal of the Philosophy of Sport 43 (2)*: pp. 311–326.

Gauthier, Ryan. 2017. *The International Olympic Committee, Law, and Accountability*. Routledge.

Hall, Ann. 1990. 'How Should We Theorise Gender in the Context of Sport?' In *Sport Men and the Gender Order: Critical Feminist Perspectives*, edited by Messner, Michael, and Donald Sabo, pp. 223–240. Champaign, IL: Human Kinetics.

Hall, Ann. 2016. *The Girl and the Game: A History of Women's Sport in Canada*. 2nd ed. Toronto: University of Toronto Press.

Hargreaves, Jennifer. 1994. *Sporting Females: Critical Issues in the History and Sociology of Women's Sports*. London: Routledge.

Harper, Joanna, Emma O'Donnell, Behzad Khorashad, et al. 2021. 'How Does Hormone Transition in Transgender Women Change Body Composition, Muscle Strength and Haemoglobin? Systematic Review with a Focus on the Implications for Sport Participation'. *British Journal of Sports Medicine 55 (15)*: pp.1–9.

Heidari, Shirin, Thomas Babor, Paulo De Castro, Sera Tort, and Mirjam Curno. 2016. 'Sex and Gender Equity in Research: Rationale for the SAGER Guidelines and Recommended Use'. *Research Integrity Peer Review 1 (2)*: Article 2. https://doi.org/10.1186/s41073-016-0007-6.

Hilton, Emma, and Tommy Lundberg 2021. 'Transgender Women in the Female Category of Sport: Perspectives on Testosterone Suppression and Performance Advantage'. *Sports Medicine 51*: pp. 199–214.

Hind, Sally 2017. Cycling legend Robert Miller says she should have ditched bike and masculinity as a teen. *Daily Record*, November 3. https://www.dailyrecord.co.uk/news/scottish-news/cycling-legend-robert-miller-says-11458827

Human Rights Watch. 2020. '"They're Chasing Us Away from Sport" Human Rights Violations in Sex Testing of Elite Women Athletes'. https://www.hrw.org/sites/default/files/media_2020/12/lgbt_athletes1120_web.pdf

HM Government. 2010. Equality act. London: TSO. http://www.legislation.gov.uk/ukpga/2010/15/section/195

International Association of Athletics Federations. 2019. 'IAAF Eligibility Regulations for the Female Classification [Athletes with Differences of Sex Development]'. IAAF.

Ingle, Sean. 2021a. 'World Athletics' Rules Threaten to Leave More Female Athletes Stuck in Limbo'. *The Guardian*, September 13. https://www.theguardian.com/sport/blog/2021/sep/13/world-athletics-rules-threaten-to-leave-more-female-athletes-stuck-in-limbo

Ingle, Sean. 2021b. Sport's trans issue is here to stay. But at last, the debate is starting to change. *The Guardian*, December 13. https://www.theguardian.com/sport/blog/2021/dec/13/swimming-trans-debate-starting-to-change?CMP=Share_iOSApp_Other

Ingle, Sean. 2021c. Laurel Hubbard's Olympic Dream Dies under the World's Gaze. *The Guardian*, August 2. https://www.theguardian.com/sport/2021/aug/02/laurel-hubbards-olympic-dream-dies-under-worlds-gaze

Ingle, Sean. 2022. 'Shelly-Ann Fraser-Pryce Fixes Wig Mid-Race but Still Qualifies in Worlds 200m'. *The Guardian*, July 19. https://www.theguardian.com/sport/2022/jul/19/shelly-ann-fraser-pryce-fixes-wig-mid-race-but-still-qualifies-at-world-titles

International Olympic Committee. 2003. 'Statement of the Stockholm Consensus on Sex Reassignment in Sports'. Stockholm, October. https://olympics.com/ioc/news/ioc-approves-consensus-with-regard-to-athletes-who-have-changed-sex-1

International Olympic Committee. 2015. 'IOC Consensus Meeting on Sex Reassignment and Hyperandrogenism'. Lausanne, November. https://stillmed.olympic.org/Documents/Commissions_PDFfiles/Medical_commission/2015-11_ioc_consensus_meeting_on_sex_reassignment_and_hyperandrogenism-en.pdf

International Olympic Committee. 2021. 'IOC Framework on Fairness, Inclusion and Non-Discrimination on the Basis of Gender Identity and Sex Variations'. https://stillmed.olympics.com/media/Documents/News/2021/11/IOC-Framework-Fairness-Inclusion-Non-discrimination-2021.pdf?_ga=2.244885574.2123514635.1644508765-930040168.1637087907

Lapchick, Richard, with Erin Davison, Caryn Grant and Rodrigo Quirarte 2016. 'Gender Report Card: 2016 International Sports Report Card on Women in Leadership Roles'. The Institute for Diversity and Ethics in Sport. https://www.tidesport.org/_files/ugd/7d86e5_47dc0dc55b294fe185d1392e676b6a51.pdf

LTA. 2019. 'Policy and Guidance on Trans People Playing Tennis'. https://www.lta.org.uk/globalassets/about-lta/equality--diversity/lta-transgender-inclusion-policy-_-september-2019.pdf?_t_id=1B2M2Y8AsgTpgAmY7PhCfg percent3d percent3d&_t_q=transgender&_t_tags=language percent3aen percent2csiteid percent3af3862a05-6b76-4b3c-9179-c99ae142b858&_t_ip=2.98.12.85 percent3a50793&_t_hit.id=Lta_Models_Media_Pdf/_0ea5a600-f9ae-45b8-bf12-88c81b9ffe86&_t_hit.pos=2

Lister, Ruth. 2003. *Citizenship: Feminist Perspectives*. New York: New York University Press.

McDonagh, Eileen, and Laura Pappano. 2009. *Playing with the Boys: Why Separate Is Not Equal in Sports*. New York: Oxford University Press.

Murray, Kath, and Lucy Blackburn. 2019. 'Losing Sight of Women's Rights: The Unregulated Introduction of Gender Self-Identification as a Case Study of Policy Capture in Scotland'. *Scottish Affairs* 28 (3): pp. 262–289.

Nicholson, Raphaelle. 2022. *'Holding a Gun at Our Heads': The Sports Council's Role in Merger–Takeovers of Women's Sport, 1985–2000*. Bingley, UK: Emerald Publishing Limited.

Pateman, Carole. 1988. *The Sexual Contract*. Cambridge, UK: Polity Press.

Rugby Football League. 2022. 'RFL Board Approves New Gender Participation Policy for Rugby League'. https://www.rugby-league.com/article/60634/rfl-board-approves-new-gender-participation-policy-for-rugby-league

Rugby Football Union. 2022. 'RFU Gender Participation Policy – Frequently Asked Questions'. https://www.englandrugby.com//dxdam/cc/cc222f52-677f-43f8-a4f9-75735f120986/RFU percent20Gender percent20Participation percent20Policy percent20FAQs.pdf

Sailors, Pam. 2020. 'Transgender and Intersex Athletes and the Women's Category in Sport'. *Sport, Ethics and Philosophy* 14 (4): pp. 419–431.

Senefeld, Jonathon, Sandra Hunter, Doriane Coleman, and Michael Joyner. 2021. 'Transgender Swimmer in College Athletics'. https://www.medrxiv.org/content/10.1101/2021.12.28.21268483v1.full

Shift. 2022. 'Sport and Human Rights'. https://shiftproject.org/what-we-do/sports/

Snider-McGrath, Ben. 2021. 'Olympic Medallist Wants DSD Athlete Category for Track and Field Events'. *Canadian Running*. https://runningmagazine.ca/the-scene/olympic-medallist-wants-dsd-athlete-category-for-track-and-field-events/

Sports Council Equality Group. 2021. 'Guidance for Transgender Inclusion in Domestic Sport'. September. https://equalityinsport.org/resources/index.html

Swimming World. 2022. 'Champion Women, WSPWG Release Results of Petitions Asking Congress, Sports to Prioritize Fairness for Biological Women'. https://www.swimmingworldmagazine.com/news/champion-women-wspwg-release-results-of-petitions-asking-congress-sports-to-prioritize-fairness-for-biological-women/

Thewlis, Tom. 2022. 'UCI Tightens Rules for Transgender Cyclists: Two Year Wait before Competition Allowed'. *Cycling Weekly*, June 17. https://www.cyclingweekly.com/news/uci tightens rules for transgender women

Thibault, Valérie, Guillaume, Marion, Berthelot Geoffrey, et al. 2010. 'Women and Men in Sport Performance: The Gender Gap Has Not Evolved Since 1983'. *Journal of Sports Science & Medicine 9 (2):* pp. 214–223.

Travers, Ann. 2008. 'The Sport Nexus and Gender Injustice'. *Studies in Social Justice 2 (1):* pp. 79–101.

Union Cycliste Feminine. 2022. Letter. April 8. https://twitter.com/UnionFeminine/status/1512323337245974530?s=20&t=qSX0v4k9tk7_-ikcxEkgAQ

United Nations. 1967. 'International Bill of Human Rights'. https://www.ohchr.org/sites/default/files/Documents/Publications/Compilation1.1en.pdf

United Nations. 1979. *Convention on the Elimination of All Forms of Discrimination against Women.* https://www.ohchr.org/en/instruments-mechanisms/instruments/convention-elimination-all-forms-discrimination-against-women

USA Powerlifting. 2019. 'Transgender Participation Policy'. https://www.usapowerlifting.com/transgender-participation-policy/

Whitehead, Margaret. 2010. *Physical Literacy.* London: Routledge.

Women and Sport Policy Working Group. 2021. 'Briefing Book a Request to Congress and the Administration to Safeguard Girls' and Women's Sport & Include Transgender Athletes'. https://womenssportspolicy.org/wp-content/uploads/2022/10/Congressional-Briefing-WSPWG-Transgender-Women-Sports-10-22-22.pdf

Women and Sport Policy Working Group. 2022. 'About Us'. https://womenssportspolicy.org/about-us/#:~:text=Our percent20Mission,girls percent27 percent20and percent20women percent27s percent20sports percent20umbrella

World Athletics. 2022'. Toplists'. https://worldathletics.org/stats-zone.

World Rugby. 2020a. 'Transgender Women Guidelines'. https://www.world.rugby/the-game/player-welfare/guidelines/transgender/women

World Rugby. 2020b. 'Transgender Meeting 2020: Player Results https://resources.world.rugby/worldrugby/document/2021/02/22/fec411ad-b1f2-4095-9779-17d07787331b/17.-Transgender-Group-2020-Player-Survey-Results.pdf

World Swimming Coaches Association. (2022). 'Position Statement on Transgender Swimming'. https://www.triathlon.org/news/article/world_triathlon_executive_board_approves_transgender_policy

Young, Iris. 1980. 'Throwing Like a Girl: A Phenomenology of Feminine Body Comportment Motility and Spatiality'. *Human Studies 3:* pp. 137–156.

15
SEX, GENDER, IDENTITY AND CRIMINOLOGY

Jo Phoenix

Sex is a fundamental consideration in criminology. There are nearly 200 years of statistical and qualitative evidence attesting to the fact that there are distinct differences between women and men in terms of lawbreaking and criminalisation, the administration of criminal justice and the experience of punishment. For as long as the evidence has been there, criminologists and other social scientists have debated how to explain these differences. The rise of queer criminology (i.e. a criminology that concerns itself with lesbian, gay, bisexual, transgender, queer and intersex [LGBTQi people] and gender-identity theory) has brought much of this into question. Both theories assume that a person's sexual or gender identity matters more than their biological sex. The implications are profound, and the challenge presented is two-fold: What counts as 'evidence' and 'truth' in criminology? and what is the relationship between activism and academic rigour? Criminology is a theoretically informed empirical discipline (i.e. the purpose of criminology is not just to count but to *account* for what is observed). The evidence base largely draws on descriptive statistics provided by governments, surveys and the like and small-scale qualitative research that examines the sense- and meaning-making systems of those involved in crime and criminal justice.

Some criminological schools of thought are concerned with matters of social justice and attempt to account for what is observed whilst also noting social structural inequalities (such as those of class, race and ethnicity and sex). Despite a well-established empirical evidence base about the social determinants of crime and justice, both queer criminology and gender-identity theory challenge the relationship between agency and social structure, positing that matters of subjective identity are as important if not take precedence over the role of material and structural inequalities in determining the shape, nature and character of criminal justice. More problematically however both are also primarily political projects in

DOI: 10.4324/9781003286608-15

that they *prioritise* the injustices of LGBQTi and/or transgender people specifically over other aspects of social life and seek to change the discipline of criminology and the administration of criminal justice in ways that reflect their assumptions about the importance of subjective identities. Finally, and as this chapter suggests, the arguments and assumptions of both queer criminology and gender-identity theory in relation to criminology are without as robust an evidence base as that pertaining to the salience of sex and verge on empirical methodological nonsense (i.e. not operationalisable). This is best argued by demonstrating how and why sex matters in relation to crime, criminalisation and victimisation. The argument of the chapter is that we must retain sex as a key factor for description and analysis in criminology particularly in societies that are structured by profound sex-based inequalities.

Sex, Sexual Differences and Criminal Statistics

Statistics on crime and justice are the end products of complex social processes, including the creation of laws that constitute criminal violations, police recording decisions, reporting behaviour and decisions made by agencies responsible for the adjudication of guilt or innocence and carrying out court-mandated punishments (courts, probation service, prisons). In England and Wales, the police are responsible for recording data about *reported* crime. Recorded crime data are highly partial. It excludes all criminal acts that go unreported. Some examples include 'victimless' crimes (such as purchasing illegal drugs), incidents in which the victim has chosen not to report a crime (e.g. a sexual assault victim might feel too ashamed to contact the police or a person might feel a crime is too trivial to report) and situations in which the victim is unaware that a crime has taken place. Other statistics collected by criminal justice agencies include information on prosecutions, convictions, sentencing, and the prison population. Separately, large-scale surveys such as the Crime Survey of England and Wales (CSEW) provide estimates on the prevalence of victimisation for a range of crimes and are generally viewed as a more reliable measure of offending trends.

Despite the limitations of police-recorded crime, the stability of particular patterns within official criminal statistics has given rise to several 'truisms' about sexual differentiation in crime and justice.

Truism 1: Women are, in comparison to men, a law-abiding lot.

Based on a head count of arrest and conviction data, the single strongest predictor of criminal activity is sex. Since criminal statistics were first collected in the mid-19th century, across many countries, the male:female arrest ratio has remained relatively stable. Approximately 80 to 85 percent of people recorded in criminal justice statistics will be male, irrespective of changes in the overall arrest rate. For instance, in 2006/7 in England and Wales, there were just over 1.3 million arrests for notifiable offences. Of these arrests, 80 percent were of men and 20 percent were of women. Yet by 2019/20, the number of people arrested had fallen to less than half (i.e. 640,000) and yet women made up 17 percent of those arrested (Ministry of Justice [MoJ] 2020).

Truism 2: The types of crimes women and men get arrested and prosecuted for are patterned by sex.

Statistics on arrests and convictions tend to be grouped into offence categories. Examination of these categories (including a broad category of 'sexual offences') indicates that there are no categories that are male only or female only. Notwithstanding this, statistics on arrests and convictions are strongly patterned according to sex. As a rule, women are usually arrested for petty property offences; 'survival crimes', such as soliciting and loitering for the purposes of prostitution and sleeping rough; and crimes of poverty (such as benefit fraud, failure to pay fines, failure to purchase a TV licence and so on). Conversely, men are over-represented in arrests for violence, burglary and robbery.

In 2019, 27 percent of all those convicted of a crime were women (MoJ 2020). The most common offence was TV licence evasion, which accounted for 30 percent of all female convictions, compared to only 4 percent of male convictions. An analysis of prosecutions for TV licence evasion is telling. Between 2003 and 2013, the number of prosecutions against women had increased by 6 percent compared with a relative decrease in the number of prosecutions against men. The MoJ (2015) stated that this was driven by increases in the number of prosecutions for TV licence evasion. Whereas in 2003, females constituted only 39 percent of all TV licence evasion, by 2015, they constituted 74 percent. It is difficult to know whether this shift is a result of more TV licences being put in women's names, more women evading paying their licence or changes in policing and prosecution priorities. The important point is that those prosecutions for non-payment of TV licence (a crime typically related to poverty and survival) are highly patterned by sex.

Figure 15.1 shows the extent to which prosecutions in England and Wales are sexed. As noted earlier, statistics on prosecutions are gathered into offence categories in which similar offences are recorded together. The main offence categories are violence against the person, sexual offences, robbery, theft offences, drug offences, possession of weapons, public order offences, miscellaneous crimes against the person, fraud offences, summary non-motoring offences (these are offences tried in a magistrates' court that are not related to motoring and do not fit into any other category, such as begging, soliciting or loitering for the purposes of prostitution, non-payment of TV licence) and summary motoring.

The figure demonstrates that males are disproportionately overrepresented in offence categories. Of all prosecutions for sexual offences, 98 percent were against men. The pattern seen in the figure remains relatively stable over time.

262 Jo Phoenix

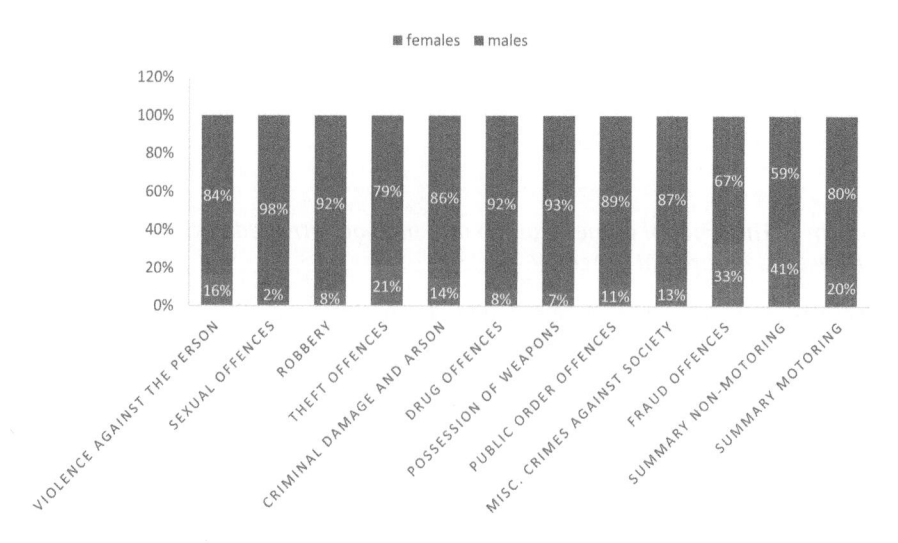

FIGURE 15.1 Proportion of defendants prosecuted for selected offences 2019, England and Wales

Source: Derived from 'Women and Criminal Justice Statistics 2019', Ministry of Justice

Truism 3: Sentencing is sexed.

Most offenders are processed through the magistrates' court, which adjudicates offences that attract up to 2 years' imprisonment, typically theft, violence against the person and drugs offences. In 2020, about 70 percent of magistrates' court defendants entered a guilty plea (derived from MoJ 2021). Most defendants received a fine, with a higher proportion issued to women than to men (86 percent and 72 percent, respectively).

Overall, and without reference to offence category, women received a higher percentage of fines than men, with a concomitant smaller percentage of community service, suspended sentences and custody. Furthermore, when women are sentenced to custody, they are given shorter sentences. In 2019, the average custodial sentence imposed on females was 11.3 months, compared to 19.7 months for males (MoJ 2020). It is easy to think of this as women receiving more lenient treatment.

However, many women suffer additional pains of imprisonment, compared to men (Prison Reform Trust 2019). Notably, they are likely to lose their accommodation and children. That such losses are experienced for comparatively *short* sentences is controversial and can be seen as an example of unjust treatment against women (Trebilcock and Dockley 2015). One of the long-running concerns of feminist criminology has been about sentencing. Establishing exact comparisons between men and women has proved elusive for a variety of reasons, not least of which is that there is no direct relationship between the type of offence and the sentence given. Sentences are the result of judges or magistrates weighing up the full mitigating and aggravating circumstances on a case-by-case basis and working within a rubric (known as sentencing guidelines). Given this, a like-for-like quantitative comparison is challenging. That said, we know from qualitative studies in which sentencers have been interviewed that sex matters when making their decisions, and this might be why we see these differences in overall patterns of sentencing (see Worrall 1990).

Truism 4: Male violence is a significant problem in women's lives with the most dangerous place for women and girls being the home.

Self-report data (see Sullivan, Murray and Mackenzie, this volume) from the Crime Survey of England and Wales (Office for National Statistics [ONS] 2017) show that a higher proportion of adult males experienced violent crime within the last year, compared to adult females (2.1 percent and 1.3 percent, respectively). However, the prevalence of sexual assaults amongst women (aged 16–59) was four times higher than that amongst men (3.1 percent and 0.8 percent, respectively). Just over a quarter (28.9 percent) of all females (aged 16–74) had experienced sexual assault since the age of 16, compared to 13.2 percent of males (ONS 2018). The homicide rate for men is much higher than for women; of the 671 homicide victims recorded in England and Wales in 2018/2019, the proportion of male victims was almost double that of female victims, at 64 percent and 36 percent, respectively (ONS 2020). There are also significant differences in context. Whereas most male homicide victims are killed in a public place, female homicide victims are mostly killed at home by acquaintances and partners. In 2018/19, female homicide victims were most likely to be killed in or around their home (77 percent), compared to 39 percent of male victims (ONS 2020). Most perpetrators of violence (including homicide) are male. For female victims of violence, most perpetrators are men who are known to them (ONS 2020).

The prevalence of violence against women at the hands of their husbands, fathers, brothers and other familial, friendship and intimate relations has given rise to the criminological truism: the most dangerous and risky place for girls and women is their own home. As Stanko (1990) states:

> Women's lives rest upon a continuum of unsafety. This does not mean that all women occupy the same position in relation to safety and violence. . . . Somehow, though, as all women reach adulthood, they share a common awareness of their particular vulnerability. Learning the strategies for survival is a continuous lesson about what it means to be female. (85)

Truism 5: Women victims of male violence are under-protected by the criminal justice system.

Responses to women's victimisation in the UK and many other countries are woefully inadequate. Domestic violence (also known as 'intimate partner violence' or 'wife battery') and rape provide two illustrative examples. Until the late 20th century, the physical assault and rape of wives within marriage were not criminalised. It took until 1976 for English law to provide clear legal protections for female victims of domestic violence, and even then, police routinely failed to respond to such violence (see The Law Commission [1990] for a full discussion). In England and Wales, rape within marriage was made a crime in 1992. Until then, a man could lawfully rape his wife (Westmarland 2004).

Even when police do act, five decades of criminological research shows that the attrition rate for sexual violence is higher than for any other crime type. Attrition refers to the gap between the number of reports for a specific crime and the eventual number of convictions achieved. Take rape for instance. In England and Wales, the Sex Offences Act 2003 defines rape as the penetration of a vagina, anus, or mouth by a penis. Therefore, rape is a crime that can only be committed by males, although females can be convicted as an accomplice, and victims can be male or female. The rate of police-recorded rapes has substantially increased over the last two decades. In 2002/03, 12,295 rapes were recorded by the police in England and Wales, rising to 55,696 recorded rapes in 2020/21. This means that there were over 4.5 times more rapes recorded at the end of this period than at the start, almost certainly due to victims being more willing to report the crime. Yet, we know that rape remains one of the most under-reported crimes. The Centre for Women's Justice et al. (2020) estimate that approximately 100,000 adults are raped every year in England and Wales, of whom 85 percent are women. In 2019, the police recorded 55,259 rapes (MoJ 2020). That same year, only 1,659 resulted in prosecution, and only 702 men were convicted. This is a conviction rate of only 1.2 percent and an attrition rate of 98.8 percent. At the risk of repetition, this means that for every 100 rapes recorded by the police in England and Wales, only 1.2 percent will end in a conviction. Many will be 'no further actioned' by the police who determine that there is not enough evidence to charge or the Crown Prosecution Service on the grounds that the case is not strong enough to secure a conviction. The attrition rate for rape in England and Wales is so great that several women and justice campaigning groups have concluded that rape is virtually decriminalised in England and Wales (see also Home Office and MoJ 2021; Victims Commissioner 2020).

Sex, Sexualities, Gender, Gender Identity and Justice

Since criminology began, sexed patterns in crime were explained in reference to biological differences between men and women. However, it is important to note that linking crime and criminality to biology has an exceptionally problematic history in criminology and more generally (Hahn Rafter 1997). In late 19th-century Italy, Lombroso (2006) claimed that people who committed crime were less evolutionarily advanced than others. They were 'degeneratives'. At the same time, Francis Galton in England argued that criminality was an inheritable trait (Galton 1875). The implication of claiming that criminality is encoded in the genetics is profound. It leads to the argument that with the right social engineering programme, criminality can be 'bred' out of existence. Enter the Eugenic movement in the early 20th century. By 1922, a series of laws were passed in 18 US states that introduced forced sterilisation and resulted in large numbers of women (not men) being sterilised in the name of securing 'purity of race' (King and Hansen 2013). Galton's ideas were not implemented in the UK, but they did underpin that other deadly manifestation of eugenics: the Holocaust perpetrated by Nazi Germany. This is why, within criminology, any suggestion that criminality is linked to biology is subject to intense scrutiny and scepticism.

There are other problems with biological determinism (i.e. arguing that biological traits are a determining cause of a non-biological phenomenon). Such arguments fail to take account of the socially, politically, economically and ideologically specific nature of crime. Such explanations focus on individual characteristics and present criminality as being only marginally affected by social, political or economic forces. Yet the majority of those who populate the criminal justice system of England and Wales are also young, disproportionately drawn from ethnic minority communities and from economically marginalised and poorer backgrounds. Biological explanations fail to account for the relationship between criminal justice policy and what we understand as 'the crime problem'. So, for instance, biological explanations ignore how laws change and how changes in policing, in guidance given to the Crown Prosecution Service about what to prosecute and in guidance given to courts about sentencing shape what appears in the statistics. Biologically deterministic explanations further fail to account for how governments shape how particular types of social problems are seen as criminal justice problems. Finally, they fail to account for the fact that lawbreaking is ubiquitous. Take speeding for instance. It is an offence. Most drivers at some point will break the law. Yet few of those who do so will find themselves arrested, prosecuted and convicted for a motoring offence. And the idea that those who speed have some type of biological difference that accounts for their failure to adhere to the restriction of velocity in a car seems more than a little far-fetched!

Yet despite the problems of explaining crime in relation to biology, biologically deterministic explanations for sexed patterns of crime persisted long after they had been discredited as explanations for male criminality. The argument ran that criminality is a male trait, and thus, women who commit crime deviate from their biological make-up. At various points in the last two centuries, explanations for male aggression, violence and lawbreaking have argued that biological and presumed psychological differences between men and women can account for the sexed patterns outlined earlier. Perhaps the most well-known of these accounts was that put forward by Cowie et al. (1968) in which they explained women's criminality in reference to chromosomes. They claimed that violence is associated with the possession of a Y chromosome whereas social passivity results from XX chromosomes. They argued that:

[d]ifferences between the sexes in hereditary predisposition (to crime) could be explained by sex-linked genes. Furthermore the female mode of personality, more timid, more lacking in enterprise, may guard her against delinquency. (167)

They went further: 'Markedly masculine traits in girl delinquents have been commented on by psychoanalytic observers . . . we can be sure that they have had some physical basis' (171). In other words, female criminality is a result of chromosomal abnormalities.

However, such explanations were thoroughly discredited by a feminist scholarship that began in the late 20th century. Dorie Klein (1973), in an early critique of the main theories of female criminality, demonstrated how a century of explanations for female criminality was based on assumptions about women as socially and sexually passive, compliant and emotional. She concluded that the 'economic and social realities of crime – the fact that *poor* women commit crimes, and that most crimes for women are property offences – are overlooked' (178, emphasis added). The critique was a devastating one. A decade later, Leonard (1982) summed it up nicely:

> Theories that are frequently hailed as explanations of human behaviour are, in fact, discussions of male behaviour and male criminality. . . . We cannot simply apply these theories to women, nor can we modify them with a brief addition or subtraction here and there. They are biased to the core, riddled with assumptions that relate to a male – not female – reality. Theoretical criminology is sexist because it unwittingly focuses on the activities, interests and values of men, while ignoring a comparable analysis of women. (181)

Since then, there has been a proliferation of studies that have moved ever farther from linking sexual differences in crime and criminalisation to biological pathology in the study of crime. Yet, and as the next section demonstrates, this has not been without problems. In order to understand what these problems are, however, it is necessary to describe the multitude of meanings given to the notion 'gender' in theoretical criminology and to chart the shift from using 'gender' to talk about sex-based inequalities to a version of gender almost completely devoid of analytical, explanatory power.

Feminist Pathways

Feminist pathways explanations adopt the assumptions of life-course analyses which track the way that offending, victimisation and contact with the criminal justice system develop in the life course, through an examination of their antecedents and consequences. They start from the assumption that women's broad life disadvantages and social circumstances *qua women* can lead to criminality (Daly 1992, 1996; Belknap and Holsinger 2006). Biological sex is important in feminist pathways analysis but only inasmuch as the basic unit of analysis is 'sex' (i.e. females). The main explanation offered is that being *women* in societies structured by sex-based inequalities creates a chain or sequence of events that for some, especially female victims of violence and economically marginalised women, produce criminality. Hence, the most common risk factors for female offending include childhood abuse, substance abuse, unhealthy intimate relationships and a lack of self-confidence as they combine with possible mental health issues and familial relationships.

By highlighting male violence and women's victimisation, early feminist pathways research tended to overlook other structures of inequality (class, race) and so more recently there have been attempts to correct this. Davis (2011) and Richie (2018) explore the way personal experiences of male violence interlock with structures of racial and class inequalities to 'entrap' minoritised and economically excluded females into US criminal justice systems.

Leaving aside the theoretical problems, feminist pathways and risk factor analyses have had a tremendous impact on criminal justice services. The Corston Report (Corston 2007), which shapes current criminal justice policies regarding women, started with an understanding of the 'fundamental differences between male and female offenders', including sex differences in types of offending and crime rates, the over-representation of victimised women and women with severe mental health issues in the criminal justice system and the differences in the 'pains of imprisonment' between men and women (i.e. women often lose their accommodation and their children whereas men do not, the high rates of self-harm in women's prisons and so on).

Sex, Gender, Social Roles, Ideologies of Femininity and Masculinities and Criminalisation

There are theories that start from the assumption that men and women commit crimes for the same reasons but that they are treated very differently by criminal justice. These theories are rooted in sociological analyses of the sexual division of labour. Until the postmodern, textual 'turn' of the 1990s and early 2000s, the basic analytical framework of sociology distinguished between social institutions (such as governments, schools, families, economic institutions, or workplaces), the social roles that comprised those institutions (such as the role of 'student', 'educator', 'mother', 'father') and the cultural norms that underpin these institutions and roles.

Early sociological analyses of the social institution of 'the family' noted that the division of labour by sex (with male breadwinners and female carers/housewives) often accompanied industrialisation as it was an efficient way of ensuring the reproduction of the labour force (daily and generationally; Parsons 1960). Feminist scholarship of the 1980s made particularly good use of these conceptual distinctions to argue that women's oppression within societies structured by sex-based inequalities is directly related to the social roles women occupy as a result of the sexual division of labour (i.e. the social role connected to childcare and care of older relatives) as well as normative expectations of 'gender' (those being the ideologies that render the socially constructed nature of women's oppression invisible; Fergusson 1989; Bristol Women's Studies Group 1979).

These conceptual distinctions (between socially constructed sex-based roles and the ideologies of gender) provided fruitful ground for thinking about sex differences in crime, criminalisation and victimisation. It prised open a space to recognise that *opportunities* to commit crime and the processes of criminalisation are shaped by sex-based social roles as well as gender ideologies. For instance, Heidensohn (1985) argues that sex differences in rates and types of criminality between men and women can be easily explained by women's sex roles in the domestic sphere:

> Burglary is rendered more difficult when one is encumbered with a twin baby buggy and its contents; constant care of a demented geriatric is not a conducive situation in which to plan a bank robbery. (174)

Social control theory argues that people are more likely to conform to the law when they perceive a vested interest in conforming. This is different to rational action theory because the emphasis of the theory is on how the individual is bonded to and embedded within their community rather than the rationality (or otherwise) of the individual outside of their immediate social context. The strength of social control theory is that it can explain the lawbreaking of the rich and the poor (see Carlen 1988). Two centuries of criminological research tells us that most people who populate Western European criminal justice systems 'drift' into crime and that lawbreaking is tied to friendship, financial gain and excitement (Matza 1964). It also tells us that most criminality is age-related and that people 'grow out' of crime at those moments when they settle down with jobs, form partnerships and have children. For some women, however, the appeal of money, friends and excitement may outweigh the alternative of conformity to a life of poverty, economic marginalisation, marriage and domesticity.

Framed in this way, Carlen (1988) argued that in general working-class men are 'controlled' through the disciplining routines and structures of work which produce social conformity, whereas working-class women are 'controlled' through the disciplining routines and structures of work *and* domesticity. Both work and domesticity are exploitative social relations (one of class, one of sex), although this is concealed by discourses and ideologies of familialism and consumerism. After analysing the life histories of 39 criminalised women, Carlen concluded that under certain conditions, women will not commit to male-dominated domesticity, often because of the effects of victimisation at the hands of men or because they are lesbian. Likewise, some women commit to consumerism at the same time as recognising their exploitative class position. Most women who end up in criminal justice systems are economically marginalised to such an extent that they have few, if any resources, to alleviate problems such as bereavement, isolation, ill health, drug or alcohol problems and housing. This is as true today as it was 40 years ago when Carlen did her study (Phoenix 2021). In such circumstances, many women feel they have absolutely *nothing* to lose and perhaps something to gain by engaging in criminal activity.

There is a rich seam of criminological empirical research on the processing of women through the criminal justice system and their unjust treatment. While we know that there is no ordinary typical female offender (Carlen et al. 1986) offending women are nonetheless viewed as 'doubly deviant' and 'doubly damned'. They deviate from the law through offending and from ideological norms of behaviour associated with their sex (one of the key norms associated with women is conformity!) and then are damned for their lawbreaking and for breaking normative ideological patriarchal expectations. The courts, probation officers and lawyers tend to make sense of female (but not male) criminals by using discourses of pathology, domesticity and sexuality. Women who fail to conform to gendered norms about being 'good women' or 'mad women' or 'troubled' women often receive harsher sentences.

'Gendering' Criminology: Shifting the Focus away from Sex-Based Injustices to Gender as a Performance

In the five decades since these studies, the concept of gender (and how it relates to justice) has taken on fundamentally different meanings. As seen in the earlier examples from Klein, Leonard, Heidensohn and Carlen, the concept of gender was first and foremost a *theoretical* construct that enabled a critique of the biologically essentialised and reductionist theories proffered by earlier generations.

Using the concepts of sexual social roles and ideologies or discourses of gender as a set of related analytical categories therefore provided the framework for the argument that when women do break the law they tend to do it in conditions quite different from men and that, for the most part, women's crimes are predominantly crimes of the socially powerless (for instance, Carlen et al 1986; Sharpe 2013). From there, it was then possible to empirically demonstrate that biologically essentialised notions of womanhood, femininity and female sexuality shaped how welfare, criminal justice and penal systems treated female offenders. Much of this research was then used by academics and campaigning organisations to push for better treatment of women in conflict with the law.

Yet even as these studies of women, gender, crime and justice were being produced, the concept of gender was already losing some of its analytical purchase within criminology. There was a parallel exploration of the notion of gender within an emerging sociology of sexualities and gender. Until the late 20th century, gay men and lesbians were understood within the social sciences through discourses of abnormality. But the new sexualities studies sought to understand homosexuality, especially gay men from an anti-pathologising and social constructionist point of view (for instance, Plummer 1981). By the early 1990s, a new field of criminological studies had emerged, heavily influenced by these developments and specifically Connell's (2005) theory that gender is a performance and that there are multiple ways it can be performed depending on one's place in a social hierarchy and one's sexuality. Conceived in this fashion – as a social practice and performance linked to social hierarchies – the study of masculinity turned more accurately into a study of dominant and subordinate masculinities. The case was made that crime, especially low-level violent crime, is a resource that young men draw on to demonstrate (i.e. perform) masculinity, just as it was argued that heterosexual activity is also a way to perform masculinity. For instance, Messerschmidt (2012) argued that sex, gender and sexuality interweave in complex and unpredictable ways and are co-constitutive of each other. They are a matrix made up of (largely) binary possibilities for performance, recognition, and reflexivity (or ways of 'doing' sex, gender and sexuality). Within this matrix, crime becomes a particularly potent resource for 'doing gender', and 'gender' is little more than performance and connected identity.

Abandoning Biological Sex and Sex-Based Inequalities in Favour of Identity Categories

As the previous two sections described, by the early 2000s, there were two parallel frameworks within criminology with two distinct ways of defining gender. The first used the highlighted social roles, sexual differentiation and ideologies or discourses of femininities to make sense of the routine injustices experienced by women, namely criminal justice administration and male violence. The second highlighted the performativity aspect of gender and connected it with individual identity to explore the role of crime in the performance of masculinities. Sitting somewhere between is a set of questions about sexuality and how best to theorise sexual and gender identities and justice. In both the perspectives outlined earlier, lesbianism and homosexuality are positioned as epiphenomenal. They are non-normative dimensions of human sexuality and human sexuality is only one dimension of sex-based social roles and ideologies of gender. The last 40 years have witnessed profound socio-cultural and political changes for entire categories of individuals Othered for being sexual minorities of one type or another. Early gay and lesbian liberation movements of the 1970s and 1980s fought to end both discrimination against them and the heterosexist ideologies that constructed them as sexual deviants (such as Section 28 of the UK's Local Government Act 1988 which prohibited local authority schools from 'promoting homosexuality' as an acceptable lifestyle). Latterly, the struggle of many different categories of people seen as deviant for their sexual preferences or identities have been combined into a larger social movement. This rainbow coalition is often denoted by the tags 'LGBT', 'LGBTQ' or 'LGBTQI'.

There can be little doubt that a criminology that addresses sexualities and gender identities is necessary. Worldwide, 70 countries criminalise private consensual same-sex sexual activity, 15 criminalise transgender people (using cross-dressing laws) and of those 11 impose the death penalty for consensual same-sex sexual activities, with 6 of those actively implementing it (Human Dignity Trust 2021; see Auchmuty and Freedman, this volume). Even today, large parts of the US still routinely discriminate against lesbians, gay men and transgender individuals in matters of employment, housing and criminal justice (see Burt, this volume). In short, sexual preference and gender identity have been and continue to be subject to criminal sanction.

In this context, some saw the development of a queer criminology (drawing on the concepts of queer theory) as a way of theorising normative expectations about sexual preference and gender identity in relation to law, crime and justice. Queer criminology offered the promise of explaining a range of issues, including the ongoing criminalisation of non-normative sexualities across the world; the routine exclusion of sexualities and gender identities from criminological theories; the routine injustices experienced by many lesbian, gay, transgender and bisexual people regarding treatment by victim services, the police, the courts; and the reliance of criminal justice agencies on notions of normative sexualities and gender identities when processing individuals. Others saw queer criminology as charting the different experiences of sexual minorities vis-à-vis crime and justice, like, for instance, the different pains of imprisonment experienced by lesbians, gay men, bisexual people, transgender individuals and those identifying as 'queer' and non-binary (especially when access to health and medical care for trans people is concerned) or the victimisation of people on the basis of their sexuality – such as the practice of corrective raping of lesbians in South Africa, and the assault, battery and murder of transgender sex workers in the US. As Buist and Lenning (2015) make clear, queer criminology was seen as filling the gaps in criminological knowledge as well as providing a platform for activism.

But queer criminology is problematic. Many contemporary versions of queer criminology are framed by the notion of gender as a set of free-floating discourses and practices (femininities, masculinities) that attach to and facilitate ways of identifying and being (see Butler 2002; Stock, this volume). Queer criminology distinguishes between biological sex and gender only to render biological sex irrelevant and biological sexual differentiation as a discourse created by the categorisation of bodies at birth. Gender becomes a performance and identity with 'queer' being a moniker for the identity that disrupts dominant discourses of biology and social roles (see Sullivan and Todd, this volume).

The problem of this framework is exposed by asking a relatively simple question: Who is 'queer'? Most queer theory scholars would agree that this includes lesbians, gay men, bisexual people, transgender men and transgender women, intersex, asexual, queer, gender diverse and gender non-binary and everyone else who is not 'cis' or 'heteronormative'. But can we treat these different categories as sociologically the same? Do lesbians and gay men have similar enough experiences to warrant being included in the same category even though we have 50 years of solid empirical evidence attesting to the way that biological sex shapes life opportunities and chances? Given that the category 'queer' is associated with identity, how long does one have to identify as such to be included in a queer criminological analysis of crime, justice, victimisation or discrimination? If we claim that inclusion into the category queer is not based on identity but sexual practice, are all those individuals who have, at some point in their lives, had sex with a person of the same sex queer and to be included in empirical studies of, for instance, queer victimisation? And if it is the case that a queer identity is fluid, then given that all identities are fluid (not just queer ones), does that not mean that we are all a little queer? If everyone is a little queer, then 'queer' ceases to be a useful descriptive or analytical category. Put simply, the category 'queer' cannot be empirically operationalised with any degree of robustness as any attempt to do so inevitably denies the social realities and sociological distinctiveness of the many subcategories or risks reifying one aspect (their identity) of an individual over all others (the material and social structural determinants shaping their lives).

Returning to criminology, however, some sexual identities have never been criminalised. To my knowledge, asexuality is not a crime anywhere in the world. Some sexual practices are not routinely criminalised. Same-sex female sexual activities were never criminalised in the UK. More than this, however, as I have argued elsewhere, the governance and (criminal justice) regulation of sexual practices and sexualities is a boundary-setting exercise (Phoenix 2017). Sexualities and sexual practices are always bounded by notions of 'normality' and 'abnormality', permissible and impermissible. There is no escape to a place where all sexualities and sexual practices will be forever liberated and arguably such a place would not be one that is desirable.

Translating queer criminology into criminal justice policy is even more contradictory. There is both a call for recognition of difference *and* a call to deny difference. This is particularly evident in relation to the placement and treatment of prisoners who are male people who identify as women. The claim is repeated that prisons must recognise the different needs such prisoners have, like a greater risk of illnesses, such as cardiovascular disease and osteoporosis because of hormone treatment; the disproportionate reported disabilities and chronic health conditions; or even the higher rates of autistic spectrum disorders (Webster 2017) while providing for their need to be socialised as and with women. Or, for instance, the many male prisoners who claim a trans identity are fearful to 'come out' (Lamble 2012). Yet activist and campaigning groups also call for prisons to deny any differences between males who identify as women and to accommodate such individuals (regardless of the legal sex status) in the women's prison estate because it is discriminatory not to recognise their chosen gender identity. Hence, the political project pulls in two irreconcilable directions: validation and recognition of difference and denial of difference.

Biological Realism, Justice and Prison Placement Policy

The preceding section traced multiple ways that criminology has theorised the links between crime and justice and sex, sexualities, gender and gender identity. Queer criminology has raised the question of specialist criminal justice services and provisions to cater for the unique needs of trans and non-binary people, respectively. Before proceeding, it is important to note that the last few decades have seen significant changes in the way that individuals express their gender identity and specifically in relation to what 'trans' now means. *Trans* refers to several sociologically distinct groups of people – from those individuals who have gone through the process of gender reassignment and who may have also made physical changes to their bodies to those who only change pronouns or wear clothing associated with the opposite sex (Halberstram 2018; Stryker 2017).

In the UK, the prison estate in England and Wales was segregated into female and male prisons in 1823. This was done as a means of reducing risks to female prisoners' safety and security and reducing the chances of prison pregnancies. In practice, female prisons have never been female only because they are often staffed and governed by men. As the preceding sections in this chapter described, women's lives and social experiences, their 'pathways' into lawbreaking and the conditions in which their lawbreaking is criminalised differ from that of men.

These differences accrue to a sex class (females), but they are not *determined* simply and directly by biological sex. There are physical differences and size and strength. These do, in certain circumstances matter, but the differences between men and women vis-à-vis crime and victimisation are also social differences that arise because we live in social structures that provide one group (males) with political, economic and social *advantages* over another (females). In the context of criminology, failure to recognise the realities of biology *or more specifically the social and political consequences arising from biological sexual differentiation*; that is, failing to adopt what I would call a position of 'biological realism' is antithetical to *any* social-scientific analysis that is concerned with justice of any kind (and see Jones, this volume).

My justification is as follows. One might argue that sex-based differences between criminalised men and women do not matter and, at any rate, ought not be the justification for excluding male people who identify as women from the female prison estate. However, one of the guiding principles of justice is that criminal justice must be fair and one of the dominant ways of thinking about fairness is by treating like things alike (known also as 'the Aristotelian Principle'). This raises tricky questions. Do we, in accordance with the Aristotelian Principle, apply the same rules and processes to men and women knowing that, as a demographic in societies structured by sex-based inequalities, they are *not* alike? Do we recognise that doing so might cause *injustice* and thus develop special and specialist treatment and rules? Do we seek only formal justice, or do we aim for substantive justice? Baroness Corston (2007) grappled with this and wrote:

> I have seen little evidence that much preparatory work is in hand in respect of the imminent statutory duty or of any real understanding that treating men and women the same results in inequality of outcome. Equality does not mean treating everyone the same. The new gender [*sic*] equality duty means that men and women should be treated with equivalent respect, according to need. Equality must embrace not just fairness but also inclusivity. This will result in some different services and policies for men and women. (3)

The same or similar arguments have been made by, for instance, Carlen (2013), who called for woman-wise sentencing, and Covington and Bloom (2007), who called for gender-responsive treatment programmes.

The question of fairness becomes more complicated when thinking about the prison placement of male people who identify as women. Are they sufficiently 'like' women to be considered 'the same' regarding the principles of fairness? We have no evidence base *at all* that analyses the relative importance of sex versus gender identity in offending, criminalisation and experiences of punishment – or rather none that addresses contemporary *British* society (see Sullivan, Murray and Mackenzie, this volume). Context here is critically important as different cultures and countries have distinct histories of law, tolerance, policing and punishment.

Prison placement policy by gender identity is problematic for other reasons. It flies in the face of a century of psychological and sociological research about identity. Identity is not the same as biological sex. Biological sex is immutable where research has confirmed, time and again, that people's identities change across time, place and in relation to social networks (Mead 1933). How an individual might identify at the beginning of a court order can and often does change. Indeed, that is exactly the logic of desistance programmes (to move an offender away from his/her 'offending identity' and towards a more law-abiding identity; see Weaver and McNeill 2015). Being mutable, identities do not provide a stable basis on which to organise complex criminal justice institutions, like prisons, which have statutory responsibilities regarding the security and safety of prisoners.

Second, everything about prisons is designed with two purposes in mind: removing individuals' liberty and maintaining the security and safety of those whose liberty has been removed. Recent Canadian research on the implementation of a prison placement policy based on gender self-identification demonstrates some of the challenges. When talking about placement based on gender identity, prison officers had concerns about placing males who identify as women but who may still have the physique, perhaps even still a penis, in the female estate. They were worried about the safety of women, just as much as they worried about the additional challenges this would create for them in maintaining security within the prison. Similarly, they were concerned about the potential for sexual and physical violence if transgender men (i.e. females who identify as men) were placed in the male estate (Ricciardelli et al. 2020). There is mounting anecdotal evidence that the placement of males in female prisons puts female prisoners at risk (see Phoenix 2022). So the question remains: How is it possible to both recognise the unique needs of female prisoners at the same time as recognising the desires of transgender prisoners to be placed in the female estate? Recognition of the needs of women prisoners can, at times, mean denying the desires of transgender prisoners and vice versa.

Conclusion

Imagine a world in which we had no data about sex, crime and criminal justice administration. In that world, nothing in this chapter would be knowable. The criminological truisms would not exist. We would lack the language to talk about male violence against females in any systematic or meaningful way. We would have no way of tracing, charting or describing women's unequal access to protection by the law, much less their unequal treatment by the law. And with that, we would have no ability to understand the extent to which trans and non-binary people are (or not) treated in a discriminatory or unfair fashion in the administration of criminal justice. For despite what is implied in contemporary cultural sexual politics (that transgender women are literal women) and within a queer penal politics (that transgender women should be counted as women in the administration of criminal justice), it is only through distinguishing transgender individuals from female and males that any assessment or claims about fairness of treatment for trans and gender-non-binary people can be made (i.e. we must recognise difference).

This chapter has demonstrated the continuing need for a criminology that takes biology and sexual differentiation seriously. The ideal of justice is not realised in societies structured by profound class, sex-based and cultural inequalities, and until those inequalities are addressed, it is vital that we continue to understand the many ways that females are denied equal access to the rule of law. For these reasons, we must continue to recognise how and in what ways sex matters where crime and justice are concerned. Without retaining the recognition of biological sexual differentiation in both criminology and penal politics justice becomes harder, not easier, to realise.

References

Belknap, J. and Holsinger, K. 2006. 'The Gendered Nature of Risk Factors for Delinquency'. *Feminist Criminology* 1(1): 48–71.

Bristol Women's Studies Group. 1979. *Half the Sky: Introduction to Women's Studies*. London: Virago.

Buist, C. and E. Lenning. 2015. *Queer Criminology*. London: Routledge.

Butler, J. 2002. *Gender Trouble*. London: Routledge.

Carlen, P. 1988. *Women, Crime, and Poverty*. Milton Keynes, UK: Open University Press.

Carlen, P. 2013. Against the Politics of Sex Discrimination: For the Politics of Difference and a Women-Wise Approach to Sentencing. In *Feminist Perspectives on Criminal Law* edited by L. Bibbings and D. Nicholson. London: Routledge-Cavendish.

Carlen, P., Hicks, J, O'Dwyer, J. Christina, D and C. Tchaikovsky. 1986. *Criminal Women: Autobiographical Accounts*. Cambridge, UK: Cambridge University Press.

Centre for Women's Justice, End Violence against Women Coalition, Imkaan and Rape Crisis. 2020. *The Decriminalisation of Rape: Why the Justice System Is Failing Rape Survivors and What Needs to Change*. November. https://rapecrisis.org.uk/media/2396/c-decriminalisation-of-rape-report-cwj-evaw-imkaan-rcew-nov-2020.pdf.

Connell, R. W. 2005. *Masculinities*. London: Polity.

Corston, B. J. 2007. *The Corston Report: A Report of a Review of Women with Particular Vulnerabilities in the Criminal Justice System*. London: Home Office.

Covington, S. S., & Bloom, B. E. 2007. 'Gender Responsive Treatment and Services in Correctional Settings'. *Women & Therapy*, 29 (3–4): 9–33.

Cowie, J., Cowie, V., and E. Slater. 1968. *Delinquency in Girls*. London: Heinemann.

Daly, K., 1992. 'Women's Pathways to Felony Court: Feminist Theories of Lawbreaking and Problems of Representation'. *Southern California Review of Law & Women's Studies* 2(1): 11–52.

Daly, K. 1996. *Gender, Crime and Punishment*. New Haven, CT: Yale University Press.

Davis, A. Y. 2011. *Women, Race, & Class*. New York: Vintage.

Fergusson, A. 1989. *Blood at the Root: Motherhood, Sexuality and Male Dominance*. London: Pandora.

Galton, F. 1875. 'The History of Twins'. *Fraser's Magazine* 12: 566–576.

Halberstram, J. 2018. *Trans*: A Quick and Quirky Account of Gender Variability*. San Francisco: University of California Press.

Hahn Rafter, N. 1997. *Creating Born Criminals*. Chicago: University of Illinois Press.

Heidensohn, F. 1985. *Women & Crime*. London: Macmillan.

Home Office and Ministry of Justice. 2021. *Review into the Criminal Justice System Response to Adult Rape and Serious Sexual Offences Across England and Wales*. June. https://assets.publishing.service.gov.uk/government/uploads/system/uploads/attachment_data/file/994817/rape-review-research-report.pdf.

Human Dignity Trust. 2021. *Map of Countries that Criminalise LGBT People* <https://www.humandignitytrust.org/lgbt-the-law/map-of-criminalisation/>, accessed 8 Dec 2021.

King, D. and Hansen, R. 2013. *Sterilized by the State: Eugenics, Race and the Population Scare in Twentieth Century North America*. Cambridge, UK: Cambridge University Press.

Klein, Dorie. 1973. 'The Etiology of Female Crime: A Review of the Literature.' *Issues in Criminology* 8 (2): 3–30.

Lamble, S. 2012. 'Rethinking Gendered Prison Policies: Impacts on Transgender Prisoners.' *Howard League for Penal Reform ECAN Bulletin* 16: 7–12.

The Law Commission. 1990. *Working Paper No. 116: Rape Within Marriage*. London: HMSO.

Leonard, E.B. 1982. *Women, Crime and Society: Critique of Criminological Theory*. New York: Prentice Hall.

Lombroso, C. 2006. *Criminal Man*. Durham, NC: Duke University Press.

Matza, D. 1964. *Delinquency and Drift*. London: Wiley.

Mead, G. H. 1933. *Mind, Self and Society*. Chicago: University of Chicago Press.

Messerschmidt, J. W. 2012. *Gender, Heterosexuality, and Youth Violence: The Struggle for Recognition*. New York: Rowman & Littlefield.

Ministry of Justice. 2015. *Statistics on Women and Crime, 2015*. https://www.gov.uk/government/statistics/women-and-the-criminal-justice-system-statistics-2015.

Ministry of Justice. 2020. *Statistics on Women and Crime 2019*. https://assets.publishing.service.gov.uk/government/uploads/system/uploads/attachment_data/file/938360/statistics-on-women-and-the-criminal-justice-system-2019.pdf.

Ministry of Justice. 2021. *Criminal Court Statistics Quarterly: October to December 2020*. https://www.gov.uk/government/statistics/criminal-court-statistics-quarterly-october-to-december-2020.

Office for National Statistics. 2017. *Crime in England and Wales: year ending March 2017*. https://www.ons.gov.uk/peoplepopulationandcommunity/crimeandjustice/bulletins/crimeinenglandandwales/yearendingmar2017.

Office for National Statistics. 2018. *Domestic Abuse: Findings from the Crime Survey for England and Wales: Year Ending March 2018*. https://www.ons.gov.uk/peoplepopulationandcommunity/crimeandjustice/articles/domesticabusefindingsfromthecrimesurveyforenglandandwales/yearendingmarch2018.

Office for National Statistics. 2020. *Homicide in England and Wales: Year Ending March 2019*. https://www.ons.gov.uk/peoplepopulationandcommunity/crimeandjustice/articles/homicideinenglandandwales/yearendingmarch2019.

Parson, T. 1960. *Structure and Processes in Modern Society*. Chicago: Free Press.

Phoenix, J. 2017. 'The Politics of Sexuality: Alternative Visions of Sex and Social Change'. In *Alternative Criminologies,* edited by P. Carlen and L. Ayres Franca, 135–149. London: Routledge.

Phoenix, J. 2021. 'Women, Poverty, Violence and Justice: The Need for a New Research Agenda'. *Howard League for Penal Reform ECAN Bulletin 48*: 34–37.

Phoenix, J. 2022. 'What Do We Stand For? Criminology, Politically Induced Ignorance and Gender-Identity'. https://jophoenix.substack.com/p/what-do-we-stand-for.

Plummer, K. 1981. *The Making of the Modern Homosexual.* London: Rowman & Littlefield.

Prison Reform Trust. 2019. *Why Focus on Reducing Women's Imprisonment? England and Wales Fact Sheet.* http://www.prisonreformtrust.org.uk/Portals/0/Documents/Women/Why%20Women%20England%20and%20Wales%202018%20data.pdf.

Ricciardelli, R., Phoenix, J., & Gacek, J. 2020. '"It's Complicated": Canadian Correctional Officer Recruits' Interpretations of Issues Relating to the Presence of Transgender Prisoners'. *The Howard Journal of Crime and Justice 59*(1): 86–104.

Richie, B. E. 2018. *Compelled To Crime: The Gender Entrapment of Battered Black Women.* New York: Routledge.

Sharpe, G. 2013. *Offending Girls: Young Women and Youth Justice.* London: Routledge.

Stanko, B. 1990. *Everyday Violence: How Men and Women Experience Sexual and Physical Danger.* London: Sage.

Stryker, S. 2017. *Transgender History: The Roots of Today's Revolution.* New York: Seal Press.

Trebilcock, J. and A. Dockley. 2015. 'A Very High Price to Pay? Transforming Rehabilitation and Short Prison Sentences for Women'. In *Women and Criminal Justice: From the Corston Report to Transforming Rehabilitation* edited by Jill Annison, Jo Brayford, and John Deering, 213–230. Bristol, UK: Policy Press.

Victims Commissioner. 2020. *Rape Survivors and the Criminal Justice System.* https://s3-eu-west-2.amazonaws.com/victcomm2-prod-storage-119w3o4kq2z48/uploads/2020/10/Rape-Survivors-and-the-CJS_FINAL-v2.pdf.

Weaver, B., & McNeill, F. 2015. Lifelines: Desistance, Social Relations, and Reciprocity. *Criminal Justice and Behaviour 42*(1): 95–107.

Webster, R. 2017. *Caring for Transgender Prisoners.* https://www.russellwebster.com/caring-for-transgender-prisoners/.

Westmarland, N. 2004. *Rape Law Reform in England and Wales,* School for Policy Studies Working Paper Series, Paper no. 7. University of Bristol. http://nicolewestmarland.pbworks.com/f/Rape+Law+Reform+in+England+and+Wales+-+Westmarland+2004.pdf.

Worrall, A. 1990. *Offending Women: Female Lawbreakers and the Criminal Justice System.* London: Taylor & Francis.

INDEX

Note: Page numbers in *italic* indicate a figure and page numbers in **bold** indicate a table on the corresponding page.

administrative data 105–109
anatomy: brain sex 42–45
androcentric citizenship 234–236
Athena Swan Charter 108–109
athletes: with DSDs 239–241; transgender 239–241
atypical sex development 25–26

binary 28–29
biological determinism 63–64
biological realism 272–274
biological sex 2–7, 12–13; and criminology 270–275; data 106–107, 114–117; and gender dysphoria 156–157; history of sex 69–74, 80–82; and sport 236–237
biologists 30
bisexuals 9–10
bodies 21–22
bodily autonomy 234
brain 41–48; brain sex theory 35–36; 'normal' distribution and difference 36–37; view from the brain 37–41
brain scans 45–47

children's literature 214–215, 227–228; gender identity in the twenty-first century 220–227; gender as a social construction in the twentieth century 215–220
citizenship *see* androcentric citizenship

cognitive functions 40
conflict 142; of rights 147–148
confusion 149
consequences 142–145, 148–153
crime 106–107
criminalisation 267–269
criminal justice system 263–264
criminal statistics 260–264
criminology 259–260, 262–266, 268–273, 275
curriculum 203–207

data 104–105, 118–119; arguments collecting data on sex 109–119, **117**; asking sex as violation of privacy 113–114; conflating sex, gender, and gender identity 110; gender identity trumps sex 112–113; losing data on sex 109; more than two sexes 111–112; numbers 115–118, **117**; sex categories as oppressive 110–111; sex change over time 113; sex as self-identified 114–115; UK surveys and administrative data 105–109
definitions: gender 3–5; and law 127–130; sex and gender 3–5, 17–22; woman 59–63
demographic change 161–162
detransition study 166–169
development: atypical sex development 25–26; embryonic 23–25
dimorphism 237–239

disorders/differences of sex development (DSDs) 239–241
domestic law 130–133; *see also* law
DSDs *see* disorders/differences of sex development
Dutch protocol: creation of 176–179; international adoption of 181–184; scrutinised 179–181; subsequent evidence 184–186

embryonic development 23–25
empathising brains 38–40
equality 139–143; foreseeable negative consequences 148–152; legislative backdrop 143–145; reformulating 153; sex-based protections regardless of sex 145–148, *146*
equal opportunity 152
explicit curriculum 203–206

facts *see* social facts
fairness 152
felt security 151–152
femalehood, adult human 63–64; meaning of 59–63; as social 53–59; and subjective states 64–65
femininity, ideologies of 267–269
feminism/feminist critique 194–195, 210; gender-critical framing 195–198; of sex denial 75–82; 'trans-inclusive' framing 199–202; ways forward 202–209; *see also* second-wave feminism
feminist pathways 266–267

gametes 19–21
gay men 9–10
GD *see* gender dysphoria
gender 110, 236–237; in children's literature 214–228; competing understandings of 5–7; and criminology 259–275; defining 3–5; and equality 139–153; in law 125–137; and schools 202–209; and second-wave feminism 86–100; womanhood as 63
gender-critical framing 195–198
gender dysphoria (GD): conceptualising 160–161; definitions and context 156–160; demographic change 161–162; online observation 162; psychosocial factors 162–170
gender identity 110, 112–113, 220–227, 232–233, 253–254, 264–266; historical exclusion 233–236, *235*; and sport policy 243–253, *249*, *251*; theoretical debates 236–241, **240**; values and rights 241–243

gender identity ideology 69–70, 83; radical materialist feminist critique 75–82; and sex-denialist arguments 70–75
gender-identity theory 194–195, 210; gender-critical framing 195–198; 'trans-inclusive' framing 199–202; ways forward 202–209
gendering 195–198; criminology 269–270
gender-non-conforming people 207–209
gender order 198–203, 206–210
gender pay gap 106

heritage 125–127
Higher Education Statistics Authority (HESA) 107–108
history 69–70, 83; radical materialist feminist critique 75–82; and sex-denialist arguments 70–75; sport 233–236; U.S. Equality Act 144–145
hormones *see* sex hormones
human rights 130–133; international human rights law 133–136; sport and/or gender identity as 242–243
human sex 22–26; *see also* sex
human sexual dimorphism 237–239

identity 259–260, 272, 274; categories of 270–272; and justice 264–266; *see also* gender identity
ideologies of femininity 267–269; *see also* gender identity ideology
implicit curriculum 206–207
inequalities, sex-based 270–272
injustices, sex-based 269–270
international human rights law 133–136; *see also* human rights law; law
IQ: and brain sex 38

justice 264–266, 272–274

law: definitions 127–130, 136–137; domestic law and human rights 130–133; international human rights law 133–136; and sexed heritage 125–127
legislation 143–148
lesbians 9–10
LGBT 135, 139–143, 147, 153, 164–165, 270
LGBT+ 129, 135, 139, 142–145, 153, 204
LGBTQ 270
LGBTQ+ 70
LGBTQI 259, 270
literature *see* children's literature

masculinities 267–269
materialist feminist critique 75–82
microscopes 45–47
myths *see* sex myths

National Health Service (NHS) 107

online observations 162
oppression 75–76, 80–83, 89–90, 94–95, 98–100, 110–111, 267

parent-report study 163–166
pay gap 106
performance, gender as 269–270
personality 40–41
policy, prison placement 272–274
policy, sport 232–233; historical exclusion 233–236, *235*; recognition 243–246; redistribution 248–253; representation 246–248; theoretical debates 236–241, **240**; values and rights 241–243
prison placement policy 272–274
privacy 113–114
psychological well-being 151–152
psychosocial factors 162–170
puberty 25; suppression 175–187

'queer' people 9–10

radical materialist feminist critique 75–82
rapid-onset gender dysphoria (ROGD) 169–170
realism, biological 272–274
recognition 243–246
redistribution 248–253
representation 246–248
reproduction 18–19
rights 241–243; conflict of rights 147–148; *see also* human rights
ROGD *see* rapid-onset gender dysphoria

safety 149–151
schools 194–195, 210; gender-critical framing 195–198; 'trans-inclusive' framing 199–202; ways forward 202–209
secondary sex characteristics 25
second-wave feminism 86–87, 99–100; 1968–1978, 87–92; 1979–1989, 93–98; backlash against 98–99
security 151–152
self-determination 234
self-identification 114–115, 146–147
sentencing 262–263

sex 16–17, 30–31; and the brain 35–48; competing understandings of 5–7; and criminology 259–275; data on 104–119; defining 3–5; and equality 139–153; gametes and sexes 19–21; history of 69–83; human sex 22–26; in law 125–137; reproduction 18–19; and second-wave feminism 86–100; sex myths 26–30; sexual systems and bodies 21–22; and sport 232–254; *see also* biological sex; brain sex
sex-based inequalities 270–272
sex-based injustices 269–270
sex-based protections 145–148
sex denial 69–70, 83; arguments 70–75; radical materialist feminist critique 75–82
sex determination 23
sex hormones 45
sexism 262–263
sex myths 26–30
sexual differences 260–264
sexual dimorphism 237–239
sexualities 264–266
sexual systems 21–22
social construct/social construction 29–30, 215–220, 233–234
social facts 51–66
social influences 162–163
social roles 267–269
sport 232–233, 253–254; historical exclusion 233–236, *235*; policy 243–253, *249*, *251*; theoretical debates 236–241, **240**; values and rights 241–243
statistics: criminal 260–264; educational 117, **117**; labour market 106, 113, 116; sex 111–116; sexuality 113
subjective states 64–65
surveys 105–109
systematising brains 38–40

testosterone 45
theories: brain sex theory 35–36; debates 236–241; gender identity 156–162; psychosocial factors 162–170; *see also* gender-identity theory
transgender athletes 239–241
transgender-identifying children and young people 207–209
'trans-inclusive' framing 199–202
trans people 7–9
truisms 260–264

United Kingdom (UK): data 105–10
UK Equality Act (EA) 5, 69, 105, 129, 137, 248, 250

United States, equality in 139–143; foreseeable negative consequences 148–152; legislative backdrop 143–145; reformulating 153; sex-based protections regardless of sex 145–148, *146*

U.S. Equality Act (EA) 139–143; foreseeable negative consequences 148–152; the legislation 145–148, *146*; legislative backdrop 143–145; reformulating 153

Universal Declaration of Human Rights (UDHR) 133, 136

values 241–243

violence 263–264

well-being 151–152

womanhood 51–53; and adult human femalehood 53–59; two meanings of 59–65

Women's Liberation Movement (WLM) 86–87, 99–100; 1968–1978, 87–92; 1979–1989, 93–98; backlash against second-wave feminism 98–99

Taylor & Francis eBooks

www.taylorfrancis.com

A single destination for eBooks from Taylor & Francis with increased functionality and an improved user experience to meet the needs of our customers.

90,000+ eBooks of award-winning academic content in Humanities, Social Science, Science, Technology, Engineering, and Medical written by a global network of editors and authors.

TAYLOR & FRANCIS EBOOKS OFFERS:

- A streamlined experience for our library customers
- A single point of discovery for all of our eBook content
- Improved search and discovery of content at both book and chapter level

REQUEST A FREE TRIAL
support@taylorfrancis.com

Routledge
Taylor & Francis Group

CRC Press
Taylor & Francis Group